3-10

Happy Bi[rthday]!
From Te[... fam]ily

6-10

That's What I Am

That's What I Am

AL WAXMAN

[signature: Al Waxman]

MALCOLM LESTER BOOKS

Copyright © 1999 Tobaron Productions Limited

All rights reserved. No part of this publication may be reproduced, stored in a retrieval system, or transmitted, in any form or by any means, without the prior written permission of the publisher, or in the case of photocopying or other reprographic copying, a licence from CANCOPY (Canadian Copyright Licencing Agency), One Yonge Street, Suite 1900, Toronto, Ontario M5E 1E5.

Canadian Cataloguing in Publication Data
Waxman, Al
   That's what I am

Includes index.
ISBN 1-894121-26-0

1. Waxman, Al.   2. Actors – Canada – Biography.   I. Title

PN2308.W39A3   1999   792'.028'092   C99-931602-8

For kind permission to reprint, the publisher would like to thank:

Steve Allen, for permission to quote from "This Could Be the Start of Something Big." Copyright © 1956, renewed 1984 Meadowlane Music, Inc. ASCAP International Copyright secured. All rights reserved.

Aubrey Tadman and Garry Ferrier, for permission to quote from the theme song for *King of Kensington*. Lyrics by Aubrey Tadman, Garry Ferrier and Bob McMullen.

Book Editor: Meg Taylor
Book Design: Linda Gustafson/Counterpunch
Author Photographs (front jacket cover, spine and p. ii): Jim Allen
Spine Background Photograph: Robert Burley/Design Archive

We acknowledge the support of the Canada Council for the Arts for our publishing program.

Malcolm Lester Books
25 Isabella Street, Toronto, Ontario M4Y 1M7

Printed and bound in Canada
99   00   01   02   5   4   3   2   1

For my daughter, Tobaron, and my son, Adam

Acknowledgements

No, I did not have a ghost. But yes, I did have a spirit—the very gifted and skilful editor Meg Taylor. Meg was determined to make me sound like a writer, while preserving my "voice." It was that voice that caught the attention and commitment of my friend and publisher, Malcolm Lester. The commitment was mutual. Just as Malcolm responded to the material and its potential, I was encouraged by his expertise and integrity. As well, my thanks to Barbara Coven of Malcolm Lester Books, who along with Malcolm and Meg championed my efforts from Chapter 1 on. Also my gratitude to Donna Dawson, my loyal and talented assistant, who was much more than secretarial support.

Lastly and always, there is my love, Sara, who was constantly there for me, even when her patience was tried. She once shouted in exasperation after reading some of the manuscript, "Haven't you ever heard of a period?" (Happily, Meg has.) Still I could, as I have for over thirty years now, count on Sara's counsel when needed, her courage when mine flagged, her memory when mine lapsed—as always, she is my wife, my partner in life.

Contents

Acknowledgements *vii*

Chapter 1 My Dad 3
Chapter 2 The Mona Lisa 17
Chapter 3 Destination Unknown 31
Chapter 4 A Watershed Year 41
Chapter 5 And Revelations Still to Come 52
Chapter 6 I Aced Ec. 20 the Second Time Around 73
Chapter 7 An Actor Prepares 84
Chapter 8 Whatever Method Works 107
Chapter 9 Passage and Pilgrimage 121
Chapter 10 115 Levinsky Street 138
Chapter 11 The End of the Beginning 152
Chapter 12 *Nachis* and Neon Lights 158
Chapter 13 A Job-Job 167
Chapter 14 Epiphany in an Enchilada 174
Chapter 15 *Tviggy* 184
Chapter 16 A Oneness: SARAL 198
Chapter 17 Hunger versus Desperation 205
Chapter 18 And Now We Were Four 220
Chapter 19 Kensington, By Way of Rosedale 238

Chapter 20	Where Do I Sign? 250
Chapter 21	A Commoner's Kingdom 253
Chapter 22	The Road Broadens 276
Chapter 23	The Party's Over, but the Feast Goes On 288
Chapter 24	A Winning Streak 295
Chapter 25	Long-Distance Love 306
Chapter 26	A Mansion of Love 320
Chapter 27	Bicoastal Paradise 328
Chapter 28	Adjustments: Arterial and Attitudinal 342
Chapter 29	A Frame Freezes, but the Film Advances 353
Chapter 30	From *Persona Non Grata* to Patagonia 360
Chapter 31	And Master of None? 372
Chapter 32	Bottom of the Barrel 389
Chapter 33	A New Perspective 402
Chapter 34	The Playwright in the Sky 415
Chapter 35	Conversation with My Dad 423

Index 432

Photographs after pages 134 and 278

That's What I Am

CHAPTER 1

My Dad

As a kid, I loved winter. I guess I still don't mind it, but back then I really loved the snow, tobogganing, skating, snowball fights. Early February of 1945 was heaven on earth for me. One of the heaviest snowfalls in recorded history blanketed Toronto that month. People skied to work. There were no cars on the roads. Kids were excused from school. Mind you, that didn't stop me and my friends from going out to play, digging tunnels from one side of the street to the other. After we tired of digging, we would clear some snow off the road, the snow that remained being high enough to serve as natural goalposts for hockey practice. It may have been a nuisance to some, but for me, as the song says, it was a "winter wonderland."

And of course February brought Valentine's Day. Hearts and flowers, candies and cards. Romance for those who knew what that was about, like my parents. My older brother, Benny, and I could feel the excitement as "Won't you be my valentine?" filled the air. For my family, you see, it was particularly special, because February 14 was my mother's birthday. I'm not sure if it was in fact her birthday, but for as long as I can remember, that's the day on which we celebrated it. It was fitting because for me and my brother, and for my father too, my mother meant love. So there was, for me, indeed, something so clean and pure and personal about all that snow.

But early in the morning on February 15, 1945, it was still dark, just a few hours after Valentine's Day and about three weeks before my tenth birthday, I was awakened by my mother's crying and wailing. When I came to my parents' bedroom, only a few steps from the little room shared by me and Benny, I saw my dad flat on his back and our doctor leaning over him with his hands on my dad's chest, vigorously, desperately, pumping a rhythmic artificial respiration, trying to restart my dad's heartbeat. To no avail.

My mother said to me, in Yiddish, "Give your daddy a kiss goodbye." I will never forget what to me looked like an army of blue in bold relief against my daddy's white skin, marching up his chest and surrounding his heart. *Attack.* An accurate description. *Massive heart attack.* Accurate and ugly. I kissed my daddy goodbye.

Following Jewish tradition, my father was buried on the same day he died, probably at midday or in the early afternoon. It seemed like morning. It was certainly as cold as morning.

The cemetery is way up on north Bathurst Street, near Steeles Avenue. It was quite a journey then. Today it's surrounded by highrises, supermarkets and shopping plazas; in 1945 it was a lonely trek. North Bathurst Street was a single-lane country road, and a few miles before we reached the cemetery, the funeral procession had to abandon automobiles in favour of horse-drawn sleighs.

I will always remember the snow. Horses' hooves, crunching snow and gliding sleds, all have such a jingle-bell sound, but on that day they struck a chord of resounding loneliness against the strange stillness of what seemed like a world of white. White as far as my eyes could see. White in all directions. I will always remember the snow. Perversely pure. I threw myself on the ground and, reaching into the grave as the casket was being lowered, I cried out, "I want my daddy back!"

Kaddish. The Hebrew prayer for the dead, recited aloud every morning and every evening for the rest of the year; and every year on the anniversary of his death for the rest of my life. Why not? I loved him and choose to remember him in this prescribed way.

My Dad

I also remember images of him and moments, a precious few, that I shared with him. Snapshots, or impressions, of him. And like snapshots, these memories capture a truth that can run deep, a truth that is as much about me as it is about him. A truth within the snapshot and, as well, a truth within the viewer, namely me, projected onto the subject of the snapshot, my father.

There was the time my brother and I, as adults, were playing chess. I must have been in my late twenties at the time; Benny was of course almost four years older. He was beating me. I've never been very good at chess. Now my son beats me. I never had the patience. While we were playing, Benny and I talked about how each of us had learned to play chess. For me it was probably during rest period or rainy-day programs at summer camp. He, on the other hand, remembered specifically that it was our father who taught him. He told me of how Daddy would remove his queen and with that handicap play my brother until he learned.

I don't think I let on, but I was immediately jealous. If he learned how to play chess from my father, that means, I concluded, that they had had conversation together, grown-up conversation, at least more adult conversation than I had ever had with my father. Why didn't I get to have that? I often felt my father cheated me by dying when I was so young. I later appreciated that it was he who was cheated to have died so young, at only forty-five.

Of course there were times of special attention—not long enough and not often enough, but nevertheless quite the opposite of being cheated. Sunday meant for me the "day of the son." It was the day when time, however limited (probably only a couple of hours) was dedicated by my dad to me and my brother.

We virtually never saw him during the week. He left for work before we got up and returned around the time we went to bed or when we were already asleep. He worked from 6 a.m. to 8 p.m. or later at the Melinda Lunch, a restaurant in the basement of the old Telegram Building on Melinda Street. The *Telegram* was the precursor of the *Toronto Sun*, and Melinda Street, now mostly swallowed up by downtown restructuring, was in the heart of the Bay Street business and stock exchange district. That district still flourishes, and so does the memory of Melinda Street and the old Telegram Building. And so does the memory of my dad, at least in me.

My dad mortgaged and borrowed, and bought the Melinda Lunch, and as a result of his energy, smarts and drive it was turning into a profitable business venture. He was obsessive about work. I remember him banging his fist on the kitchen table, shouting, "A man works! A man who doesn't work is a lazy bum!" It is an image that came out of the filing cabinet of my mind and into the character of Frankie Walls in the CBC's award-winning 1981 drama *The Winnings of Frankie Walls*, about a labourer automated out of his job.

I remember my dad saying that a certain neighbour was a big baby because he shaved at night before going to bed so he could get a few more minutes of sleep in the morning. My dad woke early, and in the winter would open the window, pull a handful of snow from the ledge and wash his face with it. On the occasional morning that he was still home when I began moving around, fogbound with sleep, he would grab some snow off the window-ledge and say, "Nah," which means "Here" in Yiddish, as he shoved it into my face, abruptly and mercilessly snapping me out of the warmth of sleep.

When I tell that story, some people think he was being mean, but the memory brings a fond smile to my face. As does the memory of sitting at the breakfast table, still in the haze of sleep, my elbow resting on the kitchen table and my face propped up in the palm of my hand. Suddenly my dad knocked my elbow out from under me, and my chin dropped with an eye-opening bang onto the table. Rude awakening? I guess. But although I wanted to cry, I knew better, preferring instead to sit up straight and look awake.

His hard work and long hours all week meant that Sunday was special, not just for Benny and me, but for my mother as well. Perhaps her Sunday started Saturday night, but I do remember that early

My Dad

Sunday morning was still hers, and in retrospect I would think his too. One Sunday morning I ran into their bedroom with the intention of getting an early start to my "Sonday." They had twin beds in their room when we lived on Burnside Drive, but this particular morning they were in the same bed. And as I was running into their room, shouting with enthusiastic anticipation, "Daddy, Daddy!", he, without looking away from my mother or diverting his attention from their togetherness, manoeuvred his leg out from under the blanket and thrust his foot in my direction, catching me in the stomach as I reached the bedside and sending me flying backwards right through the door and out of their room. I noticed that my mother, who had always protected and soothed me, seemed blissfully unaware of my wounded feelings. They were not wounded for long, though, because later that morning I got to spend time with my daddy.

Our time together would start with the gift of a toy, maybe a cop on a motorcycle which, when wound up, would race around in a circle on the kitchen floor, sirens blaring. Later—this was when we lived on Spadina Avenue—we would walk in the park in Kensington Market, then up to Brunswick and College where the YMHA was and next to it the Talmud Torah, a Jewish school, or over to the corner of Spadina and St. Andrews, where the Labour Lyceum was. In either location, the sidewalks were wide and packed with men who all seemed to have on the same dark grey overcoat and light grey fedora that my father was wearing. These intersections were always teeming with discussion and argument about the war, the economy, the workers and labour, the bosses, owners and management.

My father, I was later told, had resisted joining a union when he had been a furrier, soon after he first arrived from Poland. He successfully resisted even when physically ambushed, outnumbered and overpowered. He was tough. He came home bloodied, but got his licks in, too, and kept the money he had worked so hard for, money they would have wanted him to part with for union dues.

I can guess what side my father was taking in those Sunday-morning arguments at the corners and crossroads of Jewish life in Toronto then. Of course, when it came to the war, friends and family overseas, and anti-Semitism, they were all on the same side. Regardless of the subject of discussion, however, my dad would get intense and involved, and I would get tired and restless and want to go home. One time I was hanging on to his sleeve as he was caught up in an energetic exchange. I pulled on his arm and whined, "Daddy, let's go home!" But he was getting more carried away. Or perhaps I was. I suddenly noticed that the sleeve I was hanging on to, however familiar it looked, belonged to the arm of another man. My dad's arms, a few shoulders away, appeared ready to throttle someone in order to make a point.

He had an explosive temper. I remember one night waking up very late to find my father jumping into his trousers and pulling his suspenders on over his naked chest, all the while complaining about being awakened by our noisy and drunken upstairs neighbour. My dad worked hard and needed his sleep. He was tough and he was disciplined, and sleep was a necessary part of his daily regimen. So he was going to subdue this loud lush who, it just so happened, was twice my dad's height. And my mother was very concerned about that. She was holding on to his suspenders the way you would try to rein in a horse, all the while begging in Yiddish, "Aaron, please!" My dad, who was as strong as a horse, was in turn yelling in Yiddish, "I'll give it to that drunken goy, I'm going to give it to him!"

In spite of my mother's efforts, he made his way out the door and she was pulled along with him. I don't remember the finish of that story—whether the drunken neighbour won, or whether my dad won, or whether my mother won. I do know that it was quiet soon after that; and that there were no marks or blood or bruises on my dad. He was tough, feisty and strong. He could rip a telephone book in half with his bare hands. Toronto was smaller then, but so was I, so the telephone book looked very big and thick and bulging to me—just like my dad's biceps.

My Dad

There certainly was a vitality in the Kensington Market area at that time. There is today too, but the conversation then covered sports, especially Jewish boxers and ballplayers, gambling, bookmakers and bootleggers, as well as the more serious topics of war and politics. I knew none of that, of course, but I did know it was an exciting time. It was fun.

We lived in what was considered a two-room apartment on top of what is now a Chinese restaurant on the west side of Spadina Avenue, 414A Spadina. The two rooms were a living room, where Benny and I slept in beds that were folded up during the day, and a dining room, which was never used as a dining room but rather served as my parents' bedroom. There was a short hallway leading to the bathroom and a little kitchen. The kitchen was, in effect, our living room, because that's where we spent most of our time.

In those days 414A Spadina Avenue was on top of Pearl Produce, a chicken and egg dealer. Next to Pearl's was Imperial Tobacco. I'm still allergic to feathers and smoke. Down the street, at the corner of Nassau and Spadina, was Halpern's Drug Store, where they sold what I remember as the best ice cream in the world. Up the street, at the corner of Spadina and Oxford, was Goodman's Hardware, and across the road, on the northwest corner, there was an empty field where the older Jewish boys and the Ukrainian boys would get into fist fights and brawls.

Although anti-Semitism was rampant by all accounts, I didn't see it much or really know what it was—yet. The first time I heard the words "dirty Jew," they were directed at someone very much like me and I thought, "Isn't everyone?"

Yes, those days were fun, and our little apartment was, as far as I knew, a mansion. Certainly, when I look back, I know there was enough love and warmth in that little apartment to fill a mansion. We didn't have a lot of material things, but that didn't seem to matter. Benny and I each had a drawer in our all-purpose kitchen where we could store our playthings, like toys or paper and pencils. It seemed sufficient space and indeed provided fertile lift-off for our imaginations. We were always playing on the floor. I remember my mother having to step over us as she went back and forth getting dinner ready.

There is a family photo I cherish. It represents a couple of realities. Firstly, my father isn't in it; he was probably at work. There's just my mom, Benny and me. Secondly, it's in the kitchen, of course. I remember my mother feeling the need to fill up the picture; she covered the kitchen table with as many empty soda-pop bottles as she could find so that black-and-white photographic history would not record our lives as being meagre. But as far as I knew, our lives were full.

And my mother never turned hungry people away. At that time there always seemed to be needy people knocking on our door asking for food. My mom would always make them a sandwich. She lived by a philosophy that sounds biblical, but I've heard these words only from her mouth: "If you have a slice of bread, break it in three pieces. Eat one piece today, put a piece away for tomorrow, and the third piece give to someone who has no bread at all."

If we had to do without something, I would always ask if we would be able to have it "when the war's over" or "when we get rich." There was no question that both of those eventualities would happen. I guess I was always told that it was for one of those two reasons that we didn't have one thing or another. Which is why I thought we didn't have spaghetti because we couldn't afford it. Only years later, when I was an out-of-work actor in New York and all I could afford to cook was spaghetti, did I realize that the reason we didn't have it when I was a kid was simply that my mom didn't like it. We seemed to have all the basic necessities—no luxuries, but we were never in want.

We were optimistic. I've always said that as a Canadian, as a Jew and as someone in Canadian show business, you've got to be optimistic. Well, optimism existed in that mansion of a little apartment. I remember playing on the kitchen floor with a neighbourhood friend who noticed that we had two portraits on the wall above the kitchen table. They were black-and-white pictures of the King and Queen. My mom had cut them off a calendar and tacked them up on the wall for decoration. My playmate looked up at the crowned heads and said, "Who are they?" I answered, "My mom and dad."

We were not in want of companionship. Most of all, we had each other. My parents had friends and relatives, some already successful, who were from the same towns in Poland that they had come from, and who generally shared the same circumstances and the same ambitions as my parents. My dad didn't seem to have a lot of time for these people, but he went along with my mom's efforts to keep us focused not only on ourselves, but on the wider family and community as well.

They were simpler times. There were problems, yes, and there were obstacles in our path too. But they weren't problems that couldn't be solved or obstacles that couldn't be overcome. And that, when I look back, is what Canada, the freedom and the good fortune in being Canadian, meant for me. Sure, there was anti-Semitism, but it could be addressed, confronted and ultimately surmounted; sure, there was poverty, but there was also opportunity.

It has taken a while for some of us, especially in the entertainment industry, to discover the power in the freedom of being Canadian; my dad and many of his generation discovered it quickly. Perhaps he was an example of what was called, in those days, rugged individualism. That phrase is usually associated with the great outdoors, but I think it could apply just as well to the jungles of the city. He certainly was his own man.

He commanded respect, and probably some fear too. Not only our upstairs neighbour but my brother and I too could sure be afraid of him. When Benny and I misbehaved, my mother would say, "I'll tell your father when he comes home tonight." As soon as we heard that, we'd stop whatever we weren't supposed to be doing and plead with her not to tell Daddy. Of course, she never did.

I remember one time when Benny, who collected stamps, was caught stealing from a stamp store. My dad beat him with a belt. I didn't see it. They were either in the kitchen or the bathroom, and I was down the hall, probably cowering in the front room; I didn't want to be near it. But I heard the commotion, the whacks of the belt, the screams and the crying. Benny never stole again and I never stole for a first time. This is not to say that I endorse this kind of punishment. If the desired outcome is honest behaviour, then perhaps children should learn by following the examples given by their parents and teachers. Perhaps that's the ideal. But in this case the operative method was a beating, and it worked. And we didn't love my dad any the less for it.

Ironically, I was playing Willy Loman in *Death of a Salesman* at the Stratford Festival when I wrote these passages about my father. Although I am never judgmental about a character I play—rather, I try to love every character—I couldn't help but notice a certain contrast between Willie and my father, particularly in how they brought up their sons. Willie wants so much to be liked and respected, whereas my father was apparently concerned solely and unsentimentally with duty and responsibility.

When Willie learns that Biff, his elder son, has stolen a football, he waffles and laughingly suggests, "I want you to return that," but also adds that his son, a budding young quarterback, needs it to practise with, and that the coach will probably congratulate his initiative. Well, as we learn later in the play, Biff has lost every job he's had in the past ten years because of stealing, and even spent some time in jail "for stealing a suit in Kansas City." It seems my dad's swift decisiveness helped to clear a more productive path for his two sons to follow.

In light of this discipline, I wonder where I found the courage to defy one of his strict orders, namely, an eight o'clock bedtime. On Saturday night he would get home a little earlier than during the rest of the week and have his dinner, after which he'd remain in the kitchen reading the papers with his back against the frame of the open door that led into the hallway. (This was when we lived on Burnside Drive.) I would dare to sneak out of our bedroom and down the hall, crawling literally inches behind him, on the way to the huge Stromberg-Carlson radio in our living room. I would turn the sound on until it was just barely audible to my ear pressed against the speaker, and listen to Foster Hewitt welcoming me and the rest of the country to *Hockey Night in Canada*. I wonder now if I was getting away with it or if he knew, and admired my guts.

On the day of Benny's bar mitzvah, I was walking beside my dad into the reception hall on College Street where the party was being held. I asked my father what would happen if Benny misbehaved. Would he, on this, his once-in-a-lifetime day, still get a beating? Without missing a stride, my father replied, "Yes, if he deserved it, yes." Then he stopped and fixed me with look. There was a long pause before he said quietly, "I would take a hundred lickings from my father if I could see him again." I was nine years old then. He would die later that year.

I remember my dad in an argument with someone who was proposing a business deal. They were meeting in our kitchen on Spadina Avenue, and we were down the short hallway in the front room. There were hot words, and suddenly my father commanded, "Get the hell, gerroutta here!" whereupon the frightened and embarrassed fellow quickly departed. I'm afraid that I must attribute to my father, although the Hollywood movies of the time were not without influence too, my belief that it was manly to be tough and quick-tempered.

But he was not just a man to be feared. He was also a man to be respected, for his intelligence and hard work. And a man to be loved, for his generosity, kindness and even tenderness. I was told by my mother that when Benny was a boy of three or four, certainly before I was born, my father had been touched by the sight of him moving his little fingers along a wall as though he were playing the piano. It was then that he vowed to buy Benny a real piano some day. Years later, he loved to sit and listen to my brother practising.

Whether or not he would have approved of my career choice, I'm not sure, but I do know that he gave me my first taste of the theatre. When I was probably less than five, my parents took us to see *Abie's Irish Rose* at the Royal Alexandra Theatre. We sat way up in the second balcony. So steep and up so high that it was scary, but I was on my daddy's lap, so I felt safe and excited. Mostly I remember being surrounded by laughter, and that my parents were happy.

My parents were always loving and sexy and full of fun with each other. He knew that my mother used to say, "When I argue with your father, I have the last word—but I let your father speak it." This was contrary to his attitude towards Benny and me, however, where the last word would always definitely be his.

Benny was the first person in the family to bring into our home something that approximated correct English. He was, after all, learning it in school, and he was a bright student. So his use of English was closer to correct than my parents' fractured speech. One day my father, referring to a place he had visited, said, "I wore dere." Benny dared to correct him by saying that the word was "were," not "wore," and that in this instance he should really say, "I *was* there." My dad slammed his fist on the table as he roared, "I wore dere!" And that was that. But I noticed quiet laughter on Benny's face, bringing a smile to mine too. I think maybe even my dad noticed. Last word aside, I do know he wanted us to be good students (and he appreciated evidence of that).

My father became quite successful with the Melinda Lunch and so was able to assist my mother's two brothers in their new venture. He didn't think too highly of them as businessmen, I remember, but because she wanted him to, he helped them financially. As a result, my dad became part-owner of a tavern called the Beresford Hotel on Queen Street East, as well as being the full owner of the Melinda Lunch. He made enough money to buy a house for us.

In those days, as soon as a Jewish family could afford it, they moved "up the hill," or with a Yiddish accent, "op deh hill," which then meant Forest Hill. We didn't get quite that far, but we did make it partway up the hill, onto a lovely little circular street called Burnside Drive, on the crest of the hill that climbs up Bathurst Street from Davenport Road. As a matter of fact, the school opposite our street was called Hillcrest.

We bought a duplex on Burnside Drive and lived on the first floor, renting out the second floor and the attic space on the third floor. Our living quarters now consisted of two more rooms than we had had on Spadina Avenue: a living room and a dining room, neither of which had to serve as bedrooms, because now there was a bedroom for my parents and one for me and Benny to share. There was also a little kitchen, a little hallway and a washroom.

The living room was big enough for a piano. A baby grand— that's how much my dad believed in my brother's talent. Benny became what was considered a child prodigy on the piano, and my father derived great joy from listening to him. My father deserved to have some *nachis*, some joy in his son's achievement, reaped from his extraordinary efforts to build a life for his family in a free country.

He came to Canada to escape oppression in Poland and to seek opportunity. He apparently wanted to be a lawyer, but because of circumstances—certainly not want of ability—that would never be. He and my mother were married in Poland in 1927, and then he came over here alone. He worked as a furrier, his chosen profession at the time, for three dollars a week. To augment his income, he also worked as the caretaker in the building where he was a furrier, for five dollars a week. After three years of making eight dollars a week, he could finally afford to bring my mother over. She arrived in 1930. Evidence perhaps of their deep love for each other and sense of romance, they chose to get married again in Canada. I have a wedding picture of them taken in Poland in 1927, and I also have, symbolic of a new life and a renewed love, their certificate of marriage in Canada in 1930. Benny was born March 16, 1931, and I arrived March 2, 1935.

My dad was a "man's man." I don't mean those words the way they are used in so many of the Mob movies I've acted in. I use them to refer to the way he lived: his aspirations, his ambitions for himself and his family, his energy, integrity and resourcefulness—all ploughed into an all-consuming thrust to achieve his goals. He was a man's man, but he was also a family man, a provider for me and Benny and especially for my mother. Years later she said about him, with a wistful smile on her face, that he was "clean in the bedroom and he never hit me." I was taken aback when she said that. I would have thought that would go without saying. Well, apparently not in those days. And the way she spoke those words somehow conjured up the man I knew him to be, good and loving and caring.

One day when we still lived on Spadina Avenue, my brother and I were looking out the front window of our apartment onto the street. I had just asked Benny what he thought God looked like. He answered, "Like an ordinary man." Just then, we caught sight of our father crossing the wide avenue and walking towards our apartment. Benny pointed to him and said, "Just like Daddy."

I wish my dad and I could have had more conversation.

Chapter 2

The Mona Lisa

My mother was such a beautiful woman that her friends called her the Mona Lisa. Although I certainly agreed that my mother was beautiful, I didn't think the Mona Lisa was much of a looker. Gradually, I became aware that her beauty was not the flashy kind promoted by Madison Avenue or Hollywood. Mona Lisa's beauty had the weight of history and the wisdom of the ages behind it. It meant classic, unchanging beauty. Just like "mother," it meant forever. So I too began to consider the Mona Lisa beautiful.

Indeed, there were secrets of the soul in my mother's beauty. I have a photograph of her in which she is serene strength and mystery personified. It is a picture that justifies the "Mona Lisa" compliment. Gordon Pinsent, a long-time friend who happens also to be as talented a painter as he is an actor and a writer, gave me a gift, back in the 1950s, of an oil painting of my mother. The painting is based on that photograph, which I call the Mona Lisa, and it still hangs on my wall.

Yes, she was beautiful, and after a period of mourning suitors came, or rather, were allowed to visit. They came mostly through well-intentioned matchmaker friends of my mother's, but Benny and I were the only people my mother would consult about them. There was no way she would allow herself to become the subject of gossip or, as she would say in Yiddish, "to fall into the mouth" of one of the matchmakers.

It seemed that almost every Sunday another guy would show up, dressed in his Sunday best and carrying a box of chocolates. Apart from the candies, I didn't like the sight of any of these men. Nevertheless, each of them would be ushered by my mother into the living room. I would be around the corner in the dining room, peeking from a vantage point behind the sheer-curtained, glass-panelled door, standing guard, as it were, for my mother's honour. I didn't have to worry. All I ever saw was my mother and her guest seated at a respectable distance from each other in polite conversation over tea.

After each gentleman caller left, my mother would ask us, "Well, what do you think?" My brother and I always got the candies without having to commit to an answer. Regardless of what we might have thought, my mother was particular, and she didn't want to encourage suitors if she did not see a future in the courtship, so Benny and I didn't get to know any of them as well as we got to know Laura Secord.

In the meantime, a living had to be made. My dad had been the kind of man, not uncommon at the time, who believed that a man goes out to work and a woman stays home and takes care of the house. In his lifetime, the possibility of my mother going out to work would never have been considered by him or even, however much she may have wanted to, by her. But after the seven days of shiva in February 1945, that edict changed. Life goes on and dictates its own edicts. My mother suddenly had to work, as well as take care of the house, and she certainly rose to that double challenge.

The challenge was mine and my brother's too. Benny carried on with his music and his schooling. I, on the other hand, just carried on. Benny was at Oakwood Collegiate from 9 a.m. till 3:30 p.m., while I spent the same hours at Hillcrest Public School, right across the road from our house on Burnside Drive. Afterwards we both went to the Orthodox Jewish school, the Yeshivah Torath Chaim. It

The Mona Lisa

was about a half-hour streetcar ride away, and we were supposed to be there from four till six. We were home for supper by seven, which we made ourselves if Mom wasn't there, and then it was time for homework, both Hebrew and English, till bedtime. As well, there were part-time jobs now and then, such as cutting grass, or raking leaves, or shovelling snow, or delivering *Liberty* magazines, or delivering bread—from a horse-drawn wagon, believe it or not. I sat right behind the horse's rump. The part-time jobs were OK. They gave me some spending money and were even fun—except when the horse farted. But put the whole schedule together—public school, Jewish school (which we called it then), homework, prayer time for Kaddish, travel time between schools and part-time jobs—and I had a regimen that prevented me from getting into any trouble. That is, if I stuck to the regimen. But if I had stuck to the regimen, when would I have had the time to swing a bat, shoot a puck or kick a ball?

Hillcrest School was only minutes from our front door, even if I went up the street to cross at the lights, but I was seldom there on time. And while Benny went religiously to Jewish school, I preferred to play hooky. I didn't hang out in pool halls or anywhere conducive to getting into trouble with the law; truancy was delinquency enough, and there were truant officers in those days. No, I played hooky in order to play hockey.

The rabbi at the Yeshivah, who was never completely in control of his exasperation regarding my poor attendance, would phone my mother at the restaurant and ask, "Where do you think your son is?" She'd answer, trying to sound confident but likely only sounding hopeful, that I had, of course, gone to *cheder* (Jewish school). Now the rabbi's control went right out the window—the window that he happened to be staring through at that moment, as he screamed into my mother's ear that I was lying to her, because he could see me playing hockey with the "*goyim* in the *gus*," that is, with the Gentile boys in the street.

I never heard those conversations, but they were relayed to me by my embarrassed mother. I can well imagine the rabbi building into an apoplectic crescendo. His only satisfaction was telling me to "assume the position" and then wildly swinging his yardstick, or even a cane, across my butt. That didn't scare or deter me. I don't know why, but he just made me laugh.

Before shiva was over, my father's ring and wristwatch, both with my father's initials—the same as mine and therefore intended for me—suddenly disappeared. If a thief had broken in, it was certainly a clean and skilful job because he left no traces. As far as we knew, they simply vanished. If I could not have my father's watch and ring, I believed it was *bashert*, that is, fate, that I should never have any watch or ring at all. From that day till this, I have never worn jewellery.

Despite not wearing a watch, time and punctuality at some point became high priorities in my life. Indeed, in my adult life, some of my colleagues and co-workers, and particularly my family, have said that I'm obsessive about schedules and promptness. But back then, when I was ten, eleven, twelve, I was oblivious to time.

It wasn't an easy battle for my mother, trying to oversee our life on two fronts. Just days after she took over the running of the Melinda Lunch, an accident occurred in its kitchen one night. We were awakened by a phone call for her to come and see her main source of income burnt into a charred and stinking mess. Again, *bashert*.

Her strategy then was to take partners, experienced in the business, to help rebuild the Melinda Lunch. Her spirit was indomitable. If she cried, it must have been in private. On the contrary, I only remember her standing behind the counter, wearing a flowered smock, always with a happy smile.

That's a look that she tried to produce on my face too. Happy smiles, happy birthday. Fifteen days after my father's death, eight days after shiva, March 2, was my tenth birthday. In spite of all that was happening in her life, she planned a birthday party for me. She made a cake with icing and candles. And of course there were gifts

The Mona Lisa

and guests, probably some family but mostly neighbourhood kids. It was not a surprise party, but there was unfortunately one surprise—it was for my mother: I never showed up.

I can't remember why I did that. I felt unworthy and embarrassed, I guess—unworthy because there was now, since my father's death, something incomplete and inadequate about me; embarrassed because, although I loved my mother deeply, her heavy Yiddish accent, particularly in front of other kids whose parents didn't have accents, sometimes made me wish I were somewhere else. So, before the party guests arrived, I ran out of the house and hid somewhere down the street, but close enough to keep an eye on the house so I could see when the last unwanted guest had left—unwanted by me, that is. When they had all gone, I returned home. My mom must have been hurt, probably perplexed, but mostly I remember she was disappointed for me.

Later that afternoon a boy who couldn't make it to the party showed up to give me a gift. I opened the front door, and standing there was this new kid on the block. He didn't know anybody yet and nobody knew him. He introduced himself and reached his hands out to me, offering his gift. I didn't want his gift, but I was mesmerized, so I took it, thanked him, watched him leave and then closed the door. I was impressed, not just because what he did was nice, but more because I thought how confident he was in himself. The gift was a book. I never read it, but it's still on my shelf today. I've always been intrigued by that moment and by the book's title, which was, appropriately, *Destination Unknown*.

Being deprived of my father was inexplicable and unfair—like suddenly having to feel my way in the dark—but, strangely, there were benefits as a result. Sometimes I would feel special. At school, for example, because of the rabbi's instructions to my mother, as a gesture of respect during the year of mourning I was forbidden to see movies or listen to the radio for at least the first month. Hard done by? Maybe. But on the other hand, I would be excused from the classroom and allowed to sit in a privileged place, the teachers' lounge, while my classmates had to listen to what I believed to be, as did most of them, some dull radio program. They had to take notes and would be required to respond to questions or write a report. I got out of that, and the other kids envied me for it.

Sitting in a comfortable chair in the teachers' lounge, watching the sun stream through the window onto my shoe and gazing at the shadow my foot cast on the polished hardwood floor, I would think of my father and how I lived in his shadow. Years later, that image would often serve as one of the devices in my bag of tricks, to create or trigger a "sense memory" or "emotional recall," if the feeling that it produced in me fit the mood of the moment and the behaviour of the character I was playing at a specific point in a play or film. I didn't know at the time that by living my life I was building up an inventory of emotional, sensory and intellectual equipment for an acting technique; I just thought I was getting out of doing a boring assignment.

Before my father died, my mom used to bring a *siddur*, a prayer book, to our bedside so that Benny and I could read the appropriate prayers in the morning and at night. Now, with her working so hard, it was up to us, and after a while there seemed to be not enough time or energy—or in my case, not enough inclination. But I did say Kaddish every day for the remainder of the year.

I continued to be late for school and play hooky, but somehow I passed from one grade to the next, even though I never read. Reading was for sissies. Not only did I not read *Destination Unknown*, but I didn't read anything—not even Classic Comics.

Perhaps I was lazy, but I think not. You can't go at sports with the kind of energy I gave it and be lazy. I guess I just didn't like school as much as I liked sports. I loved baseball, football and hockey. I played catcher in the spring and summer, centre (or snap, as the position was called in Canadian football then) in the fall and goalie in the winter. It made sense; there's something similar about each of these positions, and I was pretty good at them.

The Mona Lisa

I loved thrusting myself feet first or headlong in front of the net to stop a shot or prevent an oncoming player from slipping the puck into the goal. It was thrilling for me to catch a sizzling shot out of the air, particularly a low one; the higher ones were easier, like catching a baseball. Equally fun was to block a shot on my other side with my goalie stick.

I noticed that a lot of Jewish kids came out for baseball, but when I played football and particularly hockey, more often than not I was the only Jewish kid there. It used to disappoint me and even make me mad that none of the Jewish kids at my school would come out for hockey. They were scared of the game, I thought. This impression led me to think of Jews as sissies—brainy, sure, but physically, afraid of confrontation.

Like my brother. He wouldn't go near any kind of sports, let alone hockey. With that kind of attitude it was difficult for me to see him as a big brother. Although I didn't appreciate it at the time, I'm sure in retrospect that he was involved with his own search for self; after all, he was only fourteen. It was unfair to expect him to be a father figure for me when he needed one himself.

Being tough was what hockey was all about, so I was determined not to be scared when I played in the Toronto Hockey League. Most of the games were scheduled to be played at an indoor rink called Icelandia, at Yonge and Davisville. The building is still there, but it's now a Speedy Muffler King. Icelandia was restricted, which meant there was a "gentleman's agreement" that Jews were not welcome. Hockey was a very Catholic game in those days. Most of the young players came out of schools like St. Mike's and De La Salle. "Fuck 'em," I said. "I'll just play better than they do." Frankly, I was not that gifted, but I sure tried hard.

In those days, 1945 to 1948 when I played pee wee, minor bantam and bantam hockey, there were approximately eight hundred boys in the THL. To the best of my knowledge there were only two Jews amongst them. The other was Alan Cherry, now of the Yorkville women's fashion store. Cherry, whose nickname was Buster, was quite a good hockey player. Whether Buster Cherry ever made it into any record books, I don't know, but I do know that I never did.

The only statistics recording my playing days that I know of are in former NHL player and coach Billy Harris's diary. When I played against him, we were eleven and twelve years old. You could tell even at that early age, when he easily skated and deftly stickhandled through our whole team, that he would make it to the NHL; and indeed a few years later he started an illustrious career with the team I had dreamed of playing for, the Toronto Maple Leafs. According to Billy's diary, when he played for a team called the Cooper Combines and his nickname was Hinky, he single-handedly beat my team, the Hillcrest Camerons, by scoring four goals on me. Actually, I'm not too embarrassed by his official record, because I seem to remember, unofficially, that it was closer to seven goals.

So professional hockey was not my destiny. But I sure had a lot of fun, and I learned a little about myself and even more about how the world works. I don't know where my know-how or drive came from, but I organized a bunch of the kids who played together at Hillcrest School into a hockey team. We didn't have enough money, so we needed a sponsor. There was only one building in the neighbourhood, a leather factory, that looked substantial enough to take an interest in some kids in the community, so I approached the old gentleman who owned the factory, a Mr. Cameron, to sponsor our team—to be called, I suggested, the Hillcrest Camerons. He liked that. He was kindly, but he was firm. He would contribute, but we had to contribute a little as well. A "little contribution" was a lot for us, certainly for me and my family. Mr. Cameron would pay to have us registered as a team in the Toronto Hockey League, pay for ice time at the venues around the city that the league played in, and supply us with our team sweaters. Oh, and one more thing: our coach was to be Mr. Cameron's son.

Sounds like nepotism, but it really wasn't so bad. Mr. Cameron's son had played hockey. He was a man in his twenties, a fair-haired, freckle-faced, wholesome-looking, well-built rock of a man. He looked like a good-natured jock, like comic-strip boxer Joe Palooka. Maybe he would be a good mentor. I don't know that I was aware of it, but in retrospect I can see that since my father's death I gravitated towards authority figures, perhaps looking for a big brother.

My teammates and I were expected to pay for rental of practice ice if we ever used an indoor rink, so we mostly practised, catch-as-catch-can, on outdoor neighbourhood rinks. Getting ourselves to and from arenas was a combined effort. The ones in town meant just a streetcar ticket, but the ones on the outskirts of the city or in surrounding towns meant meeting at a designated place and then hopefully getting a lift from the coach or one of the few parents who had a car and was willing. This is a way of life today, but then it was not always easy to organize.

Lastly and most importantly, we were responsible for our individual equipment. This was expensive, especially if you were a goalie. Most teams provided goalies with their pads, but I had to get my own, so I borrowed the pads from school. This still left me with goalie gloves to buy: twenty dollars. My earnings from part-time jobs wouldn't be enough—I needed help. Twenty dollars was a lot of money in 1946, particularly for my mother. She was reluctant, but I was persistent. She was disappointed, because I'm sure it caused a dent in her savings and sports was not high on her list of priorities for me. She would rather have made the sacrifice for violin lessons. But although she saw no need for hockey, she did see a need for me not to be unhappy, so I prevailed and she gave me the money to buy the gloves.

The young Mr. Cameron, our coach, was probably a nice-enough guy. I thought he was impressive. I wanted to like him and wanted him to like me. Like his dad, though, he was also firm of purpose. I remember being in the locker room of, ironically (or perhaps appropriately), the "restricted" Icelandia, when Coach Cameron came in and told us to choose a captain. The choice was ours, he said. He would leave the room and return a few minutes later, at which time we would tell him who was to be the captain of the Hillcrest Camerons. Well, the boys chose me, and I was exultant. This was my team.

When informed of this, Coach Cameron disagreed. It was as though I had been punched by a fist I didn't see coming! Moreover, hurt by someone whom I had hoped would fill a void in my life. Why this reaction, we all wondered? After all, he said the choice was ours. There was no lobbying or politicking for it. I didn't ask for it. The boys just instantly and unanimously said, "Waxman." It seemed right, so what was wrong?

The coach said firmly, but without any obvious meanness (which made it hurt even more), that we had twelve boys on the team, eleven of whom were Christian. Only one was Jewish, so therefore it was not a fair or realistic representation of the makeup of the team. Never mind that we were twelve hockey players, never mind that we were twelve Canadian boys; the captain simply could not be the one Jewish boy, but instead must be one of the eleven Christian boys. He ordered us to choose again.

None of us responded. The team thought the best choice had been made. We didn't know who else to suggest. Well, if we couldn't choose, then he would choose for us. He pointed to one of the best players, Larry Andrews, and said, "You're the captain." Larry, in turn, a few moments later, came to me quietly and said he was sorry for the way things turned out, that he didn't want to be captain, that he would have preferred what he thought was the better choice—me. But neither of us wanted to put the team in jeopardy with the Cameron family.

I waited until everyone left, then, sitting alone in that locker room at Icelandia, where Jews were not welcome, I cried. I had been hit by flying pucks, slapped in the face by swinging sticks, smothered in scrambles around the net, but had never cried before.

The Mona Lisa

This was, of course, pre–Jacques Plante days; the goalie mask had not yet been invented. Although I considered borrowing the baseball catcher's mask from school, I ultimately decided against that for fear of looking like a sissy. No matter how much I got bruised or bloodied during the course of the game, I never let on how much it hurt. Even when the other kids would come over and say, "Are you OK? Does it hurt?" I'd be wincing or groaning on the inside, but I'd say, "No. It doesn't hurt. Let's keep playing."

I had been in a lot of fights when I was a kid, and I handled myself well. As a matter of fact, when any of the Jewish kids in school were being harassed by the tougher Gentile kids, they'd come to me for protection. Perhaps a physical blow is, in the short term, more damaging, but that incident in the locker room at Icelandia stung me deeply, and while cuts can heal, breaks can mend and swellings can subside, an insult can penetrate your spirit and remain with you forever.

Still, I think that the Camerons were decent people, when understood in the context of that time. I'm sure that young Mr. Cameron intended me no evil, but rather believed that he was only being fair. Yet to any truly fair-minded person, like the rest of the kids on that team, he would be considered unfair and anti-Semitic.

But we played on. Hockey was what it was all about, even though I would occasionally encounter minor instances of prejudice, such as, "You're Jewish, but you're OK" or "You're Jewish, but you're different than the other Jews," or when our team lost a close one and we were moping in the dressing room, one of my teammates would say, "Aw, we got jewed by the ref." I didn't even have to cock my fists and an apology would be forthcoming—not because I was tough, but because the boy realized that what he had said was wrong.

Perhaps even more damaging than an insult, and certainly just as memorable, is self-insult. I recall one time when I was on my way to Varsity Arena at two-thirty in the morning. Remember, the financial responsibility for paid practice time was ours, not our sponsor's, so if we ever needed concentrated practice, over and above the time spent on public outdoor rinks, we had to pay for it ourselves. The cheapest rates for Varsity Arena were in the early hours of the morning. I considered it a feather in my cap to be skating there—next stop, Maple Leaf Gardens. Well, I got on the Bathurst streetcar, carrying my skates and with my goalie pads strapped to my stick. I was eleven or twelve years old. There was no one on the streetcar except for the conductor and a crony of his. I deposited my ticket and took a seat. I was close enough to the front to hear the conductor say with a smile and a lilt, "There's a good Irish lad, getting up in the wee hours of the morning to play hockey."

I didn't have the heart to correct his impression; I didn't want to disappoint this charming-sounding Irishman. I say heart, but perhaps I didn't have the courage to tell him the truth. And I was secretly pleased that I didn't look Jewish. I'm ashamed to say it, but I felt less inferior because I didn't fit the stereotype: my eyes were blue, my skin was fair and freckled, my hair was brown and my nose was not big or crooked. I remember thinking, My skin and eye colour are pretty good, if only my hair were blond! Mind you, I'd still have been Albert Waxman, though I often wished I were Wayne or Watkins.

I wasn't the kind of kid who could cope by finding some humour in the situation. I took it all so seriously. But years later, in 1996, I acted in the CBC TV movie *Net Worth*, about a conflict between NHL owners and players, in which I played Jack Adams, the general manager of the Detroit Red Wings during their Stanley Cup days in the 1950s. The film won awards, and I made strong impact. As a result, I was invited to host the prestigious Conn Smythe Dinner in aid of physically challenged children. I didn't want to do it because I didn't want to honour the former owner of the Toronto Maple Leafs, who was known to be anti-Semitic. On the other hand, he did accomplish a lot for hockey and therefore for Canada, and of course the charity being supported was very worthy. As I was deliberating,

The Mona Lisa

they told me, perhaps as an enticement, that the invitation to host included an honorarium of $2,500. I said that I never take money for charity work. They then suggested that I could donate it back to the Conn Smythe Foundation. I said, "Wait a minute. Does the cheque say Conn Smythe anywhere on the face of it?" The answer was yes. "Good," I said. "I'll do it, but only if you make the cheque out to the United Jewish Appeal." Done!

When I was a kid, anti-Semitism was hard for me to address, let alone put in perspective. And it certainly was prevalent, not just in hockey—it was in the air. You heard about it all through the war. The war seemed sometimes to be only about the Jews, as if it was our fault. It seemed prudent, at the time, not to draw unnecessary attention to yourself; this was certainly often advised. When the war was finally over, the birth pangs of the soon-to-be State of Israel caused one to fear for the vastly outnumbered Jews. Here at home, I had heard often enough of other kids getting into violent confrontations, and although I was born after the infamous Christie Pits riots, there would be knots of fear in my stomach whenever I was at Christie Pits to play baseball, or just walking by on the way to Jewish school. Paranoia? Maybe. Persecution? Definitely. Fear and reason for fear? Definitely.

I certainly needed the steadying hand of a male authority figure. It wasn't going to be my hockey coach or my rabbi or any of my teachers, with whom I would rather have spent less time. My brother, as good and as intelligent as he was, couldn't be that for me. I had two uncles, my mother's brothers, with whom we were at times friendly and at times feuding; neither of them could fill that void in my life.

My mother was strong and ultimately became a powerful influence and guide in my life, but at this time she too wished that I could have had more conversation with my father. However, she probably had a different kind of communication in mind than I had. I remember once, around that time, coming home from school after having been given the strap. I was, in a way, proud of myself because all of the kids were impressed that I didn't cry. But it hurt, and I showed my mom the bruises that were still on my hands. "Good," she said. "At least someone is doing it."

The need for control and example in my life was presumably very much on my mother's mind when the gentleman callers would make their candy-coated visits. She wanted happiness for herself, of course, but even more, she wanted happiness for us. And this didn't mean just financial security; it meant an emotional stability in our lives.

I remember a very rich-looking man coming to visit my mother, and the box of chocolates he carried was different. The box was pale green and it said Jenny Lind. He had apparently known my mother in what they called "the old country." He now lived in Cincinnati. He was handsome and successful, and I thought sharp—perhaps too sharp—but nevertheless impressive. He wanted to reacquaint; he wanted a second chance with my mother. And now he had so much more to offer. He wanted Mom to accompany him back to Cincinnati, with or without Benny and me—preferably without. But not to worry, he reassured, we would be taken care of financially.

My mother was not only beautiful, she was smart, loving and loyal. We came first. My mom, the Mona Lisa, decided she would only marry a man who could convince her of his interest in being a father and a family man. That was a basic requirement, which resulted in many boxes of chocolates over a four-year interval before she graced a decision with her secret smile.

CHAPTER 3

Destination Unknown

Perhaps more inexplicable for me than an eleven-year-old organizing a hockey team is a twelve-year-old writing, producing, directing and acting in a play—especially if I am the twelve-year-old. From out of nowhere! So much of what I did, (namely sports) and what I did not do (namely arts and academics) made it highly unlikely that I would write a play. After all, I had never read one. I hadn't read anything yet. And what would I know about directing? I don't think I'd even seen a play, apart from *Abie's Irish Rose* viewed from the rafters of the Royal Alex, and although it was a memorable event in my life, I was too young to remember anything that happened on that illustrious stage. No, the only drama or comedy I saw would have been at the movies—or, better still, in my imagination, conjured up by radio shows like *Lux Theater of the Air*, *The Jack Benny Show*, *Fibber McGee and Molly*, *Wayne and Shuster*, *The Red Skelton Show*, *Duffy's Tavern* and, of course, all the serials: *The Lone Ranger*, *The Green Hornet*, *Suspense*, *Inner Sanctum*. So many trips into fun, fright and fantasy.

Movies? Their influence would not have been to turn me on to acting, but rather to encourage me to enlist in the US Marine Corps. All those movies with stars like John Wayne, tough and courageous and heroic and never crying: "From the halls of Montezuma to the shores of Tripoli." Movies like *Back to Bataan* and *Guadalcanal*

Diary, movies that taught us how good it was to be American, how right it was to be American, and how wrong it was to be anything else.

Hollywood was another planet altogether, full of names beyond the reach of a mere mortal like me: Jimmy Cagney, Robert Taylor, Loretta Young, Joan Crawford, Jack Benny, Fred Allen, George Burns and Gracie Allen, Bing Crosby, Bob Hope and Dorothy Lamour (she was my first crush; actually, I think Bambi was my first crush, but then I graduated to Dorothy Lamour), Abbott and Costello, Wayne and Shuster, Laurel and Hardy—but wait a minute, one day I found out that Wayne and Shuster did not come from another planet, as I had thought. They did their radio show just a streetcar-ride away, at a CBC studio on Mutual Street. They were Canadian. Wow. Maybe things *were* possible.

But nevertheless, acting didn't happen in the tiny circles that I moved in, filled with sports and young jocks. Girls might be impressed with acting, but not guys. It might have been expected from my brother, not me. Benny's precocious musical talent was maturing into a potential career as a concert pianist; he, rather than I, demonstrated a sensitivity towards the arts in general.

I was certainly not a likely candidate for involvement in writing, acting or directing. Producing? Well, if I organized a hockey club—that is, assembled a team, raised the financing by finding a sponsor, then ran the show, as it were, by seeing to it that we had regular practices, as well as making sure we were all present and on time for every game—then producer, maybe.

What prompted me to do it, I still don't know. The play was about Dagwood Bumstead, Blondie and their kids and dog going on a day trip to the summer cottage. I wish I had kept it, but I do remember it was about Dagwood rushing everyone. He wanted to leave as early as possible because they had only the one day for their holiday, and the later their arrival in the country, the less time for fun at the cottage. Dagwood, exasperated by their dawdling, feels they will have a holiday only because of him, so he badgers and hustles and finally gets them all into the car and on their way.

Cut to Act 2. They arrive at the cottage, get their bags out of the car and unload at the front door. Hooray! Everyone is happy and can't wait to unpack and get into their bathing suits. But wait! Dagwood can't find the key to the cottage. Oh no! In all his haste to get everyone packed and going, he forgot to take the key to the cottage. Embarrassed, apologetic and the laughing stock of his family and our audience, Dagwood has to take his family home without their holiday. That is, rather than having a holiday only because of him, they instead have no holiday at all and, yes, only because of him.

I consider that little play about Dagwood Bumstead, Blondie and their kids the start of what is now a career of more than fifty years. I wrote it, cast it, played Dagwood, directed it and produced it in a neighbour's house across the road on Burnside Drive. Bruce Alexander's house. They had a rec room in their basement; we just had a coal bin. Mr. and Mrs. Alexander were happy to have us putting on a play in the basement because, they felt, the rec room had been built for just this kind of activity for their kids and their kids' friends. Today, whenever I meet any of the Alexander family, I always thank them for that and more, more than they or I could have been aware of. I certainly didn't know what it all meant—I just liked what I was doing even though I didn't know what I was doing.

The fact that I didn't create the characters in my play but chose instead to take established characters with familiar and lovable foibles and comic characteristics may have been more by chance than design, but in either case was not at all unwise—there was an immediate recognition factor for the audience. I certainly had never heard of the word "plagiarism," but no matter, there was no financial gain for me.

As for remuneration, we charged the adults a nickel and the kids two cents; we raised $2.50 and gave it to the Red Cross. The latter was my mother's influence. She always taught us that if you live in a community, you don't just take from it, you also give back to it. For her it was the true understanding of the Hebrew word *tzedakah*—a concept that contains in it not just the will to give but more importantly, the duty to give, which exists regardless of your wealth or willingness.

In one stroke at the age of twelve, without knowing it, I had touched on a number of vocations that I would later embrace for the rest of my life: acting, directing, producing, writing, even charitable and community work.

I wasn't smitten yet, but the taste was there. The next day I had to get back to the more mundane meal of life. Particularly now, as I was in my thirteenth year (as my mother used to say), it was time to prepare for my bar mitzvah. Attendance at Jewish school was still a problem. As a matter of fact, my mother went to the extra expense of bringing the rabbi to our house, where absenteeism would presumably not be a problem, although lateness still was. However, once the class began in the privacy of my own home, with just the one-to-one of me and the rabbi, I was captive.

In public school I was not so captive. In a classroom of approximately thirty students, there was a lot more room for mischief. Mischief gained the respect of the boys and the attention of the girls. Some went in for slingshots and spitballs, others for paper missiles and missives. I preferred pigtails and inkwells, flirtation and exploration. I couldn't wait for the parties on the weekends. Mischievous in school, I was shy and reticent at parties. Nevertheless, I anxiously anticipated the kissing games: Postman, Doctor and Nurse, Spin the Bottle. Delights and, unfortunately, dilemmas were the result. I was still playing hockey, and more often than not I would come to these parties with a cracked lip and my mouth swollen out to here, and would wonder why, when it was my turn to spin the bottle, the girls suddenly lost interest.

Reason enough for my passion for hockey to wane? A little, but something else happened, something that put a new charge of electricity in me.

I was going to the movies one Saturday afternoon and the streetcar conductor asked me if I was going where everyone else seemed to be going—to the Tivoli on Richmond Street, to see a movie called *The Jolson Story*. Well, I didn't like the look of the lineups outside the theatre and the name Jolson didn't mean anything to me, so I was going instead to a movie house around the corner from the Tivoli and a couple of blocks up Yonge Street called the Loews Theatre, which now houses the Elgin and Winter Garden theatres. Both those spaces existed then too, but the building was known only as the Loews. It was showing a movie called *The Beginning or The End,* which I felt at the time was probably a more important picture because it was about the atomic bomb; conflicting feelings of devastation and triumph aroused by that weapon were still very strong in 1947.

Well, there is good reason I don't remember the picture about the atomic bomb. The picture itself bombed and was soon forgotten, as is perhaps the now-defunct Tivoli—forgotten by some, that is, but not by me. I will always remember the Tivoli because *The Jolson Story*, unlike the picture about the bomb, just kept on running week after week. Much as I hated the lineups, I finally had to go and see it, and when I did, I couldn't leave the theatre. I sat and watched the next showing and the next, until the last showing that day. And then I came back every Saturday with a lunch that I had packed so I wouldn't have to leave the theatre until the last showing was completed. All told, I saw *The Jolson Story* at the Tivoli Theatre twenty-seven times.

I was smitten. Not like a fan or a groupie—I wasn't in search of an autograph or some piece of memorabilia. Rather, there was something about the way Jolson could electrify an audience that touched me to the proverbial core. I think "electrify" is a better word for the energy Jolson generated than "turn on." His rich voice and magnetic personality and performance didn't need the enhancement of electronic equipment. Blackface? Yes. But put it in perspective: to consider that politically incorrect or even a gimmick would be judging him by the standards of today. Besides, I liked him better without the makeup. His was just pure, raw talent, musically rushing out in sadness or gladness to connect directly, viscerally, with an audience—like he said in song, "to start your feet tapping" or "lift you out of your seat."

It was the first time a movie personality had come off the screen and touched me personally. And he was Jewish. That didn't make a difference to most people, nor at first to me, but it certainly was a bonus. I was part of a worldwide audience who thrilled when Jolson shouted, "You ain't heard nothing yet." But more important than being part of that audience, he touched me in terms of the direction my life was to take. I wanted to do what he did—not sing (I couldn't sing) but touch an audience. Maybe I could somehow do that? In retrospect I now know why I chose to do that little play about Dagwood Bumstead. What Jolson's talent and energy touched in me was in there to be touched; fertile ground, as it were, in which to grow and make of me a living instrument of dramatic and comedic expression. I didn't know it then, but this meant a lifetime of cultivating this potential in myself.

I bought all his records, 78s and then LPs. Decca stock went up, and I certainly contributed. I began to imitate him *à la* Larry Parks (the actor who played Jolson in *The Jolson Story*)—that is, in front of a record player, playing his songs. I did it for myself, but it was exciting when I did it for guests in the house or at community functions at the YMHA. I got really good at it. And if I touched the audience who were watching, I felt, obviously, that it was mostly Al Jolson who was doing it. But maybe it was a little bit of Al Waxman too. Although I was impersonating Al Jolson, I wasn't trying to be him. Mind you, I am confident that I had him nailed every bit as much as Larry Parks did. But I wasn't trying to lose myself in him. Rather, I was projecting my own energy, creating with my timing, talent and feelings a portion of the total performance that was touching the audience.

Now I really wanted to be an actor, but I didn't know if I was good enough, and I didn't know how it could happen: did I have to put out energy to make it happen, or was it to be a passive thing, a dream of being discovered? Just as then, I would often over the years alternate between driving confidence and wishful thinking.

I may have done smooth performances of Al Jolson, but my bar mitzvah reading, speaking and singing did not exactly go without a hitch. The selections from the writings of the prophets that are appended to every sabbath Torah reading are usually read by the bar mitzvah boy, and constitute the Haftarah reading. Thankfully, my Haftarah portion wasn't a long one. Still, it was long enough for my mother to sit on the edge of her seat up in the gallery with the other women, hoping I would make it through without a mistake. Well, I sang somewhat haltingly, but somehow not without confidence, perhaps because most of my guests (that is, friends I'd invited) would not have known the difference because they weren't Jewish; they were the kids I played hockey with. At the finish I was rather proud and my mother was relieved that I had stumbled only twice over the Hebrew words in the scroll. Her joy rained down on me, mixing with the sweet shower of nuts and candies thrown from all the women up in the gallery. It was finally fun, and I will remember it forever.

My bar mitzvah was not the splendid affair that many kids have, which takes place over two days, that is, the Saturday-morning service and the Sunday-evening celebration. The reason was that my dad was not there, and so Mom and I agreed we would just have the Saturday-morning service at the Henry Street synagogue—which, by the way, was subsequently a Chinese church and is now a Russian Orthodox church (I love that aspect of Toronto: continuity within change). We had a luncheon after the service in the small reception area of the synagogue, during which I delivered a speech in English and Yiddish. Nothing inspirational was said, nothing momentous or memorable, but sincere thanks were given and respectful promises made. Although I am sure I was nervous, I can now look back on that moment with affection, knowing even then that I was not yet a man but merely embarking on the journey to manhood.

I knew enough at that time not to have the audacity to say, "Today I am a man." Rather, the popular bar mitzvah joke at the time better suited my speech, namely, "Today I am a fountain pen." I think I must have received three or four Parker 51s, the status pen in 1948.

I can't remember ever writing with any of them. I think I leaned too heavily on the nib. So, until the advent of the ballpoint, I didn't write much. As I've already said, I didn't read much either, but I was pretty good at arithmetic. Without writing the numbers down I could rapidly and accurately go through the multiplication tables. Division, addition and subtraction problems, even with large numbers, were easy for me to solve in my head. Decimals and algebra were fun. When the teachers held math competitions, I was usually the winner in our class. For that matter, even though I was a poor reader, I did well in the spelling bees.

Inevitably, though, the time came when I finally had to read a book. I was told that even though I would probably pass, I would not be promoted if I didn't read the novel that was on the curriculum. Fortunately for me, it was *A Tale of Two Cities*. I read that book slowly, and fell in love with it. And then I read it again. I think I felt that if I kept on reading it, I might become Sidney Carton: "It is a far, far better thing that I do, than I have ever done..." Not even John Wayne, or any member of the United States Marine Corps, had the loyalty in his character, the romance in his soul or the courage in his heart to make such a glorious sacrifice. That book became a trophy for me. I think there is a copy on every bookshelf in our house. Mind you, perhaps because I started reading so late, I am still a slow reader. Whenever I finish a book, any book, it becomes a trophy on my shelf.

I think my mother and I were very much alike. Certainly, reading slowly was one of the things we had in common. My mother, who had very little formal education in her native Poland, didn't start reading in English until after she came to Canada, when she was in her thirties. I think it was difficult for her to keep up at night school, so she abandoned that effort in favour of reading the novel that was the basis for a movie she loved. That novel was *How Green Was My Valley*. Like me rereading *A Tale of Two Cities*, she would reread *How Green Was My Valley*, but in her case it was starting in her mid-thirties and continuing for the rest of her life. It was the only book in English that she ever read. *How Green Was My Valley* was in the night table by her bed for over thirty years; before she turned out the lights, she would read just a few paragraphs from her frayed-at-the-corners, maroon-coloured hardcover copy. When she reached the end of the book, she would immediately go back to the beginning and start again. I love the sight of her in my mind's eye, under the blankets, propped up against the pillow-covered headboard of the bed with her glasses on. I can still hear her mouthing each word quietly to herself but audibly struggling with some of the words—less, presumably, with each go round, but always, always, divinely *kvelling* (radiating joy) with the huge humanity of the story. After a few paragraphs she would close the book, the same well-worn copy for all those years, and place it in the night table beside her *siddur*, which she also read regularly, and then turn off the lights and go to sleep.

Happily, I was finally introduced to reading. I discovered that books offered not only rich experiences and ideas, but characters that could inspire me. I didn't have a mentor or father figure at the time, so I was searching, whether I was aware of it or not, for guidance and inspiration. From the movies came a dynamic motivator like Al Jolson, while books provided a model in the character of Sidney Carton from *A Tale of Two Cities*.

Of course, in real life, right in my own house, there was the inspiration of my mother. She was strength and sensitivity, wisdom and *saychel* (practical, good common sense) personified. At this time in my life, however, I collided with her practical, good common sense.

I had decided that in order to find out about dreams and destinations, in order to find out whether I could be good enough, in order to learn something about acting, I had to take some acting classes. My mother wouldn't hear of it. This, she claimed, was not only more expensive than goalie gloves but even more unnecessary. I countered by saying she always wanted each of us to have an artistic hobby. Benny had piano, why couldn't I have acting lessons? Sure, an artistic hobby, she said, sure, if you take violin lessons. She had always wanted Benny to play the piano and me to play the violin. I again said no to that, but argued that if she were willing to pay for violin lessons, why not pay for me to study an art form I wanted to learn something about and maybe pursue professionally?

But actors, for her, were ne'er-do-wells, gypsies, bums, she said, unreliable, unstable people, and unlike the piano or violin, acting was not a respectable art form, it did not have the dignity of music or literature. No, don't ask again, she reiterated. She would not hear of it.

My earnings from part-time jobs were not enough. Without my mother's help, I wasn't able as yet to take the necessary steps towards a possible career in acting.

CHAPTER 4

A Watershed Year

My mother successfully steered our ship through waters that she charted. The waters may have on occasion been rough, but she stayed her course. She knew what she wanted and where she was going—so much so that I have to wonder whether she was just having fun with us whenever she asked our opinion about any of the gentleman callers. I don't think she was insincere; I'm sure she wanted us to be happy with her choice. But it was definitely *her* choice, because when the real thing, as she saw it, came along, we were not so much consulted as informed. Why not? It was her life. But it was ours too, and it took some getting used to. She seldom saw any of these would-be suitors more than once, which was reassuring in a way, at least for me. But suddenly we noticed that she was going out with one man more than she had with any of the others. At first it was usually in a foursome, probably with the friends who had introduced them. His name was Jack Leipciger. Eventually we noticed there were no others, just Jack.

Jack Leipciger was a strong, nice-looking man. He must have been strong, not just physically, but in terms of character and determination too. How else could he have come through five years of the Holocaust, including Auschwitz, in one piece and in good health? Not only that, but to have successfully protected and guided his teenage son, Nathan, through that murderous maze—that, to me, even though I didn't want to be impressed, was most impressive.

Jack was always well dressed (he was a tailor by profession), even fashionably, and would come to pick up my mother smelling like a cosmetics counter. I would later kid him about that, but I'm sure it made my mother feel good. He was respectful too. When we had dinner, for example, no sooner did my mom serve soup than I'd be halfway through it, but then I'd notice that Jack hadn't yet picked up his spoon, and he wouldn't until my mother sat down to eat.

As much as my mother had strength and smarts, a woman alone at that time could easily be taken advantage of. Business partners could disregard her even if they were friends or worse still, as in my mother's case, blood brothers from whom loyalty should be expected. Even the law worked against her: for her own good, it was claimed, she was prevented from freely entering and working in the tavern or "beer hotel," as it was colloquially called, a business of which she was now half owner.

By this time, because of friction in the family between my mother and her brothers after my dad's death, there had been a parting of the ways. My mother and one brother, Uncle Moishe, were bought out of the Beresford and became the new owners of the Simcoe Public House on Eastern Avenue.

Those were the days when there were two entrances to these establishments, one for men and the other for "ladies with escorts." The assumption, of course, was that the escort was an able-bodied man. The floors were all tiled, like a public lavatory, to make it easier to mop up the blood after the fist fights every night. The proprietors, for their own safety, tapped beer behind the counter of a caged-in bar—not an ideal place for the Mona Lisa. In the company of a proud husband, her presence could be better registered. It made her, in her own right, even more to be reckoned with.

A woman alone could easily be overlooked socially as well, but Jack looked good beside her, and together, they were quite a couple.

Friends of my mom's, particularly the matchmaker types, would take me aside for whispered and earnest conversations about me not wanting my mother to be lonely ("You don't want that, do you?") or me wanting my mother to be happy ("You do want that, don't you?").

Of course I wanted the best for her, and of course I knew that this new relationship didn't mean she loved my dad less. Still, I didn't like it. As much as I knew there was nothing wrong with Jack, I didn't take to him at first, or to Nate, my new brother-to-be, my stepbrother (a description I never liked—I think there's something mean about it—but still that's how the relationship was defined). Perhaps Nate, who was nineteen years old, a little more than five years my senior, felt the same about us. It appeared so, because he seemed sullen and reticent. I should have appreciated—actually, I'm sure that I did—that what he had gone through in his teenage years was a million times worse than an anti-Semitic insult in a hockey locker room. What he had undergone explained, perhaps justified, not only a sullen outlook but indeed a colouring of his perspective for the rest of his life. However, it was my life I was thinking about at that time.

My mom tried to make everything work out. The first night that we all had dinner together—Jack, Nate, Benny, me and my mom—was in the cramped dining room of our duplex on Burnside Drive. Mom and Jack were not yet married, but we were all aware that they would be soon. This evening was more than an audition for togetherness, it was togetherness daring to stick its toe into icy waters as a necessary preliminary step towards jumping in.

It must have been tough on both Jack and Mom as they were confronted by three adolescents who were not yet ready to endorse, let alone embrace, what was clearly in the offing. Their task was to make us all happy with each other, to win us over. And my mother, God bless her memory, led the way. She prepared a sumptuous dinner. She made our house sparkling clean and beautiful, and she prepared gifts for everyone, to make us all feel welcome within this new household.

She was on her own in doing this—no one to help her, no one to check with as she anxiously saw to everything. In her haste, she overlooked one small detail. She presented Nate with what was (as I mentioned earlier) a special gift in those days, a Parker 51 pen. But it was one of mine, one of the three or four I had received earlier that year for my bar mitzvah. Goodness knows I had more than I could possibly use, but my poor mom forgot to ask me first. She had intended to, of course, but with the inevitable last-minute rush (she was still working in the restaurant as well) she must have thought she already had.

When we were all seated at the dining-room table like a typical family gathered for dinner, the opportunity was perfect, so she gifted Nate, unbeknownst to me, with one of my Parker 51s. He, I imagine, was touched and appreciative, but the truth is I can't recall what his reaction was, because I bolted from the table and ran to my room. I threw myself face down on the bed and cried. The pen didn't mean that much to me—my mother was right about that—but it was the manner in which it had been done that shocked and hurt me. It was, I felt, symbolic of what was happening: a betrayal of, and disloyalty to, me and my father.

My mother immediately followed me from the dining-room table to my bedroom. Whatever embarrassment or awkwardness this incident caused her was secondary now to her concern for me. She leaned over me, her face pressed against the back of my head, and whispered in my ear, "I'm sorry, I'm sorry. I should have asked you. I'll buy you another one."

"It was my pen," I uttered through muffled sobs.

"I'll get you another one," she tried to reassure.

"You didn't ask me."

"I'm sorry. I should have."

"It's not the pen, Mom."

"I know."

And then it poured out, aching, just as though my father had, at that moment, died again.

"I know, I know," my mother said, as she caressed me and stroked my hair and cried with me, "I know."

I don't remember anything else about that evening except that my heart eventually went out to my mother as hers had gone out to me. She wanted everything to work out for all of us, and ultimately it did—not that night perhaps, but Nate and Benny and I would finally become resigned to the upcoming marriage. I probably knew when and where it was scheduled (City Hall, I think), but we did not attend; rather, we were informed after the fact. I thought that was wise of them, because I don't think I could have witnessed it. Recently, Nate and I discussed our mutual past for the first time in our lives (about forty-eight years after the marriage), not by way of my doing research for this book but just by happenstance. He told me that he had felt, if not abandoned by Jack, cut out of his life, certainly after having been so inextricably intertwined, and he therefore would have preferred to have witnessed the wedding. (It's often been said that no one ever taught us how to be parents; you just try your best—as they certainly did.) Ironically, when I told Nate during that same conversation of my perspective on the Parker 51 incident, he told me he was unaware of the hurt and awkwardness it had caused. I think that's a tribute to how well my mom manoeuvred to smooth things over that night.

I think they both, Jack and my mother, deserve tribute for recognizing their mutual good fortune in finding each other, for having the wisdom to seize a second chance at happiness, and for their work on the delicate task of sculpting a new family. Many thanks to them for their strength and *saychel* (good sense) and patience, for accepting some short-term pain in exchange for long-term satisfaction for all five of us.

Indeed, Jack took steps to smooth things over as well. He must have done so with Nate. Benny didn't present too much of a problem because he would soon be leaving home to study medicine at the University of Western Ontario in London. But Jack did have to contend with me. It was clear to him that I did not take to him. It was a foregone conclusion that I would not call him Dad. As a matter of fact, we all decided that for Benny and me he would be Jack and for Nate my mother would be Toby. That made things a bit easier, but Jack knew he had to do something more proactive with me (although I don't think that word existed in those days). The action he took was certainly smart of him, and courageous, knowing my mom's feelings on the subject, and for me it was very fortunate. In order to win me over he said, "You want acting lessons? You will have acting lessons."

This was still my fourteenth year, the year of my bar mitzvah. What a year! A watershed year. The year my mother met Jack. The year we would start a new family and search for a new house. The year I began acting lessons, which led to my performing roles on radio shows at CKEY and CBC. The year, now that I had finally read a novel, that I would graduate to Oakwood Collegiate high school.

My bar mitzvah year, 1948, also marked the birth of a nation that had existed as the Jewish homeland for thousands of years: this was the year of Israel's inauguration into statehood. No more need for self-denial. Jews suddenly stood tall all over the world. Jews no longer turned the other cheek. Jews were tough. And something I never knew before: it was fun to be Jewish. Most important, for Jews and for many non-Jews as well, the new Israel was a symbol of hope, an example of vision and inspiration for a world that was still trying to pull itself out of the Holocaust, out of devastation and demoralization from Europe all the way around the globe to the Far East.

My brother Benny had become a fervent Zionist, and I would sometimes tag along with him to his meetings and get-togethers. The political message was a little heavy-handed for me, but the spirit of Israel was refreshing and vital. And for me it was fun. The dancing and singing were lively, and the girls were reportedly free thinkers. They were "easier," or so I was told. Unfortunately, I never received any first-hand evidence of that, but it was worth dancing all those horas (they never slow-danced) at the Habonim Club and the even more left-leaning Hashomer Hatzair to try and find out.

In the meantime, Jack moved into our home on Burnside Drive—and into the room my mother had shared with my father. Benny and I, of course, still shared the same room, and Nate stayed with close cousins of his for the short time it took to find a new place to house the Waxmans and the Leipcigers.

I don't remember learning very much in my radio acting classes, except how to mark up a script—a slash between words to indicate a pause or a breath, for example, and underlining a word for emphasis. It was too technical and artificial for me. From the beginning I trusted my instincts. The classes, though, did in one way prove to be educational and productive: we were on the radio, and that in itself was rewarding. I don't recall any financial remuneration, but what was important was the professional, on-the-job training and experience.

My first teacher, Marjorie Purvey, was blonde, an "older woman" from my perspective, but very attractive, probably once glamorous (only fitting, I thought, for show business) and loaded with radio savvy. She held her classes on Mount Pleasant, a little above Bloor Street, in an old Rosedale-type house. The classroom consisted of a studio where we all sat around a couple of standing mikes, which were opposite a glassed-in control booth—like the real thing. And if you were any good in class, you got to do her radio show, a kids' show called *Peter and the Dwarf*. This was broadcast live every week on CKEY, a very popular local radio station.

CKEY was situated at the corner of University Avenue and Dundas Street. It was a small building compared to what's there now, but it was imposing, fronted by three two-storey-high pillars. It looked the way I imagined a studio in Hollywood would look. When I passed through those portals, I felt like I was entering another world. Imagine that! It was just CKEY, but at that time in my life, entering that building made me feel even more important than I already felt with the script under my arm.

CKEY was owned then by Jack Kent Cooke, for whom I had already worked (not that he would have known) as a delivery boy for *Liberty* magazine. He later left CKEY and *Liberty* and his other Canadian interests behind to become a media and sports mogul in the United States, where his holdings at one time included the Los Angeles Lakers and later, the Washington Redskins.

There were some very talented people assembled for the casts of *Peter and the Dwarf* every week at CKEY. One of them, older than me by only a couple of years, was Sidney J. Furie. Sid went on to become a successful film director. Although he and I, and our families, have socialized over the years, we finally worked together, forty-five years after *Peter and the Dwarf*, on a film called *Iron Eagle IV*, which he directed and I acted in along with Lou Gossett Jr.

The only thing that could have been more important for me at that time than Marjorie Purvey and her class and radio show was the classroom and radio show I moved on to next. The teacher's name was Lynn Cooke, and again I don't remember anything at all about her class, but her show was a step up. It was called *Doorway to Fairyland*. It was a better and more prestigious show, and on a network, a full network, not just a single local station. It aired coast-to-coast live on CBC every Saturday morning—live on CBC for all of Canada, just like the hockey game I would listen to that evening. I was impressed, and so were the girls at school whenever they saw the script under my arm; I made sure they did by having it right on top of the books I was carrying. Mind you, whenever any of the boys came around, I quickly shielded the cover of the script; it would not have served me well, with all the hockey pucks and jocks I hung around with, to be associated with something called *Doorway to Fairyland*, even if I did play ogres and pirates.

And what joy it was for me to play those characters. The young artist in me could let go of guarded reality and immerse himself in adventure and fantasy, all the while developing vocal characterization and projection skills. Live radio was at once intimidating and exciting:

there was no safety net. You couldn't screw up. I would stand at the mike, ready to launch, awaiting that first pointed-hand cue from the other side of the glass, drying the puddles of sweat in the palms of my hands by rubbing them against the sides of my pants just one more time before the cue came. And then it came—and with it the pulse of live performance and the immediacy of now. You knew you were making contact, touching an audience.

I still love radio drama. It was again a joy for me in the 1980s to work in those same CBC studios at 354 Jarvis Street. This time I played Canada's pre-eminent criminal lawyer, Eddie Greenspan, in the radio series *Scales of Justice*. The studio was an old mansion, formerly the Havergal Girls' School, which became at the CBC's inception its radio studios. (Since the advent of the CBC Broadcast Centre, of course, all that is past tense.) The studios in the 1980s looked the same as in the forties, but the process was different. Now there was tape and editing, stop and start, and as many "takes" as was deemed necessary by the actor and director, or allowable by schedule and budget.

What price progress? Risk, and with it the adrenaline rush of artistic expression, gone? Possibly. Now it was all the more important to hang on to purpose and integrity, because then progress in the form of technical advances can assist the actor without eliminating risk. Risk-taking goes to the essence of talent. With integrity intact—that is, never taking what it's all about for granted—and a firm grasp of purpose, progress can assist the actor to achieve greater artistry.

So I will always hold the memory of the perspiration in my palms, not just with fond nostalgia, but with strict intention. Fear signals a respect for the task, respect for the craft and art of acting in any medium. Nowadays, let's say, standing in the wings before an entrance on stage, if I feel as I usually do some butterflies in my belly, I know that they are part of the springboard; I know that to control those butterflies I have to redouble my concentration, to focus on my purpose. I know that some nervousness, therefore, will help give me lift-off to the rush of performance I will in a moment embark on.

Performing on the radio in the late 1940s made me feel almost a oneness with the performers I listened to from the other planets. There was something rarefied and glamorous and important about the professionalism of production, something exalted and special about talent, and I wanted to believe that I belonged to that, to the excitement of that.

One night I was at a skating party at the Wells Hill public rink, near the corner of Bathurst Street and St. Clair Avenue. It's still there. It was dark, well past dinnertime and cold, but we were all having fun and no one wanted to leave. But really, the truth was no one would leave as long as Mary Taylor was there. She was the prettiest girl in school, and at fourteen already built like a woman. Sexy but delicate, as I remember, in her lovely parka and white skates laced up high, she looked like Snow White, and all of us fawned around her like the seven dwarfs. As long as she was staying, I was staying. I'm sure that's what everybody else thought too. The boys wanted to be with her and the girls wanted to be like her. Suddenly, she said she had to leave. Everybody groaned, "Oh no, why?"

"I want to get home in time to hear *Kraft Music Hall*," was her explanation. "I don't want to miss Al Jolson." That pleased me. I identified with Jolson not only because I used to impersonate him, but especially because now we were both on the radio.

Then came something even better. One of the kids said, "What do you want to hear *him* for? He's Jewish."

"I don't care," was her response. "I just like to hear him sing."

I smiled with the warmth of silent victory, not only because I was Jewish but also because of the understanding that there was something very significant about talent, and I dared to believe I had it too. Over the years I would, on occasion, identify with Jolson. Even five decades after that skating party, when I would star in Neil Simon's *Proposals* at the Royal Alexandra Theatre, I was given the same dressing room Jolson used when he played the Alex, first in 1918 and many times during the 1920s and '30s. At almost opposite ends of the century, we shared the same dressing room. This realization, plus the memory of my parents introducing me to the Royal Alex as a child, brought an inner glow—it would be full circle times two. Maybe I, from that same stage, could make an audience laugh and feel good the way my parents did when they came here. And maybe I, in my own way, just as Jolson did in his, would turn on an audience from the stage of the Royal Alex.

I apparently did touch someone out there in the radio audience of Canada in the late 1940s. Perhaps not as specifically or individually as Jolson touched Mary Taylor, but there was a girl (I've since learned from a reliable source) on a farm just outside of Beauséjour, Manitoba, who never missed *Doorway to Fairyland*. She listened to it raptly every week. It was, of course, the show itself she responded to, rather than me personally. The personal connection with me came some twenty years later, when Sara Shapiro would become Sara Waxman.

CHAPTER 5

And Revelations Still to Come

A centre hall plan. That was something my mother had always wished for when she allowed herself to dream: a house with a centre hall plan. And she finally got one! 25 Glen Cedar Road. We finally made it "up the hill." Not quite Forest Hill Village, mind you. As pleasant as Cedarvale sounds, it was just outside Forest Hill Village. That was something that made a difference to some people, though not to anyone in my family, except, to be honest, perhaps me, at least once in a while. It was not so much a question of wealth as of image. No longer concerned about looking like the Joneses, I now wanted to keep up with my brethren—well, occasionally I felt like that. But certainly everyone else in the new family was thrilled with our new house, and I came to love it as well.

We had started with literally two rooms on the second floor of a house on Wales Street in Kensington Market. At 74 Wales Street, we had been tenants of Mr. and Mrs. Greenbaum. That portion of Wales Street was expropriated by the city to expand Western Hospital on Bathurst Street, which later became part of the complex now known as the Toronto Hospital.

From 74 Wales Street we moved to 414A Spadina Avenue, and then to 96 Burnside Drive. From two rooms with a shared kitchen and washroom, to two rooms plus a kitchen and washroom, to five rooms—and now, at 25 Glen Cedar Road, eight rooms plus a wood-panelled rec room downstairs and a maid's room beside it (not that we ever had a maid). Plus—another status symbol—a two-car garage (not that we had a car). There was also a long driveway that would prove helpful for my first driving lessons. Wait—I'm not sure, but I do seem to recall a car on our narrow driveway at Burnside Drive. We must have bought our first car just prior to moving to Glen Cedar Road. It was a Studebaker. The joke at the time was that you couldn't tell whether it was coming or going because you couldn't tell the front from the back. The car must have been for Jack and Benny, because my mom couldn't drive and I was too young. But soon there would be Nate and me, heavy demand on one car. Inevitably there were fights over the car, as well as arguments about whose turn it was to wash and whose to dry after supper—and in those days we had two sets of everyday dishes in our kosher home, one for meat and one for dairy, and others for special holidays, such as Passover.

It's good that we had a lot of dishes and it's good we had a lot of room, because my mother decided to answer a call put out by the Jewish Immigrant Aid Services (JIAS) for those who had room to take in Displaced Persons, that is, refugee survivors of the Holocaust, particularly those without any family here.

We each got our own room. Upstairs there were four bedrooms: the master bedroom for Jack and my mom, and one for each of the three sons. I'm sure, after the deprivation and horribly degrading experiences of the Holocaust, that Jack and Nate felt this was beyond their wildest dreams. Hey, it was beyond Benny's and mine too. Mind you, Nate's nose was a little out of joint because Benny got a bigger room than he did, and at the front of the house. There did seem to be a competitive edge to their relationship at the beginning, but I don't think that lasted for very long. After all, we each had our own room, so we were all very privileged, regardless of the room size. Because I had the biggest room, I had to share, but I was happy to. My roommate was Jack Weinberger, the first of the Displaced Persons (or DPs as they were sometimes called) to come into our fold. We were paid a nominal rent—which was facilitated by JIAS to help defray costs incurred on their behalf.

It was as though I now had yet another older brother. Jack W. was, I think, a year or two older than Nate. And soon after Jack W. came Jerry Konvoy, who took the maid's room in the basement. That room had its own entrance; many other survivors came to visit. They became like family, and visited not just Jerry and Jack but also my parents, particularly my mom. Our house was open house at all hours. At mealtime there would be the four or five of us, and Jack W. and Jerry K., plus a few of their friends, too. My mother would be feeding as many as seven or eight hungry men every night for dinner. And with Benny away at the University of Western Ontario most of the time, I'd be the only unaccented English-speaking person at our United Nations dinner table. They were from Poland and other parts of Eastern Europe, Italy, Germany, France and Israel—and I was from Canada. It was fun for me.

I now had a whole group of older brothers. They were all in their early twenties, and their hormones were raging. They had a great appetite for life. They had ambition as well as a lot of catching up to do. And they all seemed to have a sense of humour. Their stories were horrific, but they told them to me, if not with humour, certainly with a positive attitude and seldom with self-pity. For example, Jack W. was somehow able to explain his gold front tooth as a funny anecdote. In the concentration camp he had once come late for a meal and was therefore not allowed to partake in the meagre morsels the others were given. He was told that if he didn't come exactly on time, he wouldn't be allowed to eat, so he arrived early the next day. In fact, he was first in line, with a playful grin that said, "See?!" Spunky? Yes, why not? He was just a kid. For this he received a punch in the mouth that knocked out his front tooth, which was ultimately replaced by a gold one after the war. Perhaps humour does come, as some have said, from pain.

Even more painful, and told not with humour but certainly with thankfulness, was the story of Jerry K.'s saving of his brother's life. His brother, who sometimes visited, corroborated this story. The prisoners were being marched from one camp to another along a muddy road on a cold, wintry day. They were weak and starving, but were not allowed to stop for a rest. Those who fell by the wayside were left to die or were shot. Jerry's brother was weak and about to fall over from exhaustion, and would have been one of the dead ones on the roadside. Jerry wouldn't let his brother fall. He draped his brother, who was the same size he was, over his back, hanging straight down with his arms over Jerry's shoulders and Jerry hugging his brother's arms close to his own chest, so that his brother's face, over Jerry's shoulder, was almost cheek-to-cheek with his. As undernourished as he was, Jerry was able to find the inner resources to carry his brother like this for hours, the better part of the day, till they reached their destination. And they both lived! Vivid testimony to the possibility of an ordinary human being reaching extraordinary heights, and a blessed example of the timeless teaching that "I am my brother's keeper."

They did not indulge in these stories. I heard them only very occasionally. They were more future-oriented, and what they wanted in the present was to work and make money, to play now while paving the way for later. They all worked hard, saved money, bought clothes and cars (indeed, Jack W. taught me to drive), and were preoccupied with having good times after work.

One of them, Abby B., was a good-looking, athletic stud, who enlisted me, with my unaccented English, to phone beautiful women and get dates for him. One time, he somehow got Miss Toronto's phone number and asked me to call her, say that I was him and get a date for Saturday night. Well, I deepened my fifteen-year-old voice, acted smooth and confident (I couldn't have done that for myself), and got him a date for Saturday night. When he arrived to pick her up, she said he didn't sound like he did on the phone, and he nonchalantly dismissed her remark with, "I hed ah kold. I'm OK now." I'm sure he was, and not only that, I'm sure she, too, thought he was.

Those guys were always scoring, and I wanted to score too. I wanted to be a man! One Saturday night I double-dated with someone who was sixteen and could legally drive, while I rode in the back seat, necking and petting. At the end of the evening, when I was dropped off, my face and shirt collar were still covered in lipstick. As I was approaching the door of the house, I was about to wipe off any tell-tale signs when I heard all the guys inside. I quickly decided to leave the evidence, to wear it like a badge of victory—evidence that I too was a man. And sure enough, when I walked into the house and they saw the way I looked, the place erupted in cheers: "Way to go, Al! What a man!" I felt tall!

Suddenly, my mother, who had overheard, called me into the kitchen and said quietly to me, "A real man doesn't have to tell." This message, so contrary to the prevailing attitude of bragging and conquest, gave me a moment's pause, but I understood and have been guided by her honourable advice ever since.

I never heard any Holocaust stories from Jack Leipciger. He didn't seem to want to dwell on the past, at least not in any way that would be an imposition on others. But every night, he would watch the war movies after the late-night news. In those days there was only one late-night talk show, first Steve Allen for a few years, and then Jack Paar. The other channels played movies, usually old war movies. Jack would quietly watch, mesmerized, his eyes a little moist.

The only story I ever heard about Jack's wartime experiences was second-hand, from my mother. Towards the end of the war Nate and Jack were standing beside each other in a long line of men. An SS officer stepped smartly in front of the line, indicating for one prisoner to get onto the back of a waiting truck and the next to get onto a second waiting truck. As he marched along, he pointed one person in one direction and the next in the other direction, and so on down the line. None of the prisoners knew where either truck was headed. It was obvious, however, that no two people beside each other were going on the same truck. It appeared, frighteningly, as though Nate and Jack, so close to the end of the war, were finally to be separated, and to what end, who knew? They were fearful because it was known that the ovens were working overtime.

Jack, oddly enough, had on an apparently new, shiny-looking, sturdy pair of boots. When the SS officer, whose boots were worn and scruffy, stood in front of Jack and Nate, he saw two things: a father and son, and a pair of good boots. He could have simply said, "Give me your boots," and sent them on their separate ways. Instead, he said, "Give me your boots and I'll give you your son."

Nate, as well as bringing up a beautiful family with his wife, Bernice, and carrying on a successful career as an electrical engineer, has been a dedicated spokesman for Holocaust memorials and for causes on behalf of Holocaust survivors.

I was now in my teenage years, taking acting lessons once a week from a woman whom I have often called my "Madame Sousatzka" (I hope you saw the film of that name). She was Josephine Barrington, and she was for me a superb, inspired acting coach. She was elegant and beautiful, and she was herself a good actress as well as a teacher of good actors. Before me she had taught, amongst others, Lloyd Bochner, who was at Stratford when it started and later worked on movies and TV shows that came out of Hollywood. She also taught the Davis brothers, Donald and Murray, and their sister, Barbara Chilcott, all of whom were also at Stratford, and who were the founders of the Crest Theatre up on Bayview Avenue, an important interlude in Canadian theatre. I remember seeing a production of *The Rainmaker* there with a beautiful young actress in it called Kate Reid. I thought, Wow, one day I want to work with her. I did, years later, in the Academy Award–nominated *Atlantic City*, directed by the late Louis Malle. As well, Kate played my mother in one of her last performances, in an HBO film called *Teamster Boss*.

I recall preparing a scene once for Miss Barrington's class. I can't remember exactly what the scene was, but I do remember the result. So often an actor needs to be reassured that he has talent. Of course there is only one person who can answer the question "Am I talented?" Only you can finally decide whether you have talent, and yet, ironically, talent is what you need right from the beginning. You have to believe you have it! Critics can't give it to you or take it away from you. Friends, loved ones and fans can tell you you're talented, but nice as that stroking is, the answer that counts is the one you give yourself. Still, as a young, fragile-on-the-inside actor, I needed to hear something about my talent from Miss Barrington. I prepared that scene all week, to the exclusion of whatever other duties I may have had, and prayed to God before going to sleep that after I presented the scene, Miss Barrington would say something about my talent. That I was good. That I had what it takes, that elusive "it."

Well, I went to class and presented my scene, and afterwards the impact of my work caused a moment of silence in the class. Miss Barrington gazed at me with a warm, proud and respectful smile on her face, almost a look of awe, as her eyes took me in completely. And then she said, "You are a *remarkable* actor."

I shared that story later that evening with my mom, and even she, who had no love for the profession of acting, leaned over and gave me a kiss. She was moved by what I had told her, although I think she was more touched that I had prayed to God than by the content or result of my prayer.

The word "remarkable" has stayed with me through the years. It's a word I reserve for complimenting only very special talents and very special work.

It was Josephine who encouraged me to consider studying in New York rather than in London, because she felt I leaned more towards the American realistic, naturalistic style of acting that was then the rage, the so-called Method style exemplified by Marlon Brando, James Dean and Lee Strasberg. While I studied with Josephine, I did do some Shakespeare, including probably every male part in *Twelfth*

Night, from Sir Toby Belch to Malvolio to Duke Orsino, and Dunois in Bernard Shaw's *Saint Joan*. But when CBC TV started broadcasting in 1952, when I was seventeen, I chose naturalism for my audition with the CBC's head of casting, a wonderful woman named Eva Langbord. I prepared, with Josephine's help, an excerpt from Tennessee Williams's *The Rose Tattoo*. It was a speech by the character called Alvero Mangiacavello (which means "eat a horse"). That audition was recorded for their Talent Bank and resulted in my first appearance on TV, in 1954.

At the time, the closest I came to Method acting was to read the book that some people regard as the bible of Method: *An Actor Prepares* by Konstantin Stanislavsky. I didn't understand a word of it, and I read it more than once. The first time I appeared on TV (live TV—again, no safety net), what I was most concerned about was not the artistic truth of the soul, Mr. Stanislavsky, but the factual truth of that little red light on one side of that intimidating behemoth of a camera. There was no human being giving you your countdown cue; you took it from that little red light. When it went on, you started. This, in the beginning, with my sweaty palms, caused me to split my focus between my purpose in the scene on the one hand, and on the other, keeping a watchful eye on the behemoth, waiting for it to wink at me.

All I remember from that first TV show is what I've just described, plus my costume. The CBC costume department, particularly for small parts like mine, preferred to draw on the actor's own wardrobe, so I borrowed a sweater from my friend Arthur Clairman. It was a beige V-necked pullover, good-looking—a man's sweater, although his family was in ladies' wear. They had a shop on the Danforth called Willer's. When he and his family watched the show to see their sweater perform, all his dad could say about my fleeting moment was, "Why didn't he have Willer's Ladies' Wear written on the back of the sweater?"

I met Arthur Clairman and another friend, Seymour Weinstein, when we were all about fifteen years old. Art to me looked like Clark

Kent—he was as muscle-bound as Superman—and we worked out together. Seymour was probably the best natural athlete I knew in those days, and one of the strongest men I've ever known. He seemed to live his life on the handball court at the YMHA. I used to call him the Mayor of the Y. We are all, a half-century later, still very good friends. I think if I have a sense of balance in my life, one of the reasons is that I did not put all my eggs in one basket, particularly in the area of friendship. Neither Art nor Seymour is in "the business," and unlike me they are both practical and sensible, or at least more so than I am. But we have bonds of loyalty and laughter connecting us.

As I went out into the world with an artist's will to believe, like an open book wanting to fill my pages, I was fortunate to have this attitude tempered by the cautions of Art and Seymour.

Arthur is logical and lawyer-like, and always was. Though he no longer practises law, he still gives me his experienced advice in legal and business matters. As I said, Seymour was a gifted athlete, but he could never play on a school team because he never passed out of Grade 10. Still, in the area of street smarts, he was supreme. He and his brothers went on to build one of the most successful produce companies in the country. While I called him the Mayor of the Y, others called him the Watermelon King or the All-Canadian Fruit.

I was still acting on radio, and now even getting paid for it. A great achievement for me was to finally work for Andrew Allen on the celebrated *Stage* series, still considered one of the CBC's greatest artistic achievements. Equally important for me was to work in radio with actors such as John Drainie and Budd Knapp, and to work for the CBC's other high priest of radio drama, Esse Ljungh.

While I was learning about acting, I was also still in high school, at least in theory. I started out well at Oakwood Collegiate. When I graduated from Grade 9, I was taken into the select class of the tenth grade, 10-A, where the students were expected to study all the courses the other Grade 10 students took, plus an extra language. So, as well as French and Latin, I was taking German. This promotion came about despite an incident in Grade 9, a confrontation with my teacher, an apparently rigid character whose name was, ironically, Mr. Wright.

One day Mr. Wright was temporarily out of the room and left us an assignment to do during his absence. Believe it or not, I was diligently doing it while the rest of the class was not. Rare, but nevertheless true. The other students were all goofing off, horsing around, getting louder and more boisterous as I quietly, in the midst of the mayhem, concentrated on the assignment. When Mr. Wright returned and saw what appeared to be complete chaos, he was so incensed that he ordered the whole class to prepare the exercise ten times for the next morning. I went up to him to explain that I had not been goofing off and indeed showed him my completed work. He said it didn't matter, I had to do what he'd ordered the whole class to do. I said I didn't think that was right or fair, and that I wouldn't do it. He then said that I'd have to do it twenty times.

I went home and told my mother, and she believed me and sided with me and said she'd back me up. So I didn't do it, and Mr. Wright said OK, thirty times. The following day it was forty times, and so on. The class eagerly watched this contest every morning, as I kept my cool while Mr. Wright progressively lost his, and the number climbed each day by ten. Neither of us would give in, so Mr. Wright decided to take the matter to the principal. I said, good. I explained my side from the beginning and argued my case with sincerity and conviction. The principal was caught in a situation where he believed me, was impressed by my character and courage, and wisely didn't want to squash any of that, but at the same time couldn't let Mr. Wright look wrong. The principal's Solomon-like solution? He invited me to spend the rest of the school day, that is, until four o'clock, in his office, at his desk, completing as much of the assignment as I could; that would have to suffice for Mr. Wright. I lost none of my after-school time or the weekend it would have taken to complete it. I was treated specially, and the class knew it.

This, as I said, didn't prevent me from getting into 10-A. So far, so good. It was what my brother, always an A student, had done before me. But when we moved to Glen Cedar Road, I transferred to Vaughan Road Collegiate and started slacking off. I was not intimidated by physics or chemistry, actually liked geometry, was stymied by logarithms in trigonometry but not turned off by the challenge of the puzzle. And I loved languages and literature. But there was so much else happening in my life that seemed to matter more.

I was invited to join a high-school fraternity, Upsilon Lambda Phi, by my summer camp counsellor, Art Vaile. (Arthur Vaile later became what I would describe as the Walter Winchell of Canadian business TV broadcasting.) Upsilon Lambda Phi, ULP—it sounded like a burp. But it was taken very seriously, and I was elated to be invited into this snob-appeal, rich kids' club, which, despite the Greek letters, admitted Jewish fraternity brethren only. I often wondered what would have happened if a non-Jew had wanted to pledge. (It happened only once that I remember; he was someone who wanted to be Jewish, and he was accepted.) Out of fairness, though, it must be remembered that these clubs sprang into existence as a defence against exclusion.

Joining Upsilon Lambda Phi was a coup for me. I had to pledge, get inducted in a secret ceremony and learn a secret handshake, which I still remember but can't show you. No sooner was I inducted than I was elected to the executive—a big deal for me at the time.

What with all the fraternizing that was going on in my vibrant household, the socializing in my high-school fraternity, the new friends, the activities (mostly sports, but now some new-found ones like all-night gin rummy, poker and crap games), plus all the focus on acting classes and professional acting work, if something was going to give, it was going to be school. I seldom attended classes, if at all.

Twenty-five years later, by chance invitation, I joined Allen Linden at the fiftieth-anniversary celebration of Vaughan Road Collegiate. Allen had been a distinguished law professor, and at the time of this high-school reunion was on the Supreme Court of Ontario (and is now on the Federal Court of Appeal). The auditorium, corridors and surrounding grounds of Vaughan Road Collegiate were packed with alumni. There were loudspeakers in the halls and outside the building, broadcasting what was said on stage in the auditorium.

At the time of this event, I had considerable national profile as a result of *King of Kensington*. So, in spite of the academic achievements of many of the alumni present, the organizers of the event asked me to come to the stage to say a few words. I said to them, "Why me? I was hardly ever here. I hardly even remember the place. Surely there are others here more appropriate and more worthy." But they insisted.

I got up on the stage and said that I owed my career in film to these hallowed halls of Vaughan Road Collegiate because I had skipped so many classes, choosing instead to spend my time, not in pool halls like other delinquents, but nevertheless playing hooky—in movie theatres. I preferred the Vaughan Cinema at Vaughan and St. Clair, the Radio City at Bathurst and St. Clair, the Christie at Christie and St. Clair, and the Nortown at Bathurst and Eglinton rather than these hallowed halls. That took up the first four days of the week. Sometimes I would come to school on the fifth day. So I hardly ever saw these hallowed halls and the result was that by avoiding them I learned more about movies. Many thanks to these hallowed halls! Needless to say, it took me six years to get out of high school.

I certainly wasn't a very focused student—so out of focus, in fact, that Jack suggested I join the army for much-needed discipline. After about a year with the fraternity I outgrew that indulgence, but I had spiralled so far downward in terms of academics that it was hard to get back on course, so I seriously considered Jack's suggestion. I went to a local air force base on Avenue Road a little above Eglinton to try and enlist. I was seventeen years old in 1952, and they wouldn't take me until the age of eighteen without my parents' signature. My mother wouldn't sign, just as she wouldn't sign for me to play football in high school. I said I'd be back in the spring, after I turned eighteen. I didn't go back there until about 1996, when it was no longer an air force base but a makeshift movie studio, and home base for the HBO movie *Gotti,* in which I co-starred.

The reason I didn't go back in the springtime was that, happily, Josephine Barrington helped to get me my first job in summer stock, at the Niagara Falls Summer Theatre. With an interview, and certainly a word from Josephine, I was chosen to be an apprentice, and the only one with a scholarship, thereby receiving on-the-job training at the Niagara Falls Summer Theatre. Scholarship? That meant I was the only one who didn't have to pay to do the job! All I had to pay for was my room and board.

The job description was that you did everything, every day, and with your duties came the weekly opportunity to audition for one of the tiny parts left uncast by the visiting touring company. Fortunately, there almost always seemed to be a small part available for me, particularly in the musicals where, in addition to acting a small character role, I would sing in the chorus. So that summer I was totally immersed in the theatre. If I wasn't building sets, I was moving or painting them; if I wasn't putting them up, I was taking them down—usually all of the aforementioned, plus acting or singing (which I couldn't really do) or, even more implausibly, dancing (which I also couldn't do). The result was a marvellous, magical summer.

The only time away from the theatre was when it was my turn to tack up publicity posters on telephone poles and lampposts and deliver them to restaurants and bars in the community and to other public places like libraries and grocery stores. We worked all day and all night, seven days a week, and only got to sleep in on Monday mornings. Then, at noon on Monday, the whole routine would start over again.

Each show opened on a Monday and closed the following Saturday, with move-out on Sunday, as the next show moved in and opened the next day, Monday. I arrived on a Saturday, the last day of the first show, and pitched in immediately. I was totally green: when asked if I was striking that night, I answered that I had just arrived and didn't know the prevailing mood and conditions, but whatever everybody else decided to do, I would go along. I was then informed that striking, in the theatre, means taking down, as in "striking the sets." I learned quickly.

There was an opening-night party on Monday for the summer theatre season, and we, the apprentices, were invited. It was at the Brock Hotel in Niagara Falls. I went with Toby Tarnow, another of Josephine Barrington's students. Toby was and is a wonderful actress. She was in the very first dramatic TV show ever produced by the CBC. She played the kid sister of, and starred with, another special Toby, Toby Robbins, who I think was the first glamorous home-grown Canadian star. I say home-grown because while there were Hollywood stars like Mary Pickford, Yvonne DeCarlo and Deanna Durbin who were Canadians, Toby Robbins made it happen here in Canada.

These Tobys were both special, and so was my mother, whose name was also Toby. This made for some problems when I dated Toby Tarnow. According to Jewish tradition, no one is named after a family member who is still alive. That's why you will never see Junior or Senior or II after a Jewish person's name (with rare exceptions). So, if a son were to marry a woman whose name is exactly the same as his living mother, for some it would seem to violate this tradition. But in my mother's way of thinking, it would have been a mortal insult. So even though I assured her that we were only friends and classmates, and maybe dated once or twice, but nothing serious happened or ever would, my mother was still wary. I, frankly, was amused by her concern.

Toby Tarnow and I went together to that party at the Brock Hotel for the Niagara Falls Summer Theatre. In those days, summer stock was a bigger social and cultural event than it is today. People would dress up for opening night, particularly if the theatre was run by a woman like Maude Franchot, who was from a high-society family from Niagara Falls, New York. She was a first cousin to the Hollywood and Broadway actor Franchot Tone, who would occasionally visit and even play at the Niagara Falls Summer Theatre.

It was an exciting night for Toby and me, and I could write about it now, but instead I'm going to illustrate it with a short story (a vignette, really) that I found in my files. Early on as an actor I thought it would be an enriching exercise to explore writing. According to my files, I wrote the following in 1963 about that opening-night party in the summer of 1953 when I was just eighteen. The names were changed "to protect the innocent," as the saying goes, but you'll be able to tell who's who.

Alan and Nancy walked towards the ballroom. They could see many people milling about with cocktails in their hands. Alan was anxious to hold a cocktail in his hand. Some of the people were in tuxedos and evening gowns. Wow! He and Nancy were dressed pretty sharp—but not like that. So what? They were dressed pretty good, for kids their age—anybody would agree. He held Nancy's hand tight as they entered the ballroom. He was her escort. And anyway, he'd promised himself that he'd look out for her all summer. She'd just turned sixteen, that's all. Besides, he heard that you could come across some pretty unscrupulous characters in show business, and she was just a kid.

Where's Miss Hetherington, they both wondered. She had promised to introduce them to a Broadway star. The one who made famous the role Alan had excelled in, in her class. They held hands as they wandered looking for her, lost in a maze of elbows and cocktail glasses. No matter where they turned, they bumped into somebody, or knocked their glasses flying.

Boy, some party. Opening night. Big deal. And the drinks they gave ya here. Just grapefruit juice. That was bad enough at breakfast, never mind a party. And gin didn't help it any either. Boy, some party—no Cokes, no doughnuts, no sandwiches, no music. And even if there was music, there'd be no room to step around. Boy, some party.

"Hey Nancy, lookit over there. There's Miss Hetherington."
"Yeah."
"Boy, she looks like she's having a swell time, eh?"
"Yeah."
"I never saw her like that before, did you?"
"No."
"But I never saw her at a party before, eh?"
"Yeah."
"Hey, lookit that guy with her."
"Yeah. Maybe that's her escort."
"Yeah, but he's loaded. He's even got his own bottle with him. Doesn't he know he's with Miss Maybelline Hetherington?"
"Yeah."
"C'mon, I'm going over there!"

"Alan and Nancy, my darlings, there you are!"
"Good evening, Miss Hetherington."
"Alan, my darling, we're not in class anymore. Please do call me May."

Wow, what a thud. He didn't think he should even call her Maybelline, never mind May.

"Nice party, eh? . . . May?"
"Yes, do enjoy yourselves, my darlings!"
"Wow! Hey Nancy, did you hear that!"
"Yeah."
"Miss Hetherington said I should call her May."
"Yeah."
"Hey, lookit her now. Who's that guy kissing her up 'n down her back?"

"Maybe *that's* her escort."

"No, the other guy is. The lush. Boy, can't he see what that greasy guy is doing?"

"Yeah."

"Say, if he doesn't cut that out I'm gonna pound him one right in the mouth."

"Hey, Alan. Lookit."

"Yeah. Good."

Miss Hetherington was squirming around to face the guy. Probably to bawl him out. But her turning was not in anger or embarrassment. She was giggling as she glowed up at him.

"Hey Nancy, look. She likes it!"

"Yeah."

I called it "And Revelations Still to Come." I don't know why I changed the names; there is nothing offensive to anyone. I still revered Josephine Barrington. I could never call her Jo, even had trouble calling her Josephine. I am not the only one who remembers her with fondness and as an important influence in Canadian theatre. A bunch of us, former students of hers, chipped in for a wall plaque to commemorate her at the Jane Mallett Theatre in Toronto's St. Lawrence Centre.

Apropos of preferring to call her Miss Barrington, I'm reminded of my mother's first really good friend in this country, Hinda Greenbaum, her landlady at 74 Wales Street, where we lived when I was born at the original Mount Sinai Hospital on Yorkville Avenue. As a tenant, my mother always referred to and addressed her landlady as Mrs. Greenbaum. It was respect. Also, it was a formal relationship at first. Mrs. Greenbaum always referred to my mother as Mrs. Waxman. After a few years they became good friends, and were no longer landlady and tenant after we moved to Spadina Avenue. Nevertheless, they were still Mrs. Greenbaum and Mrs. Waxman to each other. It was respect. The Greenbaums never really prospered financially, while the Waxmans did. They remained on Wales Street and we moved "up the hill," but that made no difference as the two good friends became like sisters. But it was still Mrs. Greenbaum and Mrs. Waxman.

When my mother remarried four years after my father died, some eighteen or nineteen years after Mrs. Greenbaum and Mrs. Waxman first met, my mother had to change her name and could no longer be addressed as Mrs. Waxman. Their friends prevailed upon them that it was time, it was convenient and it would not be disrespectful to call each other by their first names. And so, finally, they became Hinda (Helen) and Toby. They remained good friends until their dying days.

To me, of course, she was still dear Mrs. Greenbaum, and as a matter of fact, when my mother came to visit me that summer in Niagara Falls, the Greenbaums came with her and Jack and Benny. It was well into the season. I think the show that week might have been *Carousel,* in which I had a couple of small parts and sang in the chorus. I was on stage a lot in that show, and felt at home there. This was in contrast to my first performance of the summer, in *Finian's Rainbow,* in which I had played a character called Mr. Robust (a takeoff on Roebuck of Sears & Roebuck). I was so nervous on that opening night, and it showed in more than just my palms. Apparently the other kids stood in the wings stifling their giggling as they watched my legs trembling, my trouser legs looking like they were caught in a wind storm. I don't know how Robust I was on opening night, but I was probably Robust enough before the end of the week. Certainly by mid-season when my family came to visit, I was comfortable on stage—which is why my mother's reaction was disappointing for me, but in a way encouraging.

I'm trying to remember, but I can't recall ever seeing my mother angry. Certainly I never saw her lose her temper. She didn't lose her temper this time either, but there was anger! Anger seething beneath sobering shock; quiet, controlled on the outside, but fuming on the inside. Like dry ice. She must have seen that what was once tolerated as a hobby was beginning to look like a frighteningly unstoppable future. It was a future she feared, not just because of her own distaste for it, but even more out of concern for my security. However, she couldn't say anything.

As memorable for me as the look on my mother's face that day was what happened when the visit ended and they pulled away, with Benny driving. About half a block down the road the car suddenly jolted to a stop, as though something had been forgotten. Benny didn't put the car in reverse. He just got out of the car, left the door open and ran back to me. He grabbed me, kissed me and said, "Don't stop what you're doing. Don't let anybody stop you!" He then went back to the car and drove off. I was moved, appreciative and encouraged, and I sensed something else, although I couldn't articulate it then. In retrospect I realize that, although Benny was on his way to graduating summa cum laude and Phi Beta Kappa, what I was doing reminded him of what he was not doing—pursuing his own interest in the arts.

Yes, it was a summer of revelations. I learned a great deal about my craft, about many different aspects of the theatre and theatrical production. And about professionalism.

Every week a different packaged play arrived, with one or two stars attached to it. The first had Arthur Treacher and Dagmar. I can't remember the name of the play, but it was probably concocted to take advantage of the down time these celebrities enjoyed in the summer. Dagmar was a big, blonde-haired, busty woman, one of the first cartoonish sex symbols of the television age. All I remember about her was that she doused her ample self in White Shoulders perfume, and the sexy supersweet smell of this lingered long after she left, well into the remainder of the season. More important for my learning process was Treacher. He was English and seemed to have carved out a career playing aristocratic butlers in British and American comedies, both in movies and on TV. One matinee performance of the play, they had an audience of only seven people. My job, amongst other things, was opening and closing the curtains by pulling or slackening the ropes. Before the show started, when we were informed of the sad size of the house, I made some cavalier remark, probably trying to buddy up to Arthur Treacher, about it being hardly worth doing for such a small audience. He tore a strip off me with a sharp reminder of what professionalism is all about. He said, "Regardless of the size of the house, they paid for a performance and it is my job to give it to them."

Even if the visiting stars and I didn't talk much to one another, I learned just by watching their work. One week it was the movie star Farley Granger, then another fairly new phenomenon at that time named Harry Belafonte, and then former child movie star (the only one bigger was Shirley Temple) Margaret O'Brien. That's when I stopped asking for autographs. Margaret O'Brien was sixteen or seventeen, Toby Tarnow's age. I was eighteen. Seemed silly to ask for an autograph from someone who was younger than I was.

One week I didn't get to audition for a part I wanted very badly. I wanted it so bad, I could taste it, as they say; I felt it was mine. But the stage manager had assigned me to certain tasks where he felt my services were needed and as a result there was no time for me to audition. He wasn't necessarily being mean; he ran a tight ship. He was an unsentimental man, very cold and very efficient, which is why he had the job. No one questioned him. No one dared to or needed to, because everything at that theatre, in a business full of surprises, ran very smoothly. Nevertheless, I confronted him and wanted to know why I couldn't have a shot at the part. His answer was simply that he had a show to run and could not indulge in consideration of personal feelings. I thought that was unfair and I was hurt. He said, "If you're here to learn, you'd better learn right now that this is an impersonal business."

That stopped me cold. Impersonal business? It's something that I could comprehend intellectually, but when I tried to swallow it deep into my understanding, it didn't mix well with the personal artistic ambition in my aching gut—aching because *want* unrealized leaves a hole filled instead with painful emptiness. An impersonal business that, at its core, involves a personal art form! Two powerful forces that are not always compatible; more often than not, they contradict one another. Some maturity is required of the artist in order to reconcile these two opposing notions—impersonal business and personal art form. I was too young at the time to do anything more than grapple with these concepts. I dare say that a wrestling match went on inside me for many years after that.

Every week I asked the visiting pros, the artists, the stars, what route did they take? what advice could they give? Almost every one of them answered that, in this precarious profession, it's wise to have something else to fall back on: have another skill, be able to get another job; if you can, get an education.

Unlike today, where there is tremendous preoccupation with youth in this business, when I was eighteen there was not much work for people my age. Steady work wouldn't happen for years anyway, so why not go back to school? So, for reasons different than my mother's, I took the route that in the immediate and foreseeable future was the one she wanted me to take. In the fall I went back to finish high school.

CHAPTER 6

I Aced Ec. 20 the Second Time Around

I wasn't going to give up a minute of that summer stock season in Niagara Falls. The result was that I got back to Grade 13, or the fifth form, as it was called, a couple of months into the fall session. Still, at the end of the year I finally graduated.

Off to Western. Good, my mother thought. If I stayed at the same boarding house my brother had stayed at, slept in the same bed, studied at the same desk, maybe I'd get the same marks.

The boarding house at 800 Hellmuth Street in London, Ontario, had three rather Spartan rooms upstairs, each sufficient for a student's purposes. One of them had been home for my brother until his marriage to Shirley Silbert of Hamilton. He and Shirley, a nurse, moved into a lovely little apartment near the medical school and hospital where they would be spending most of their time.

The room that served my brother's and my mother's purposes was now available to serve my purpose. And there was no reason why it shouldn't have—except for two people: me and Mrs. Forrester. Bessie Forrester was the landlady. She was a dear old lady who had become friends with my mother. They even corresponded. Can you imagine how fond they were of one another if my mother had the patience to write and Bessie Forrester had the patience to read my mother's broken handwriting? Well, Mrs. Forrester didn't have much patience with me. She looked a little like Ma Kettle and sounded a lot like Ma Kettle, and she ran a strict boarding house.

I've always been given to discipline, but I prefer it to come from within. I had trouble dealing with rules imposed by an outside authority, especially at that time in my life and especially Mrs. Forrester's rules. She had a ten o'clock curfew. The other students who boarded there had no trouble complying, but I did. And you had to come down for breakfast no later than ten minutes to eight—one second later and you missed breakfast. One morning as I was thundering down the stairs (she couldn't stand the noise I made), hungry for breakfast at 7:49 and a half, Bessie's voice crackled up from the foot of the stairs as I raced by her. "Albert, if you come home any later at night, you're going to meet yourself coming down for breakfast!" How could you not like her? And she liked me, too. But rules are rules. After only three weeks at 800 Hellmuth, Mrs. Forrester wrote a letter to an embarrassed Mrs. Leipciger informing her that for the first time in all her years she had to ask one of her boys to leave. And that boy was Albert.

I rented a room at the Beta Sigma Rho Fraternity House, where it was assumed that, because I was Jewish and it was the only Jewish fraternity on campus and my brother was an illustrious alumnus, I would pledge and become a fraternity brother. But frankly, I'd had enough of fraternities back in high school.

Fraternity houses, according to campus folklore at the time, were temples of booze and mischief. I would have expected my escapades to be a source of pride for them. Well, panty raids were fine, if you just brought home the panties, but if you sneaked the girl in along with her panties, that was problematic. Drinking bouts could make for great camaraderie, but not if your comrades were prevented from sleep and study. All this was understandable, as was the fact that the BSR brothers, as we got closer to mid-term exams, wanted this behaviour to end. But I couldn't get enough of campus partying, and finally the guys at BSR had enough of me. They asked my brother to speak to me or to advise them. Benny felt the same way about fraternities as I did and simply said, "Do what you want." I was asked to leave BSR, without having been asked to pledge.

I next moved into an apartment with an old friend from Hillcrest Public School, who had trouble paying the rent. My share enabled him to meet the payments. And because he was not a student but in business, he was seldom there, so we hardly ever saw each other. A perfect situation.

Lots to do. Girls and more girls. Besides all the coeds on campus, there were two nursing schools close by. The aroma of autumn, the air crisp with the clear search for learning and clearly the search for each other. A colourful blanket of leaves on the prettiest campus grounds ever. Rock and stone buildings with ivy climbing up the towers. Bobby socks and saddle shoes, white bucks and crew cuts, the wholesome 1950s.

Squash at Thames Hall, a brand-new game, a gentleman's game. I climbed up the squash ladder not quite high enough to make first string, but close. Lots of time spent in Thames Hall. It was like a men's club; after squash one could have a snooze in the mahogany and maroon-upholstered reading room. Sometimes I'd get up in time for a class; if not, a game of cards instead.

There were theatrical productions too. Always theatre. Costard the Clown in Shakespeare's *Love's Labour's Lost* at the University College Auditorium. Bob Acres in Sheridan's *The Rivals* at the Grand Theatre. And again at UC, one-act plays directed by me. And more romance. Falling in love, finally, even with learning.

Purple and white, Western's colours refresh and delight. Football games and pocket flasks. Goalposts and rousing cheers, bleachers and smuggled beers, knees and thighs rubbing under blankets. Later, warmer and better. Songs with lyrics like "We will have these moments to remember." But my music was still Al Jolson. They hesitated about asking me back to be a disc jockey at CFPL because I persisted in playing Jolson. Playing what I wanted, doing what I wanted—life at Western for me was like an all-you-can-eat buffet. And I kept going back up for more. Thank God, drugs were not on the scene yet. Some people called me "Cas" Waxman, short for Casual Al. On occasion I casually attended a lecture or ensconced myself in the library to write a paper. And then came the final exams.

I remember reading the questions on the final examination for a course called Economics 20. I was relaxed, munching on a candy bar, slouched in my seat with one foot up on the empty chair beside me (I always made sure I found a seat with an empty chair beside it), and I thought, this is interesting stuff. It was as though I was meeting concepts I'd never encountered before. And yet this stuff had to do with things I read in the papers or heard on the news every day. Things like GNP and GDP, supply and demand, and something called the Acquisitive Principle, which to me seemed an academic euphemism for greed, something I wanted to discuss and argue about. What interesting stuff, I thought; I should have studied this during the year, I should have attended classes. Next time out, I said to myself, I will. I finished my candy bar and handed in an empty paper.

Indeed, the next time out I aced Ec. 20. No longer "Cas" Waxman, for a while I was known as Mr. Economics. I think I am living proof that opportunity knocks more than once.

My first year wasn't a complete failure. I passed most of the subjects, but I had some catching up to do via summer school if I was going to get my BA in three years. My turnaround in attitude towards Ec. 20 developed into a love affair with studying. I didn't just catch up, I accelerated. I used summer school and the second year, plus summer school again, to get ahead and obtain my degree in two years rather than three. I had enough credits to claim philosophy or political science or English literature as a major, with economics as a minor, plus sciences, psychology and languages, and of course my continuing courtship with theatre courses in playwriting and play production.

I did well in two philosophy courses in particular: logic and ethics. This success pointed me, I thought, towards a career in law. Not because my mother would now have "a son a doctor, and a son a lawyer," not because my father had wanted to be a lawyer and so would probably have approved, but because I thought I really wanted it. No matter the reason, my mother was happy and so was I. In the fall of 1957 I was accepted into the University of Toronto Law School. The campus was in Bayview, where Glendon Hall is now.

I was twenty-two. This was the first year since I was twelve years old that I had no designs on radio, TV or theatre work in addition to my school work. I don't know whether that meant that I consciously took a pass on show business or not. I do know that I entered law school with a commitment to study law.

I soon found, however, that what interested me was not necessarily taking me in the same direction as the rest of the class. For example, at the risk of oversimplifying, if A struck B over the head with a sword because B called him a dirty name, the class was interested in how these circumstances fit with similar circumstances between C and D in a case decided in a higher court. Would the principle in that case be applicable here? Would the decision in C and D be binding on A and B? And C and D brings to mind a case between E and F that has, again, similarities, but also significant differences, when comparing C and D to A and B. And of course, when considering pertinent and distinguishing points, it would be wise to read the dissenting opinion in G and H. And so on and so on.

The class would be through the alphabet while I was still trying to talk to A and B. "A, so he called you a name. Did you have to hit him over the head with a sword? Why did you do that? Wouldn't it have been better just to walk away? And B, why did you have to call him a name?" I wanted to find a way to make A and B play nice, and if they couldn't, I wanted to find out why they did what they did, or didn't do what they might have done. The class, on the other hand, wanted to discover and accumulate precedents. They wanted to abstract themselves from the "instant case" and collect principles and similarities and distinctions at this level of court and at higher levels of court. The class was interested in parallel thinking; I was interested in thinking right into the heart of it—not just the heart of the issue but the hearts of the people—to a point where I could feel what was in their hearts. I wanted to get directly, personally and viscerally involved.

Actually, I did very well in Tort Law, because, like criminal law, it is quite dramatic. Human beings come up against each other, there is friction and conflict, ingredients that are the essence of drama.

I suspect that lawyers who are already in practice can, if they choose, pursue the questions regarding human behaviour that interested me. But in first-year law I was years away from that. I didn't want to wait that long. I preferred the immediate involvement that you get in the theatre, or in any form of dramatic storytelling.

The year of the Asian flu, 1957–1958, was dangerous for what it could trigger. The result was an asthmatic condition in me that wouldn't subside for quite a while, rendering me bedridden for most of the winter months. My poor mom. Asthma is more difficult on loved ones who have to stand by and watch helplessly as the patient gasps for breath. And she was of course concerned about my first year at law school. I already knew I was in the wrong place, but my mom wanted to salvage the year and therefore suggested that I transfer to a law school in Arizona.

I said, "No, Ma. Arizona is filled with sick people, and soon I'm not going to be sick."

At U of T law school, if you failed the first year, you were not invited back. Well, I missed one or two subjects, but it wasn't considered failure. Perhaps missing school for reasons of ill health made for mitigating circumstances, as lawyers might say. So I was invited back for the following September.

But what to do in the summer months? Josephine Barrington came to the rescue again, once more with an introduction from her that resulted in a season as an apprentice in summer stock. This time it was in Ogunquit, Maine. I remember it as an enchanting seaside colony of artists with the celebrated Ogunquit Playhouse, in the midst of New England charm and quaintness, surrounded by the rugged rock and rustic beauty of Maine, kept simple and yet made sophisticated by the Manhattanites, Bostonians and other cosmopolitan types who summered there.

It was the same deal for apprentices as in Niagara Falls: we worked on productions as crew and sometimes got minor parts. In this case, though, the visiting stars were required to give seminars to the apprentices.

One week the visiting stars were Hume Cronyn and Jessica Tandy. While Hume was working on the set, Jessica conducted the seminar. One of the apprentices was a young actor from Shreveport, Louisiana, who was as good-looking as James Dean and wanted to be a movie star. But he felt he had a problem to overcome and needed advice in overcoming it: he was short. Most matinee idols, he feared, were about six feet tall, and he was never going to be more than about five feet five inches. He took some heart from the fact that Hume Cronyn was short. When he raised his hand to ask a question, I'm sure Jessica expected it to be about the art of acting. Instead, what she heard was, "How did Hume make it in light of the fact that he is so short?" Jessica contained herself and quietly bristled this response: "My husband stands tall!" A lesson to be learned that I don't think ever reached that never-heard-from-again actor from Shreveport.

Years later I participated in a benefit for cystic fibrosis in Ottawa. Some of the other performers included the Cronyns, Christopher Plummer, and Celine Dion, performing in English for the first time. One morning the Cronyns and I shared a table at breakfast, and I reminded Jessica of that incident at the Ogunquit Playhouse. She seemed a little embarrassed and said, "Did I really say that?" I said, "Yes, you did. And in a way I'm glad he asked that question. Your answer was appropriate for him and appreciated by me and the rest of the apprentices."

That summer at Ogunquit I also met Bette Davis and Gary Merrill. They were married at the time. They had starred opposite each other in the great film *All About Eve*. Gary Merrill was at an opening-night party at the theatre, wearing a black cape over a suit that consisted of a green jacket and matching green Bermuda shorts, with knee-high black socks and black slipper-like shoes matching the cape. I had never seen Bermuda shorts before. I wondered what had happened to the rest of his pants.

He was carrying a flask under his arm about the size of a farmer's milk can. It was filled with martinis, and the lid served as a cup. Needless to say, he couldn't drive home, particularly at night along that cliffside coastline. He asked a couple of us to drive him, and he invited us into his and Bette Davis's awesome mansion overlooking the ocean. However, Bette, also inebriated, thought differently about hosting us, and unleashed a torrent of invective that scared Merrill into hiding and drove us out of the front hall and back into our car. I did get a glimpse of her house, though. The front hall was literally lined with book-filled shelves. I thought, no matter what her formal education had been, preparing for all the roles she'd played must have meant that her education process never stopped. I was impressed.

No sooner did I return to law school than I was reminded why that life was not for me. Since they had made a special case for me, I felt I should speak directly to the dean to inform him that I was going to leave law school once and for all. Dean Wright, who also suffered from asthma, was ill, so I had to report my intention to leave to the acting dean, Bora Laskin.

"So, what are you going to do?" Professor Laskin asked me.

"I'm going to go into show business!" I must have sounded like Mickey Rooney looking for a barn to put on a play, but he gave me a response of scholarly consideration.

"Show business," he said slowly as he leaned back thoughtfully.

You could see the long, lean, ascetic lines on the face of this brilliant professor and wise judge-to-be as he leaned towards me, saying, "Show business. You're going to have to want that very badly."

Years later, Prime Minister Pierre Trudeau appointed Bora Laskin Chief Justice of the Supreme Court of Canada. This was in the late seventies, during *King of Kensington*. I thought I should send Bora Laskin a congratulatory note, but then I thought, who am I kidding, he wouldn't remember me. He's getting all kinds of congratulatory notes from national and international dignitaries. How do I match them, I thought. And so I shied away from writing him a note.

One evening around that time, my wife and I had a party and one of the guests was someone I had worked with at the National Film Board in Montreal, Malca Gillson. It turns out that she and Bora Laskin were first cousins. Malca was going to arrive at our party late, because she was first going to spend some time with her cousin Bora and his wife, Peggy, in their suite at the Sutton Place, where later that evening, if memory serves me correctly, Bora was to be presented with the prestigious Benjamin Cardozo Award, named for the internationally respected New York State Supreme Court Justice. Apparently, after helping Peggy with her hair (Malca had been a makeup artist at the National Film Board), Malca said she'd better get going or she was going to be very late for a party at Al Waxman's house.

I was told by Malca when she arrived that Bora Laskin sent his regards to me and wondered if I remembered him. Wondered if I remembered him? Wow! Now I would definitely write him that letter. I felt honoured to, because I was happy for him and for our country. And then I felt even more honoured when I got a handwritten note from the Chief Justice of the Supreme Court of Canada, thanking me for taking the time to write to him!

So in 1959 I left law school. I wanted to turn what had been a hobby, sometimes a lucrative one, always a passionate pastime, into a passionate profession. And to do that I felt I needed to galvanize all of my theatrical, radio and TV experience into a realistic and productive approach through focused training. In other words, acting school. There was no National Theatre School in Canada yet, and none of the universities had theatre programs. RADA? LAMDA? There were indeed great schools in London, but I had always remembered and agreed with Josephine Barrington's advice that New York was where I should study. After some investigation I determined that the finest acting school in North America was the Neighborhood Playhouse School of the Theater.

When I look back at that moment, I think I realized that I was closing a chapter and starting a new one. While I can see it clearly now, then it was only on a subconscious level that I was aware of all that had gone into the chapter that was closing and what I was taking from that chapter into the next. For example, there are cases I studied in law school that I can still discuss with lawyers. And of course there are theories in economics and politics and philosophy that are ongoing. However, I think what made the deepest impression on me, on a gut level, although I may not have articulated it then, was poetry. I have often, even without opening a book of poetry, revisited from memory the verses that first made an impact on me in school.

A poem's music and meaning, although built by words, may be more, much more, than merely words. Poetry is, I think, the most personal art form. It is personal to the poet, who is not as concerned as other writers might be about the ultimate impact of their work on an audience. A book or a play is incomplete without a reader or an audience, but a poem is the pure expression of the artist's personal thoughts and feelings. The work stands by itself whether it is read or not, just as a sculpture or painting exists fully whether it is seen or not.

Like the act of creating it, the appreciation of the poem is personal too. No matter how completely the reader interprets, accurately or inaccurately, he may be able to take something away from it that is personal to him, whether that was the original vision of the poet or not.

Such was the case for me with two poems I studied in high-school and university years. I was personally touched, profoundly inspired and guided by both for the rest of my life.

The first is by John Milton. In some collections I've seen it called "On His Blindness"; in others it is called "When I Consider How My Light Is Spent," which is actually the first line of the poem. In either case the words that have particular meaning for me are: "And that one talent which is death to hide, / Lodged with me useless." In Milton's case he is bemoaning the fact that his talent for writing is lodged with him useless because he can no longer see to write. Before the sonnet is over, he resolves not to be stopped by his blindness. In my case, over the years I have felt that the talent to act was sometimes lodged with me useless because it couldn't be realized if there was no role to perform. Perhaps there simply wasn't much work available for me; maybe my age was a problem, or the way I looked, or the competition. I resolved—although it took me longer than a sonnet—that my talent to act would not be lodged with me useless, that I would make myself stand out, and that I would create opportunities for myself if I had to.

The other poem is "Andrea del Sarto," by Robert Browning. Andrea del Sarto is a dedicated painter who, no matter how hard he tries, can't achieve the genius of Michelangelo or the inspiration of Raphael. Yet he feels his work deserves attention. He even points out that he paints an arm more accurately than Raphael; why shouldn't he too receive praise? He resolves, regardless of what is fair or not, that he will continue to work at his art and his craft, because that—the work itself—is what it's all about. At least, that is how I interpret the famous lines from "Andrea del Sarto": "Ah, but a man's reach should exceed his grasp, / Or what's a heaven for?" That is to say, I will never stop trying, and for me heaven is in the work itself.

Chapter 7

An Actor Prepares

The Neighborhood Playhouse: how to get accepted, and then how to get there, and finally how to sustain myself once there. Tuition was substantial; New York was expensive. And on a student visa you were not allowed to take any work. I had my interview and audition for the Playhouse in Toronto, with their Canadian representative, James Doohan, himself a graduate of the Playhouse. Mr. Doohan must have been pretty impressed, and I'm sure his influence was helpful too, because what resulted was a scholarship, apparently an unusual opportunity. Indeed, I was the only student who entered that year with a scholarship. Jimmy Doohan, by the way, was a busy radio actor in Canada who subsequently moved to Los Angeles, where for many years he "beamed up" TV audiences around the world as Scotty in *Star Trek*.

So my tuition was taken care of. Now I had to come up with transportation, and room and board. I must have saved some money from either work or gambling because I had enough for travel. I figured I needed $25 a week to live on for eight weeks, by which time I would have found a part-time job, regardless of what the student visa said. Two hundred dollars for two months. That would just cover lunch today, but $200 was a lot for me to come up with then.

My mother wasn't going to give it to me. She would have gone into debt to see me through law school, but not for this. She was crushed when I quit law school, and would not allow me to sell my law books to a first-year law student. She stood in front of them protectively, insisting they were hers—after all, she'd paid for them. She would be pleased to know that those law books are still lined up on my shelf today.

My mother, as I've said, looked down upon show business. In a strange way her attitude seeped into my own outlook. I love the business I'm in, and I love actors. Sometimes when I see a certain play or film that is highly entertaining or is of high artistic or social significance, excellently produced and performed, it makes me proud to be in the business and very respectful of its artists and artisans. Sometimes, however, particularly in the early years, I would look down upon the actor in me.

In her concern for my future, my mother could be unintentionally cruel to me. She would ask, "When will I get *nachis* from you the way I get from Benny?" *Nachis* is best described as the pride and joy parents derive from their children's achievements. Benny was now an intern, apparently happily married, and as a result my mother was now the mother of a doctor—a specialist, no less—and the grandmother of a beautiful little boy and girl. When would she get *nachis* from me too? She wondered aloud what Jewish girl would ever want to marry an actor. I probably wondered that too, silently. And as for my means of making a living? She said to me, partly in jest but wholly concerned for the life ahead of me, "You want to be an actor?"

My silence was a positive response as I waited for more.

"What are you going to do?"

Still silent, still more.

"You can't sing. You can't dance. What are you going to do? Tell jokes? You're not so funny!"

That didn't hurt me. It actually made me laugh. I wish I could have written it with the music of her accent. She finished by saying, "If you're going to do it, stop talking about it already and go do it.

But not with my help!" So I had no blessing from her—yet. And of course no money.

Neither a borrower nor a lender be. I sort of knew that without studying whether to be or not to be. But if I was going "to be," I needed some money. For that, I decided to stay within the family. After my mother came my brother; but there was no point in asking him. He was interning, and interns got paid very little, and his wife wasn't working at the hospital now, with two little kids at home. That left Nate. He and his wife, Bernice, a schoolteacher, were both working, and he could possibly afford to lend me $200. So I asked. He was inclined to, but Bernice thought I was "unstable" or "irresponsible"—some word like that. Certainly I remember her saying that what I wanted the money for was "foolishness." Disappointing, and a little hurtful. To be fair, though, I think that attitude was not unusual. Maybe there was even a little bit of me that thought that way too. In the geographical and psychological district in which we lived, stability and responsible behaviour were measured by double-car garages and centre hall plans.

So I didn't have enough money to go. The Playhouse wouldn't take me halfway through the year. Should I delay it a whole year and take a job in the interim? I didn't want to. I was demoralized and didn't know where to turn. Then came a phone call from my buddy Seymour. He could hear in my voice how I felt and asked what was the matter. I remember stating, without ulterior motives but simply answering his question with a factual statement, that I needed money. I didn't expect a response and certainly not the response I got—just two words in his tough but comical Runyonesque way: "How much?"

I was taken aback. "What?" I said.

"How much money do you need?"

I thought it was still just conversation, so I said, "Oh, about $200," expecting it to end there.

But he said, like a command, "How do you want it?"

Again all I could say was, "What?"

Then he got specific, almost impatient. "What? Tens or twenties?" I couldn't believe it. He said, "I'll be there in twenty minutes."

That phone call, plus the words Seymour spoke when he arrived, are something I will never forget. He handed me ten $20 bills. And then he said, "You gonna hang around with a bunch of actors down there?"

"Probably."

"Some of them are kinda funny, aren't they?"

I knew where he was going, but I felt like playing him along. "I guess some will have a sense of humour."

"No. You know what I mean."

"What do you mean?"

"Well," he cautioned, grinning, "maybe you better put a piece of tape across your asshole!"

Let's flash forward to a couple of years later, when I was able to put together the $200, earnings derived from my chosen profession, to pay Seymour back. He was pleased for me that I was able to do so, but noted that I had not yet become a "star." I had to agree. As though to complete the conversation of two years earlier, he said, "Well, if that's the case, maybe you should take that piece of tape off your asshole!"

My apartment in New York was almost a showbiz cliché. It was a cold-water flat; that meant no heat. It was a sixth-floor walk-up; that meant no elevator. The kitchen table was a board over the bathtub, which wasn't inconvenient because the bathtub was in the kitchen; it was only inconvenient when you wanted a bath. The john was also virtually in the kitchen, because when you sat down on the toilet, your knees jutted out into the kitchen and you couldn't close the door. This made for some delicate moments when I had female guests. And there was a living room, which wasn't that much bigger than the kitchen. That was it. There was a couch in the living room that opened into a bed. There was a TV set in the living room as well, but I was warned never to turn it on. The apartment was a sublet from a staff member of the Playhouse who was doing winter stock in Florida. The good news was that it was on East Fifty-fourth Street, right next door to the Neighborhood Playhouse School of the Theater, where I would spend most of my waking hours.

From at least 9 a.m. to 6 p.m. I was at the Playhouse, and now I finally understood Stanislavsky's *An Actor Prepares,* because I was living it: voice and speech classes, acting analysis and scene study classes, movement and dance classes, surrounded by other dedicated students from all over North America and beyond. Some of the other students in my year included young hopefuls who blossomed into important talents, such as James Caan, Dabney Coleman, Elizabeth Ashley, Brenda Vaccaro, Christopher Lloyd and Jessica Walters. The place was vibrant with discovery, sizzling with energy—the energy of youth and raw talent, sexual energy, and the energy of ambition.

Acting. I had been doing it fairly well for a dozen years now, working intuitively, as well as being aided, I'm confident to say, by a natural gift. I had a fair bit of practical and professional experience under my belt. But now I was starting to learn acting as a science. I was absorbing the academic language of acting, which to this day I still speak and practise and teach. I was starting to learn technique and craft: how to analyze a scene and a character's behaviour in the scene; parallel to this, and for the purpose of achieving this, how to use yourself, that is, your body, your soul, your voice, your feelings, your memory, your mind, or all of it put together in one word—your *instrument.* You seek to become an acting instrument, an instrument that, regardless of how young you are (I was twenty-three at the time), will ultimately be regarded as your own Stradavarius.

That's taking yourself pretty seriously, but that's how serious the commitment was, particularly in the prevailing atmosphere of the time, both on Broadway and in Hollywood, dictated by the substance and style of the likes of Marlon Brando, James Dean, John Garfield and Montgomery Clift. As great as these actors were and although I'm proud of that sense of purpose and focus on purpose, I wonder in retrospect where the humour was. Happily, although I still employ the same thinking and recipe learned back then, in addition to that I now ask myself, no matter what the role, Where is the love? Where is the humour?

Thinking and recipe. There is a specific approach to analyzing and parsing a character, getting to his heart and soul: who he is, where he comes from, what he wants, what he will do to get it, and how he will do it. Of course, many of the answers to this, if not all, are in the script. More importantly, though, the script opens up avenues for the inventive actor to explore layers below and areas beyond the script, dimensions that are perhaps not in the script but could not be reached except through the script. This exploration always involves an approach or a recipe for research, probing and character building that is composed of many ingredients. These ingredients are always available, but not all are always necessary. Some are essential and common to the core of every exploration.

By virtue of Sanford Meisner's philosophy, the emphasis at the Neighborhood Playhouse was on "actions and intentions." That is, you find the underlying purpose behind a character's *raison d'être* in a scene, and then you decide what he will do to achieve this purpose. This almost always can and should be reduced to active verbs. These actions lead through ramifications to other actions or active verbs of intent, affecting the character's continuing or changing purpose, his relationships and all aspects of his moment-to-moment behaviour. This approach, one of the most fundamental principles of Stanislavsky's system, was espoused by Sandy Meisner and in turn practised in America as one of the twin pillars of what came to be known as the Method.

The other pillar, comprising "emotional tasks" like sense memory and emotional recall, became the substance of the teachings of the other master of the Method, Lee Strasberg. Neither of these great teachers taught one approach to the exclusion of the other, but each preferred one approach as the centrepiece of his respective method of teaching.

To demonstrate to students at the Playhouse how action is the life flow of character, we were told one day that we couldn't come into the classroom through the door, which was locked, yet we had to get into the classroom. Some students tried to break the door open; some begged to gain entrance; others cried and pleaded; still others scraped and clawed till their fingers bled. One former student, another Canadian, I'm happy to say, has become part of Neighborhood Playhouse folklore: Leslie Nielsen. A few years before my term there, he apparently climbed, like Spiderman, straight up the exterior brick wall (the classroom was on the fourth floor) and entered through the window. The point of the exercise was that in each case an action was undertaken, which could be described by an active verb, such as climbing, begging, breaking and so on. These were called one-action problems.

Another example of a one-action problem, this time one action for each of two students in a situation, was this: One student was "blind," that is, acting with eyes closed for the purpose of this exercise. The other's task was to come into the room, steal something and get away undetected. There was to be no dialogue. The blind actor would be preoccupied with an activity, let's say knitting (again an active verb), and would be seriously committed to completing what he or she was doing. Of course the thief's action was to *tiptoe* in, *sneak* around until he *found* what he was after, and then *get out*. Although governed by their specific activities in the pursuit of achieving their individual goals, each pursuit would nevertheless be, like it or not, affected by the other's behaviour. As each was focused on his own intention, the atmosphere would be electric with concentration, action and reaction in the tension of moment-to-moment behaviour.

From one-action problems and two-action problems we graduated to improvisations. There was no set dialogue. Whatever happened, happened, in the quest of each participant to realize his or her purpose. Although new understandings of self were achieved, the resourcefulness you reached for within yourself could as often as not be on a gut level as on a head level. Working on a gut level was better. This was quite a shift for me, because whereas in law school the year before I was dealing with conflicts cerebrally, now, most of the time, the teachers at the Playhouse didn't want the student's head to get in the way of his gut reactions.

There were variations on improvisations, like each actor being allowed only one word to achieve his or her purpose. For example, one actor could say only "please," the other only "no." The task of the first actor would be to get the second to say "yes." The point of these improvisations was to get the actors not to rely on dialogue but to use other faculties to achieve their goals, or other strings as it were, of the actor's Stradavarius.

Finally, the instrument would be ready to do scenes from established plays. Somehow, although they may seem simple and obvious, the improvisation exercises were all part of a marvellous awakening for me—sometimes intimidating, sometimes awkward, always exciting. For example, because of the conflicting interests, if both actors' needs were urgently felt and completely committed to, there could be serious friction and even, if not stopped in time, violence, as occurred in at least a couple of improvs in which I was involved.

I was doing an improvisation with an interesting guy who was an ex-marine, accomplished in hand-to-hand combat and knowledgeable about which ordinary objects can be turned into instant weapons—as in this case, a pencil. I can't remember what the improvisation was about, but I do remember it building to a confrontation between the two of us. I saw him grab a pencil from his jacket breast pocket, its point jutting out from his fist as we went for each other. Fortunately, I was wearing a winter overcoat, and I thought to myself, I'll reach for him in such a way that his fist can't go as high as my face and my body will be protected by my overcoat. While I was endeavouring to do just that, the scene was (fortunately) stopped by the teacher.

The ex-marine and I were good friends, and we were laughing about the scuffle afterwards, when he suddenly pointed apologetically to a bloodstain on my shirt, at chest level, which became apparent as I took off my coat. In the intensity of the action, during the last seconds of the improvisation, I didn't notice, nor was he aware, that he had stabbed me right through my clothes into my chest. I checked with my brother, who was then practising and teaching medicine in Washington, D.C., as to whether I should have the piece of lead that was embedded in my chest surgically removed. Benny said it would be more trouble than it was worth and no harm to leave it. So I carry with me, at all times, close to my heart, a memento of my acting classes at the Neighborhood Playhouse.

Jerry Weintraub, probably the biggest guy in our class, often chose me for a partner in improvisations because I was amongst the next biggest and he wanted someone who had a chance of standing up to him. These situations would always escalate into scary tension. Nevertheless, I was fond of Jerry. I found his declared reason for studying acting refreshingly honest, but crass. He wanted to make a lot of money, and he thought acting was the way to do it. I thought it was all about art. I thought, sure, I wanted to make money, but that financial success would come as a result of being good at what I do. So money wasn't what I was focused on; money would be a by-product of what was my only focus there, that is, becoming a good actor. Jerry said that was a lot of shit, and soon he said that studying acting itself was a lot of shit. Indeed, within only a few months, he changed his mind about being an actor and left the Playhouse; he saw that acting was not where the money was. He went to work as a delivery boy in the mailroom at the William Morris Agency and at night as an usher at *The Johnny Carson Show*. He soon worked his way up, and eventually achieved his goal of becoming very wealthy, as one of the most powerful managers in Hollywood as well as a successful film producer.

When I look back now at my ideals, I think they were worthwhile, and I think they still are. I was sincere in my dedication at the

Playhouse. But I have to admit that, however worthy my ideals, I may have been a little pompous. Inverse inferiority complex? Indeed, some of the teachers at the Playhouse would sometimes say, "Come down off those lofty Canadian heights" or "Come out of that cold Canadian shell." I didn't realize I had my guard up all the time.

Often, and for a long time, there was confusion before there was discovery. Part of this confusion arose from my Canadianness. Being the only Canadian made me different, at least I thought it did, although no one else seemed to care. In 1958, unlike today, very few acting students in New York knew of Toronto or the country it was in. So while my Canadianness made me feel different, there was nothing so very different about it as far as they were concerned. I was just another student to them—but I wanted to stand out.

At the same time, I felt that all the other students spoke an accented English, while I was capable of something possibly superior, a Canadian accent, something closer to the head office of English, namely England. After all, we were much more defined at that time, especially by the majority of Canadians, by our membership in the British Commonwealth. This self-imposed dichotomy caused me some confusion in speech and voice classes, and was also demoralizing, because the feeling around me was "Who cares?" and "What's the difference, anyway?"

Ironically, in Canada being Canadian had created the opposite problem, but with similar results. Ten years earlier, as I waited my turn to perform on *Doorway to Fairyland*, sitting there in the corridors of the CBC, with the distinguished sounds of British English echoing around me, I, a Canadian actor, sometimes felt out of place and inadequate because of my accent: it was Canadian. Feelings of personal inadequacy, for whatever reasons, could be compounded by this lack of a strong sense of national identity in Canada—that is, until I lost myself in the identity of a character, whether it was a pirate in *Doorway to Fairyland* or a character in a play we were studying at the Neighborhood Playhouse.

Fortunately, the real thrust of the Playhouse, regardless of individual stumbling blocks, carried us forward. The teachings of Sandy Meisner provided guidelines that would forever accompany me in my acting career. I was privileged to be under his influence and that of his teaching disciples, who included Sydney Pollack, himself a very good actor, who went on to become a celebrated film director. Most memorable for me, however, amongst acting teachers was someone who didn't teach acting per se. She was a dance teacher and is considered the founder of modern dance: Martha Graham.

The discipline of dance is important to the actor's attitude, and the use of the body enriches the actor's instrument. There was something not just informative and educational about Martha Graham's class, but even inspirational. Her total involvement, absorption and commitment of body, soul and mind to her work, to every move, was something to behold and learn from, an attitude to emulate. As she said, and wanted each of us to internalize, "There is vitality, life force, an energy, a quickening, that is translated through you into action, and because there is only one you for all time, this expression is unique."

When I started her class, I commented that there was little point in my taking her dance class because I had no rhythm.

She quickly set me straight. "Yes, you do," she informed me.

"No. I wish I did, but I don't."

"You do," she corrected me. "Everyone has rhythm. Each of us has his own."

I dared to be amusing, and said, "I wish that were true!"

Her patience was just about at an end. "Can you walk?" she demanded.

"Yes."

"Do you put one foot after the other?"

"Of course."

"Then you've got rhythm!"

When she taught us a move and said "So be it"—it was. And

motivation? She got to the guts of it even better than Strasberg or Meisner when she said, "If you men can't do this, it means you're impotent." We were suddenly poised.

That was something to be seen, the men in our class in dance togs. Although the women looked great, the guys in tights and leotards all looked to be in varying states of silliness. But we got used to it, because we spent fifteen hours of every week in dance class under the tutelage and towering example of that short woman, Martha Graham. Whether one achieved perfection of a certain step or move was secondary, I think, to the attempt, and to the learning of disciplined application of self and physical use of the acting instrument. Indeed, I have often used dance moves in a film or a play to achieve or convey a certain feeling. The dance step, in such a case, would happily not be noticed, but the feeling would be projected by me and felt by the audience. For example, a contraction pulling the body inward towards the middle conveys a transition from a character's feeling of bigness to one of smallness.

I did this in *Death of a Salesman* when Willy's elation over his decision to kill himself is momentarily lost in sobering fear. During that one second when he shrinks into a pleading cry for his big brother Ben, I physically went from the expansiveness of self-delusion through a Graham contraction, withdrawing within myself for a fleeting moment of frightening reality before bursting, panic-stricken, towards the inevitable conclusion. Again, I used the contraction as a tool to create a specific impact on the audience, this time physically motivated, in *A View from the Bridge*. As Eddie Carbone, I am knifed in the stomach by Marco, my cousin-in-law. The danger for the actor is not the knife, but playing a generalization of death. What's preferable is the specificity of technique: the impetus for a contraction is instant upon contact, my stomach pulled in, my back arched as I slide down Marco's legs to crumple at his feet in death.

In Martha's class one day, I, for some reason or other, wasn't wearing my tights, only my leotard, so my legs were exposed. I was having difficulty doing a certain step or move she had just spent three-quarters of an hour teaching. Because of my failed attempts to execute the move, plus my bare legs, I looked sillier than anybody else there that day. And the silliness of the way I looked bare-legged in only a leotard was made funnier by my tendency to be overweight. Nevertheless, I tried—without success. With the whole class watching, she was determined to teach me personally by putting her arm around my middle and guiding me across the length of the floor, employing the step and move she had just taught. As my foot came down incorrectly each time, she would with her free hand slap my bare thigh. With each step a resounding smack! When we finally got to the other end of the floor, the redness of my thigh almost matched the redness of my face, but I summoned up whatever wit was left in me to say to her, "Well, now, at least I can say I've danced with Martha Graham."

Despite my inexpensive apartment and the frugality of my new-found fondness for spaghetti (long before it was called pasta), I needed a part-time job. Almost with a sense of history, I got a job as an usher at the Roxy. The famed Roxy—one of New York's two great citadels of the silver screen and stage, offering both cinema and chorus line. A place enshrined in the Broadway banter of *Guys and Dolls*, which asks and answers, What's playing at the Roxy?—a very popular question of the famous place neighbouring and rivalling Radio City Music Hall for show-business lore. I got the job at the Roxy a year or two before it was to be torn down. Radio City Music Hall, of course, still stands.

Brass-buttoned vest, gold braid and epaulettes. The usher's uniform at the Roxy was very different from the buttoned-down shirt collar, tweed jacket and charcoal grey trousers that were the Ivy League uniform of the year before at the University of Toronto Law School. I found something comic in it, but I was not without concern that this great tourist attraction could draw visitors from Toronto who might notice my comedown in uniform. In my mind's eye, in spite of the abundance of the Roxy uniform, I felt undressed. And goodness knows, watching the same movie and the same stage show over and over, every night, for about eight weeks in a row (would you believe *Rio Bravo,* starring John Wayne and Dean Martin), left plenty of opportunity for my mind to wander. Of course, that paranoia of being caught "naked" by Toronto tourists only set in occasionally, because most of the time, when my mind was not on ushering, I would be concentrating on learning lines and working on the recipe and analysis of the work to be presented at the Playhouse the next day.

After *Rio Bravo* came *Imitation of Life,* starring Lana Turner, Sandra Dee and Troy Donahue, three times a night for weeks on end, interspersed with the same stage show twice every night, honouring and welcoming the fiftieth state to the union, Hawaii, with no less a personage than Don Ho singing Aloha songs as the famous chorus line wicky-whacky-wooed in hula skirts. Actually, I didn't mind that too much.

After work I'd go across the street to Hansen's. It was a drugstore, but was better known as a place where actors bought their stage makeup. It was also known for its coffee shop a few steps up at the back, where showbiz types would sit around and schmooze. I would go in there after work and hang out till approximately 2 a.m., even though my classes started at 9 a.m. I was fascinated by the collection of comics, as in *Broadway Danny Rose,* regaling each other until the wee hours of the morning. Camouflaged by the haze of cigarette smoke, I would sit at a table within earshot, ostensibly having a coffee but really eavesdropping. There'd be about a half-dozen comics, whose regular beat would be the Catskill resorts, sitting around a table exchanging stories over their coffee, or in some cases buttermilk, with that Milk of Magnesia–like stain it left on the inside of the glass. Although there was laughter, they didn't enjoy their storytelling, it seemed, but rather were competing with each other—not even trying out new material so much as one-upmanship. Each story would trigger another, like candy-coated anger—in an attempt to be funny, yes, but more like, "Oh yeah, well if you think that's funny, listen to this!" And so on until they finally dispersed, usually telling each other something like, "So you'll call me, OK? You got my number, don't you? So you'll call? All right?"

They seemed so lonely and, for funny guys, not very happy. All were reasonably successful, I thought, because their faces and stand-up routines would show up periodically on *The Ed Sullivan Show*, but still they gave me the impression that life was passing them by and comedy was painful and lonely. After they had gone, I would look for a moment or two at the buttermilk-coated glasses they left behind. Somehow, the empty, clouded glasses seemed to epitomize those comics for me, but perhaps I was just projecting my own fears about this business. Perhaps I too was lonely and scared.

One night when I went home from Hansen's, alone, I couldn't sleep and was cold, so I sat bundled up, staring at the blank TV screen that I had been warned not to turn on. Even though it was about 2:30 a.m., I was too cold to sleep. I was thinking of all the ways to try and keep warm. I once lugged scavenged wood up those six flights to create some warmth from a fireplace in my living room. The fireplace was only a few inches deep, and I merely succeeded in almost setting the whole building on fire. I could turn the gas stove on for heat, but then the danger was falling asleep and never waking up. Once in a while there would be some female companionship, shared spaghetti and wine, and then maybe I'd get lucky up there and my bed would be warm, but this was not going to happen tonight. My eyes lingered on the TV set. I wondered why I was warned not to turn it on. It seemed I had no choice but to sit there bundled up until morning. I decided, fuck it, I'm going to turn it on! I did, and it exploded! The tiny place filled up with stinking, stinging smoke. I couldn't breathe. The hell with this, I figured, I'm getting out of here.

Where could I spend the night indoors? The only place I could think of was an all-night movie house on Forty-second Street. These were porno palaces. I, of course, did not sleep there—too risky. But at least I wasn't cold. Even though I sat up and watched, I don't remember any of the movies that played that night. Instead, I was very cognizant of the other patrons—all in trench coats.

Finally it was nine o'clock and I was back at school. It was warm and the air was fresh and clean and clear at the Playhouse. I reflected on the long night: starting with my Roxy-uniformed "Second aisle on your right, please," "Follow me to your seats, please," and "This way, please," then eavesdropping on competitive comedy through the smoke-filled haze of loneliness, followed by frozen air in my apartment, warmed over by the acrid smell of burning electronics, and finally ending up at a porno picture.

Fortunately, I could look at that situation and laugh, but my moods could swing from humour to sorrow. On a day when the latter mood prevailed, I happened to be auditioning for a role in a movie or a play, I can't remember which. I only remember the woman who auditioned me, an important casting director called Marion Dougherty. She saw the self-pity I was clouded under, but was perceptive enough to perhaps see something else: talent and potential? Even though she had many appointments waiting, she was thoughtful and generous enough to take the time to talk to me. She asked me what was going on. The upshot of our conversation was that without a sense of humour you can't cope in this business, and so she advised that if you can't find something to laugh at when things aren't going exactly as you want them to, you'd better get out of the business. I never got the chance to audition for her again, but I will always remember her, and of course I always try to remember her advice (even if I don't always succeed in following it).

Immersion: the Neighborhood Playhouse all day and the Roxy all night, and on Saturdays I was invited to join some of the students I mentioned earlier at a casual class, virtually a discussion group about actors and acting with a man who had a profound effect on my life—just from my listening to the enthusiastic, loving and passionate philosophy that informed his life as an artist. His name was Howard da Silva.

Howard was a very well respected actor who had won an Academy Award for Best Supporting Actor some years earlier for his performance in a film starring Alan Ladd called *Two Years Before the Mast*, but then his career plummeted because of his confrontation with the infamous House Un-American Activities Committee. This was the tail-end of the McCarthy era, 1958–1959, a time of Communist witch-hunting that caused so much damage to some very gifted people because of their political beliefs, real or attributed. Howard was one of the victims of that shameful period. He was a man not only of courage and integrity, but with wells of resources within him from which great amounts of love and laughter would rush. At all of our discussions, only optimism was displayed. This gentle soul was quite a contrast to the villainous characters he usually played.

We met in his huge loft in the garment and factory district, at Twenty-fifth Street and Fifth Avenue, probably a comedown from his Hollywood days, although he certainly seemed to enjoy his circumstances. One end of it was his living quarters—very simple—and the other was used for scene study and group discussions. The space was not so much spare as uncluttered, directly to the point. Huge, but homey. There was something cleanly inspirational about it, like its occupant.

Our sessions would start late on a Saturday morning and linger into late afternoon. He never charged us for his mentoring; he just seemed to find joy in it, as we did. At the end of the session he'd give us each a piece of cheese to munch on as we left, a kiss on the cheek and, until the next get-together, a farewell wish of "*Zie gezint*," Yiddish for "Be well."

There was a theme that was central to all our sessions and discussions, which ultimately penetrated to the core of my approach to the art of acting. It is why so often, so many years later, I am told things like "You were born to play this part" or "You *are* this character" or

"That's acting? I thought that was you," when in fact the character referred to is so different from me. But achieving this naturalism is predicated on knowing who "me" really is.

On a personal level, I was in search of self. That was at the heart of the Beat Generation, which we were in the midst of then. That's also what being young and growing up is all about—the search for self. In essence, that inner struggle is what religious and cultural identity is all about as well. In the end, all of this is influenced by national identity, or want of national identity.

I think we non-Native Canadians inherited, from our very beginnings in this new land, a certain amount of confusion and negativism. We came into being from a status quo mentality and with the seeds of separation from our very inception, whereas the United States was born out of the positivism and unity of "wanting to be." Even when we tenuously tied our country together from coast to coast, it was as much to prevent the US from surging up the middle as it was to connect the East to the new provinces in the West. The railway that was to unite Canada was as much for the purpose of preventing our becoming American as it was for cross-country transportation.

I think that we in Canada grew up confused, or at least I did. To put it simply, we live in North America but are told we are not American. We used to be told that we were, in essence, closer to the British. Then we realized that, no matter where our loyalties lay, we were thousands of miles away from Britain, and are not British. Instead, we were and are right next door to the Americans, and not only contiguous but closer in defining characteristics to them. Nevertheless, we are different from them too. And so again, we are not American and we are not British. What are we? We swirl around like that, in a confusion defined only by what we are not.

This confusion results in a gap in the awareness of self, and in the assertion of self, that could also make for a dangerous gap in honesty at the foundation of an actor's work. So when I assumed, for example, because of preconceived notions, that Shakespeare would be best played by the British, and better played by Canadians than by Americans because we were closer to the British, Howard da Silva disagreed. He would say that trying to sound like someone else was looking to define yourself outside yourself, that I was starting from a wrong premise, a weak premise of self-denial, and then leaping to a generalization that I was trying to identify with. He would advise never to deny who you are, but rather to look within yourself for who you are. Furthermore, the example I gave would be denial of self because I would be playing a conclusion instead of building from a foundation to a conclusion. You would, in leaping to a conclusion, be *pretending* a character, not *being* a character; and good acting is about being, not pretending. So when you deny self, he would point out, you start from a foundation built on dishonesty, and that gap in honesty will show up ultimately as phoney acting. And the audience will see it, because they can always spot a phoney.

Country of origin is not what it's about; the individual actor is what it's about. As Martha Graham said, "There is only one of you for all time." Country of origin only comes into play as one of the factors that determines who the actor is, and to that extent country of origin is important. So da Silva would argue, and brilliantly demonstrate, that he was a Jew from Brooklyn who, with this mental preparation, plus that emotional understanding, this intention, that action, this adjustment physically, that adjustment vocally, this makeup and that wardrobe, would ultimately equal the character of, let's say, Benjamin Franklin—which was one of the great roles he did on Broadway when the blacklist eased (as it never did for him in Hollywood). The point is that he didn't start off thinking he had to be British-sounding in order to play an early American character. More to the point, he started building the character from a solid foundation of fact and truth—that he, the actor, was a Jew from Brooklyn. Starting from that premise of honesty, what "I am" will result ultimately in "being" the part. That is the equation: truth and honesty, with scrupulous external and internal research, plus appropriate adjustments, will equal the part, will *be* the part. From that time forward, I have always defined acting in terms of two active verbs: *being* and *doing*.

What Howard did was to encourage us as actors to be self-reliant, to believe in self and to be resourceful. This was quite different from, for example, the most celebrated of New York acting teachers, Lee Strasberg. I got the feeling in Lee's classes, at least during the time I studied with him, that the belief was supposed to be in him. I expected to be able to challenge and question and have my concerns addressed, thereby determining *what* was right, not *who* was right. In Lee's class I found actors often being told, in effect, "Don't question, just do as I say, and you'll see." And students willingly accepted this. Well, even Stanislavsky cautioned against slavish devotion and advised finding your own way. Never stop that search. So now, as a teacher, I offer myself to my class as a fellow student, albeit one who has been out in the professional world for longer than they have, and may possess more knowledge to share; nevertheless, I'm still a student, just as they are, looking to learn more.

Before the year was over at the Neighborhood Playhouse there would be a flurry of attempts to land summer-stock jobs. A buzz filled the halls with news about who was auditioning where, what plays were being packaged, what parts were available, which companies would have better people or be better places to be associated with, that is, if you could get cast in a role, any role. Some actors had agents; some, like me, had to fend for themselves. Some auditions you could go to unsolicited by an agent. Somebody knew somebody who knew somebody. Another actor was more talented, or he was taller, slimmer or better looking. It always hurt to consider yourself a failure because your natural attributes were (you gave yourself to believe) inadequate. I didn't have the maturity to see that arbitrary standards are ephemeral, whereas I would last. Disappointment sometimes clouded my vision. It was hard to remember Martha Graham's words about uniqueness, that there was only one me. I understood those words, but like so much else I learned then, it was still up above my eyebrows and would take some time to sink deeper to a level of real understanding.

There were some prestigious regional and summer stock theatres where more established actors were hired; apprenticeships were available there, but that was not appropriate for me now. Then there were less prestigious situations, but even there, not many roles for actors of my age and type. It's always possible to break through somewhere, though. I successfully auditioned for a company of so-called lesser prestige. The company may not have been considered top rate, but the role and the play were: Eddie Carbone in Arthur Miller's *A View from the Bridge*. I was too young for the part, but my reading was convincing. The director, Charles Gordone (an important off-Broadway writer and director at that time) believed that I could do it. I got the lead!

One of the students at the Playhouse had a part-time job running the coffee concession at an off-Broadway theatre called the St. Mark's Playhouse. He invited me to a special evening they were having on their dark night. It was a private performance of *A View from the Bridge* for a limited and select audience (he was going to sneak me in), which would include Arthur Miller and his agent—the targets of the effort. The actors had been denied the rights to do *A View from the Bridge* in New York, even off-Broadway, because it had been done on Broadway only a year or two earlier, and at the time I'm talking about Miller and/or his agent apparently felt there was too much Miller in New York. *The Crucible* was running, as well as Miller's adaptation of Ibsen's *An Enemy of the People*. But these actors and their director prevailed upon Miller and his agent to let them audition, as it were. They spent a month rehearsing just to give one private performance for Miller and his agent. If Miller approved, the actors would get the rights; if not, well, at least they had given it their best shot.

The St. Mark's is a small theatre at Second Avenue and Eighth Street. No matter where you sat, you would be near Miller. Anticipation. He was the last to come in. As we all waited, we wondered if he would bring Marilyn Monroe. Alas no, it was just his agent accompanying him. Still, they were like royalty. Everyone in those days was a little dressier than today, even at an off-Broadway house. The men all wore shirts, ties and jackets, despite the stifling, airless heat of the humid late-spring evening. No one loosened a tie or removed a jacket until they saw Miller do so.

The play started. For me, it will always be one of the most memorable nights in the theatre. Not only were the actors and the production phenomenal, but within earshot and within view—he was taller than everyone else—were Miller's reactions. It was as though with one eye I watched the stunning production and with my other the impact the production was having on Miller. He was shaking his head slowly from side to side in awe and appreciation of the work before his eyes, and quietly but audibly saying over and over, "Amazing!" This was a source of satisfaction and reassurance, because it always bothered me in a way that actors, as artists, were not creators but interpreters, or at best secondary creators; the writers were primary, the creators. Yet here was one of the great writers of our time, amazed by new aspects of a work he had originally created as they were revealed to him by the actors.

Well, these actors got the rights. Not immediately, mind you. I think it was about a year or so later that they started a long run at the Sheridan Square Playhouse in the Village. The cast was the same as in that private performance at the St. Mark's Playhouse, and it included unknowns such as Robert Duvall, Jon Voight and Susan Anspach. I worked with Susan years later when we both guested on *Murder, She Wrote,* and we reminisced about the importance of *A View from the Bridge* for each of us in our respective paths.

So when my year at the Playhouse was over, I was an actor still preparing, but now equipped with the example and inspiration of great mentors—the discipline of Martha Graham, the belief in self of da Silva, the language and technique of Meisner, the emotional tasks of Strasberg—all based on the process of playing the "pipes of the organ" that create the music of acting as articulated by Stanislavsky. I was ready to take on the challenges out there.

CHAPTER 8

Whatever Method Works

I was enthusiastic about implementing what I had learned, putting it all to practical use on a real stage, in front of a real audience. I couldn't wait to try out technique and measure its effectiveness—to monitor the work I was doing with a view to sustaining what worked and improving or adjusting wherever it was needed from performance to performance. That's one of the benefits of a long run—continual opportunity for observation and experimentation.

From my journal, written during the tour of the Stanley Woolf Players production of *A View from the Bridge* in the summer of 1959:

> *July 4*   I was getting quite a bit of colour in my performance, but I think there could have been deeper involvement. I must explore the script, Eddie and myself more...
>
> *July 6*   Crying... in each of the three cases is not honest—the external work is not bad, though. Must work on some images, tasks or some sort of involvement. Voice very raspy but I used it...
>
> *July 8*   I could not employ the images for the three crying scenes. I can't split my concentration. Perhaps this is a good thing. I am involved with my action and with moment-to-moment behaviour. Either my images are not close enough to

the situation or there must be some other way... there was another way—for the last crying scene, anyway. This may be heresy, but I worked outside-in. I started physical crying (externally) and then I got real tears...

Crying without a truthful inner motivation was heresy because, at that time, the Method was like a religion, and "faking it" was condemned in the theatre, the temple of the Method. So were "pretending" and "indicating" as opposed to "really feeling it!" Oh well, whatever method works, works, and that's the method to use—your own. It's good if the actor feels it; it's more important that the audience does. However, I continued to probe, explore and experiment.

> *July* 10   I must try a longer and fuller preparation tomorrow night. I must go further into Eddie's personal life—his life that is never mentioned on stage... There must be an undercurrent on stage of something deeper and further back that I haven't yet tapped...
>
> *July* 11   I worked on preparation for over an hour, made it personal... Tried to create a similar situation for me and either of my last two girlfriends. Anyway, by showtime I had a splitting headache...
>
> *July* 14   Played every action, intention and meaning fully, moment-to-moment behaviour excellent, voice still shitty. One of my best performances, probably because the whole audience was Italian—they picked up every line and innuendo in the play, they loved it. Felt great that an Italian audience accepted my Eddie Carbone.

I kept this journal as I toured the New England states, applying the academics of acting to the professional and practical world of the theatre. Every night we played a different hotel in the Catskill Mountains, the Poconos, the Berkshires. We travelled throughout New

York state, Pennsylvania, Connecticut, Vermont, New Hampshire, Maine and Massachusetts. We visited all kinds of summer resorts, from the biggest and glitziest hotels, like Grossinger's and the Concord (where we would alternate with big-time comedians like Milton Berle), to bungalow colonies where people cooked their own food and gathered at a community centre for our performance. We travelled during the day, arrived at a hotel, set up in their theatre or makeshift theatre, performed, struck the set, packed up, then slept in whatever accommodation they provided, which was, as with the food, sometimes great, sometimes not. The next day it was on to the next resort. But always, every night, the work was rewarding, and I wrote about it in my journal, assessing the job I had done, how the next performance might be affected and what I ought to do to prepare for it.

One day I decided to try what I thought was the preparation used by George C. Scott and Jason Robards. At that time, the stories about their drinking habits were legendary. And if those stories were true, then they, the actors, were absolved by the brilliance of their artistry on stage. I thought, if I'm going to explore, why not try this too? So one night, at a posh hotel where we were invited to mix and mingle with the glittering guests, I began to glitter from mixing a quick succession of pre-dinner cocktails—four, to be exact, a martini, a Manhattan, a whisky sour and a daiquiri—one right after the other, then no dinner, straight to performance on an empty stomach. Well, with extra-careful attention and commitment to my actions, although I got progressively looser, out of step and out of synch, I somehow made it through the show. But I didn't have to wait for a morning-after hangover to experience a headache, which alternated with feelings of nausea. I wrote in my journal that night that I would never use this particular preparation again.

The Stanley Woolf Players was probably close to the bottom rung of prestige in the hierarchy of summer stock. Nevertheless, working with that company gave me the opportunity to do a leading role in a terrific play. I could experiment in a professional atmosphere, just as comics have always tried out new material in the Catskills. For that alone it was a worthwhile summer.

Many young actors started at that same bottom rung and climbed up the ladder from there. The company boasted a number of actors in Hollywood and on Broadway who had started with the Stanley Woolf Players. Not the least of them was Tony Curtis, whose success they claimed some responsibility for.

My convincing portrayal of Eddie Carbone demonstrated that what I had gleaned from my various mentors of the previous season in New York had equipped me with an approach to creating a role. This was proof that the equation was, for me, the right one. I started with "who I am and what I am"—that is, Al Waxman, a Canadian Jew. Then, with commitment to the script, plus adjustments resulting from intensive internal and external research, I realized the character of Eddie Carbone, a New York Italian Catholic.

Using the same approach from character to character, I would, over the years, play other New Yorkers. Some twenty-five years later, when I played Lt. Bert Samuels on the TV series *Cagney and Lacey*, the New York Police Department named me an honorary lieutenant of the NYPD. At that point, only one other actor had received this award, and that was Telly Savalas for his portrayal of Kojak. I was presented with their coveted "shield" at a luncheon attended by a few hundred police officers, including lieutenants and other officers ranking all the way up to the top brass. On the shield is written, "Presented to Al Waxman for a sensitive and accurate portrayal of a New York City police lieutenant on the television police drama *Cagney and Lacey*."

The event was covered by CNN, and I was proud to receive the shield, which is still in my office on the wall above my desk. I was proud that both the character I created and I myself were to be counted amongst them, and proud also to say in my acceptance remarks that the character I built was the result of research started in

Canada, where I had worked with the Metropolitan Toronto Police. The representatives in attendance from the NYPD were not offended by this, but impressed and interested in my process of building a character that they approved of enough to call "one of their own." This was flattering to me because it was the real thing from the real people, not unlike the acknowledgement the night I played Eddie Carbone for an Italian American audience.

After I completed the run of *A View from the Bridge*, I returned to Toronto in the summer of 1959. I did not take any more acting classes at that time, but I did not and will never stop thinking as an acting student. I took voice classes because I always needed, and still need, to work on voice production and projection. I needed to learn how to use rather than abuse my voice; that is, to use the voice so that it emanates from a deeper source than the throat. Like Stanislavsky said, and I agree wholeheartedly, most of all an actor needs three things: voice, voice and voice.

As for acting classes, I preferred to work out, as it were, in an acting gym. Indeed, now, over thirty years later, my professional acting class is called Al's Gym. The same sort of philosophy infused the group I assembled in 1959, a group that got together to do improvisations, scene studies and character studies. That group, by the way, included budding young actors and directors like Gordon Pinsent, who became one of our country's poets of dramatic storytelling; Perry Rosemond, who later created and produced *King of Kensington* and is, at the time of this writing, the producer of *The Royal Canadian Air Farce*; Don Owen, who directed some significant films as our country's then-embryonic film industry was emerging, such as the National Film Board's feature film *Nobody Waved Goodbye*; Martin Lavut, who directed me years later in the CBC's *The Winnings of Frankie Walls*; and Toby Tarnow, who acted in *Nobody Waved Goodbye* and with whom I had studied at Josephine Barrington's and worked at the Niagara Falls Summer Theatre. There were others in the group, amongst them one of my dearest friends, George Sperdakos, a true classical artist of an actor. George has been my travel companion in Canada, in London and Europe, in New York and Los Angeles, with, as a result, many great memories of wining and dining.

Back in Toronto after the summer with the Stanley Woolf Players, I had to find work. Looking for work is part of an actor's work, so I went to work. I would make the requisite rounds, but there wasn't that much pavement to pound here in Canada. This was before CRTC-enforced content and programming requirements put progressively more Canadians into more Canadian productions. There was some regional theatre across the country; some private-sector film work, including commercials in Toronto and drama or industrials by the likes of Crawley Films in Ottawa; the occasional theatrical touring company, like the Canadian Players; and occasional work at the National Film Board in Montreal, as well as the CBC in Montreal. The main game, however, was still CBC radio and TV in Toronto.

This meant regular rounds of the casting directors, the script assistants and the directors, or producers as they were called at the CBC. This could sometimes be demeaning because some of the producers, with their entourages of script assistants and casting directors, were cavalier in their use of the power that came with their position, as we actors paraded by for inspection, as it were. I needed to look like I was on top of it all as I struggled to overcome feelings of inadequacy. It was time to remember what I had learned to date, from da Silva, saying believe in yourself; from Dougherty, saying if you don't have a sense of humour, you might as well get out of the business; and from the Niagara Falls Summer Stock stage manager, saying it's an impersonal business, so don't take it personally, it's part of the job, so be a professional and get on with it. Putting all that together, I handled it fairly well most of the time.

Some of the CBC producers were very thoughtful towards me, like Harvey Hart and Leo Orenstein. As a matter of fact, Leo advised that an actor in his quest for work has a right to be everything short of a pest. So I had a Rolodex mentality in scheduling recurring visits or phone calls at regular intervals, to remind producers and directors of me. Frankly, I would sometimes take it further and say, the hell with it, I'm going to be a pest. Why not, I reasoned. If work is dignity, and I believe it is, then any effort short of hurting someone else, any attempt to get it, no matter how demeaning, is dignified. That wasn't always the case, but it was a rationale that helped buoy me up.

There is always a far greater supply of actors than there is demand for them—it's the nature of our business. Back in 1959, there was even less demand for someone like me, because unlike today, when the culture and particularly advertisers and sponsors are so youth-oriented, all the work involved characters in their thirties and forties and up. So for me, at age twenty-five, there was either no work or only small parts, like background characters or extras. When I was an extra, I always gave my character a name like Joe Wallpaper or Ben Background in an attempt to create characterization and not be just part of the crowd.

Actually, I didn't do too badly, but if memory serves me correctly, in the whole community of young actors there were only a few who managed to make a living from it. Two of those were Gordon Pinsent and Lawrence Dane (a handsome man whose name was then Larry Zahab, a Canadian of Lebanese descent—Jews weren't the only ones with identity problems in show business). Larry was and is one of Canada's successful go-getter actors. He and Gordon and I were probably the only actors I knew who were paying the rent from earnings derived in this business—and I don't know about them, but the only reason I could pay the rent was that I was living at home and the landlady loved me.

Pinsent shared a rented room at a fraternity house with Perry Rosemond and Allan Blye. Blye went on to produce successful TV variety shows in Los Angeles, such as *The Sonny and Cher Show*, but at that time in Toronto he was probably singing as a cantor in local synagogues between TV gigs. Still, it was show business. Years later he sang a beautiful rendition in English of "Hatikvah," at a dinner the B'nai Brith gave to honour me as humanitarian of the year.

As for my friend George Sperdakos, he was always renting a basement apartment, but only in upscale areas like Rosedale, and he somehow had the knack, with food, wine, books and music, of giving the most cramped and damp quarters a spacious, sophisticated and cultured feeling.

Another problem faced by up and coming actors was in the very nature of the system at the CBC. Producers were, in effect, civil servants; they certainly functioned within a bureaucratic atmosphere. Unlike in show business, they didn't have to compete for ratings or audience. They were generally, it seemed to me, more interested in maintaining the status quo rather than building an audience; I suspected that they didn't foster the emergence of stars or personalities for fear of giving up power or position.

Ideally, a show rides on its own merits. However, stars do help attract an audience, and without them there is less opportunity to build up a following—not just for the individual, but for the industry as a whole. That is, without producers of courage and commitment to initiate a TV or film project, plus stars and/or reputation to attract attention to the project, it's difficult for a TV show or film to even exist, let alone succeed.

The term "producer," as it was used at the CBC, following the example of the BBC (where it may have worked), was in my opinion a misnomer. Ultimately, the industry in Canada suffered from this mistaken notion. The producers at the CBC were really directors. They didn't produce shows in the sense of shepherding a project from inception through to broadcast, initiating a project both creatively and financially, then peopling and packaging it, overseeing production and finally presenting it to a pre-targeted audience.

At the NFB, on the other hand, directors were called directors, but they had unrealistic power, like the European auteur director—unrealistic, that is, in the TV industry they would all eventually work in, at least part time, in order to survive. Television operates most effectively as a producer-driven industry, but every good producer knows that viewers don't turn on the TV to watch a producer. So whereas at the NFB directors had too much power shaping the film, at least as it pertains to television, at the CBC producers did not "produce" in the show business sense of the word.

So a vacuum was left in the essential function of producership in the TV industry, which would not be filled except through trial and error for many years—not until the advent of producers, distributors and broadcasters in the private sector, companies that demonstrated the possibilities of artistic and financial success. We in Canada produced good actors, good directors, good editors, good lighting people, good crews, and even good writers—I say "even" out of respect, because writing, a difficult and essential ingredient, is (with producing) where the project starts. But we did not for some years develop producers or stars. The TV industry led the way in this, but the parallel endeavour of feature film has not kept pace.

The factor that was flawed or missing in both the TV and film industries can be summed up in one word: entrepreneurialism, or lack of it. It certainly took me a while to learn that entrepreneurialism is not a dirty word, and that it doesn't necessarily mean there's less artistic content. I'm talking about the entrepreneurialism of energy and resourcefulness, the entrepreneurialism of ambition to create and achieve—not the entrepreneurialism of greed.

Entrepreneurialism was the farthest thing from anyone's mind at the CBC or the NFB, and perhaps understandably so. How could they have had, and why should they have had, that industry-wide perspective and foresight? Still, I think that the private sector, and indeed Canada itself, as we approached a world of culture and communications where borders would be virtually obliterated and where hundreds of channels would vie for attention, would have been more constructively served with producers who were artistically, creatively and commercially more entrepreneurial. Indeed, the making of stars requires entrepreneurialism not only from producers but especially from actors and their agents. It might have succeeded in creating a demand, at least within our own marketplace for our own product. Entrepreneurialism should have been back then, as it is finally becoming now, as integral to the art itself and to the promotion of the art as any other aspect.

Producers in Canada didn't have to worry about attracting or keeping an audience, nor were they concerned with enhancing talent or developing new talent to achieve decent ratings. There were some, however, who seized the opportunity to build their own ladder by using established stars from abroad in order to reach beyond Canada. Many of them would import guest stars, thereby creating attention for themselves in New York or Hollywood. I personally didn't mind competing with British or American stars, because I believed in and wanted to be part of an international industry. What I minded was not getting the opportunity to compete, because most of the time, if the part *could* attract a star, it wouldn't be put out for tender through the casting department to agents for local talent; the casting people went right to the stars.

If you hang in, however, sooner or later opportunity knocks, and in my case it didn't take long. It was a show called *Sun in My Eyes*, to be produced for CBC's TV anthology series "General Motors Presents" in 1959. I know that they were at one point considering international names, so I am forever indebted to the author, Jack Kuper, and the director, Harvey Hart, for allowing me to compete. I got the lead role in what turned out to be one of the most important shows of my career. It certainly gave me, as an artistic vehicle, great challenge and reward, and in terms of my career it gave me a substantial push forward.

Sun in My Eyes was a true story, based on a portion of the memoir by Kuper called *Child of the Holocaust*. It offered a great character for me to bite into, a character whose life is related to the audience through the eyes of a boy, based on Kuper himself during the war.

The character I played was the uncle of the young boy, himself barely an adult and going through the growing pains that any young man would experience, but compounded by the threat and terror of Hitlerism and of the Polish ghetto to which they were eventually confined. He ultimately sacrifices his life for the sake of the boy, his nephew. It was a touching story of the tragedy, triumph and dignity of sacrifice, and it affected audiences across the country.

Sun in My Eyes gave me the opportunity to work with Harvey Hart and with Jimmy Doohan, who played a sadistic police officer. It was good to be able to work with Jimmy after he had been so helpful to me at the Neighborhood Playhouse. And I was able to work closely with Toby Robbins, who played my older sister. As I mentioned before, Toby had become a home-grown star in spite of the system—which, while providing opportunity for stardom, at the same time hampered any potential star from taking off. Toby was one of the first to come along who would not be held back. Indeed, I moved ahead by virtue of working with her.

I think most of all I'll always be grateful for *Sun in My Eyes* because it was something both professional and artistic that my mother was able to see me do and appreciate. The Polish background and ambience, the Jewish characters, the persecution, the fear, the terror, the hope—it was all something she could relate to. And she was proud. It was as though I were the sun in her eyes—certainly a light—perhaps, dare I say it, even a star—in her eyes. Mind you, she thought for having so drained myself emotionally I should have been paid much more. I got paid minimum scale. For the lead in an hour-long show that took ten days to make, the pay was something like $227 after tax. She thought I should have been paid at least a thousand dollars. I said to her that I didn't care, that I would have paid to do the job—this was a logic she couldn't understand.

Sid Furie had watched the taping of the show in the control booth and was probably the first person who came down to see me when it was over. He said he was flying to London within days to start work on a feature film, for Twentieth Century-Fox, to be called *During One Night*. It was about a young air force pilot on the night before his twenty-fifth mission, the last on his current tour of duty, who is fearful it will be his last mission in life. A clever premise, written by Sid himself. After seeing *Sun in My Eyes,* Sid said he wanted me for the lead. He was effusive and sincere. Jack Kuper cautioned me that "Someone might mean what he's saying tonight, but not have the power to do anything about it tomorrow." It turned out that Jack was right. Oh well, close counts not just in horseshoes but also in morale building as well. Being close was better than nothing at all. By the way, the fellow who got the part, a very handsome actor, was hardly heard from again. Fate is funny.

After making a significant impact on the critics, audiences and people in the business, you might think that I had it made, that leading roles would naturally follow, one after another. Not so. There simply weren't enough roles available. I had to go out and hustle as though *Sun in My Eyes* had never happened, and accept small roles, if I wanted to work again. It was too easy to say, well, that's Canada, but I don't think that would be fair or accurate; I think that's the nature and reality of the business anywhere. If the roles weren't written, then they just didn't exist. If I had negative feelings as a result, they weren't particularly about Canada but about the business of acting itself. It seemed that acting could not always provide a sufficient challenge to my energies. I wanted to use more of myself than was being used, especially when the feast of *Sun in My Eyes* was followed by a lean period.

Happily, an interesting challenge came my way, this one back on stage: *The Connection*. It was at the House of Hambourg on a sidestreet a block or so above College, between Bay and Yonge. That theatre no longer exists. It was a space that was the love of Clem Hambourg, a local jazz impresario, who was fondly regarded by loyal followers of his after-hours and jazz sessions. I remember his theatre space as a special place, a refreshing memory along my path. The play at the House of Hambourg was Jack Gelber's *The Connection*, and it was produced by the multitalented Don Francks, who also played the lead. *The Connection* was a play about drug addiction. Because of its content and the kind of play it was structurally (an extemporaneous feel, together with contemporary music performed live on stage), it made significant cultural, social and entertainment waves in New York, and was in the process of repeating its impact in Toronto when its leads, I think by virtue of contractual commitments, had to be replaced. Bruno Gerussi replaced Don Francks, Percy Rodriguez replaced Roscoe Lee Browne, and I replaced George Sperdakos in the role of Solly, the philosophical Jew, who was one of a group of characters, including the Gerussi/Francks character, awaiting the arrival of their "connection," played by Rodriguez/Browne.

There was no curtain. The characters wandered, apparently aimlessly, onto the stage as the audience took their seats. I was sitting on a window sill, facing offstage into the wings, ostensibly looking out for the arrival of the connection. On my first night, I looked out front and noticed an imposing, flamboyant figure, a large man wearing a cape and carrying a walking stick, coming down the aisle towards his reserved seat near the front row. I thought, "Oh my God, it's him!"—not the connection, of course, but the eminent theatre critic Nathan Cohen. I panicked. I didn't know if I'd be able to speak. This was the big leagues, I thought. Our off-Broadway. More than a few rungs above the Stanley Woolf Players. Was I ready?

By redoubling my concentration on my character's purpose, on my intentions, actions and relationships. I made it through the evening, well enough to get a positive, albeit perfunctory, mention. I thought that was better than a kick in the ass—certainly as much as can be expected from a re-review of a supporting role, and from the man who is still considered probably the foremost theatre critic in Canada in this century. He was well respected beyond our borders, in New York and in the traditional pre-Broadway try-out and post-Broadway touring destinations.

Nathan Cohen was the kind of critic you could learn from. Whether it was a pan or a rave, he usually said something illuminating. I've forgotten the play he was reviewing—I was not in it—when he made one specific critical comment that I, as a result, consider part of my arsenal of approach, along with what I learned from the great mentors I mentioned earlier. He said that if a character doesn't go through change, from Act 1 through to the final act, the character is either not well written or not well performed, or both. Change is a necessary ingredient in the dramatic development of a character. A synonym often used by story editors and dramatists for change is *metamorphosis*, or more recently, in TV in particular, the word used is the character's *arc*.

I was concerned about my own arc in life. I wanted to move on. I wanted change. I wanted challenge. It wasn't just that Canada wasn't enough; like any young man, regardless of where his home is, I had wanderlust. I wanted adventure, and acting in Toronto just wasn't providing enough challenges. Maybe if more great roles had come my way, I would have felt differently. But after Solly in *The Connection* and a small but challenging role as a French Canadian priest in the CBC TV special *Riel*, if and when I got work, the parts were Ben Background and Joe Wallpaper.

I wanted more than acting anyway. Directing? Was I smart enough? And what about the education and training I would need to be a director? Writing? Was I gifted enough? Did I know enough? Did I know enough about anything? About life? It was time, as the Beat philosophy of the day said, to be "on the road." Life itself meant being on the road, so why not? It was time to get further out into the world than I had ever been before, and then... and then all sorts of "and thens."

CHAPTER 9

Passage and Pilgrimage

I wanted to be lost in a foreign land, in a country where I didn't speak the language. So I went to England.

Actually, it made sense to start off in England and use it as a launching pad. I had friends there already, many from my undergraduate days at Western. As well, Canadian writers, actors, directors, sculptors and painters were drawn in large numbers to England, and a natural networking resulted. Writers and artists went to Paris in the 1920s and '30s. In the '50s and '60s (this was 1961) the lure seemed to be either London or New York. And as Canadians we were in a sense exploring our heritage. A proud kinship still existed with England, not to mention the practicality of being able to work in England with a Canadian passport.

My friends from the University of Western Ontario came from, as they said, "London Ont" and were now living in "London Eng" (both pronounced as spelled). I intended to visit them, and spend some time soaking up hip and historic London. Indeed, everywhere I went in England, I was in the midst of lore and legend, a land of great literature and ancient architecture, multilayered and multimythed, and I wanted to see it all. Then I planned to wander around Europe, perhaps even behind the Iron Curtain to explore other roots in Poland, maybe ending up going even deeper into my heritage on a pilgrimage to Israel. But I had lots of time, and everywhere I went, I'd be seeing something new to me; so I went with the attitude, I'll take my time and breathe it all in before I move on, and not worry about what I might be missing elsewhere, because I'll be back again. This was the era of the phenomenon known as the Ugly American. Some North Americans would offend Europeans by saying things like, "I've got two weeks to do Europe. I'll do Paris in three days, Rome in four and squeeze the rest into the remaining seven." So they could say back home, "I've been there." Quite apart from insulting their host countries, they were doing themselves and their budgets a disservice. With just two weeks, you'd be better off spending it all in one country. I travelled everywhere then, and still do now, with the attitude that I'll be here again. There was no panic. I could drink it all in. In fact, I've often returned more than once to many places I've visited.

I moved in with friends who allowed me to share a house they were renting in Battersea, on the other side of the Thames from the "with it" village of Chelsea. Battersea at that time was not just on the other side of the river but, as we would have said in North America, on the other side of the tracks. But I didn't care, because that skinny little row house they let me share with them was as romantic as *La Bohème*. My two landlords were both intellectuals and would often, if not always, be on opposite sides of a debate. The disagreements could start first thing in the morning, as they took turns preparing tea for the household. One would say tea tastes better with the milk poured into the cup first, while the other would argue that the tea should be poured in first.

I had gone to school in London, Ontario, with these two fellows. One was in England to take advantage of the National Health Service (there was no Ontario Hospital Insurance Program yet), by availing himself of psychoanalysis five times a week while attempting to write a novel. The other had apparently done a dissertation on Joseph Conrad and now was doing one on George Orwell. No one ever knew for sure. There was a young woman who shared the row house with us, and hers was yet another reality. She was a waitress from Paris. Apparently you couldn't get an abortion in Paris, but you could in London. She needed an abortion, so she was in London.

The first historic place I wanted to see was not the British Museum or St. Paul's Cathedral or the Tower of London or any of the palaces. I would, of course, eventually visit them all, but because of its impact on me in *A Tale of Two Cities* and out of fondness for my law school days, I wanted first to see the Old Bailey. While I was there, a man who was considered one of the most skilful and eloquent barristers of the day—his name was Victor Durand—was arguing a case in court. I came back to the Old Bailey day after day and sat in the gallery, watching and listening to him "holding court." The ongoing history of the law: right and wrong, knowledge, reason and humanity, a process handed down from these wood-panelled halls and spread throughout the civilized world. I sat listening in deep appreciation; you could say I was *kvelling*.

I travelled up and down London—by foot, by tube and by bus—to hear accents, see sights and maybe meet people. I never had a watch, so I could talk to people, ask them what time it was.

Show business, acting, was not the primary thing on my mind. But guess what? *Sun in My Eyes* had played in England, and by chance, or perhaps through an intermediary, I met a Canadian director who had seen it, Alvin Rakoff. There were many Canadians directing in England then. As well as Rakoff, there was Sidney Furie, and Sydney Newman, who was in charge of programming and production at the independent TV network and had brought many Canadian directors over. Ted Kotcheff, Mordecai Richler and Norman Jewison were in London too, but I didn't meet them until much later, back in Canada. Author/playwrights Ted Allan and Stanley Mann were also there. Ted and I would soon become very much involved in each other's efforts.

My first job in England was for Al Rakoff in an American Western, a TV movie he made at Granada up in Manchester. George

Sperdakos had a part in it too. My part was originally the husband of a character played by the well-known older actress Bessie Love; instead, the character became Bessie's son. Good luck didn't stop there; it also resulted in my getting an agent, a very good one—Elspeth Cochrane, who represented many other Canadians, particularly actors who had worked at Stratford, Ontario.

I was glad to have the job and the agent, because not only was I still an actor, but I was going to make some money, which would help me in my travels. The show itself introduced me to a new place: the north of England. What a way to travel and learn—being paid to work on my craft, and having my craft in turn serve me as a vehicle for discovery.

The next logical step would be to tour England with a repertory company. I heard of one that wanted an American actor to alternate lead roles in three different plays, which would tour the provinces. It was called the Wimbledon Repertory Company, and they paid me close to £15 a week. That was pretty good—an average salary, I believe, in England at that time. That was when the pound was worth three dollars, and in those days it went quite a distance in London. My rent was only £10 a month (the rule of thumb was your rent should be a quarter of your income) and I had only myself to support, so if I was careful, I could live well.

Close by the celebrated tennis courts, the Wimbledon Repertory Company was based at the Wimbledon Theatre, a huge ornate structure like so many theatres throughout England. It was intimidating for a Method mumbler, particularly in the company of RADA-trained, technically honed actors. Would I be heard in these theatres? There were no mikes, just the voice, supported by vocal training. Would someone in the back row stand up and shout, "We paid for our tickets too. We can't hear the Yank!" (I was always thought of as a Yank.) There was no way that the competitive streak in me was going to allow the RADA-trained actors to out-volume me. I practised my vocal exercises and came on stage with boom and bombast. Why not?

I was always playing brash Americans anyway, in farcical war and postwar plays like Terence Rattigan's *While the Sun Shines,* or a play called *Hot and Cold in All Rooms*. They all depended on visual and vocal vitality and precision timing, with doors opening and closing on cue, revealing titillating moments full of sexual innuendo. Lots of entertainment for people who in those days valued their night at the local repertory theatre as much as their "telly."

The Wimbledon Repertory Company was run by a grand old gentleman named Peter Haddon, a farceur of fantastical skills. He and I got along superbly. While we both had discipline regarding our professional work, within it there was an inclination towards mischief. I quickly learned the meaning of the English colloquialism "taking the mickey" out of someone, that is, to make fun of or send up—something we were always doing to one another, particularly on stage. We would try to make the other person break into laughter or somehow fall off course through tricks and practical jokes of one kind or another, while staying on course yourself. I think it was understandable and perhaps even necessary to maintain sanity while speaking the same lines every night, plus two matinees—eight shows a week, week after week. The challenge seemed to be first and foremost to entertain the audience and, within that primary responsibility, to entertain ourselves. In order to do this, you had to walk a fine line. While your colleague was trying to stay on course (with the play and his dialogue), tiptoeing along the edge of a cliff, as it were, you would try to push him over, all the while having the confidence that he would not be a pushover. I never succeeded in making Peter Haddon, that old trouper, laugh off-course, but he more than once caused me to slip and hang on by my fingertips. It was fun, and the audience was always unaware and entertained.

The good relationship I had with Peter Haddon is the only reason I can think of for the Wimbledon Repertory Company arranging for a big article about me to appear in the *Yorkshire Post* before we arrived at our first destination, the Bradford Alhambra, in Bradford, Yorkshire. It was a flattering piece that compared me to the strength of Canadian oak trees; at least, I think that's flattering. So, apparently, did a darling little old grey-haired lady, probably in her seventies, who worked at the pub hotel where we were billeted in Bradford. In the theatre, unlike the movies, you get to sleep in, and after a hard night's work (my parts were all leads) followed by a hard night's play, sleeping in (or "lying in" as they called it) was deliciously welcome—indeed, the body required it. My first morning there, at 7 a.m., without so much as a knock on the door or a "May I come in?", my door sprung open and this sweet little old lady placed a cup at my bedside and announced, "'Ere's your coop a' tay, loov!" I told her I hadn't ordered it. She said, "Aye, loov," and left. I didn't touch it, and went back to sleep. The next morning, the same time, the same thing: "'Ere's your coop a' tay, loov." I said I hadn't asked for it and to please never wake me again. She said simply, "Aye, loov," and left. The next morning I got a little impatient and said, "There must be some mistake. I don't even like tea, so please don't do that again." She sweetly said, "Aye, loov." The next morning I got angry and shouted, "That's it! No more! Don't do that again!" Now she looked hurt and a little dismayed, and she said, with that lovely North Country musical lilt, "You're not as nice as they said you were in the newspaper."

The next morning I was up and waiting for her when she said, "'Ere's your coop a' tay, loov." I thanked her and she said, "Aye, loov," just as sweetly and matter-of-factly as on the first day. Like I said before, I wanted to be in a land where they spoke a different language.

The reviews were good, with phrases like "tip-top performance" attracting some people to the theatre who otherwise might not have come. One night, a stagehand gave me a business card with the name *Albert A. Waxman* on it. I said I didn't have a business card. He pointed out that the card wasn't *from* me. Then I said, "And my middle initial isn't A." Again he pointed out that the card was meant to be given to me. The light in my head finally went on; after all, you come off stage after a round of applause pretty full of yourself. The back side of the card had a handwritten invitation to tea from someone who suggested we might be cousins.

The Waxmans lived in Shipley, near Bradford. They were textile magnates. Their beautiful, baronial home made me feel like I was in a Jane Austen novel. I made a faux pas, evidently, when admiring the grounds, I said, "What a beautiful backyard you've got." My host responded politely, "You mean the gardens?" I said, "Oh yes, of course, the gardens." They weren't snobbish and I wasn't foolish, but this wouldn't be the last time in England I was made aware that there is apparently a more accurate and precise choice of words used. When I visited a dentist in London, for example, and he asked what was the reason for the appointment, I said my teeth needed their regular cleaning (which is what both my dentist and I would have said in Canada). The British dentist replied, "When you go to the doctor, do you ask for a bath?" This cracked me up, although I don't think he intended a joke. He then explained, "If you mean scraping and polishing, then get in the chair."

The Yorkshire Waxmans and I, and later my wife Sara too, agreed to agree that we were cousins. Both the wife of the Shipley Albert and the wife of the Toronto Albert concur that there is a family resemblance, and we do know that both of our immediate ancestries trace back to Poland. Nice people, my British cousins. We've visited each other and corresponded often over the years.

After Bradford there was Nottingham, the sheriff of, and Robin Hood and all that. As well as lore, there was the living legend of Lincoln's Abbey close by, which was interesting to see after Fountain's Abbey in Yorkshire. I was still in tourist mode. Next we played Blackpool, the Coney Island of the north of England, a city that seemed in its entirety like the midway at the Canadian National Exhibition.

Acceptable as part of tourist mode was a new phenomenon for me, "actors' digs," boardinghouses that catered to travelling actors—although part of me would hear my mother's voice saying, "Actors...

nomads... gypsies!" Maybe I even agreed with her. Although it may sound too pat an explanation, perhaps my parents' generation was so committed to establishing a solid foundation under their feet, and maintaining it under ours, because they were closer to the history of the "Wandering Jew" and wanted our future to be firm—hence the importance of owning a piece of land. Perhaps this is also why, quite apart from the history of the Holocaust, Jews worldwide, no matter where we live and travel, are so committed to a secure future for the state of Israel. Symbolically solid ground. More than symbolic: make the desert grow! I would soon visit Israel.

My next job settled me back home in Battersea for a while. It was a movie based on John Hersey's air force novel *The War Lover*. I had acted in some movies made in Canada, at the Kleinburg Movie Studios just north of Toronto and at the Lakeshore Studios west of Toronto, all forgettable—not because I'm trying to pass judgment, but because I really don't remember them, other than the fact that in one I was a cowboy and in another a sailor. Now I was to be a tail gunner from Detroit in a B17. Of course I had already acted in front of the cameras on TV, but this was my first film for a major Hollywood studio, Columbia Pictures. It starred Steve McQueen and Robert Wagner. I had a good supporting role, along with Michael Crawford, who later would star as the Phantom in *The Phantom of the Opera*. My buddy George Sperdakos got into the film as well. We celebrated by drinking too much apple cider, which I thought was going to be like apple juice, but what a punch! Soon we were unable to stand up straight, nor could we tell which of the lookalike row houses was mine. We were crawling on all fours before we found my little row house.

I spent eighteen weeks at one of the great studios, Shepperton, and on location at Bovingdon Air Base. Eighteen weeks at £75 a week: that was a princely sum. Remember, my rent was only £10 a month. I could even save while I was spending freely. And I had my own chauffeur-driven limousine! The car that picked me up was longer than our house in Battersea was wide. The first morning it arrived, even though it was still dark out, the neighbours up and down the street all stood outside their front doors and applauded as I got into the back seat of the car. I was a little embarrassed to have a car door held open for me, but it was good to know that the neighbours felt, because of this posh treatment, that "one of them" had made it.

Working on the film exposed me to aspects of moviemaking I hadn't encountered before, particularly the jockeying for position exhibited by Wagner and McQueen. Wagner was part of the Hollywood establishment, as it were, a product (one of the last) of the studio system, while McQueen, an upstart from television, was making the difficult crossover from TV series stardom (*Wanted: Dead or Alive*) into movie stardom (this was before *The Great Escape*). Wagner, outside the studio system for the first time, seemed a little unsure of himself (this was long before the smooth style he acquired on the successful TV series *Hart to Hart*), compared with feisty, street-smart and very likeable (and he knew it) McQueen.

Steve would argue, "Lookit, Wagner's getting the girl [Shirley Ann Field], so I should get all the sympathy. After all, I'm the lead." Ironically, McQueen's need for sympathy for his character (which was legitimate) cost me my death scene. The scene was between me and Wagner's character; it was filmed and it was effective. McQueen argued that there were three death scenes—his, Crawford's and mine—which was two too many! Overkill (my pun, not his). His argument was that the sympathy quotient would be sapped by the time he was killed at the end of the film. He may have been right. Crawford's freckle-faced character was the youngest in the flight crew, the ball-turret gunner. My character was the sensitive, scared one, and scared for good reason: our research showed that, more often than not, the plane returned with the tail gunner (my position) and the ball-turret gunner both dead. But to hell with factual truth, when you're dealing with artistic truth and entertainment, not to mention career building. Point made: the two deaths together took too much sympathy away from McQueen's character. Arguments ensued, then compromises. Crawford's death scene stayed, mine was cut. All I have to show for it is a black-and-white still photo of my face, bloodied for the scene, and this anecdote, which I've dined out on quite often over the years.

As a result of *The War Lover* I went into another war film, also in black and white, called *Man in the Middle*, a Twentieth Century-Fox film. I seemed to be getting a good reputation as an actor and professional with three of the most important casting directors in London: Rose Tobias, who before London used to cast for David Susskind in New York, where I could never get in to see her; Irene Howard, an actress in her younger days and sister of Leslie Howard (who played Ashley in *Gone with the Wind*); and Maude Spector, probably the most important casting director in all of Europe.

Man in the Middle starred Robert Mitchum, Trevor Howard, Keenan Wynn, American transplant Sam Wanamaker, another Canadian, Alexander Knox, and a Eurasian beauty called France Nuyen. My scenes were all with Mitchum, Wynn and Howard, three solid, gifted and experienced pros. Trevor Howard had an illustrious career, which legend has it was soaked in booze. Indeed, if you look at him in a close-up, it seems like every vein in his face went to acting school. But I wasn't about to try that preparation again; it was sufficient just to watch the simplicity and at the same time the grandeur of his acting. And Keenan Wynn? Acting and show business had been in his blood from birth—his father was the great clown and comic Ed Wynn. He was suffused with the practicality of vaudeville and Broadway, not to mention character after character in both comic and dramatic films. Keenan Wynn always delivered straight-ahead, no-bullshit good acting.

Bob Mitchum was the biggest surprise of all. His movies always seemed to show the same side of him, the sleepy-eyed tough-guy movie star. I didn't think of him as an actor, but I was wrong. He had an excellent sense of comedy, as demonstrated alongside and in between Cary Grant and Deborah Kerr in *The Grass Is Greener*. Similarly, he made a lasting impact in his dramatic roles, like the lead in *The Story of GI Joe*. His accents, such as the Australian one in *The Sundowners* (again with Deborah Kerr), were simple, unadorned and accurate. As for storytelling on the set, Mitchum's tales, like his accents, were endless. His Jewish accent (can you imagine a Jewish accent from Bob Mitchum?) was as funny as Jackie Mason's or Myron Cohen's.

Mitchum wasn't just a funny raconteur, he was also a mischievous practical joker. The only time in my life that I ever got into trouble on a set was because of one of his pranks. It all started out with him surprising and impressing me on *Man in the Middle* with his discipline and punctuality. I thought movie stars came to work whenever they wanted to and the hell with the schedule, like the gossip we were hearing about Elizabeth Taylor, who was at that time also in London, shooting *Cleopatra*. We heard stories about her not showing up till 4 p.m. for an 8 a.m. call. Mitchum, on the other hand, was there promptly in the morning, just as I was. One day, I and a few of the other cast members were invited to a pub lunch with him. After the lunch hour was up, we were still enjoying ourselves, not too concerned about returning to work as long as Mitchum didn't; after all, he was the lead and probably in every scene. He seemed to know what we were thinking as he regaled us with stories, all the while drinking triples of Scotch and chasing them with beer. He knew he had us mesmerized. After another hour passed, I guess he figured the game had gone on long enough. He suddenly looked down over his big chest at his watch, and said, "I don't know what you guys are doing here, but I was broken [released for the day] before lunch!"

I raced back to the set. Waiting for me was Kip Gowan, one of the best assistant directors I have ever worked with. The assistant director is responsible for running the operation of a movie set; the schedule is one of the things uppermost in his mind. Some ADs were given to screaming and yelling, particularly the English ones—things like "I'll have your guts for garters!" Kip Gowan, on the other hand, was calm, yet just as effective as any AD I can remember. When I came on the set after my extended lunch with Bob Mitchum, very late, Kip simply looked at his watch and said quietly, "Waxman, I thought you were a professional." As the saying goes, I wanted the ground to open up and swallow me whole. What he said was a reprimand, but it was also a reminder of the importance of professionalism and an acknowledgement that I was capable of professionalism. I was never late on a set again in my life. That was the first, last and only time.

Before I finished my film work, I was already signed to do a play. Back to the theatre. One advantage England has over the United States is that the film capital and the theatre capital are the same city, not three thousand miles apart on opposite coasts. Mind you, my interest in the play I was signed to do was kindled three thousand miles from London, back home in Toronto. It all started with Rose Kastner, an energetic friend of the arts and artists, and mother of a family of artists: Peter Kastner, one of Canada's bright lights of film acting, who starred in *Nobody Waved Goodbye* and Francis Ford Coppola's early film, *You're a Big Boy Now*, as well as guesting on *King of Kensington* a couple of times; Kathy Kastner, former on-camera TV reporter and now video producer; Susan Kastner, *Toronto Star* columnist; and John Kastner, Emmy Award–winning documentary maker. Rose Kastner brought Ted Allan and me together and virtually cast me in his play *Secret of the World*, in the part of Alex Alexander, the juvenile lead, as they would say in London. It was a great supporting role in a wonderful play, and one that proved to be an important personal experience for me, and a milestone in my career.

The seeds that were sown back in Toronto came into full bloom with the official approval and endorsement of producer, director and casting director in London. I was cast in *Secret of the World*, a production believed to be headed to the West End, London's Broadway, because it was being launched at the Theatre Royal in Stratford East.

This theatre was at a level of importance, in my opinion, above off-Broadway but not quite Broadway or the West End, like the Royal Court on the west side of London, in Chelsea's Sloane Square. Both had earned special respect in the hierarchy of London theatre. So with the right kind of reviews, this production, which already had virtually West End importance, would in fact move there.

Theatre Royal in Stratford East was the workplace of the chain-smoking, tough iconoclast Joan Littlewood, a new creative force in British theatre. It was her space, and our producers were renting it. Joan Littlewood had nothing to do with our production, but the theatre had her mark. This happened to suit *Secret of the World*, which was about a union leader who becomes disillusioned with Communism as a result of Krushchev's 1956 revelations of Stalin's crimes. I think it's fair and flattering to say that Joan Littlewood's company was to London in the 1950s and '60s what the Group Theatre had been to New York in the 1930s. Her ensemble was sometimes called Theatre of Action or Theatre Workshop and, like the Group Theatre, was left-leaning and drew energy, artists and ideas from the working class. The company of artists and the theatre she forged wanted to break from the traditionally structured theatre and content seen in the West End. She and her group were part of the muscle of a new energy in British theatre and filmmaking. This was the time of Britain's "angry young men" and "kitchen-sink drama"—plays such as John Osborne's *Look Back in Anger* and Shelagh Delaney's *A Taste of Honey*. Acting talents were emerging, like Albert Finney, Tom Courtenay and Alan Bates. Also amongst the angry young men was Arnold Wesker, whose play *The Kitchen* was a superb example of the kind of work identified with theatres like Theatre Royal in Stratford East and the Royal Court in Sloane Square.

We were in good company. I was in good company. And not just with regard to the theatre, but especially the cast, author and director of *Secret of the World*. The woman who played my mother, the star of the show, was Miriam "Mims" Karlin. She was a terrific talent in drama, comedy and musical comedy, and had often been associated with Joan Littlewood. Her co-star, the man who played my father, was also the director of the play, John Berry.

I was privileged to work in those days with a number of talented people who had all been targeted, some directly, some indirectly, by the Hollywood blacklist; that is, some were publicly "named" and some were just "on lists" and found themselves curiously unemployed. I say I was privileged because the ones I worked with were all intelligent, courageous and sensitive people; all were important to the art and the industry, and particularly to me. The whole industry was affected by the blacklist, by its impact on popular entertainment, but none of us had our personal and professional lives affected like some of these artists I worked with. In addition to Howard da Silva, whom I have already mentioned, I worked with Ted Allan, Carl Foreman, Sam Wanamaker, Anne Revere, Lionel Stander and, in *Secret of the World*, John Berry.

John Berry's last work in Hollywood was *He Ran All the Way*, a black-and-white film he directed starring John Garfield and Shelley Winters. It was a successful film, but the blacklist prevented him from working for the foreseeable future in his own country. He told me he felt "so betrayed that I didn't want to hear English spoken again." He went to France. In Paris, he learned French and began directing for the theatre. He directed Jean-Paul Sartre's *No Exit*. After its success in Paris, it was brought over to the Royal Court in London, and he was prevailed upon to direct the English version. As a result, the door was now open for him to continue working in English theatre. He was also a fantastic actor, very much like Garfield and very Garfield-looking. So he was asked not only to direct but also to play the co-lead (the role of my father) in *Secret of the World*.

He and I began bonding, during rehearsal and after rehearsal. A friendship was formed—professionally and personally. We were like father and son. It was partly because I always seemed to be looking for a father figure, and he seemed to welcome it. I held him in high

My mother, the Mona Lisa.

A family portrait, circa 1937. Can you believe me, camera shy?

The Mona Lisa at the Melinda Lunch, about 1947.

My mother, Benny and me (on the left) at the kitchen table in our apartment at 414A Spadina Avenue, around 1939. My dad, as always, was at work.

1960. CBC TV production of *Riel*, with me as a priest (still haven't played a rabbi yet).

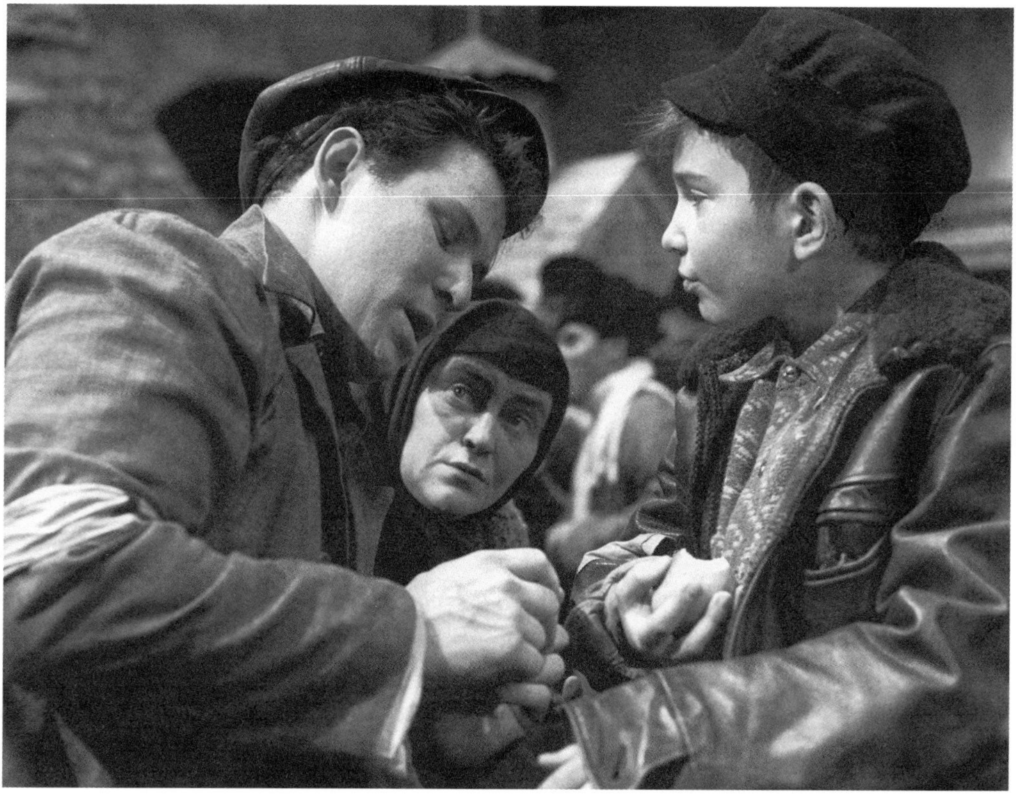

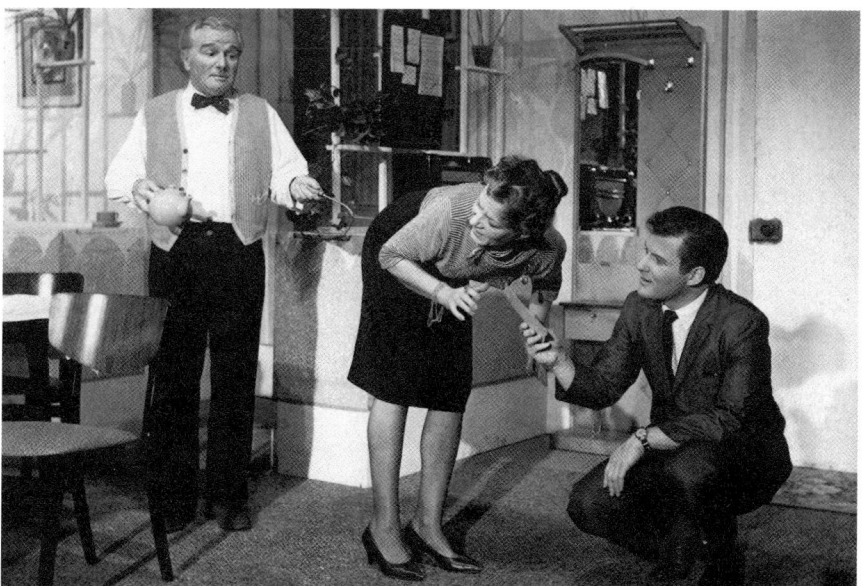

1959. CBC TV production of *Sun In My Eyes.*

Conway Studio

1961. *Hot and Cold in All Rooms*, with Wimbledon Repertory Company at the Bradford Alhambra in Yorkshire, England.

1961. *The War Lover*. Flight crew, including Robert Wagner, Steve McQueen and me, about to embark on a mission.

1962. Another military campaign for Columbia Pictures, this time in *The Victors*.

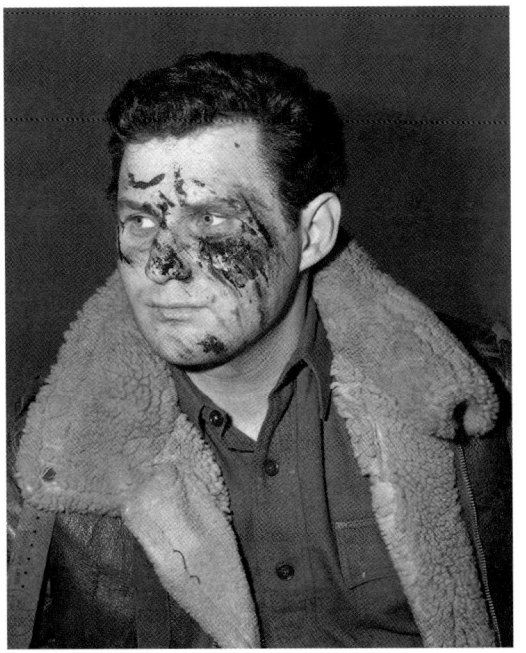

1961. *The War Lover*. My first death scene in a film ended up on the cutting-room floor. This publicity still is all that remains.

1967. Directing a scene for the theatrical short film *Tviggy*.

1968. Just outside the chapel of Holy Blossom Temple, after our wedding ceremony.

Stratford Beacon-Herald

At a Stratford opening in 1970.
One of us was pregnant.

Adam, me, Tobaron and Sara on a charity walkathon in 1977.

1976. Promoting *King of Kensington* from coast to coast, starting at a grocery store in St. John's, Newfoundland.

With Fiona Reid—a publicity still for *King of Kensington*.

esteem and leaned on him, and I was getting used to that. Then the play opened, and suddenly, apart from the time we spent together on stage, the relationship was abruptly severed. Whatever time we had shared was well worth it professionally, because it served the texture of the play well, but once established, once we opened, as far as John was concerned, it was on to the next thing. I was hurt. I thought he was supposed to be sensitive. Well, in truth he was; he had his own family, his own son. I was more than three times seven, and I was a professional. He was not really a people user as the scorned part of me wanted to think; it served him and me and the play well. And with some distance I was able to see that this experience was another example of the lesson that stage manager in Niagara Falls had taught me—that this, albeit a personal art form, is an impersonal business,.

Secret of the World provided other revelations. Rehearsals were rich and full, as were the characters and relationships. I was able to employ myself and all I had learned at the Playhouse in New York and from books I had read since then, which included not just Stanislavsky but other great acting teachers like Boleslavsky, Robert Lewis, Harold Clurman and Michael Chekhov (nephew of Anton), resulting in a rewarding five or six weeks of rehearsal and previews.

Rehearsal is a personal process. An embryo opens up. A character comes into being. Characters interact. Life happens. Growth and development and "change," as Nathan Cohen used to say, happened for me and my character, from my first entrance in Act 1 through to completion in Act 3.

As a matter of fact, the play opened with my entrance in Act 1, which, if it hit the right note, gave the play its lift-off. I was meant to come on stage and share with my mother some eagerly awaited important news, good news. My character, a young writer, had just sold a story. My first two words, the first words of the play, as I came onto the empty stage looking for her were, "Hi, Mom!"

An actor's preparation for a scene can relate to feelings or intentions, that is, moods or actions, which can be achieved or expressed through the senses, like sense memory or emotional recall; or through activities, like a physical action that generates mood or feeling; or through a combination, as in what Michael Chekhov called "psychological gesture." In my case, as Alex Alexander, wanting to share my exciting news, the sense I chose was *hearing*; the means was music. I found the right note, literally, for my entrance. Steve Allen had recently written an optimistic song with lyrics that started, "You're walking along the street..." and at some point arrived at the words, "This could be the start of something big." I timed it so that I started walking in the wings to the beat of that song in my mind, and as I was making my entrance, I would arrive at the words, "This could be the start of something big!" Then, on stage, as though it were the next line of the song, out would come the words, "Hi, Mom!" It gave everyone—the play, the characters and the audience—an overture of love and optimism.

One aspect of that unforgettable rehearsal process was not the way I would have liked it to be. Still, it is a memory I cherish. During the week of previews the producers were concerned that the play was too long. They had to make cuts, and it was decided that the cuts should come out of the second act. The cuts affected me directly; as a matter of fact, I was no longer in the second act—a cut that stunted my character's growth and rendered not only me, but in my opinion the play itself, a casualty. Suddenly I went from a major supporting lead to a minor part, from a reviewable role to a "mention." I was a bit depressed, and Ted Allan noticed. He offered me a lift home after the last preview before opening so we could talk. I will always love him for the aphorism he created in his successful attempt to cheer me up: "When you make a fabulous entrance in the first act, you can drop out of the second and we'll still love you when you come back in the third."

We opened to mixed reviews. Within a week of opening—too late for the reviews—I was reinstated into Act 2, which nevertheless was a great joy for me and the play. But because the raves didn't come in, particularly from two key papers, we couldn't pick up the necessary momentum, in spite of Princess Margaret's morale-boosting attendance, to merit a move to the West End. We closed in five weeks. Still, it was a great experience, but now it was time for me to move on.

If I felt let down by the turn of events resulting from the cuts prior to opening night, it was only because my expectations had been so high. I think I wanted to prove to my mother (and myself as well) that respect was building for me in my profession, that there was the possibility for me to make a solid life, a good living. I was making money, so much so that I phoned home whenever I wanted to, and never collect. I didn't know if my mother was proud, but I did think I could detect confidence in me in her voice.

It was just about time for Passover. I realized I had been in England for eight or nine months, that London was supposed to be my point of departure, but instead I had fallen into work. In fact, one job after another had come up. I now wanted to travel again. I wanted to do what I started out to do when I came over to England in the first place. I wanted to be on the road again. I phoned home to discuss Passover—and I sensed some disappointment when I told my mom my plans. I wasn't coming home for Pesach. But when I told her why, she was pleased. I wanted to go to Israel. *Aliyah*—the Hebrew word for emigration. For Diaspora Jews it has an additional meaning: pilgrimage. To Israel. *Aliyah*!

Chapter 10

115 Levinsky Street

I was thinking as I walked in Tel Aviv that where I come from, downtown streets have names like Queen, King and Victoria, with Glen Cedar, Glencairn and Russell Hill appearing in residential areas. There was never anything remotely like Levinsky Street—even though the Toronto Maple Leafs, I am always eager to point out, had a celebrated defenceman in the 1930s by the name of Alex Levinsky. So here, in Tel Aviv, looking at a street sign with the words Levinsky Street on it made me chuckle. The very idea of a street called Levinsky! But why not? There was apparently an Israeli pioneer hero called Levinsky—a captain, I think. I finally found 115 Levinsky Street, a storefront with an upstairs apartment. The look of it reminded me of 414A Spadina Avenue. What a welcome! Semitic street names, Ashkenazic addresses and now a facade with a familiar face.

The door opened onto a narrow hallway with stairs going straight up to the second-floor apartment, again not unlike 414A Spadina. I waited at the foot of the stairs as eighty-three-year-old Moishe Fuchs descended halfway, then stopped and stared down at me. I looked up at my great-uncle, the patriarch on my father's side of the family. He was my father's uncle, brother to my father's mother. Short and stocky, like my father, he had white whiskers and wore a yarmulke on his bald head. He seemed charming and cherubic, like a Jewish Edmund Gwenn, but tough. Miracle on Levinsky Street.

I identified myself, saying in Yiddish, "I am Aaron Waxman's son."

"Who?" He sounded gruff and impatient, as he cupped an ear in my direction.

"Aaron Waxman's son."

"Who?" he commanded again.

I held back laughter as I tried to articulate slowly and clearly: "Aaron Waxman's son!"

Suddenly, lights of recognition went on. Generations passed through his mental abacus, the globe spun before his incredulous but accepting eyes. As much as he had seen in life and travel, there was still wonderment, as he said slowly, shaking his head from side to side, "*A veltel, a veltel*" ("A little world, a little world").

Moishe Fuchs had not seen his nephew, my father, since 1912, fifty years earlier, when my dad was twelve years old. My great-uncle left oppression in Poland to find himself unwelcome in Canada. He returned to Poland and was reminded of why he had left in the first place. Then, before 1914, he emigrated to Israel, at the time called Palestine, which made him an Israeli pioneer. He had seen so many of his family die, in so many wars, and yet he was still living. The globe spun from Poland to Canada and back again, and then to Israel, and the years passed and now he was eighty-three and still living, and there I was, yet another generation before his eyes. It was obvious to me that as much as he had seen and certainly understood, life itself was still inexplicable, something to be in awe of and amused by as it continues to outfox us. "*A veltel, a veltel.*"

They wouldn't let me stay in a hotel. Normally, I would have resisted their generosity because of the cramped quarters; I would not have wanted to cause inconvenience. But this was going to be special. I was to share Moishe Fuchs's double bed. They insisted and I accepted.

At the Passover Seder, I was seated at his side. He was at the head of a long table, leaning against a large pillow, as Orthodox custom requires. When the prayers were over and dinner was served, he nudged me, almost mischievously, and said in Yiddish, in reference to all the others around the table, "The greenies here don't understand English. So let's you and me speak some English."

I said "OK. What would you like to say?"

He leaned into me, as though confiding, and said, "Punch you in the mouth, fucking Jew!" I was shocked, but he was trying to be funny, so I tried to smile, but it was bitter for me as he said again, "Punch you in the mouth, fucking Jew!"

Trying to take the conversation in a different direction, I said in Yiddish, "What else can you say in English?"

And in Yiddish he answered, as though boasting, "Oh, I remember English very well from my visit to Canada in 1912." And again he said to me in English, the only English he knew, the only English he had learned and still remembered from Canada: "Punch you in the mouth, fucking Jew!"

Ironically, my father, whom I remember veering away from orthodoxy, had relatives in Israel who ranged from mildly orthodox to quite orthodox, whereas my mother, who was an observant Jew, had relatives in Israel who were not only left of centre but in fact flew a red flag over their kibbutz—the kibbutz Kfar Menachem.

There, on the last night of Passover, I sat on a hillside with my cousins Abraham and Luba Greenbaum and watched a different interpretation of the Passover Seder, a celebration of the harvest. Singing and dancing—horas and folk songs, slacks and sweaters, blouses and billowing skirts, wholesome and sexy. They were all young, some in age, all in spirit and energy. By evening's end the music and merrymaking were quieter, a lullaby to the land.

The next day my cousin Abraham picked up a piece of wood that had fallen from a tree and, carrying it like a makeshift walking stick, took me for a stroll and showed me the rolling hills of farmland at Kfar Menachem. He had come here with Luba from his native Poland around the time my mother went to Canada. Here, he and Luba and other pioneers forged a settlement. On this very land where we stood, a kibbutz was established named for Menachem Ussishkin, who had headed up the Jewish National Fund for years and held many posts in the Zionist leadership in Russia and later in Palestine, as it was then called. Avram raised the stick he was carrying. He held it up like a weapon and said that in those days this was all they had; they used whatever they could to fight the Arabs for the land. He gazed across that stretch of land like a Texas rancher overseeing his spread, but the look was not one of pride in individual ownership; rather, it was a look reflecting the quiet passion behind the collective creed. "This land is ours," the pride of patriotism, the *nachis* of nationhood.

Romantic? Yes. But that was the spirit of the kibbutzim, the spirit that helped to build a nation, a new nation based on an old belief, a constant commitment over all the years to the old belief. It was energizing to be in Israel. Oh sure, there were things one confronted every day that could be off-putting, whether it was didacticism on a communist kibbutz or bulldozing bravado in the cities or even the arrogant attitude of its artists. Still, no matter; a country can't be created without assertiveness, especially with so much time to make up for, and time working against them, particularly in these hostile surroundings. Aggressive assertiveness was needed, and the resolve must be rough and ready.

Of course, I visited the theatres. When I was studying at the Neighborhood Playhouse in New York, one of the outstanding students was Amnon Meskin. His father, Aharon Meskin, at the time considered by Lee Strasberg to be one of the five best actors in the world, was one of the founders of the Habimah Theatre. The Habimah was started when Meskin was a student of Stanislavsky at the Moscow Art Theatre. It was founded under the aegis of one of Stanislavsky's colleagues, Vakhtangov, as a nucleus within the Moscow Art Theatre. This nucleus ultimately moved, in its entirety, to Israel and established the Habimah there.

It was a joy to visit Meskin, to be hosted at his home in the company of his contemporaries, all great artists. Meskin, in his huge stature, reminded me of Howard da Silva—and like da Silva, his rich baritone sang when he spoke.

I went to the Habimah, which in the early sixties was already considered old-fashioned and "establishment" by the younger artists. The more avant-garde theatre then was the Camarie, where I saw a remarkable production, performed in Hebrew, of one of Sean O'Casey's one-act plays. And of course alternative theatre was popping up everywhere. It was amazing to me how this little country could produce enough theatre to cover the spectrum from traditional to avant-garde, not to mention cabaret, concerts, symphony, dance and opera. Besides the performing arts, there were galleries and museums. In fact, the whole country seemed to be filled with archaeologists and antiquities, discovered and soon-to-be-discovered. I marvelled at all the activity. I would mix my sojourns between the old and the new, like Caesaria, outside Tel Aviv, on the one hand and the Knesset in Jerusalem on the other.

I had spent three weeks in Israel, proceeding at my leisurely pace, when I received a telegram in Beersheba from my British agent. It was urgent, regarding a meeting with Carl Foreman, who had just produced *The Guns of Navarone*. He was now casting the most talked-about film in London, *The Victors*. Reluctantly, I returned to London.

Elspeth Cochrane's assistant, Brian, was handling this; he was the one who had sent the telegram. This man always dressed like a country gentleman in tweed jackets and corduroys, combined unsuccessfully with Turnbull & Asser shirts and ties—he seemed to be trying for some kind of signature look. He always struck me as being preoccupied with veneer, without much going on up here (I'm pointing at my head). I came into his office as he was calling Foreman to set up the appointment—only to be told that Foreman didn't need to meet with me just yet, to call back and set the appointment for about three weeks hence.

Well, you can imagine the state I was in. I was livid, with this little fop cheering me on from behind. It wasn't just a tantrum; I was genuinely, and I felt justifiably, filled with indignation. My time and money had been wasted. Further, I had been ripped away from a long-anticipated, passionate pilgrimage. So what if he was the man who made *High Noon*? I was furious, I was cooking—and the adrenalin wasn't going to let up.

I stormed down to Foreman's office, which was at 25 Jermyn Street, ironically just across the road from Turnbull & Asser. I took the ornate elevator up to the second floor, thundered into the receptionist's office and demanded to see Carl Foreman—now!

A woman, apparently the head of his office staff, Eve Smith, who later became his wife, politely informed me that it wasn't possible to see him now; he was in an important meeting.

"Well, my life's important too," I countered, indeed attacked. "I was thousands of miles away from here in Israel, and I came rushing back because he requested a meeting with me. That," I emphasized, with my finger almost in her face, "is an important meeting too! Now he either comes out here or I go in there and rip him out of that meeting." And with that, I headed for what I correctly surmised was the door to his office.

Eve Smith, still polite, got in front of the door, not so much guarding it as trying to reason with me. "He'll see you, I promise. Not today, but he *will* see you!"

"Not good enough," I said. "He's cost me time and money. Now you get him out here or I'm going to go in there and get him out myself." She begged me to wait and said she would be right out.

True to her word, she was out a moment later and placated me with the promise that she would phone my agent right away to arrange a meeting for all of us to attend the next day.

When I spoke to Elspeth, she asked, "What did you do? There could be a lawsuit here. Foreman claims you threw furniture around, cursed and used abusive language, and generally terrorized his office staff. But before he takes any legal action, he wants to see us all, tomorrow." I said I didn't remember throwing any furniture around, that I may have cursed—I am given to colourful language—but I didn't threaten anyone in his office, he's the only one I wanted.

Carl Foreman's office was huge and elegant. His desk was placed at an angle in one deep corner. Elspeth Cochrane, her assistant and I sat in Queen Anne chairs in a semicircle around the desk, as he sat facing us. He wanted to know how I was given, and who in fact gave us, to believe that he and I had a scheduled appointment the day before. Elspeth and I looked at her assistant for an explanation. He was totally stymied. I thought he was going to piss himself and soak his veneer. It turned out that all Carl Foreman's office had said to him was that we could possibly have met the day that the assistant had telegrammed me, because Foreman was free that day, but that was not said with any urgency—nor was anyone in his office, contrary to what I was given to understand, informed that I had been in Israel at the time of that possible meeting. He really wasn't interviewing for that part yet. It had been a casual reference to Foreman's interest in meeting me for the part. For my agent, however, an expression of interest for one of his clients from one of the most powerful independent producers in the film world was more than his British reserve could handle.

My agents had a strip torn off them. Carl Foreman said he was sorry that my trip had been cut short. Then he said he wanted me in his film *The Victors*, if only to beat my brains in as my director. The part was mine. He stood up and offered me his hand. We shook and he smiled his admiration, and there started a very fond friendship. A new mentor in my life.

The Victors was to start filming in September in Salerno. It was now May. I had the money, but it didn't make sense to go back to Israel. I would go another time. Instead, I would work in England and travel on the Continent.

London was overflowing with women that summer. There was a

popular song at the time claiming, accurately, that "England swings like a pendulum do," except the pace was quicker than that. This was the time of style-setting for the world from Chelsea and Soho; the time of Mary Quant and Vidal Sassoon, with Carnaby Street waiting in the wings; the time of mini-skirts, high boots and psychedelic colours and patterns. And talk about swinging, this was also the time of the Honourable John Profumo, Minister of War and husband to movie star Valerie Hobson, society procurer Stephen Ward and call girls and party girls Christine Keeler and Mandy Rice-Davies. "England swings like a pendulum do." Sexy and scandalous. A high time, and my digs reflected that: I moved from Battersea, and lived successively in Chelsea, Hampstead and St. John's Wood. A high time, and my wardrobe reflected that: I got my shoes made to order by Tuczek, a centuries-old shoemaking establishment in Mayfair's Clifford Street, and my clothes were from Bond Street, Savile Row and King's Road. A high time in London, but still I travelled and worked.

Peter Haddon flattered me by inviting me back to the Wimbledon Repertory Company any time I wanted. This time we travelled and worked in the south of England, along the coast, places like Weymouth-by-Sea and a lot of other names ending with "by-Sea." But the supreme compliment from Peter came when he invited me to play the title role in *Billy Liar* in the North Country. This was a play that had made a big impact. Famous actors had played Billy Liar, such as Tom Courtenay and Albert Finney. It was a highly regarded, highly entertaining play, and a coveted role. And he offered it to me over and above all the British-trained actors, who would have been particularly skilful with the North Country accent. The accent was especially important as they were touring it in the North Country. That would be like playing Eddie Carbone in a theatre filled with Italian Americans, as I had once done in New York. And I knew I would have been just as successful. But I was on the horns of a happy dilemma. The run of *Billy Liar* overlapped with the start date of *The Victors*. It was one or the other. Great opportunities in either direction. But there was in fact no question, because a commitment had already been made to *The Victors.*

I arrived in Salerno in the company of George Hamilton, George Peppard, Vince Edwards (who was very hot at the time because of the TV series *Ben Casey*), Eli Wallach, Peter Fonda and James Mitchum (Robert's son). It was an exciting time for me. This was one of the two most important pictures being made in Europe at that time. The other, also a war saga, was *The Longest Day*, about D-Day. Our story was meant to be an odyssey covering and chronicling the lives of a squad of American GIs from their landing in Salerno, in 1943, through the horrible upheaval of the next three years, climaxing with victory in 1945. But what price victory? Who were the victors? It was an ambitious and worthy project Carl Foreman had embarked on, an important statement he wanted to make. He had *The Red Badge of Courage* and *All Quiet on the Western Front* in mind, but with more to say about human relations and global politics, about our future, than just "war is hell." It was not only a major film, with lots of movie stars, publicists, clicking cameras and popping flashbulbs, but also a worthy mission.

As we got into the filming, however, it seemed that there was more statement than story happening. The man who had so skilfully carved three-dimensionality with the lead character in *High Noon*, was now creating a vast mural on the broad canvas of four years of war. Individual characters were used as instruments to convey the message of the film rather than having their own raison d'être. We were always marching or crawling on our bellies as we climbed and took a hill, slogging in muck and dust and sweat. I remember scarcely any scenes of character development or connection.

Foreman attempted to mix fiction with fact, a fascinating device when it works, and tried to give the film a documentary look. Sometimes he succeeded. I remember one scene in which we were marching into a town in the Campania Mountains—the very spot where GIs, who looked just like us, had marched nineteen years earlier. The townspeople were the extras, and some of the women, dressed in mourning black, were old enough to remember the actual event. Some of them were so emotionally caught up that they couldn't distinguish between us and the real soldiers of 1943 as they waved and cried tears of joy and relief. Memory transformed the past into the present.

I remember another scene, in a sweaty town, meant to be in Sicily, where we, the squad, were cautioned about booby traps by our sergeant, gruff and caring Eli Wallach. We were getting set to do the scene. The usual procedure was in progress. We heard the English assistant director (always dressed, no matter how hot and sticky, in a navy-blue suit) and the Italian one (always casually chic) as they each checked with the lighting department: "Lights?"

Answer: "Ready!"

We heard them check with the sound department. "Sound?"

"Ready!"

Then came the ultimate order in the world of film. It came loudly and clearly through the English AD's megaphone—a sharp military command: "Action!" And similarly, almost instantly resonating and echoing through the Italian's megaphone: "*Azione!*"

And then, instead of Eli's dialogue, we heard a plaintive expression of injustice: "Cut! Hey! What about me?" Everyone was shocked. An actor is not supposed to stop a scene; that is the director's and *only* the director's prerogative. So his yelling "Cut!" was unusual—but particularly in this case, with a producer/director the stature of Carl Foreman. But Eli spoke with controlled indignation regarding, as it were, the rights of and respect for an actor. Unlike the sound, lighting and camera departments, he was not consulted for his readiness to do this delicate scene. Eli demanded that he be consulted too before action is called because his motor had, as he put it, "a much more elusive switch." Foreman agreed and apologized. It was a lesson to watch Eli work. I have remembered that often, both as an actor and as a director.

An illustrious graduate of the Neighborhood Playhouse some twenty years before I was a student there, Eli would often come to the Playhouse to talk to us about the practical process of applying the academics of schoolwork to the reality of professional work. He remembered me from the Playhouse. We talked often on the set of *The Victors* about acting and the life of an actor. It was from talking with him that I began to use the word "recipe" for a concept I was already committed to, that is, a recipe of ingredients necessary in the approach to analyzing and building a character and a scene.

When I wasn't engrossed in conversation with Eli, my attention was focused on Carl Foreman. He wanted us to look real, not like Hollywood soldiers, he said. So we were instructed not to shave (rather than use makeup to create stubble). There was to be no pampering, no perks or comfort on the set—no canvas director's chairs, for example, no "craft services" (constant snacks) to munch on.

One day there was a delay before we could make a certain shot. The sun was blistering, and we were in an open field with only one tree for shade. All the actors gravitated towards that tree and sat on the ground under it, trading stories and gossip while we waited. Some of the group were arguing over who was the fastest draw in Hollywood, a debate prompted by the release of *How the West Was Won*, which starred George Peppard and Eli Wallach facing off in a climactic gunfight on top of a moving train. Although they were now sharing the shade, they had been mortal enemies in the movie. George was the winner, and Eli couldn't have cared less. When asked his opinion on who was the fastest, Eli (absorbed in the Paris *Herald Tribune*), looked over his granny glasses and mused that if the script said he was the winner, why should he care how fast the other guy is, and if he was to be the loser, he simply fell down on cue—sort of took the steam out of everyone else's argument.

In the meantime, I noticed that Foreman had a table and chair set up for him and, while waiting to do the next shot, he was working at his typewriter, making script changes. The director was suddenly wearing a writer's hat. Then a portable phone appeared; a Columbia executive was on the line. Now he was the producer. And when it was time to do the shot, the director's hat came back on. He never stopped working.

From watching him, I learned that essential functions proceed along parallel paths. That is, certain work must be done coincident with other work; for example, good production must be accompanied from the beginning by good promotion. This is something it took us a while to learn in Canada, but now, finally, it is very much in evidence—witness the success of contemporary Canadian-produced television shows.

Acting in *The Victors* was a learning experience, which was heightened by my forays into the surrounding area. The Amalfi Way is one of the most spectacular coastline drives there is. I took it often down to Positano, at the time one of the hot spots of the European and international jet set, which included counts (although, according to the British amongst us, an Italian count is a "count of no account") and high-society types, complete with entourages. Being part of a big-time movie, you were feted even if you weren't one of the stars. In Italy, if you work in a movie, you're a movie star. One of the counts drove me in his Ferrari to a point along the Amalfi Way from which we got onto a motor launch and powered across the bay to a rock jutting into the Mediterranean, accessible only by boat. Carved into that rock was a natural cave, but with man-made finishing touches making it the most exciting and exotic nightclub I had ever seen. It was called L'Africano. So there I was "twisting the night away" alongside the other stars of *The Victors*, and Ferrari-driven home in time for work the next day.

It was a hot time in that part of the world. Italy was in. Jackie Kennedy was reportedly vacationing just down the Amalfi Way, in Ravello. After filming was finished, I stayed on and did more travelling in the south of Italy—Naples, Pompeii, as well as seeing more of Positano and Amalfi. Then it was back to London.

There was another big American film coming up that my agent was angling for. This time he was going to wait for the opportune moment, but in the meantime, behind-the-scenes manoeuvring between him and the casting director made it look like a real possibility for me. They were sure, when the time came for me to meet the director, Stanley Kubrick, that it would happen. The picture was to be called *Dr. Strangelove*.

It was November and I was getting tired of the greyness of London. The only colour seemed to be in the party scene, and I was tiring of that too. I could dignify self-involvement as part of the Beat Generation, but so much of it was just "me me me." This was pre-Beatles, before the hippies, who also broke with the establishment and sought personal freedom but valued political awareness as well. What had gone on during the 1950s, a time of clear lines, of boundaries not yet blurred, was over.

I had been away from home for over a year. I'd made a lot of money and spent it all, but I knew I would make a lot of money again. I would come back to London and get a part in this new film, *Dr. Strangelove*. But now it was time to go home. I looked great, my weight was down and my clothes were excellent. I missed home, I missed my family, particularly my mother. Yes, it was time.

I was awakened by a phone call well past midnight on November 23. Many of my friends considered me an American, so perhaps they thought I would know. "Is it true?" they asked.

"Is what true?"

"Was President Kennedy assassinated?"

How would I know? But I had to know. How would I find out? I didn't live far from Grosvenor Square, where the American embassy was located. I would go down there. I got out of the cab as it approached the park. And then.

We each have our own "Do you remember what you were doing at that moment?" story, and this is mine. As I approached the steps of the U.S. embassy, there was a small gathering, which grew steadily larger. People were gravitating towards the steps but not going up them. At the top of the stairs was a little transistor radio, popular at the time, about four inches by eight inches, standing on its end and facing out towards the growing crowd. No one was talking; everyone was listening.

Suddenly, Carl Foreman and I simultaneously noticed one another. We shook hands and held on a little longer than one normally does with a handshake, in a mutual message of solace, and then, abruptly, we turned our attention back to the information emanating from the transistor. Everyone was riveted, anticipating, dreading the imminent confirmation of what we all feared. Hundreds and hundreds of people, layer after layer, fanned out across the park. I don't know whether they could all hear that transistor or whether news was being quietly passed backwards, but the voice issuing from the radio was the only discernible sound in the morning air. There was something symbolic, indeed a grandeur in that simplicity and directness, as all of us faced forward, held by that little radio. We were dead quiet, and finally numb when we heard the news that Jack Kennedy had been shot dead in Dallas.

Strange how this man had so quickly won over the world. Despite revelations that have emerged since that time, it is undeniable that he, in his short period in office, had passed the torch forward. Only a few months earlier I had heard people in Israel mocking the Americans for electing such a young president. Not only in Israel, but everywhere in a world of Macmillans and Adenauers and de Gaulles, all old men, the Americans had been thought of as naive. Soon, though, it all turned around; soon they were all turned on. Now, the world over, people of all ages, but especially the young, personally grieved the loss of an inspiring leader.

Yes, it was time for change. It was time to regroup. It was time for me to go home and be with my family and friends.

Chapter 11

The End of the Beginning

Paths of Glory, with its riveting execution scene and the unforgettable buildup to it, and Ralph Meeker's performance as a desperately real and bewildered victim, made a powerful impact on me. I was looking forward to meeting the director of this great antiwar film, Stanley Kubrick. Casting decisions for *Dr. Strangelove* would take place in about a month. I had plenty of time to travel and still get back to London to fight for a nice part in *Strangelove*. In the interim, I would go back to Toronto.

On the drive from Malton Airport to Glen Cedar Road, I drank in the view out the car window. After a year and a half away, I found myself looking through the eyes of a curious visitor. All I could see was endless suburb, like a giant parking lot. But I realized that it was too easy to think of myself as the sophisticated traveller, too easy to sound condescending. Important to remember that a place is not just a place; a place is also people. And it sure felt good to be home.

How wonderful it was to see my mother. Traces of the Mona Lisa, always. But now, at sixty-seven, she was Mamoushka, a Polish endearment I would sometimes kid her with. More often I called her Mammashie or Mammaleben, Yiddish words, cute and cuddly. My desire was to hold and protect and cherish her, and to make her laugh. She was adorable when she laughed, and her laughter was infectious. My desire was to give her *nachis*. I think she was proud of my achievements; I think she finally saw the possibility of a good life for me in my chosen profession. My future was still indefinite, but I think she sensed something definite in me. And in turn, for me, my mother was part of my drive to succeed.

I regaled my family with stories and gifts, and the same of course with my friends, particularly Art Clairman and Seymour Weinstein. My family enjoyed learning about *mespucha* (family) in Israel, the possibility of *mespucha* in the north of England, high holidays at the Marble Arch Synagogue (where the elders wore top hat and tails on Yom Kippur) and Friday-night meals with Jewish families in London (where the tradition was not roast chicken, although there was chicken soup, but rather a main course of breaded plaice or halibut—different, but still reminiscent of a Jewish home like ours).

Art and Seymour were more interested in other exploits. I think I was a bit of a conquering hero to them too. Mind you, the battles weren't big enough yet; I still wasn't the star that Seymour contemplated when he lent me that $200 four or five years earlier. But lots of laughs. The three of us went up to the Fairlawn Theatre on north Yonge Street that evening, to see *The War Lover*. A major Toronto movie house, and their buddy was one of the stars of the movie. Certainly Columbia Pictures of Canada saw it that way. When we arrived at the theatre, we were delighted to be met by a magnificent, eye-popping marquee that read "THE WAR LOVER starring AL WAXMAN." We swaggered up to the box office. Seymour, full of fun and charm, demanded that we be allowed in free.

"What?" the ticket seller countered.

Seymour said, "Yeah, we're with the star of the movie."

And then the ticket seller said "Where?" Seymour, with great panache, indicated, or rather presented, me. To which the ticket seller replied, "Who's *he*, Rock Hudson?"

Seymour was going to press the argument further. "Come outside and look at the marquee." I held on to him because, although it was fun, it was starting to get embarrassing, so we were each about to pay for our own ticket when Seymour said, "I'll pay." In reference to Art, he said, "He's a student, he hasn't got with what to pay." And in reference to me, he said, "He's a star, he shouldn't have to pay." And with that he picked up all three tickets.

I can't remember whether we enjoyed ourselves inside the movie house as much as we had outside, under that glorious marquee, but "Who's *he*, Rock Hudson?" became a joke at my expense for some time.

My mom was scheduled to have surgery, for something known in those days as "a woman's problem." Luckily, my brother was now an obstetrician gynecologist at George Washington University. As a matter of ethics, Benny would not interfere in her doctors' decisions; still, it would be reassuring to hear from him about her prospects. And we, that is, my mom, Jack and I, were now going to visit Benny and his family just prior to her surgery.

Benny's home in Arlington, Virginia, was the American dream come true, with a swimming pool no less. It was only a short drive from where he worked in nearby Georgetown, and an even shorter drive to downtown Washington, where noble Classical-revival monuments, museums, and government buildings are grouped in formal, symbolic relation to one another (yet only a stone's throw away from some of the worst slums in America). We toured all the sights, at least I did, and had a wonderful holiday in Washington. In the evenings, we'd gather around the barbecue and play with Benny and Shirley's three very beautiful, all-American-looking kids, Aaron, Deborah and Elana. (A fourth child was born some years later.) Benny assured us that the medical procedure mom was to undergo was completely straightforward, nothing to worry about. Indeed, that's what all the doctors back in Toronto were saying too.

When we got home, my mom was mentally prepared, and we were all confident that it was indeed a routine operation and that things would proceed as they should. As a matter of fact, my mother told me to go back to London right away to make sure I got that part in the upcoming picture she had heard me talk about. My agent had called to say that the *Strangelove* project was going to commit to casting soon; in fact they had already done some of the casting in New York. They were bringing over a young unknown actor called James Earl Jones to be one of Slim Pickens's crew members on the flight that is cut to throughout the film, and from which the bomb is ultimately dropped. They had apparently left a couple of parts open— one of which, a character called Goldberg, I think, my agents and the casting director felt sure I could get. I told my agents I would be back in London as soon as I brought my mother safely home from the hospital, and I assured my mom that there was still time. I knew I would get the part, but first, and more important, I would accompany her to the hospital, keep her company while there and then bring her home.

The operation was a success. My mother looked as delicate as an angel as she recuperated at the Mount Sinai Hospital over a period of about a week. One day she said to me that it was clear everything had turned out fine, and I could now stop worrying about her and go back to London to be in that picture. I again said no, not until she was safely at home.

The next day she said she was glad I was there because she had something to say to me. She told me that Jack was not in her will. Everything that was to be inherited had been acquired by my father and so would go directly to Benny and me, but still she wanted Jack to be left something. Talk of a will surprised me. Why, suddenly, now? It wasn't necessary. She insisted. She said that she wanted Jack to have one-third of the house, the other two-thirds to be shared equally by Benny and me. She also said she wanted Jack to have a job for as long as he needed or wanted one. That meant, she said, that even though Benny and I would be equal owners of her share of the Simcoe Public House, we could not sell it, even though neither Benny nor I had any interest in running the place or even keeping it;

we must maintain her interest as long as Jack wanted to work there. Only then, when he no longer wanted that, could we sell it. I promised her that we would follow her wishes.

At the end of the week my mother was discharged. Shortly after Jack and I brought her into the house, she needed to go to the washroom. We were still downstairs, on the main floor; we hadn't settled her into her own room yet. A moment or two after she closed the door to the powder room, I heard a thud from within, as though she had fallen. I knocked, didn't wait, just opened the door and, sure enough, she was slumped over onto the floor. She needed room to breathe. She deserved dignity. She had to be moved quickly. I got my arms under hers as I tried to lift her. I would have preferred carrying her, but she was too heavy. The heaviness of dead weight. I needed help, and called for Jack. I was frantic, but the awkwardness of her position in this tight little room made it impossible. Her underwear was down around her knees. My mind momentarily detoured as I realized, while trying to manoeuvre her out the door, that I was looking at where my life began. I was looking at the beginning, and this was the end. God forgive me. Jack tended gently to dignity as he pulled her underwear back up. We moved her to the adjacent room, the den, lifting her, trying to carry her, but I'm afraid almost dragging her. God forgive me.

Was she dead? Jack and I looked at each other with eyes that tried to reassure. Was there still time? Phone for help. The look on Jack's face—he had been here before. I tried to give her mouth-to-mouth resuscitation. Nothing happened. Was I doing it correctly? I had heard you should punch the heart with your fist. How could I hit my mother like that? Jack was calm, almost apologetic. I called the fire department, the police department, the hospital emergency department—wrong numbers. Finally, frantically, I got through. More mouth-to-mouth. Where were the medics? Why weren't they here yet? I couldn't pound her heart, but I did lean down on her chest with both my hands, applying heavy pressure, rhythmically. Artificial respiration, like the doctor had done years ago to my father, trying to restart the heart. But my father had died. And now my mother was dead. None of it had helped. I was comforted by the medics. I was told she had died within the first seconds; she was dead from the beginning. The beginning? She was the beginning, and this was the end.

CHAPTER 12

Nachis and Neon Lights

Snow. I remembered the snow at my father's funeral in 1945. It covered the earth. And now, in late January of 1964, I sat alone in the living room, looking out the window at the snow falling, delicate crystals dancing, glittering in the sun, hovering just above the earth. The ice crystals related to the snow on the ground just as my mother's tomb related to my father's, not touching but somehow making an ethereal connection. She of course had to be buried with a different last name, but the relationship between her and my father was well and quietly understood, and so she was buried, not beside my father—that was not possible—rather, one row ahead but directly in line with him, so no matter what your vantage point is, you are facing either headstone and you are positioned immediately and directly in a relationship with both. A force field of fidelity. A love connection. Pure, like the crystals of snow.

Shiva was packed at our house at 25 Glen Cedar Road for morning and evening prayers. Rabbi, cantor, friends and family. Rabbi Monson led the prayers every morning and every evening. In doing so, he honoured my mother. She had thought highly of him because he was always attentive to each of the members of his large congregation; he visited the sick, and as she said of him, he did a lot of good work for the Jewish community both here in Canada and in Israel. It pleased me that he honoured her, especially in light of the fact that she once chided him when he queried why she had not bought her usual front-row high-holiday seats; instead (because of tough economic times that year) she had bought less expensive seats, way up in the balcony. She said to him, "Excuse me if I'm mistaken, Rabbi, but isn't God everywhere? Upstairs in the balcony too?" He smiled at her with thanks and said, "Of course you are correct."

After shiva, I had no interest in any films back in London. It was as though all incentive had been removed. There was no need to prove anything any more. But was that the reason I wanted to be an actor? I knew I wanted to act whether my mother was for it or against it. Still, with her gone, there was suddenly no drive in me; acting somehow seemed insufficient. I had been thinking about writing. Maybe I would start studying directing. I thought often of the image of Carl Foreman at that makeshift desk, moving seamlessly from directing, to writing, to producing, while waiting for the next shot to be set up on that field near Salerno. Acting seemed insufficient. But I didn't possess drive enough to muster energy in any direction. For weeks I sat staring through crystal-shimmering windows into tomorrow.

Symmetry and self-indulgence. Gazing into the sun-sparkled ice formations on the windows was not unlike living in that shadow that my foot cast on the polished hardwood floor way back in the teacher's lounge at Hillcrest Public School while in mourning for my father. Strange—my mother, so strong, was able to build a bridge of transition for me fairly successfully after my Dad died, but now I felt his death and departure once again. Even more: with both gone, I now felt like an orphan. Orphan? I was twenty-seven years old. How could I say that? But I did feel like the foundation had been knocked out from under me in spite of the look I presented to the world, which, I was told, resembled a calm and confident structure, like a mansion. Powerful. But I knew that inside that mansion there were many empty rooms, and there was a tiny little person, me, frantically running from empty room to empty room, desperately searching for something.

It was devastating to have been so close to her and my very essence when she died, yet I realized it would have been much worse had I gone back to London to be in something as ephemeral as a motion picture (at least that was my feeling at that moment). No, it was better that I had been with her when she died; I would never have forgiven myself. There was anger in me. Things didn't unfold as I thought they should. I was supposed to make it big before my mother died. She was supposed to meet, approve of and love the girl I would marry. Even grandchildren... I would bring her *nachis, nachis* and neon lights. But the universe unfolds according to its own laws.

Time to do something. Time to go back to England. In the meantime I acquired a book on the principles of writing, *The Art of Dramatic Writing* by Lajos Egri. To this day, I refer to it and recommend it to my acting students. I recommend it as much for the study of acting and directing as I do for the study of writing, because it deals so clearly and comprehensively with three-dimensionality of character and character motivation and behaviour in the development of plot. It has become as much one of my bibles as any of the Stanislavsky books. This book was about the only thing taking me away from gazing through those sequin-covered squares of frozen windowpane in our living room. It did take me to a pad of paper, a pencil and a desk, but I found that it wasn't that easy to make things happen on the page. Frustrating, yes, but worthwhile. But where was I going? Anywhere at all?

One of my friends suggested that it was time to get socially active again. Specifically, it was suggested that it was "time to get laid." So I took out a woman I had dated for years. We had had good times together, and as they say, "no strings attached." But at the end of the evening, I was left with an even deeper feeling of devastation.

In retrospect, with the clarity of distance, there is humour in what happened. But I was without humour at the time, without distance, because what happened isolated and consumed me totally, at one and the same time emphasizing me and negating me. What happened was, *nothing happened.* And for me, that wasn't funny. She was surprised at first, then quickly offered reassurance, but I refused to be consoled or encouraged. The nothingness left me confused and numb with fear. At the same time, I didn't like the dramatic or psychological implications, the Freudian interpretations.

Back in London, I went to a Harley Street psychiatrist. I can't remember how I found him or who recommended him, but I was sure impressed, even with myself, that I was seeing a Harley Street specialist. Harley Street specialists were to medicine what Savile Row was to sartorial splendour. But what was I to me?

I've forgotten the doctor's name, but I'll never forget his appearance, and ultimately his unsentimental but sympathetic help and good common sense. He was tall and lean and very sensitive. One of his legs was withered and encased in a huge brace from his foot to above his knee. I suddenly felt foolish bringing him my petty problems, so much so that after the preliminaries, I was unable to talk. He waited, but I was unable to proceed. He continued to wait. I still couldn't talk. It was his last appointment of the day, so he continued to wait. I was embarrassed, not only because I didn't want to talk, but also because I wasn't talking. Finally, I blurted out, "I feel foolish."

He asked, "Why?"

"Because my problems are minor. Look at you, look at your leg. You've got real problems, mine are picayune."

His eyes, even from across a room of subdued lighting, were penetrating. He said, with quiet purpose, "I am physically crippled, but I am dealing with it. I know who I am. You are emotionally crippled, and you're not doing anything about it. You don't know who you are."

Well, the talk flowed after that. And the upshot of it was that he encouraged me to actively pursue my talents and appetites again, and to continue seeing him, but only on a once-a-month basis, because intensive analysis was not deemed necessary. The few sessions I had with him over a period of a few months were encouraging and proved most helpful.

I attacked life with energy again. And strangely, although I missed my mother, I experienced a kind of freedom. This came without any guilt; indeed, it was more like an understanding or even a revelation. They were with me, my mother and father, but it was *my* journey now. My mom and my dad accompany me forever. I welcomed them as guide and influence, to be consulted but not in the driver's seat. That was reserved for me as I resumed my journey, my exploration, my learning, my odyssey, down the excitement and attraction of the open road. My life.

I found a job working for Carl Foreman again, on the post-production end of *The Victors*. I didn't know anything about post-production. I was hired as an actor, to make sounds, desultory dialogue, throwaway lines that didn't belong to specific characters, just crowd sounds, grunts and accents, or, as they say in the business, "rhubarb rhubarb rhubarb." I was paid well and it was a wonderful learning experience.

I worked on *The Victors* in the daytime and went to film school at night. I enrolled at the London School of Film Technique, and while studying directing there, I continued to get acting jobs in TV and film. The school in Brixton was located above a grocery store (somehow always a significant symbol for me), the market district of southeast London, and near the notorious Brixton Prison. There were courses in every facet of filmmaking: writing, directing, producing, production managing, assistant directing, continuity, all aspects of camera work, from loading film to lighting a set to operating the camera, and, of course, editing, which in those days (pre editing tape, pre-videotape, pre-digital), believe it or not, involved the tedious process of gluing film clips end to end (imagine how sticky you got working on a montage!). Each class member made at least one film of one or two minutes' duration, both interior and exterior, night and day shooting. Each student rotated and got to work on every stage, on every aspect and in every job of the filmmaking process.

There was a beautiful young woman there, also a student, with whom I worked closely, or at least I gravitated towards her, not unintentionally. She was dark and dazzling, and looked Israeli, and her accent made me guess she was a sabra. Both of us worked in the industry during the day. I worked for Columbia Pictures, while she was at the BBC. At night we both wanted to learn more. Soon we were spending time together away from school. She thought of me as European and apparently not Jewish. I thought of her as Israeli, but I was no longer sure. Soon I found out she was not Israeli, but Jordanian. She worked for the branch of the BBC that broadcast to Arab territories. At about the same time, in a private moment, she discovered that I was not European, and I told her that I was in fact Jewish. She said that had she known, she would not have let it go this far.

She hated Jews, or at least Israelis. She had once lived in what she called Palestine, in Jaffa, the suburb of Tel Aviv on the coast. Her home had been expropriated by the Israeli government. Although it had been paid for, it had been done against her family's will; she felt that they had been robbed and thrown off their land. How could I argue with that? Delicate at any time. I certainly didn't want to start a debate at that moment. I was much more interested in the immediate situation, here in her London flat. And so was she. She said she never knew that Jews could touch as sensuously as Arab men. So I said, "So why do you hate me?"

"Because you're a Jew," she answered. "I want to kill Jews."

I found the threat in this made the intimate darkness we were sharing even more exciting—but baffling. I asked her, "Do you want to kill this Jew? We are lovers. Do you want to kill me?"

"No," she softened.

"Good," I said. "Because I couldn't kill you even if we met on the battlefield. What would you do," I asked, "if we ever did meet on the battlefield?"

Her lips gently brushed my ear as her breath whispered, "I would kiss you, and then I would kill you."

I stayed the night but chose not to fall asleep. I learned an awful lot about filmmaking at the London School of Film Technique, but somehow this is my strongest memory.

I also began putting a lot more words down on paper. Although I was studying film, the manuscript was headed in the direction of a novella. The process was more therapeutic than artistic, but I was moving ahead with it, and that was good. And I continued to work in film and TV, always in American roles. I did a small guest role on an episode of a series called *Espionage*. The episode starred a yet-to-be-honed but still impressive actor, albeit too self-indulgent at that time for my taste, named Dennis Hopper. But he was encouraged in this by the director, Stu Rosenberg. It was interesting for me to be able to recognize differences in taste and still acknowledge talent.

I resumed travelling, all over the continent: Germany, Switzerland, Italy, France. Sometimes I took a girlfriend with me, sometimes I was on my own. I had made a lot of money in England and I was going to spend it all. At the end of it I intended to return to New York and then Hollywood. I wanted to compete where there would be true competition for the acting work I wanted to do. It was as though the field had been tilted in my favour in London. Mind you, the parts available as a result were smaller. I wanted the playing field to be levelled; maybe the competition would be tougher, but the prizes would be bigger. I was anxious to find out. But there was still an important event for which I wanted to remain in England—the world premiere of *The Victors*.

The Odeon Leicester Square was splendidly turned out with floodlights and red carpets and cordonned-off areas to hold spectators and fans back as the stars (including me) arrived and were ushered to their seats. As sparkling as the European and American stars looked, they were outshone by the royalty in attendance, including Prince Philip. It was everything I had always heard world premieres were supposed to be. I was elated but not without trepidation—and not because I was one of the only men not wearing a tux. Although I was aware of that, I was very proud of, and knew I looked good in, my dark blue Savile Row suit. I felt it was good enough. But I was nervous, nervous for Carl. I had premonitions—not artist's paranoia, but rather an intuition, and my instincts are usually right.

First off, Carl made a speech, almost like a lecture, in which he articulated his concerns for where the world was headed. He talked of human rights and humanitarianism and political causes. It seemed to me, and probably to many others, that the film would embody these thoughts and should speak for itself. Then, there was no intermission. In those days the big movies had a ten- or fifteen-minute intermission. Perhaps it was just another opportunity to sell popcorn, but often the movie needed it. *The Victors* certainly did. Sitting through three hours of a vehicle seemingly designed for the sole purpose of allowing Carl Foreman to express his views on many issues, including hot war, cold war, East-West relations, fascism, racism and anti-Semitism, with only the barest thread of a story as a clothesline on which to hang these issues, proved tedious for this posh audience. And this from the screenwriter who had crafted his earlier films with scalpel-like precision. I hadn't yet learned the phrase that I would come to regard as a maxim when I worked on *Cagney and Lacey*: Less is more. This wise adage serves as a guide for many in achieving dramatic art in film and TV, and would have served well here.

Perhaps I exaggerate, but in my excitement at being there I was observing more than participating, and I was sensitive to all that was going on around me. I remember that some in the audience yawned audibly. People grew impatient. They tittered, they snickered, they shuffled restlessly—and I cried. Literally. I was hurt for Carl. It did not have the effect, at least on this audience, that he wanted it to. Mind you, I saw it a few months later in New York, at a Forty-second Street movie house around the corner from Times Square with a street-tough crowd in attendance, and they loved it and cheered it.

But that night at the Odeon Leicester Square, sophistication reigned and the only cheers raised were for drinks—drinks and derision.

I chose to skip the parties. I preferred instead to go off on my own, be by myself, to contemplate the fact that a man I still respected very much, still looked to as a mentor, had his feet where everyone else's are, down on the ground and not on some pedestal where I had placed him. Out of fairness to Carl, I must point out that a lot of people liked that film, and it should be understood within the context of a body of work like his. What an important filmmaker he was. If I could make only one film like *High Noon* in my life! Ultimately, it was good for me to discover that he was as human as me or the next guy, yet still so knowledgeable and accomplished that I would always consider him an important influence in my life.

CHAPTER 13

A Job-Job

New York, New York—what a wonderful town. My ambitions were up, but my finances were down. I had to get a job. I rented a bachelor apartment that came with certain conveniences and accoutrements, minor substance creating major pretensions—like a part-time doorman. It was a newly built high-rise, that is, newly thrown together at Fifth Avenue and Fourteenth Street, just on the edge of the Village. I bought some furniture, just the necessities, and then I was broke. I had rent to pay and a splendid wardrobe to support. I auditioned everywhere I could—unsolicited open calls—because I couldn't get an agent and there wasn't, as a result, much opportunity for me to get an acting job. Not that there was much acting work in New York at the time anyway, which is why most actors were going out to Los Angeles, or "the Coast," as they would say.

One day I noticed, in the trade papers, what I thought would be a sure thing. The Yiddish theatre downtown on Second Avenue was looking for a young leading man who could speak fluent Yiddish. That's me! They were going to do a Yiddish translation of Ibsen's *Ghosts*. No agent necessary, just call for an appointment. What a lucky day for me! And what a lucky day for them too, I thought. I had a thick head of hair, pompadoured like Elvis Presley; and I looked like a young Julie Garfinkle (John Garfield). Not since the Adlers or Paul Muni had the Yiddish theatre had an opportunity like this!

I think it was called the National—at any rate, it was located right near St. Mark's Playhouse, where I had that wonderful experience watching *A View from the Bridge* some years earlier. I walked into the Yiddish theatre anticipating a fantastic and successful interview. I knew it was going to be different than any I'd ever had before. It was. I knew it was going to be fun. It was. But not for the reasons I'd anticipated.

The first question rang out in a rich, resonant voice, heavily accented. I though I heard correctly, but to be safe I asked him to repeat the question. This time it was almost an order, "Can you sing?"

"No."

Now almost perfunctorily, ready to dismiss me, "Can you dance?"

"No."

And now like a rabbi's ruler being smacked down onto a school desk to make each point, he dismissed me with "In deh Yiddish teater, evreh acteh muhst be uh singher, und uh denseh too. Get out!"

"Wait a minute," I said, "I thought you were doing Ibsen's *Ghosts*."

"Yes!" (like he'd discovered something that he was going to let me in on), "but a musical version!"

Well, rejected—but not without a laugh! Now he was going to let me in on his discovery. He began to show me, with song and dance, as though he had a straw hat flipped onto his head and cane in hand, a visual synopsis of his musical version of Ibsen's *Ghosts* in Yiddish. Like I said, not without a laugh!

Still, I was broke, and that wasn't funny. I had to get a job. This was the first time since the Playhouse that I was not gainfully employed within the profession. I had always had a job, whether on

A Job-Job

stage, on radio, or in film or TV—sometimes a high-paying job. This would be the first time I had to get what we used to call a job-job, that is, a part-time job outside the profession in order to pay the bills and make ends meet.

I found employment where a lot of out-of-work actors worked, at the Village Gate. The Gate was a very "hip" place in Greenwich Village. Young comedians, such as Woody Allen, Godfrey Cambridge and Dick Gregory, would try out new material there. It was on MacDougal Street, the heart of the "in" area. Across the road at the Bitter End another new comedian, Bill Cosby, tried out his act. And down the street at other clubs would be Lenny Bruce or Mort Sahl. As for the Village Gate, it was like a revolving door for actors between jobs, looking for temporary job-jobs. Mind you, I don't know what "temporary" meant, because every time I asked a waiter what he really did, the answer would of course be that he was an actor, and that this was just temporary. I would then ask, "How long have you been here?" Answer, six years. Same conversation with another waiter. Answer, nine years. And yet another, answer, seven years. I knew I was not going to let myself stay here long.

My career as a waiter turned out to be short-lived regardless of my plans. I got fired on the first night. Actually, it was the first night, the opening night, of a new place on top of the Village Gate, a restaurant called Top of the Gate. I remember when I was interviewed for the position, I stood there in my impressive Savile Row suit and told of my schooling, training and travels, law school and university background and degrees—to which the response was, "So what makes you think you can be a waiter?" I chuckled and smiled. "OK. Touché." They must have found something worth trying in me, though, because they gave me the job.

On the first night, however, the very first party of guests sat at a table in my station and I had to wait on them. A series of firsts: first night for us all, first party of guests, my first time professionally waiting on tables. The first order I served was coq au vin, for which I had to ladle between spoon and fork a piece of chicken from a clay pot onto the guest's dinner plate. The chicken was steeped in thick sauce, and I knew disaster was just ahead as I transported the chicken from the pot to the plate. I figured, what the hell, and said, "Pardon me, ma'am, here comes a first," and of course dripped sauce on her lap. The chicken finally, thankfully, landed on her plate. For some reason or other she found it funny, and I got a big tip—but I got fired.

That party of guests turned out to be friends of the owners, and their camaraderie and conviviality overpowered the owners' anger, because although I was fired from the Top of the Gate, I was told I could stay on downstairs at the celebrated Gate itself—as a bouncer. I didn't know anything about being a bouncer, but I needed the money and was always interested in new experiences, so I said yes.

It was good that I got that job-job, because amongst the bills I had to pay was tuition at the New York School of Motion Picture Production as well as acting classes with Lee and Paula Strasberg. The acting classes were important not only because of studying and practising "one's instrument," but also because of networking. I must admit I found the guru-ism of the Strasbergs to be tiresome and infuriating. Lee Strasberg was apparently—and evidence supports this—a keenly perceptive teacher in his early years. But at the age at which I met him, he seemed to be full of circular reasoning, like "Wait, you'll see I'm right" or "Because I say so." That authoritarianism does not encourage a constructive, creative search. Still, the ensuing arguments were worthwhile. So too was the continuing practise of all aspects of filmmaking at the New York School of Motion Picture Production, in particular the emphasis on screenwriting. I didn't know that I would ever have the gift necessary for screenwriting, but I did know I was learning the essential ingredients for film story construction.

As a novice bouncer, the first thing I did was make friends with all the real and trained bouncers. The next thing I did was learn that courteous and constructive communication was more effective than being tough. If you informed someone of circumstances without challenging his masculinity, as in, "This is a no-smoking area, but you're welcome to smoke over there if you like," rather than threatening or ordering (particularly if he is with a woman he is trying to impress), the likelihood is compliance and not defiance. I learned all the right moves, because there was no way I was going to risk getting roughed up for the sake of even the Village Gate.

I was apparently good at my work, so they made me an offer: $3 more if I spent the night covering the "john." I was getting only $15 a night, so this would be a big raise. I said yes. The increase in pay, however, was not commensurate with the increase in danger. Drugs and booze were involved now. For example, an underage patron would go into the john with a half-full bottle of Coca-Cola and come out with a full bottle of Coca-Cola—the difference being rum. Sometimes I would notice on my regular patrols that there were two pairs of feet rather than one underneath the door of one of the cubicles. This usually meant two guys turning on, and sometimes with pretty serious drugs. Well, humour and courtesy worked, but on occasion I found it necessary to rely on the friendships I'd made with the trained bouncers. It was good experience, but happily I soon got a film to do, as well as an off-Broadway play.

The film was a documentary feature called *The Inheritance*, sponsored and produced by the International Ladies Garment Workers Union. The ILGWU was a solvent and strong organization that often supported the arts, but this was specifically a story about the birth and growth of that industry and especially that union. This was the mid-1960s; had it been the mid-'50s, I might have got into trouble just by virtue of association, so many of the cast members were formerly blacklisted. Frankly, I was proud to work with them, not only because of their political integrity, whether I agreed with them or not, but also because of their talent and prominence. The cast included Robert Ryan, Lionel Stander, some of the Adler family, and Anne Revere. Amongst the reasons for Ms. Revere's fame was her dignity and depth of talent, as well as the perception that she was everybody's mother. She was John Garfield's mother in *Body and Soul*, Gregory Peck's mother in *Gentleman's Agreement* and Montgomery Clift's mother in *A Place in the Sun*. In *The Inheritance*, I'm proud to say, she was Al Waxman's mother.

The play was an Equity Library Theater production of Arthur Miller's one-act union play *A Memory of Two Mondays*. This was the third Miller play I had done; the first was the summer-stock production of *A View from the Bridge*, then the CBC-TV production of Miller's version of Ibsen's *An Enemy of the People*. It was a limited run, but it was wonderful to be back on stage, especially in New York. Mr. Miller came to see the play and brought his new wife, a German photographer, who had read all his plays and had seen all his work except this one. They came backstage afterwards and we had a lovely conversation, during which I found him to be a gracious gentleman and also very appreciative of the work he had just seen. This meeting also challenged my preconceived notions; it surprised me to hear a super-intellectual speak with such a heavy Brooklyn accent.

There were only two television series being shot in New York in those days, and I worked on both of them. One was *For the People*, the successor to, but not as successful as, *The Defenders*. It starred William Shatner, whom I had met some years earlier on a CBC-TV production, and Jessica Walters, with whom I had studied at the Neighborhood Playhouse. But my connection there was Stu Rosenberg, who had directed me in the TV series *Espionage* back in London. I'm not trying to suggest that connections are what it's about; no, talent is what it's about, but because there are so many talented people, there is no denying the importance of relationships and networking to buoy up opportunity. But make no mistake, this is an unsentimental business; no one with any self-respect gets or gives a job simply because of friendship. First comes talent and being right for the part, then friendship can enter into it. I believe that was the case for me with Rosenberg. After *For the People* he cast me in a pilot he was shooting called *Trials of O'Brien*. It was a detective show, very funny, starring Peter Falk and Elaine Stritch. It didn't sell, but in a way it was successful in that it proved to be a precursor to the very successful and long-lived *Columbo*.

It seemed I had exhausted the current work potential for me in New York, and I really wanted to go back to Canada. But first I had to compete in Hollywood. I caught a lift with two women I knew and drove from New York to Los Angeles along the popular road of TV folklore fame, Route 66. What a way to see America!

CHAPTER 14

Epiphany in an Enchilada

If I thought Toronto from the airport to Glen Cedar Road looked like a parking lot, Los Angeles in the mid-1960s presented a landscape of parking lots, stretching to the horizon in all directions. It wouldn't be until I came back for *Cagney and Lacey* about fifteen years later that I would get to see the incredible homes in Beverly Hills, Bel Air, Hancock Park or Malibu Colony. Only then would I experience the pleasure of drives down to the beach or up the coast (my car in the sixties might not have made it), only in the eighties that I would get to know out-of-the-way places specializing in fabulous food and discover phenomenal shopping from bargain spots to Rodeo Drive, or have the caché to gain entry to the "in" clubs and restaurants, or take the time to visit the galleries, museums and theatre.

When I was first there in 1964–1965, Los Angeles was a city of wide, barren streets, without texture apart from sleaze strips like Hollywood and Vine. I could detect no sense of contiguity or closeness—no neighbourhoods. The only congestion came from cars driving down Sunset Boulevard on a Saturday night. But people? What a contrast, immediately after New York. In LA, people seemed to move in parallel lines; I felt that about Los Angeles even when I was successful there. The lines didn't bend or cross to meet each other.

Rather, each person was running in his or her own lane, with blinders on, focusing on the inevitable race for career success or chase for stardom. It's not just a question of geography, it's a question of attitude. In New York or Toronto, life is layered in concentric or overlapping circles, with your social group, your sports group, your professional group, your religious group, your family group, your cultural group, all either coinciding or on top of one another, creating a fabric of textured life.

When I came back for *Cagney and Lacey*, during the height of the success of that series, I was often interviewed in the press and on television talk shows. One of the talk shows I was invited to do was CBS's *Two on the Town*. This was meant mainly for California audiences (that's potentially 20 million people), but the host, Melody Rogers, asked me, would I like to do the interview in Toronto and, if so, where did I hang out? What would be an ideal place to conduct the interview? I said that what might be interesting for her California audience was what I consider one of the fundamental differences between Los Angeles and Toronto, and that's that Toronto is a people city while LA is an automobile city; Toronto is a walking city while LA is a driving city. I asked if her cameraman would be able to handhold and track with us as we walked and talked. She said yes, and it turned out to be a very successful interview, set against a backdrop of some of Toronto's streets and landmarks, particularly old architecture juxtaposed against new, like the new City Hall between the old Romanesque-revival one on one side and Osgoode Hall on the other, or the Flatiron Building against skyscraper office towers, or an old church against a new condominium building. It played many times on CBS in the California area.

Back in the mid-1960s, apart from the occasional trip to the beach, I hung out during the day at an actors' bar called the Raincheck. It was cool inside, but the atmosphere was thick with desperate actors and it was so dark that when you walked out you had to squint until your eyes adjusted to the hot sun. It was like film noir in colour, the look of *L.A. Confidential* or *Chinatown*. I lived in a type of apartment hotel that resembled a motel. I bought a very cheap used car for $150, which was listed under a category simply called "transportation." I paid the salespeople their money, drove off the lot and turned the corner; about a block and a half away, it died. I single-handedly pushed it all the way back to the lot and demanded my money back. They said a deal's a deal, "let the buyer beware." But I was so hot and pumped up from pushing, and they were so impressed with my adrenalin-driven strength, augmented by my rightful indignation, that they thought better about who should beware and to my surprise refunded my $150. I then bought, on an instalment plan, a Volkswagen bug, a lovely little stick-shift car, for $1,200. It was an ugly pea-green colour, but I loved that car and named her Brunhilde. I made rounds and of course took my inevitable acting classes, as much, this time, for networking and socializing as for studying. At night I would frequent the Hollywood landmark Barney's Beanery.

I was soon broke and needed a job. A friend of mine, Otis Young, was also an aspiring actor. He and I had met when he worked at the Limelight Café in Greenwich Village, where I and some friends hung out and solved the problems of the world. Otis had had a lead role with Jack Nicholson as one of his sailor buddies in the film *The Last Detail*, but was now between jobs and working as a short-order cook at Barney's Beanery. He said he could get me a job cooking there. But I didn't know how to cook, particularly the Beanery's specialty, Mexican food. He said, "Don't worry about it, we'll tell Barney you cooked at the Hilton in New York." I was, like all actors, constantly revising and updating my résumé; now I had to fake one in order to get a job-job. But it worked.

It turned out to be a lot of fun. It was show business. I worked like a juggler within a U-shaped counter, the customers sitting all around me. With one hand, I was jiggling the wire-mesh container in the deep fryer to get the right crispiness for the french fries, with the other hand I was flipping burgers or turning over eggs, all the while carrying on lively conversations with the patrons, who generally were out-of-work actors in the daytime and successful or famous and usually inebriated actors slumming at night (a shot of Scotch was 45 cents and rye was 35 cents). It was like being on stage, theatre in the three-quarter round, with me performing in the middle.

Nevertheless, performing as a short-order cook in a beanery, no matter how much fun or how celebrated the beanery was, was not what I had envisioned for myself at the age of thirty. I should have won my first Academy Award by this time. Apropos of the renown of Barney's Beanery, there was a remarkable replica of the bar section of the Beanery being sculpted out of papier mâché on the adjacent parking lot by an artist named Edward Kienholz. It ultimately toured galleries across the States, ending up with a showing in New York at the Museum of Modern Art. You could actually walk into it, as though you were going into a bar. Then you got the feeling of every bar you'd ever been in in your life. I thought this was more inspired and had the potential to reach more deeply into the viewer of the work than Andy Warhol's Campbell's soup cans or Claes Oldenburg's puffed-up canvas hamburgers. Inside Kienholz's replica of Barney's Beanery you stood between customers at the bar whose faces were clocks that read ten after ten. It was at once amusing and desperately lonely—sort of like the ambivalence I felt while unwrapping prepackaged steamed burritos, or stirring ketchup into a pot of anemic-looking beans, or listening to a drunken movie star talk about a curve ball, or even, to impress me, a hockey puck. Why was I doing this? Was this what I wanted? Suddenly, I would hear a voice in my ear, and it was Professor Bora Laskin reminding me, "Show business? You're going to have to want that very badly." Then I would smile with new understanding of the truth of what he'd said.

I succeeded in arranging to meet two very powerful agents. At least one of these meetings, if not both, was facilitated by correspondence from Carl Foreman, but my entree was enhanced in both cases by my own track record of training and experience. The first meeting was with Saul Krugman, a senior executive at the Ashley Famous Agency. Ashley Famous was an offshoot of the then recently defunct Music Corporation of America (MCA) Agency. MCA could no longer function as an agency because of antitrust laws; it then became the parent company of Universal Pictures, which is currently owned by Seagram. Ashley Famous would later fold into a larger organization, becoming part of International Creative Management (ICM), but at this time it was one of the most powerful agencies in the country. To raise interest from anyone there was a coup in itself. The problem was that in a big agency, one agent, no matter how high up, was not enough, because they each covered different specialized areas of the business; one agent was your point man, but a lot more than one had to see potential earning power in you. Well, I had Krugman in my corner, but he had to get, if not all the others, at least a few of them on side. To that end he had a strategy. He arranged a meeting in the Ashley Famous boardroom, where I would meet all the others, woo them and wow them, while he, unbeknownst to me, would spring his strategy on us all.

At the prescribed date and time I knocked on the imposing boardroom door of Ashley Famous, was beckoned in by Krugman and was momentarily thrown by what I saw. Sitting around a huge, long, oval-shaped table were about thirty young Ivy League-looking graduates, all men, all Brooks-Brothered with buttoned-down shirt collars, and all, or at least most, I would guess, Jewish. Somehow I found the situation humorous. Saul Krugman, the host, as it were, makes an introduction: "Gentlemen," he says, "I would like you to meet the talented actor I've been telling you about, Mr. Albert Gardiner." I'm not sure if I did a Jack Benny-type take, but I did slowly turn my head to look behind me, in case there was someone else in the room to whom he might have been referring. Clearly, he meant me. Gardiner? Interesting. I wondered how Krugman had arrived at Gardiner. It was not the Wayne or Watkins I would once have wished for. Still, a nice, safe non-Jewish name. I smiled and said, "Gentlemen, I'm sorry, but I'm not an Albert Gardiner. I'm an Al Waxman. That's what I am. And there's nothing you can do about that." And then I added, I think quite contentedly, "Nor is there anything I want to do about that." As I left Ashley Famous, I thought of my Harley Street specialist. He would have approved.

Happily, I still had a meeting with the other agent, Abby Greshler, to look forward to. This one I know Carl Foreman set up, and the meeting was scheduled for a couple of days hence. In the meantime, back to the Beanery. From the perspective of career and ambition, my time at the Beanery could be considered one of the low points in my life. But immediately after the incident at Ashley Famous, I experienced an epiphany of sorts at Barney's. It dawned on me one night somewhere between tacos and enchiladas that I had "made it"—that all-important phrase, that all-consuming show-business concept, "made it." And why? Because I realized something I probably had known all along but had now digested deep enough in living understanding that I could articulate it clearly and simply: "making it" is a never-ending process, and only when you know that have you got it made. In other words, "made it" is a past-tense concept, and I don't want that said about me until after I'm dead, because making it, like life itself, is ongoing. And therein, I believe, is the fountain of youth. Indeed, as an artist you never stop learning and wanting to learn, and if you've still got learning to do, you're still a student, and if you're still a student, you're still young—at least in attitude.

Even now, as I have said, I start off my classes by identifying with the students. I tell them I too am still a student, that we're pretty much the same. The only real difference is that I've been at it years longer than they have, so perhaps I have more insights and experiences to share, but otherwise I am, like them, a student, still learning. And in every job I do, whether challenging and inspirational or just mundane and pedestrian, I try to learn something new. So that night at Barney's Beanery, I "made it"—forever.

Abby Greshler was the quintessential Hollywood agent, a one-man William Morris Agency, probably the most inventive, ahead-of-his-time deal-maker there ever was, with a car phone before they were even heard of. As a matter of fact, his access to multibuttoned phones was his office tower. Because he had that, the only other thing he needed was himself and, of course, his clients—and I was going to be one of them.

Abby represented Vince Edwards, the star of the hottest TV series at the time, *Ben Casey*. I think he also represented two or three of the regulars in the cast. As if that wasn't leverage enough, I had worked with Vince Edwards on *The Victors,* and I think even more important than that, the director of an upcoming episode was Stu Rosenberg. Still, I had to audition, but I felt very confident about getting the part, and indeed I did get it. One of the scenes involved me as a hospital orderly trying to prevent two thugs from breaking into a locked drug cabinet. They were both taller than me; nevertheless, I was apparently very convincing in my attempt to overpower them. The resulting impact would prove interesting for me after that show aired.

In the meantime, I was still making an impact as a short-order cook at Barney's Beanery. Not the right kind, though, as far as Barney was concerned. As I mentioned earlier, during the day, out-of-work actors would frequent the place. I understood that most of them didn't know where their next meal was coming from. These were the days before the portion-control phenomenon of the fast-food era. Hamburger patties were stacked on top of each other, separated by squares of waxed paper. So when I saw a friend come in whom I knew was out of work, who maybe even had people to feed at home, if he ordered a hamburger, I would plaster three patties together so that he would be able to cut it in half or even thirds, and then take some home for his family or his next meal. Barney caught me in such an act of philanthropy with his burgers, and I was fired on the spot for over-portioning.

I didn't care. I was about to be paid for my *Ben Casey* episode, and I was confident there would be more work to follow. I got a cheque that I thought was quite substantial: $300 for a day's work. That's what I would get in a week for filming in London. I was so happy when I got that cheque, so proud to pay my first commission in Hollywood, that I made out a cheque to Abby Greshler for $30 and took it to his office.

Although Abby Greshler appeared soft around the middle, his upper body was lean and his face was gaunt and slightly anemic-looking. He always had on dark sunglasses, dressed in a dark-blue suit and drove a black Lincoln Town Car. This dark ensemble made one uncomfortably aware of the pasty-white pallor of his skin. Scary. Abby dressed like a funeral director, but looked like the corpse. His office was equally dark; in fact, I don't remember any windows at all. I'm sure it was luxurious, but it was too dark for me to remember anything except the buttons lighting up on all the phones on his desk.

"Thirty dollars!" he blurted out. "What am I going to do with this *imglick* money?!" (*Imglick* is the Yiddish word for catastrophe.) "Listen," he sighed, "if you weren't such a nice kid, I wouldn't take the time to talk to you. Look at all the lights popping. I got Paris on this line, Tokyo over here and London on that one. What the hell am I going to do with $30?"

"Well, it's your commission," I said, "I owe it to you."

"You're not only a nice kid, Carl says you're talented. Everybody says you're talented. Will you look at the sand I got in my shoes? I was on the set of *Wackiest Ship in the Army*, they got sand all over that goddamn set. I'm never going on that set again. I got the star of that show, they can come to me! Look, kid, I gotta take these calls. Thanks for the cheque, but you gotta understand, you're no good to me unless you're making upwards of $2,000 a week..." (This was 1965; it would probably be more than ten times that today.)

"Well, maybe one day I'll make that kind of money."

"Sure you will. You just gotta wait it out until it happens. Park cars in the meantime. You know Vince Edwards, right? Well, Vinnie worked in a parking lot for years. I gotta take these calls now!"

"Goodbye, Mr. Greshler."

I guess I could have stayed and been one of his clients who waited it out. Friends tried to encourage me to do just that. Dabney Coleman, although never needing to park cars himself, endorsed that course of action if necessary and advised me to stay the course. He persisted in his career, tenaciously climbing the ladder rung by rung. Jimmy Caan, equally talented, and who was climbing the ladder as well, also tried to convince me to stay, because "Hollywood needs good character actors." Flattering friends, and maybe they were right, but I think I was right, because the path I preferred had to do with my identity, and "home" is a key element in my sense of self. I don't mean to sound holier-than-thou when I say that. I'm not preaching. It was a personal choice; it's what I wanted and needed. My foundation. I decided to go home to Toronto.

What clinched it for me was the airing of the *Ben Casey* episode I did. I got a phone call the next day from one of the most important casting directors in Hollywood at that time, Lynn Stalmaster. He was apparently very impressed with the fight scene I'd done, in which I squared off against two big actors. He asked me to come meet him right away.

When I entered his office, he was sitting behind his desk, surrounded by a bunch of suits, like a family portrait. Presumably, they were the producers to whom he had been touting me. In a sense, actors are like a casting director's currency: the more "on the money" he is, the better his judgment looks, and the better he looks. For the casting director, then, there's an element of risk in showing an unfamiliar actor to prospective employers. As I approached his desk, he came around from behind it with hand outstretched to greet me. We were on the verge of shaking hands when he suddenly withdrew his and almost yelped, "I thought you were over six feet tall."

"I guess that's the way I looked last night."
"Yes," he said.
"Well, I'm not six feet tall, only five feet eight and a half inches, maybe five nine on a good day, but I can act tall."
"No. Not good enough." Not only did we not shake hands, but he turned his back on me and returned to his desk. That was the end of our meeting.

I was far from hurt. I genuinely found him and the entire situation hilarious. Yes, that was the end of our meeting and the end of my first Hollywood experience. I really didn't want to be there any more. I wasn't retreating; on the contrary, I was moving forward.

I packed my bags, got into Brunhilde with an actress friend of mine who wanted a lift to Chicago, and drove across America and back home to build a future in Canada.

CHAPTER 15

Tviggy

As I said earlier, acting at times didn't seem enough for me. I wanted to do more, or at least try. This was one of those times. The first thing I did upon my return to Canada was apply to the National Film Board in Montreal for a job. I listed all my training and experience academically and of course in film as an actor, particularly the studies I had pursued at the London School of Film Technique and the New York School of Motion Picture Production—part-time in both cases. I wanted to study full time now, but there were no film schools in Canada as yet. I said in my letter to the NFB that I was willing to start at the bottom, in whatever capacity they would assign—an apprentice, an assistant, a joe-job of any sort. When I finally got a response from them, it was a short letter of rejection, perhaps only one or maybe two sentences on Government of Canada stationery from which you couldn't tell whether I had applied to the NFB or for a job as a customs officer at the Rainbow Bridge.

There was, however, one job that I did get from the Film Board—as an actor. I still needed to make a living, after all. Most actors had something else to fall back on; I had acting to fall back on. It was a short film called *Inmate Training*, directed by Peter Pearson. We would work together again on films and on the executive of the Directors Guild of Canada.

Inmate Training was made for the Department of Corrections, to be used by prison personnel. It was shot in Montreal's St. Vincent de Paul Penitentiary, now defunct; then, in 1966, it was said to be Canada's San Quentin—a dangerous place. One of the other actors in the cast, someone else with whom I would work again, was Richard Monette, who would go on to do great work at Stratford, becoming its artistic director. Richard's character in the film was sensitive and withdrawn, while I on the other hand played a tough, hard-to-control inmate who was doing time for aggravated assault, a character not easily confined. I understood what claustrophobia means, but as part of my preparation for the role I had myself locked into a cell for a few hours to get a feeling for what might lead to what's called stir-crazy.

As an actor, I've always been attracted to the real thing, to what is called "personalizing." So it was an exciting challenge for me that none of the inmates who worked on the film (for cigarettes as remuneration) knew that we were actors. They were given to believe that we too were inmates. This suited me fine, as it did the style of the film as well. It was shot very cinéma-vérité, the camera often positioned so that the inmates didn't know they were being photographed. For example, in one scene in the gym we were playing a game called Ballon-Boo (French for broomball), with the camera hidden high in the bleachers. I played goal (some things you don't forget) and as planned, during the course of some rough play, sticks were dropped and a fight ensued between me and one of the inmates.

Peter had asked me to pick someone to get into the altercation with and to choreograph the fight. This fellow would be the only inmate who would know that I was not a fellow prisoner. Naturally I wouldn't play it safe and pick a small guy to fight with—not like when I was a bouncer at the Village Gate, where to side-step confrontation was the better part of valour. Here, instead, I had to wade right in, but I wasn't crazy enough to pick a big guy either. I found someone exactly my size and instructed him in some moves and then rehearsed them with him, but not so exactly that there wouldn't be some spontaneity and even some danger in it. Indeed, when we got going, all the other inmates encircled us, creating a human boxing ring, and started shouting, some in English, but most in French: "Give it to him! Give it to him!" As I was the new guy, this would be a kind of initiation rite. It looked too real to our crew, like it was getting out of hand. They became alarmed and said we'd better go down there and break it up before Al gets the shit kicked out of him. Peter assured them it would be OK. (Easy for *him* to say!) Finally we heard, "Cut!" and only then was I introduced to the inmates as an actor. One of them sized me up and said, "Funny, he don' look no more honest dan me!"

The fact that I was now known as an actor to some at the NFB was no help in gaining me entry into whatever training in directing they may have offered at the time. But directing was not a whim for me. Even though I was fortunate enough to support myself as an actor, I really wanted to get into filmmaking, ultimately to direct.

Next I tried the CBC. This time there was no stationery, just rejection. But the encouragement to freelance was there—applications or auditions on an ad hoc basis would be welcome, I was told: "Just show us on film what you can do." Easier said than done. It's not like practising the piano every day; it costs money to practise filmmaking. And unlike playing the piano, filmmaking requires buying or renting equipment, not to mention the cost of supplies and studio time, adding up to a chunk of money. And when it's gone, there's no way you can practise again tomorrow.

So I was on my own, a freelancer (nothing new), and I had to make it happen. I decided to write a screenplay for a theatrical short. It was a Walter Mitty-esque story about a plain, skinny Jewish girl who daydreams of becoming a famous international model. This was the time of that ultra-skinny phenomenon in international modelling called Twiggy. I called my story *Tviggy*.

I went to the Canada Council for a grant. I don't remember the reason given, but the response was negative. I do remember the reason for the response I got from the Ontario Arts Council. It too was negative, and the reason was that I had not yet done any film, outside of my participation in one- and two-minute shorts at film school, and so did not have enough experience or expertise to justify a grant or loan.

"But how do I get experience without doing work, and how do I do work without help? I'm just beginning."

"Well," they responded, "we're interested in helping those who are at the beginning of their careers, but in order to qualify, more credentials are needed than you have." All the acting I had done and all the training in film schools I had had was not, apparently, enough to consider me a qualified beginner. Strange, but what was stranger and more comical was yet to come.

A year later, after writing, producing and directing *Tviggy*, I went again to the OAC, now with a short film to my credit. I was fully confident that I finally "qualified" as I sought some financial help for a second short theatrical film. This time I was told, "You're a successful professional. We have to help those who have some experience but are not so advanced as you are." From novice to establishment in one year.

Back before I started *Tviggy*, I was at ground level, a neophyte faced with the question of how to gain experience. There were no schools in Canada, just the CBC in Toronto, the NFB in Montreal and perhaps an occasional opening with not much upward mobility at Crawley's in Ottawa, or piecemeal work at some small commercial production houses in Toronto. It appeared as though I indeed had to make it happen myself.

How was I going to make *Tviggy*? How was I going to raise the necessary money? The banks? Forget it. Family and friends? How dare I risk their money on such a precarious prospect as a film investment, particularly with no guarantee of distribution. It had to be my own money, but I didn't have any.

Sometimes fate's timing is so good that fate should be in show business. Maybe it is. My stepfather, Jack, had decided not to work any more, and my brother and I were therefore free to sell the "beer hotel." It couldn't have come at a better time for two reasons: first, in the three years since my mother's death the value of the business had deteriorated by half (to be fair, this business was not Jack's natural inclination; his talent was tailoring); and second, after debts had been paid and obligations met, my share of the proceeds would comfortably cover the cost of making and selling *Tviggy*—approximately $15,000.

Incidentally, my brother had gone along with my word, even though there were no witnesses, about my mother's wishes regarding Jack. We both felt right about honouring her wishes, and we both felt good about Jack's satisfaction. Jack had remarried, and his circumstances were comfortable and conducive for all of us to move on. So there may have been a loss, but Jack had been taken care of, my mother's wishes had been honoured, and just in the nick of time I suddenly could afford to produce a theatrical short.

I was determined to make it a success. In order for that to happen, I had to first of all be clear about my purpose. To make a good film was important, to make back my money was important, but perhaps most important was that it should further my career. If I didn't make all my money back, it would still be a success if it were a piece of film that would encourage producers to consider me worth hiring as a director.

Well, it was a success story in every sense. The critics were mostly positive, the industry applauded me, and the public talked about it. This was remarkable because shorts at that time seemed to exist solely for the purpose of selling popcorn before the main feature. *Tviggy*, however, caught people's attention. Unfortunately, there was no category in the Canadian Film Awards (as they were then called) for theatrical shorts, nor was it financially feasible for me to search out international festivals.

With *Tviggy* as my calling card, I was now acceptable for the occasional directing assignment at the CBC. Remuneration for these assignments would ultimately more than cover the cost of making *Tviggy*. But *Tviggy* made back its money on its own. The financial reward was extraordinary for a short. As a result of distribution and sales (both in theatre and TV), in Canada, the United States and a number of European territories (dubbed or subtitled), it more than covered its costs within a couple of years.

For all this I owe a great debt of gratitude to the head of Columbia Pictures of Canada at the time, Harvey Harnick, a man who advised and guided many of us in the fledgling Canadian film industry. As well as helping here in Canada, he used his influence with his contacts abroad. We did a deal here in Canada that saw *Tviggy* attached to the huge hit *Guess Who's Coming to Dinner?* starring Spencer Tracy, Katharine Hepburn and Sidney Poitier. Wherever *Guess Who's Coming to Dinner?* played in Canada, and for however long it played, *Tviggy* played with it. The two ran for weeks and weeks and into many months, all across the country. I may have broken even in Canadian theatrical distribution alone.

Tviggy was also a success because I learned a great deal about production, promotion and distribution—in other words, about the process of filmmaking. I learned enough to know that I still had so much more to learn, or at least that I needed to keep doing again and again what I had already done—no matter how well I had done it. It was good to be proud of my work, but I knew that now was the time to build on it, not rest on it.

I didn't rest; the next work I did was not in film but on the stage again. I played the lead in an original play, a union story called *The Dodo Bird*. I couldn't resist the offer, because I had done the play the year before, immediately upon my return from Los Angeles. It had been produced in, of all places, the Colonnade, the Bloor Street building which at that time (1965–1966) had a theatre in it. *The Dodo Bird*, a rather raw story for the very chic Colonnade Theatre (it also housed fashion shows), was very well received—the production, the play itself and myself in the lead role. I had performed it at night, while in pre-production for *Tviggy* during the day. The run of *The Dodo Bird* finished in time for me to devote all my time to *Tviggy*.

When principal photography for *Tviggy* was completed, as though fate were again dovetailing schedules for me, *The Dodo Bird* was to be produced again, this time in New York, off-Broadway at the Martinique Theatre, with a new director and cast, except for me. I was invited to play the role in New York that I had, as they say, "created" in Toronto. I was more interested in editing and post-producing *Tviggy*, but this was New York, an important off-Broadway house, reviews by important newspapers, a dream I had always had. How could I say no? I looked up into the sky and said to the heavens, "You may think you're dovetailing schedules for me, but I think with these coincidences, you're really a B-movie writer."

Well, I went down to New York, travel and accommodation and expenses paid by the new producer. Pretty good for budget-conscious off-Broadway. That troubled my conscience, because midway through I felt my heart wasn't in it, as far as the role was concerned, regardless of New York and off-Broadway. To use a current phrase, "Been there. Done that." I wanted to be back in Toronto, editing my first film. No matter how hard I tried to focus on *Dodo Bird*, I couldn't concentrate because my mind was on the film.

I gave notice, but promised to stay until they found what they would consider a suitable replacement. It was a very New York play, and there's lots of talent in New York. Soon Richard Castellano took over the role. Castellano subsequently got a major supporting role alongside Jimmy Caan in *The Godfather*. I found that amusing remembering what Caan had said to me about staying in Hollywood because they needed good character actors. Crossroads and coincidences. But still, I was glad to get back to Toronto to complete the post-production on *Tviggy*.

Amongst the benefits that flowed from the success of *Tviggy* were directing assignments. The first of them was one of the treasures of CBC-TV history, *Quentin Durgens, MP*, starring Gordon Pinsent as the pride of the House of Commons. Funny thing is, I was a guest star on this series when it started, around the time of my return from Los Angeles, at which time it was in black and white and on tape. When I finally got the chance to direct an episode, it was one of the last of the series and it was in colour and on film, with a great deal more texture than in the beginning. Gordon admitted that he was at first reluctant to be directed by me, perhaps because I was a fellow actor, but before it was over he came to me and said he wished it wouldn't end.

Although the star of the show was unsure of me directing, I got the job because John Trent was such a strong producer, and he wanted to work with me. John was a cautious, tough businessman of a director. Actually, he was a producer/director, and pretty damn good at both. I learned a lot from him, as did many others in our young industry, and yet he was just learning himself. If it weren't for his untimely and tragic death at fifty, he probably would have gone on to become one of the continuing powers in the Canadian film industry. In the beginning we were good friends. We both served on the executive of the Directors Guild of Canada in its early years, and together wrote an episode of *Wojeck*, one of the greatest series the CBC ever produced. Later, I got involved as an actor with one TV series after another, and we went in separate directions, both professionally and artistically.

When I think of John Trent, I'm also reminded of Peter Carter, who was another force in the early years of our industry. Peter was one of the best assistant directors in the world, easily in the same league as Kip Gowan, and he went on to become a damn good director too. But it was in his capacity as an AD that I and others learned from him. I think most of the assistant directors in the east, if not all across the country, have been trained by the practical apprenticeship network under experienced mentors, who had themselves once been apprentices. I would guess that all of these people can trace their training through this chain of mentoring back to PC, as he was known. Strangely enough, Carter, like Trent, also died at the tragically early age of fifty.

These were two talents who, although they achieved some stature during their careers, would have gone on to even higher levels. Still, considering what they had in fact done and contributed, I think it's a shame—and typical of us here in Canada—that their names, along with people like Budge Crawley, are not venerated as pioneers who paved the way for the rest of us. It's not so much about public recognition, but about members of our industry not knowing enough of the history of their own business. The Academy of Canadian Cinema and Television has been working to change that attitude, but we still have a long way to go.

Whereas I got to direct one episode of every series going (there were only three), others got "multiple deals" to direct three or four of the thirteen or twenty-six episodes in each series. It was a kind of tokenism, and I don't think that's paranoia; indeed, the ones I got were given reluctantly. It's, if I may say, a tribute to my drive and obstinacy that I directed even the few shows that I did. But considering the "practising the piano" analogy, I needed more directing assignments. All together, I think over a period of two years after the release of *Tviggy*, I got to direct exactly four TV episodes.

I acted as well, and continued writing my novella, entitled *About Tomorrow*, only now it was taking on the shape and structure of a film script. Again, I was writing because I needed to have a project on the go, not because I thought of myself as a writer with a gift or with something I was passionate to say. Writing certainly expanded my talent as an actor and director, but it didn't necessarily follow that a good script would result from my writing exercise. A better and more beneficial exercise for me would have been more directing—more chances to fail and fix.

Unfortunately, I was not part of the small core group at the CBC who got all the work that was going. This was after the era of Harvey Hart, Leo Orenstein and Henry Kaplan, and before John Hirsch. The group at that time included Trent and Carter. I was only on the periphery, a tokenism not necessarily the result of anti-Semitism, but reflecting, I believe, a type of self-preservation. The fact that we are, and certainly were then, a very nervous business is owing to the basic reality that there's not a lot of work available. Those in power will see to it that they get the bulk of whatever work there is. To create an illusion of fairness, those on the periphery get an occasional handout.

I remember saying to a member of this core group that I believed the CBC, as a public broadcaster, should be open to new talent, and that fostering new talent is one of our duties. He replied that his only duty was to make sure he got another job after this one. One of the executives in charge of assigning directing commitments was the second generation of a family that had worked for the CBC, although his talent as a story editor/producer rose above the level of nepotism. Nevertheless, he said very clearly to me once that his friends were the people he favoured—not necessarily judging how good the work was, but rather how good people were to him. He didn't mean payoffs or kickbacks, he meant that he and the people he was referring to were in a circle of established friendships, and that I was not anywhere near the centre of that circle. Even though I recognized that his friends were talented, I still saw this as insular and unprofessional—and resulted in some of the lacklustre work that marked that period. For me, the ultimate reference was then, and will always be, the work itself.

Trent and Carter were also very guarded, cautious about the information they imparted. Trent once said to me that I was like a sponge, soaking everything up. To his credit, though he felt threatened by me, he did share his knowledge with me and others. Carter was just as careful. After one of the shows I directed turned out quite well, he said that he would have to start looking at me as though I were competition. Crawley, by contrast, was very generous—with work, though not with remuneration. But who cared? The relationship was rich with friendship and humour, as well as work experience. And I thought he went some distance for me a little later when I was married, as evidenced by this contract between Budge and my wife Sara:

SUB-CONTRACT BETWEEN:
FRANCIS RADFORD CRAWLEY
(hereinafter referred to as Budge)
and
MRS. ALBERT S. WAXMAN
(hereinafter referred to as Sara)

to be annexed to the Agreement between Crawley Films Ltd. and Tobaron Productions dated February 17, 1969.

1. That the husband of SARA be permitted by BUDGE as "expenses" one long-distance telephone call to SARA each day that he is away from home on business for Crawley Films Ltd.
2. That as some compensation for "loss of loving attention" of the husband of SARA while he is away from home on business for Crawley Films Ltd. (on which SARA is unable to accompany him), he is permitted by BUDGE to charge as "expenses" one dozen roses to be sent to SARA each week (or portion thereof) of said absence from home.

But work was what I needed. The absence of it not only meant no pay, but the absence of the intrinsic joy of working and, most importantly, the loss of the chance to get better at my craft. The lack of opportunity became painfully more evident as time passed without work. Once again, I had to make it happen.

The dearth of directing work didn't mean that I had time on my hands. On the contrary, my time was consumed with creative activity. I was into many different endeavours, and they were all intertwined. In addition to whatever directing I got, I would go and observe other directors at work, and of course there was always acting and writing and studying. And then there was my social life.

It was around this time that I almost got married. I met a beautiful young woman in England, a Canadian. We had actually known each other before we met in England, but the relationship was kindled over there, and it ignited as we travelled around Europe together. The heat continued in New York. Back in Canada, we decided to get married, at city hall. I discovered I'd forgotten one of the documents when we arrived at city hall, so we left unmarried, with the intention of going to pick up this particular document. I don't know whether, as we exited city hall, I looked relieved or what, but she suddenly said, "You're heart's not in this, is it?" My tacit response, emotionless, was neither agreement nor disagreement. It was obvious that she was right. It was a very painful moment for both of us as we parted company on the steps of city hall. What an image—as comic as soap opera, but as poignant as truth can be. She believed I didn't want to go through with it because she wasn't Jewish. She probably would have converted, but that was not a requirement as far as I was concerned. I think I just wasn't in love enough.

Marriage to me meant finality. To clarify, I don't mean that some aspect of my life would be over and finished with. No, marriage would be the beginning. But it was only going to happen once—that's what I meant by finality. There was going to be only one choice. It would be the one and only. Like motherhood, it was, regardless of imperfections, perfection. It was *it*. In the Talmud, there is this saying: "When a young man marries, he divorces his mother." Well, I guess that's fraught with implications of complexes. But the way in which it has meaning for me is in the concept of oneness, the oneness of continuity, the oneness of relationship, the oneness of marriage, the oneness of two people becoming one. It also means that the young man has given himself a standard, not of comparison, but of expectation. He could as a result be a loser in life—or he could be a winner. A big winner.

One night I got a phone call in my new apartment. I had graduated from a steamy apartment above a laundromat on Avenue Road (not unlike my beginnings on Spadina Avenue) to a cool "pad" in the stylish Colonnade on Bloor Street. With all the deals coming as a result of *Tviggy*, I could afford this new apartment—albeit only a bachelor. I would often have to remind myself that in spite of chic boutiques downstairs, I was still living in an apartment above a store.

The phone call came from a friend and his date, who had brought along her girlfriend, recently arrived from Winnipeg. They wondered if I'd like to come downstairs to Club 22 in the neighbouring Windsor Arms Hotel to join them and make it a foursome. I said no, because I was expecting a long-distance call. Instead, I invited them to come up and have a drink in my apartment. They accepted.

When they had gone out earlier in the evening, it was a mild winter night and the young woman from Winnipeg dressed accordingly. I guess, coming from Winnipeg, she must have considered Toronto winters to be tame, which by comparison they usually are. As it turned out, that night was different. While they were having a drink at Club 22, a blizzard of a storm whipped up, and although the Colonnade is virtually next door, it was a far enough walk without gloves, hat or boots across the slush-covered sidewalk for her feet to get wet and cold, and the piercing wind to cause her eyes to tear.

When I opened the door, her mascara was running and she was angry at her misfortune. We were immediately introduced, but neither of us said hello. The first thing she said was, "My hands are cold." I didn't say anything. I just took her hands in mine and massaged them to make them warm. Sara has always said that my welcoming smile was equally warm. When she tells the story, she says, "He took my hands in his, rubbed them to make them warm, and we lived happily ever after!"

Frankly, I wanted to massage more than her hands. When I helped her take her coat off, I noticed an incredibly sexy body—truly, as they used to say when there was only one Coke and it was classic (her figure, I mean), a Coca-Cola bottle figure. I always like to say I fell in love with her waistline: it was nineteen inches. And in spite of running mascara, or maybe because of it, I found her face adorable. I wanted to see her again. I asked her out to lunch the next day.

I can't remember terribly much about that lunch, except that it got me even more interested. I admired her directness when, from out of nowhere, she asked me why I allowed myself to be so overweight. In those days I had long hair and wore caftans, not so much because I was so hip, which I wasn't really, but because I was so fat. Those big tent-like caftans, I felt, streamlined some of the roundness out of my appearance. Apparently not. "Bitch!" I thought to myself, "she cuts right to the truth!" But I soon realized she wasn't being mean. She seemed to care. I quickly found her straight-goods demeanor admirable and even attractive. "Straight goods" was a Winnipeg phrase and new to me—refreshing, just like this Winnipeg girl.

I asked her out to a party that weekend. I discovered that her directness comprised not only honesty and good clear thinking, but also wit. She looked nervous as we were approaching the party. I asked her if she was OK, and she said she was a little nervous, actually scared. I asked why. She asked if there would be a lot of show-business people where we were going. I said yes. She then said, "They're all probably such bright, sparkling personalities, I won't know what to say."

Chivalry, here I come. "Oh," I said grandly and protectively, "you'll be OK, you'll see. Just stick by my side."

At which point she said, "But you don't have any sides!" Wow, I thought, and she looks great, too!

Our next date was very special. Marvellous and memorable. We had dinner and went to the movies. It was particularly portentous, a good omen, because I made the movie and she made the dinner.

CHAPTER 16

A Oneness: SARAL

We were married about half a year later, in October 1968. October 24, United Nations Day. I must admit there were times I was wondering, what the hell am I doing? This was the 1960s, a time of social, political, sexual revolution—nobody was getting married. But there must have been some inner wisdom that I wasn't even aware of that drew me to marriage with Sara. Maybe that wisdom was Sara herself. Certainly what drew me was Sara. *Bashert?* Perhaps. But without a doubt it's the best, most important and most wonderful thing I've ever done in my life.

We were close to marriage well before we finally decided on the date. So close, so soon, so scary. Fortunately, I had to go down to picturesque Mahone Bay, Nova Scotia, to do a film for a few weeks for the National Film Board. It was a story for the Department of Fisheries about safety in boats, to be directed by Peter Pearson. Peter wanted to use it to kick-start his feature-film career. I think the film served him well; I know it served me well.

The story was about a young man, played by me, caught in a dilemma: he was in love with a girl and in love with his boat. For some reason or other, if he were to choose the girl, he would have to give up the boat. Confusion resulted from his indecision, leading to sloppiness regarding certain basic rules of boating safety. When he was out on the high seas, thinking, "Should I or shouldn't I?" his boat, because of procedures overlooked, blew up, and he went down with it. So I came back from beautiful Mahone Bay with some fresh lobsters and frozen swordfish steaks, knowing that my decision would be to choose the girl. As a result my ship would sail.

If I wanted out, there was still ample opportunity. For example, the night I asked Sara to marry me, I found that the fabulous Colonnade had some downsides that I had never before considered, namely noise from Bloor Street. We were sitting on the couch together when I summoned up the courage to ask her to be my wife. At that very moment police sirens and fire trucks raced by on the street below. I waited for her answer, which I had every reason to be optimistic about. But there was no response. I waited, expectantly. She looked at me and smiled, apparently having nothing to say. Finally I said, "Well?"

"Well, what?"

Deflated, incredulous, a little wounded, I said, "I just asked you to marry me."

"Oh, I didn't hear you!" she said.

Seek not to know for whom the siren blows. It blows for thee? No. In life, just like in drama, it's good to remember, "Where is the love? Where is the humour?" Well, it was right there between the two of us.

The answer was yes.

After she said yes, I noticed I had a severe headache. I often had headaches, because I smoked cigarettes then, three packs a day. I started smoking when I was ten years old, trying to be tough, I guess, just like in the movies. Soon after I started smoking, I started trying to quit. At thirty-three years old, I was now up to sixty cigarettes a day—and I never smoked before noon! I was so preoccupied with my decision, the proposal and acceptance, and my splitting headache that I forgot about cigarettes. I didn't light up even once during the whole time I had the headache, a headache that lasted for three days.

When it was gone and I became aware of the fact that I hadn't smoked for three days, I said, "Hey, this idea of marriage can't be all that bad." I tried not to smoke for another day—and succeeded. The same the next day. And every day thereafter. I finally said, "Marriage? What a good idea. I'm glad I'm doing it." The marriage has lasted, and I've never been tempted to start smoking cigarettes again.

Formalities. The prerequisite visits to respective families—Washington and Winnipeg. Sara claims that her mother, in a way, approved of me even before she met me. The weekend before Sara and I met for the first time—the night before she left Winnipeg for Toronto—Sara and her mother were watching a late-night movie on television. It was *The War Lover*. They both cared for the nice, frightened, doomed-to-die character that I played. Even though my death scene was cut, there was enough reference to my demise by other characters that the audience could be touched by the tragedy of my having been killed in action. Sara's mother went so far as to say to Sara, "You see, in a war the nicest boys get killed." Just a day or so later, Sara and I met.

In case Sara's mother didn't remember *The War Lover*, Sara found another celluloid opportunity for her parents to see their future son-in-law. A Canadian film I had done, *Isabel*, which Paramount distributed at that time, was playing in Winnipeg. Sara told her folks to go see the film and then they would be able to see me. Too late, she realized that in *Isabel* I didn't play what her mother would consider a nice boy. In fact, in one scene in the film I and a couple of other guys sexually assault Isabel, the character played by Geneviève Bujold. Fortunately, the film was made by Geneviève's husband, Paul Almond, and either for that reason or for artistic reasons, the incident occurred out of sight, behind a haystack. Still, this was not a nice boy that I played. Sara would have preferred her mother to remember me as the nice boy from *The War Lover*. When she phoned to tell her parents to forget about *Isabel*, they had already been to see it. Sara asked, "Oh, do you know which one he was?" To which her father replied, with a tone suggesting his stony expression, "I know which one he was!" Well, we would all eventually meet and, I trusted, erase that impression.

When we met face to face, Mendel Shapiro asked me, with a directness that told me where Sara Shapiro got hers, how much I weighed, and then he guessed an astronomical figure that was painfully close to the truth. I was exposed. I tried to take it in stride, and asked him how he knew. He answered, "*Ich hob gehandled mit cattle*" ("I used to deal in cattle"). Straight goods. I found humour to be the best way to cover my embarrassment, and indeed, humour became the foundation for my relationship with my father-in-law.

More flattering to me was probably the most important thing he told Sara about what he saw in his future son-in-law. At least, both Sara and I thought he intended it to be flattering. He said to her that I was a good man but that he believed I would never be a millionaire. Sara asked him why, and he replied, "because he's too honest."

Mendel Shapiro actually was a farmer, or rather claimed to be, although in fact he became one only when he got to Canada. In Poland the closest he ever got to farming was the buying and selling of farm products, such as wheat. In 1938, with Hitler breathing down their necks, he realized it was time to get out of Poland. His family, particularly his in-laws, disapproved; had they known of his intentions to take their daughter to a strange and foreign land, they would not have approved the marriage. He begged them to reconsider; he begged all his family to come with him. Some did, but most refused. Those who remained perished.

Sara wondered, particularly after reading Irving Abella and Harold Troper's *None Is Too Many*, how her father succeeded, at a time when Jews were not welcome, in immigrating to Canada with his wife and two tiny daughters. He was a man of courage and cunning. When the representatives of the Canadian government in Poland said, "You can't come to Canada unless you're a farmer," he immediately replied, "*Bin ich* a farmer," that is, "So I'm a farmer." He signed a contract to farm some land a few miles outside Beauséjour, Manitoba, for a period of at least five years. He came in 1939 with his little wife (she was barely five feet tall) and two young children (Sara was just a year old) on the last boat to leave Poland before Hitler invaded.

Mendel Shapiro had the foresight and will to overcome the fear of the unknown. Instead of being diminished by this huge expanse of cold and distant land, instead of being overwhelmed by the enormity of the task ahead, he and his family flourished. I think it is this kind of courage with which families are built; it is also the kind of courage with which countries are built. Mendel and Annie Shapiro were not unlike Aaron and Toby Waxman. They came to Canada in tough times, faced enormous odds, but benefited and gave back. Canada was good for them, and they were good for Canada. Sara and I may have grown up 1,500 miles apart, but in a very real sense we were in the same neighbourhood, just around the corner from each other.

So I married the farmer's daughter.

I just wish my mother and Sara could have met. They would have liked each other very much. My mother would have approved and I'm sure been very happy.

I think because of my mother I avoided the otherwise obvious choice of having Rabbi Monson officiate the ceremony. He was so fond of speaking of the memory of my mother that he, out of the best of intentions, would have inadvertently reduced me to a puddle of tears right under the *chuppah* (wedding canopy). A solemn occasion, yes, but meant to be as joyous and magical as it is serious. *Mazel tov*. I believe, indeed I know, that Sara and I achieved that solemnity and that magic when we committed our love to each other in our eyes and in our hearts, regardless of the place and the procedure. *Mazel tov*!

For some reason that I can't or don't care to remember, no rabbi would marry us, probably because we weren't members of any synagogue and didn't necessarily want to join. Neither of us wanted to go to city hall, particularly Sara.

Fortunately, Sara worked at *Saturday Night* magazine for the editor Arnold Edinborough. He knew Rabbi Abraham Feinberg of the Holy Blossom Temple. Rabbi Feinberg, once a crooner of love songs on the radio in the US, was now a celebrated scholar, author and journalist. He was especially well known as an activist who had supported John Lennon and Yoko Ono when the two were bedding down together in a Montreal hotel room and invited the world to join them in giving peace a chance.

Among the many reasons for the rabbi's popular reputation was that he seemed to specialize in, or at least had the inclination to conduct, interfaith marriages. Still, if one of us was a Jew, that one would have to be a member of the Holy Blossom Temple. Neither of us was. Arnold Edinborough joked and promised that if Feinberg would marry us he would review the rabbi's next book in *Saturday Night*. I don't know if that was the reason, but Rabbi Feinberg welcomed us to be married at the small chapel in the Holy Blossom Temple even though we weren't members. First he asked which one of us wasn't Jewish. After we pointed out that we were both Jewish, his task was simplified and we could proceed. *Mazel tov*. Then Mr. and Mrs. Al Waxman purchased an autographed copy of his latest book, *Storm the Gates of Jericho*, and voluntarily joined the Holy Blossom.

Our wedding celebration was a series of parties that lasted over a whole weekend. Each of my aunts had parties that would have done my mother proud, one a little closer to orthodox, the other not so close. Nate and Bernice also had a reception for us, and my friends in the film industry threw us a party as well, hosted by film editors Havelock Gradidge and George Appleby, along with casting director Karen Hazzard. We honeymooned in our new apartment in the Colonnade—a new two-bedroom suite.

A few months later, having saved enough money, we took a trip to New York, and stayed at the Plaza Hotel. When I was a broke out-of-work acting student I'd always hoped to one day make love in the Plaza Hotel. So now that I was no longer a broke out-of-work student but had graduated to the status of broke out-of-work actor—but happily married—we checked into the Plaza. It didn't matter that we had the smallest room in this prestigious palatial place. We were together at the Plaza. It didn't matter that our window looked out at a brick wall. The curtains were drawn anyway, and we were together at the Plaza. Saw some sensational shows on Broadway and returned to the Plaza. Museums and galleries briefly, then back to the Plaza. Fabulous food in famous restaurants, and back to the Plaza. That would be the first of many great hotels in our life together—bigger rooms, better views and lots of honeymoons.

We were off to a wonderful beginning. And it continues. Today, over thirty years later, I think one of the secrets of our successful marriage is that the courtship has never stopped.

CHAPTER 17

Hunger versus Desperation

Perhaps I should have learned something more than economics when I aced Ec. 20 the second time around. Perhaps I should have learned that trial and error, lots of experience, learning the lay of the land, is necessary before the big leap. I'm not talking about marriage, I'm talking about movies. I think maybe I did know that, but desperation to make a feature film superseded practicality.

That, happily, was not the case with marriage. Not that I had been married before, but I had gone through some life experience before marriage. Sara had too. I was thirty-three; she was thirty. We both had lived a little, travelled a lot, seen some of the world or, as they said in Hollywood, we'd "been around the block." We were not without youthful infatuation, but our romance was not blind; we were both guided by experience and maturity (and luck), and the result was a passionately wise and wisely passionate move for both of us.

I did not conduct myself with the same good sense when I made my first feature film. I had lots of passion and even more impatience to jump in, so I made the big leap without really knowing well enough how to jump, or where and what I was jumping into.

I was dedicated to more hands-on learning, but in the absence of opportunity, the glow of my few successes outshone the dark holes in my experience, and I allowed myself to be encouraged by that lustre, blindly catapulting myself forward. *Tviggy* was a successful first film, but it was a short. Each of the few television shows I had directed was quite good, but I had been protected by the structure and discipline of the series format, although two of them had a certain degree of individuality because they were part of an anthology series.

The second of these, *Black Phoenix*, was a tough story and a strong script, written by Martyn Burke and John Hunter. This one-hour film gave impetus to their careers too. *Black Phoenix* was in a way a first effort for each of us. It was closer to long form than any of us had done before. As a matter of fact, the CBC contemplated making it a ninety-minute special. There was enough footage and the material was strong enough to carry in the longer slot, but in the end, because of network scheduling commitments, it was cut to fit the hour-long series.

Black Phoenix was raw, abrasive talent showcased in a docudrama whose subject, neo-Nazism, was based on the riots that had just occurred in Toronto's Allan Gardens and were still fresh in people's minds. It was as real as our talent, and breathed with the pulse of "now." It was the kind of show that makes television entertainment different and special, and it merited the attention it received.

Although we searched, there was no one who was right for the lead role here in Canada. It was the part of an old Jewish Holocaust survivor who is frightened and infuriated by the Nazi demonstrations in his neighbourhood park, and cannot conceive of this kind of free speech being a so-called democratic right. Fearing that history will repeat itself, he reacts personally and violently. The project was explosive enough to attract a talented, highly respected and well-known character actor from New York and Los Angeles, Simon Oakland, and still stay on budget.

Simon and I hit it off creatively and struck up a friendship that lasted long after the filming of *Black Phoenix*. I still have a framed picture of him on the wall in my office. When he gave it to me, we shook hands and his parting words, which have stayed with me to this day, were, "Don't ever lose your hunger." In retrospect, I wish he had pointed out what I ultimately learned myself: there's a distinction between hunger and desperation, and one should never mistake the latter for the former.

Hunger is important. Nothing good ever happens in film without the passion of hunger. Hunger is constructive. With the hunger to do a job, there is the need to do it right, and that need is satisfied through the search for and application of the appropriate strategy and craftsmanship. With desperation, you are reduced to obsession. You deceive yourself into thinking your obsession is the same as passion, and with that you believe you have what's necessary to make the film. All you really have is a driving need to make a film, any film, without having honed the skills with which to do it right. When I made my first feature film, there was in me more desperation to do it than hunger to do it right. I just had to make a film.

The Crowd Inside was based on the novella I had been writing, *About Tomorrow*, restructured into a film script. It dealt with four young people, the youngest of whom, a woman, is an innocent, afraid of facing her life and potentially a victim at the hands of others. The story involves her and her three housemates as she goes through a period of inner turmoil. She is affected by the housemates, who either give to her or take from her, resulting in her emerging from this house and this period in her life with the will and knowledge to face the future. Her housemates include a woman, a little older and more experienced, a reliable friend who gives her good counsel. The other two residents of the house are men, one of whom she seems addicted to, an evil character, and the other whom she would like to be more involved with because he is good to her. These three characters represent forces that push and pull within her, and all four represent cross-currents of tension and behaviour within the house, which in itself is a kind of character.

This sort of allegory is no basis on which to build popular entertainment, never mind how sexy and hip you dress it. The concepts, existential and pedantic, were probably significant only to me, and the dialogue was pedestrian, probably evident to all but me. There was the seed of a good story here, but I hadn't yet resolved it or realized it on paper, so there was no way it was going to arrive on film.

Although I lay no blame on any of the actors, in the casting of it I was not as precise or as exploitative—in the best sense of that word—as I might have been. For example, the distributors and even the executives of the Canadian Film Development Corporation (CFDC) wanted me to cast with so-called "marquee value," that is, imports. But the furthest I would go was still within Canada: a celebrated Québécoise actress, the beautiful *vedette* Geneviève Deloir. (She'll always be grateful—because it was through this film that she met and married a budding young filmmaker, Ivan Reitman.) I felt that I was being given an opportunity by the Canadian government, and therefore believed I was obliged to share that opportunity with the local Canadian film community. This attitude was not exactly unprofessional, but perhaps it was misguided and naive. I was on a crusade.

In *Tviggy*, which I also wrote, produced and directed, I knew where the love was, I knew where the humour was, I knew where I was going, I knew the subject matter, the characters, the throughline, the market for which it was intended and the purpose for which it was being made. In the case of *The Crowd Inside*, I didn't really know as much of the aforementioned as I should have; all I knew was that I had to make a feature film. I felt I had catching up to do, as if I should have been further ahead than I was. I was so paranoid and precious about the process that I wanted to do it all myself. To trust others takes more knowledge and confidence than I had at that time, so I never benefited from delegating or collaborating. I was obsessed. I wrote it, I directed it, I produced it, I production managed it, I wrote the words to the music, I acted in it, and one day I noticed I was the only person standing in line to see it.

Feature filmmaking—I now knew in my gut, not just theoretically—is a collaborative art form rather like a benevolent dictatorship, in which all the talents of the team are, ideally, free to express their own gifts in their respective disciplines and functions. At the same time, they are all aware of, and reconciled to the realization of, one purpose, which is embodied in and articulated by the film's director. The director, in turn, while never wavering from the thrust of his purpose, welcomes ideas and expertise from whatever source to help realize the film. Rather than feel threatened by help or diminished by the need for it, the director appreciates that the film will be enriched and enhanced as a result of the input of others.

To want to work for nothing reflects desperation; besides, it's just not smart. Perhaps when I was younger and had only myself to look out for, it seemed romantic and full of artistic dedication to want something so bad that I'd be willing to do it for nothing. At this time in my life, however, with a wife who became pregnant during the making of this film, it was absolutely impractical to struggle to put food on the table and pay the rent and still want to consume myself in the creative process of filmmaking. It was disrespectful to myself, not at all helpful to the film, and most unfair to Sara.

In order to get *The Crowd Inside* (budgeted at $300,000) financed, I had to match the initial investment of the core company of four shareholders (myself and three others) of $15,000 each. This would get the ball rolling towards other private-sector investors, a distributor and the Canadian Film Development Corporation, with a view to raising one-third of the budget from each. Since I didn't have $15,000, the only thing I could do was turn back $15,000 of my salary of $20,000 (for writing, producing, directing and everything else I did), leaving me an income of only $5,000. This, despite the fact that all of my time was committed for close to two years to overseeing *The Crowd Inside* from inception through to exhibition, with no other source of income. It's what I wanted, though: to be a hero.

Actually, that $5,000 was all I earned for much more than two years, because I couldn't get any work after the film came out. The good I had done myself with *Tviggy* and TV directing was abruptly and completely cancelled out. The cliché "You're only as good as your last picture" is perhaps true. I remember Sid Furie saying to me around that time that he didn't want to work in Canada because in the United States, if he made a failure, it would be part of his career, but here in Canada it would be the end of his career. Well, I wasn't going to let it end my career. Nevertheless, as the saying goes, I couldn't get arrested. There was no directing work for me.

Somehow, the failure of *The Crowd Inside* tainted my acting career as well, in spite of the fact that I was considered one of the best character actors around. Perhaps because *The Crowd Inside* was one of the first films to be produced under the aegis of the CFDC (later called Telefilm Canada), and because I did so much on the film, I was a big target. And I took a big fall. I remember the thoughtfulness of Eric Till, a very fine director, who said to me, "You did OK, Al, but you did too much." I appreciated hearing that because it was an exception to the comments going around at the time about my work. I say this not with bitterness but as a simple observation: I may have, in the process of making this film, served another purpose in the industry, because there are lots of people in it who don't feel tall unless somebody else falls down.

Fortunately for me, there was one person who never saw me as down. Sara, my wife, my partner in life, was always there with her firm belief in me, and her encouragement. Ironically, when we got married, I was emphatic that marriage came second and my career came first. But happily, Sara knew better. She said, "uh-huh, okay" and went about her life. And every day was a new day, and soon there was a day when that order was reversed—the marriage came first, the career second—and "whaddya know," the career benefited!

After two years of lots of work that produced negative results, little remuneration and even less prospect of future work or income, I would often worry at the end of yet another unsuccessful day that what "they," that is, the critics and detractors, were saying was true,

Hunger versus Desperation

that I was not talented. I would wonder aloud whether I should get out of the business. And there were nights when macho me would even cry in bed in fear of what looked like more futility the next morning. Sara was always there beside me, to reassure me that something good would happen tomorrow. We were broke.

Sara, who had been an editorial assistant to Arnold Edinborough and then Robert Fulford at *Saturday Night* magazine, stopped working in the latter part of her pregnancy. One might have expected her to think that I'd go out and get a job-job. But no, she was always positive and optimistic that I would come out of this and make a living from my chosen profession. It's as though she again knew better, as she'd reassure me that "Tomorrow is another day."

Fortunately, there were indeed other days, other tears in our household besides mine. And they were joyous tears, tears of life. While I was in production, so was Sara. And hers, happily, was a triumph! September 14, 1970, she gave birth to a beautiful baby girl. Every child is beautiful, but there was something so immediately special about her that I wanted to acknowledge her with a name that would be hers alone. I wanted to make up a brand new name for this brand new person and at the same time honour some of the ancestry that flowed in her veins. As both of Sara's parents were, thankfully, still alive, I asked Sara if we could combine the names of both my parents to create a new name, one that had never existed before, for this special child of ours. Sara agreed. We named our daughter after my mother, Toba, and my father, Aaron. We named her Tobaron. I wished for the baby's sake that my parents could have known her and she could have known them, but they are indelibly linked by her name. Tobaron.

Broke as we may have been, that didn't stop me from buying a baby carriage that was the Rolls Royce of prams. An English one, of course, something out of *Mary Poppins*. Sara and I would promenade up and down our block, whispering, oblivious to the sirens and traffic on Bloor Street. Sometimes I would admonish loud passersby with a "shh" because my beautiful baby was sleeping. And when she was up, I'd be handing out cigars to anyone at all. And what cigars! I didn't know anything about cigars then, I just knew that, because of my beautiful Tobaron, I had to hand out the best Cuban cigars available. Any wonder that I was, then, sometimes referred to as the Mayor of Bloor Street.

On occasion I was accompanied by a dear friend, Henry Ramer, a wonderful guy, wonderful actor, certainly one of the best ever in the business of voice over. He was, at the time, a cigar smoker, and we were both, at that time, size huge. We had just acquired buffalo coats from the Winnipeg police department at a deal-making discount price. Apparently, the Winnipeg constabulary considered the coats too bulky and awkward for modern policing purposes, and determined that it was no longer necessary to keep the coats simply for the purpose of maintaining tradition and image.

Well, what an image Henry and I created wearing those coats and walking behind that elegant pram. Henry and I, buffalo-coated and cigar-chomping, covered half the width of an otherwise wide sidewalk. We looked like a stampede. Passersby were concerned. There were sidelong glances and searching stares from heads craning to see if there was a baby in the pram and if so, was the tiny thing safe in the care of these two large beast-like characters?

Indeed Sara was right, one morning something good did happen: commercials. I did a lot of them. And I was good at them. I'm not sure that the sponsors would agree with that, because no matter which commercial was on the air, whether it was for crunchy breakfast cereal, a watch that never stopped ticking, a tax advice firm or a super-solid sedan, people would stop me in the street and say that they really liked me in that beer commercial. In fact, I never made a beer commercial.

There was, however, one spot (as they are called) that really stood out, which played for a long time and brought me significant residuals, even fan mail and prestigious awards in the commercial industry (the Clio). It was a Kleenex commercial. It began with a big close-up of me advising people, if they had a cold as my character did in the spot, to trust me, to use Kleenex and stay inside. Then the camera pulled back revealing me, behind bars, in prison.

As a result of the success of the Kleenex spot, more were made—same cast, same location and situation for the same product, like a series. More important for me was the relationship it spawned with Paul Herriott, the director of the commercial. It was actually Paul's production house that made the Kleenex spots, as well as many other successful commercials at that time. Paul was so in demand here and in the United States that his production house was committed to more work than Paul could personally handle. His company was not about to turn away lucrative contracts, so he would assign them to different directors, who were accepted by the clients because of Paul's word. I became one of these directors.

They were hand-me-downs, but I didn't care; I was directing again. The first of them was a sausage commercial. The point of the commercial was to show that this product shrank less than other makes of sausage. At this time Canadian CRTC and American FCC regulations required you to actually do what the spot says you can do—you couldn't just paint the product the right colour. To prove our claims, there was a digital clock in the corner of the frame counting down the twenty minutes of cooking time in a thirty-second commercial. The sausages were shown through matching dissolves, progressively cooking to delicious-looking, golden-brown completion—without the size of any of the sausages having diminished very much from beginning to end.

There was a problem. In order for these match dissolves to work, the sausages had to be on the exact same marks from shot to shot. For them not to burn, on the other hand, but rather cook to an even golden brown, they had to be turned with tongs. (Like I said earlier in this book, I try to learn something on every job I do.) But if you turned them with tongs, they weren't on the same marks as the previous shot.

Catch-22. And if, instead, you turned them on their sides, as you would a hamburger, they weren't evenly cooked. Oy! Another Catch-22. I had seven grown-up men and women, executives in suits, standing around me, expecting some definitive word on the proper cooking and colouring of sausages, as the camera trained down on the pork-filled frying pan. Finally I said, "Look, ladies and gentlemen, I don't know anything about cooking pork sausages. I'm Jewish."

Nevertheless, they were willing to follow my lead as we browned and sometimes burned sausage after sausage throughout the day. While the executives relied on me, I came home very worried about whether the sausages had stayed on their marks or not, which we wouldn't know until I saw the dailies the next day. Sara said to me, "Why do you care?"

I was indignant. "Because I have to care. If I don't care, it doesn't get made!" And then I added with the passion of confidence, "I care because I'm good."

A sausage commercial and I'm good!? It took a couple of minutes for me to catch up to Sara, who I think was already laughing. Then we both laughed out loud. But the suits must have thought it was pretty good, because I was rewarded with another assignment: a bacon commercial.

From pork to pork feed—specifically rapeseed (now called canola). Paul Herriott had been contracted to do an industrial for Canadian Pacific on their participation in the planting, harvesting, processing and finally shipping of rapeseed products and rapeseed oil to the marketplaces of the world. He asked me to direct it. This was a step up, at least time-wise; it was way longer than a sixty-second spot. And it was a different type of film work for me. I was delighted with the prospect and the challenge—even the Prairies location. From combines in farmers' fields to grain elevators to laboratories in Saskatoon for separating and filtering, then finally to the grain terminals in Thunder Bay and Vancouver for distribution around the country and the rest of the world.

Hunger versus Desperation

I was ambitious, determined to turn what some might think of as boring subject matter into an information piece that would also be entertaining. In Melfort, Saskatchewan, when I was shooting in grain elevators I put myself and the cameraman at the bottom of a chute so that the grain would thunder right past the lens of the camera, like an avalanche, in the hope of creating an exciting shot. Being an asthmatic, I couldn't breath in all that dust. I spent my days in breath-taking (or should I say breath-depriving) circumstances like that, and my nights literally sleeping in an oxygen tent at the local hospital. But I cared to do it right. My ambition every day was to get dramatic and energetic shots and to physically be there, on the one hand trusting, on the other, working closely alongside the cameraman.

One night after work I was too energized to go straight to the hospital and call it a night, so I stopped with the crew at a local bar to watch the Russia–Team Canada hockey game. This was the 1972 series and that night was the last game of the series that was played in Canada. The game was in Vancouver. Team Canada lost—again! The country and the fans were disappointed, even angry at their team. But the Team Canada captain, Phil Esposito, who had just played almost sixty minutes of all-heart hockey, was undaunted. In a memorable moment during a post-game interview, although physically exhausted, he looked straight into the camera and tore a strip off the nation for their lack of morale and support. His was an ambitious message. Indeed, Team Canada demonstrated exemplary ambition as they came from behind, winning the series on Russian ice with Paul Henderson's history-making goal.

While watching the Vancouver game, the waitress in the bar was hovering around our film crew. She wasn't really flirting, nor was she star-struck. She just sensed that there was something more to life than what she had known so far, and maybe we represented that "something more" to her. She was wholesome and pretty; reminiscent of Judy Garland singing "Over the Rainbow." Finally she got into some conversation with us during which she said that she didn't intend to always be in Melfort waiting tables. I asked her what she wanted to do one day, and she answered with dreamy-eyed ambition. "One day," she almost whispered, paused for a second, thought a little more, and then dared to be confident: "One day, I want to make it to PA."

PA was how the locals referred to Prince Albert, which as far as other Canadian cities go is pretty small, but nevertheless bigger than Melfort. As for a goal or destination, it was about fifty miles down the road from where we were.

I couldn't help but smile with wonder and fascination at the different manifestations of the phenomenon we all had in common, ambition—hers, Team Canada's and mine.

I was burning with ambition as I graduated from pork and pork feed to people. People travelling: trains, planes, shipping and hotels for CP—probably got the work as a result of the industrial. Followed by commercials for other products, services and people. Hair products for beautiful women with flowing hair; gum that produced fresh breath so that a guy could successfully pick up a girl in an art gallery; same guy, same girl, same gum on a streetcar; lively and adorable children of all complexions playing at a summer day camp as a result of donations to the United Way (I was actually very pleased with that one). I didn't knock any of them, not only because they provided me with a living, but also because they presented a challenge: to make your point, to touch a specific audience in an entertaining and artistic way, within the discipline and economy of twenty-eight seconds. Frankly, I wish I had done a lot more.

I was asked to do another feature film. What a lift for me! The producer was Larry Dane. He and I were neighbours at the Colonnade and had hung out together in Los Angeles and London before that, and even earlier in Toronto. It was Larry's concept, entitled *Only God Knows*. Three clergymen—a priest, a rabbi and a minister—rob the Mafia and give the money to a charitable institution for needy kids. A good concept, a funny concept, particularly if, as I suggested

Hunger versus Desperation

and he agreed, the clergymen use their interpretation of the Bible as a blueprint for the strategy and plans for stealing the money and disposing of it.

Larry wanted me to direct the film because he believed I had strength in understanding, realization and projection of character. To that end he wanted me to participate in the writing of the script as well, consulting and advising the writer, who was to be Paul Wayne, an expatriate Canadian living in Hollywood. Paul had worked on many successful sitcoms and variety and comedy shows.

Larry informed the CFDC and all his partners that he was hiring me to direct the film. I think they must have felt, after *The Crowd Inside*, that I was a dicey choice. He stuck by his guns, and I was committed to the project. It was official: I was to direct *Only God Knows*. I've always admired and appreciated Larry for that. He then flew me down to LA to accompany him in script conferences with Paul. He wanted me there for the purposes for which he hired me. Now I was even more impressed. Larry, as I remember it, was very careful with his money, a stubborn, tough and patient negotiator, and in that way a very good producer; so if he was flying me down to LA, covering accommodation and a per diem for me to participate in script conferences and development, then he was putting his money where his mouth was. I wanted to do a job for him, and thereby for myself.

Paul Wayne didn't see my function the same way. He thought I should await a delivered script and then start directing. That's not what Larry wanted, nor, when I saw the direction the script was going in, what I wanted. When we arrived at Wayne's house for our first meeting, I noticed an Emmy statuette on his mantel, something he had won together with a slew of other writers, each of whom had come up with a couple of words for a show like *Sonny and Cher* or *The Smothers Brothers*. In a sincere attempt to ingratiate, regardless of what I personally thought of its overblown significance (at least in that category of writing), I congratulated him on being the recipient of an Emmy. He responded, not with a thank you, but with, "I got that for writing comedy. Now, what are you going to tell me about comedy?" This was not said in jest. My return volley was a smile for the sake of trying to keep an up mood and a productive atmosphere.

I thought we had nowhere to go but up. However, it went in the other direction. I felt sorry for Larry, caught in the middle. He knew I was right, but had to stick by the track record and reputation of Paul Wayne. Larry expected loyalty and patience from me, believing that ultimately I would be able to do what I wanted. But I had learned that if you make a mistake with your first step, that is, in this case, the very foundation, the script, the likelihood is that you're only going to make more mistakes after that.

I didn't want to let Larry down, but I couldn't afford another failure. I agonized over what to do. Finally I realized that if I made this, it would be difficult for me to get another film to direct afterwards, but if I didn't make it, it wouldn't be difficult for Larry to get another director instead of me. Reason prevailed. I wrote Larry a letter in which I expressed understanding for his predicament and asked in turn for understanding of mine. I offered my appreciation for his efforts on my behalf, but explained why I couldn't proceed with this, and that it was still early enough for him to get another director without upsetting the process. Larry didn't talk to me for some time after that. Happily, that is now past, because I'm quite fond of him.

I would have thought that the powers at the CFDC and others involved, when they read that letter, would have reasoned that if Waxman, who needs another feature to direct, is voluntarily walking from the project, we had better re-examine the material and investigate what's wrong. Instead, they probably heaved a collective sigh of relief and promptly hired another director, Peter Pearson. He had just come off *Paperback Hero*, a picture that could have been, in my opinion, even better than it was. I was consulted on its script development, made constructive comments and suggested another draft; but, as was characteristic of the times, the preference was to film as soon as possible. Filmmakers couldn't wait to say "action." Understandable in a budding young industry.

Still, Peter's career was certainly, on the face of it, more promising than mine. But *Only God Knows,* because of its faulty foundation, I believe, turned out to be a failure; to my knowledge, it was not well received by the critics or by the box office, and if I remember correctly, although he continued to work in film and TV, this was the last time Peter directed a theatrical feature film. Believe it or not, whenever we meet he and I have a good laugh about that film, but Peter feels he has the last laugh, because for some reason or another the computers at the archives in Ottawa, which have memories like elephants and can't erase what they first heard, have recorded for posterity that I am the director of *Only God Knows*. But God also knows the truth, and that is, as always, what really matters, especially in this case: there was still hunger in me but this time no desperation.

Chapter 18

And Now We Were Four

Things did start to pick up, mainly because Sara and I had each other. Fortunately we were still young, and money was not the sole factor determining our wealth. We ourselves comprised the goose that laid the golden eggs. Without each other—no goose. We struggled to make ends meet every month, yet somehow the food on our table was always delicious, one of Sara's greatest talents, and as a result we were never in want of company. Neighbours and friends were always welcome—we were so centrally located—even when they showed up unexpectedly, which happened almost daily, at six o'clock. Not only that, but I had the tendency to call home later rather than sooner and say, "Honey, I'm bringing someone home for dinner. Is that OK?" This was as much an information bulletin as it was a request.

One of the times I did that was when I was working on a film in Niagara-on-the-Lake called *When Michael Calls* for ABC-TV, starring Michael Douglas and Elizabeth Ashley. Liz and I had been classmates at the Neighborhood Playhouse. As usual, I called Sara to ask if I could bring home a couple of guests.

"Who?" Sara sniffled, through a cold.

"Larry Dane and Liz Ashley," I answered.

Larry was OK, because he was a neighbour and a regular guest anyway, but a movie star? When Sara had a runny nose? Not fair. Nevertheless, she graciously agreed.

Sara was nervous, perhaps because of the presence of a glamorous international celebrity (Liz was a huge star at the time, having recently done *The Carpetbaggers*), perhaps, although I doubt it, because of the challenge of rearranging dinner for two into dinner for four. In order to deal with this nervousness straight on, Sara, in her inimitable directness, said to Liz, "You're my first movie star!"

Afterwards I pointed out that there were two assumptions in that remark. At least one was optimistic: that there would be more movie stars in her life. But the second assumption? Didn't she realize that there already was a movie star in her life? What was I, chopped liver? Fortunately, we both liked chopped liver. Also fortunately, regardless of the pressures of time, her state of health or the company, Sara had the knack of turning a dinner for two into a satisfying spread for three or four. She was so skilful at it that it ultimately became a chapter in her first cookbook, *The King's Wife's Cookbook*.

Our apartment was always "hip" (we even had a cigarette box shaped like a treasure chest filled with perfectly rolled marijuana joints), always cheerful and comfortable. Regardless of the size, our dwellings over the years were not unlike my parents' apartment on Spadina Avenue—mansions of love. But every once in a while it would become apparent that we needed to expand, like when Sara became pregnant with our second child. We would need a bigger place, but could we afford it? The answer to that question would not get in our way if Sara had anything to do with it; and that suited my philosophy too.

Sara's attitude was important because my confidence often needed buoying up, even though money was not the be-all and end-all for me. Although I didn't care about making more, I certainly worried about making less. I would say, "OK, we just had a pretty good year, but what if next year it all turns to rat shit?" To which Sara would reply, "Do you think I would have married you if I didn't have confidence in you?"

So, it appeared, did others. At the time, there were many lawyers and accountants seeking out Canadian filmmakers with whom to enter into joint ventures. This situation was the direct result of new Canadian government tax incentives to entice the private sector into investing in the Canadian feature film industry, tax incentives which supported the Canadian Film Development Corporation's initiatives. The private-sector investor, by financing one-third—let's say $100,000 of a $300,000 budget, with $100,000 coming from a distributor and $100,000 from the CFDC—could, by virtue of the way the deal was structured, be made full owner and therefore claim a tax loss or write-off (against other income) that was larger than his initial investment. That is, the loss he could claim on $300,000 was considerably more than his $100,000 investment. So it didn't make any difference to the investor whether the film succeeded or not; because of the deal, he was already a success.

As a matter of fact, a local producer captured the prevailing mood and policy by putting out a brochure with which to entice investors, entitled "You Win by Losing." This infuriated me. I thought it wasn't a very constructive way to build an industry. But it did offer opportunites to filmmakers, including me, that we would not have enjoyed otherwise.

An accountant I knew (he's married to a cousin of mine), a cautious businessman, wanted to explore this new avenue of tax savings for his clients and himself. He proposed setting up a company with me in which he would invest the majority of the money, but I had to be a little bit on the hook too. My investment would again come from my remuneration, as it did for *The Crowd Inside*—but this time the functioning of the company in its development stage would be an adjunct to my other sources of income. My services would become exclusive only when a film would actually go into production, and then I would be completely on board and fully and well paid. So what it meant was, in exchange for some of my time and effort (I determined how much), I had seed money with which to acquire and develop properties. That was really quite good, because the initial money was, and probably still is, the most difficult to get, and I had it—not a lot, but enough to get going.

I acquired two properties—sounds like real estate, and sometimes I wished they were. In film parlance, a property is a book or a concept or a script that can be developed into a film. The first was a Canadian book called *Them Damn Canadians Hanged Louis Riel*. Actually Sara found it for me. Sara devours the newspapers, always did. Except for the sports section, she reads everything, including, of course, the book reviews. She read the review of *Them Damn Canadians* and not only wanted me to read the book, but even insisted I inquire about the rights, and if they were available to promptly buy them. I wish Sara had been a producer; I would never have been out of work.

I read the review, read the book, loved it, phoned the author, made a deal and bought it. This was in 1971. Then I hired Ted Allen to co-write a screenplay with me based on the novel.

I also made a deal with Gordon Pinsent to option his completed screenplay *The Missus*. It was a story about a character called John Munn, a miner in Newfoundland. It was about John and his missus, who, like the island, like the town, like the mine, is the rock of his life. It was a perfect part for Colleen Dewhurst, who was Canadian, but I wanted to interest her ex-husband, George C. Scott, in the part of John. So I convinced Gordie that the part ought to be expanded and the point of view shifted to accommodate the newly developed character of John—and further I didn't want to go to an actor like Scott with a script called *The Missus*. With the new emphasis, it made sense to call it *John and the Missus*.

These two scripts held out the promise of reward in the future, but Sara and I felt as though we'd already become millionaires when, two years and two months after Tobaron was born, Sara gave birth to a baby boy. Adam was born November 28, 1972. First we were two, then we were three, and now we were four. We were blessed, a perfect family: Sara and me and a daughter and a son. They used to call that a millionaire's family. We never had a million dollars, but we were indeed rich.

With the commercials I was making, the financial tide was turning. There was a high daily rate for directing commercials, and acting in them resulted in a rewarding flow of residuals. As well, acting gigs in television and film were starting slowly to come my way again. Not only was the larger apartment we needed within reach, but I was able, on special occasions, to buy (on the instalment plan) gifts of jewellery for Sara. I didn't like jewellery for myself—I still didn't wear a watch or even a wedding ring—but I loved it on Sara, particularly antique jewellery.

There was a jewellery store down the block where we used to window shop, even occasionally stopping in to browse, called The Gold Shoppe. The items were exquisite works of art with interesting histories. It was a joy just to look at them. Certainly for me it was more joyful when we just looked. From our occasional visits to The Gold Shoppe, I got an idea of what Sara liked, and what she liked was always tasteful and, with a little planning, almost affordable.

When Sara went to the hospital for Adam's birth, I presented her with a cameo ring I had purchased to match the necklace and bracelet I had given her on the birth of Tobaron. I didn't want to wait for the baby to be born. Just at this point, the doctor told us to go home: it had been a false alarm. A couple of weeks later she got the signal again. I took her back to the hospital, and then went out to The Gold Shoppe. This time I bought her a marcasite ring with an intricate little watch set into the face of it. No sooner had I given it to her than the doctor told us we should go home: another false alarm. I was beginning to worry about this new tradition I had started, and I also wondered about this new kid's sense of timing. A few weeks later she went into labour, and this time it was the real thing. The brooch I gave her when Adam was born is majestic, made of agate, shaped like a medal and worthy of royalty. Why not? Sara deserved a medal after ten months of pregnancy. And Adam was worth the wait. We had a beautiful baby boy.

Buying gifts for Sara was all the more special because the first gifts of jewellery I gave her were not bought by me; they were remembrances from my mother, gifts through me but from my mother, to Sara. The wedding ring I gave Sara was a friendship ring my mother had given me to bestow during courtship on the girl I intended to marry. It was given, I'm sure, with the hope that I would soon find her a daughter-in-law. It was set with a tiny diamond. More would follow: I inherited what was called a cocktail watch with little diamonds on it, plus a very substantial one-of-a-kind flower-shaped diamond ring.

Sara created her own wedding ring from the friendship ring, using its little diamond as a centrepiece and surrounding it with all the little diamonds from the cocktail watch. As for the flower-shaped diamond ring, it was so special that I decided to wait and see if the marriage would last; only upon being convinced of that would I give it to her. So I waited—a whole twenty-four hours. The day after we got married I gave it to Sara.

The first special gift that I bought for Sara was early in our marriage, even before Tobaron was born. It was 1969. I remember the date because it was just after Dubček and his government fell in Czechoslovakia. The following week I was on location in Prague, filming at the famous Barrandov Studios. The film was called *The Last Act of Martin Weston*, a Czech/Canadian co-production. Theatre was thriving at that time, with seventeen repertory companies in Prague alone, and I was privileged to work with some of those actors in the film. Although very dark politically, Prague was a beautiful city, very romantic, particularly at night in the falling snow. The air was crisp, but I didn't feel that cold, and on the boulevard in Prague's medieval Wenceslaus Square, I could see the heroic statue of King Wenceslaus on horseback, symbolically weathering and protecting Prague against all storms. This ambiance was all the more enchanting with snow crunching underfoot.

I found myself thinking of Sara as I walked through the snow-covered square. Just then I happened by a shop where the most exquisite and delicate works of art in antique crystal were displayed. The city of Prague seemed to be filled with artists and craftspeople who worked in glass, crystal and wood. I was lucky enough to find an antique, hand-carved crystal *bonbonnière*—an elegant piece of history sculpted to suit my Sara. No more inherited gifts; from that point on, all the jewellery and other fine things like crystal, paintings or sculptures were gifts from me, although Sara likes to say when asked about any of them, "Oh, that's a little something from a man I know."

The man she knows was becoming more of a family man. For a guy who had once said that career came first and family second, I was growing more aware of how mistaken I had been. We were blossoming: we became a family of four, we graduated from one apartment to another, twice, and continued expanding. With each kid and each move, our family and surroundings took on new personality and character.

All the while, my career was expanding too. I was acting and directing and developing scripts—when it was all put together, I had substantial activity in my chosen profession. Nevertheless, despite all the activity, if it weren't for the fullness of family, I might have felt like I was marking time, waiting for something big to happen. And I knew, and Sara knew too, that that would one day happen. I had blown an opportunity with *The Crowd Inside* because I wasn't ready. Then I had walked away from *Only God Knows* because I realized it had only the appearance of opportunity. I was getting ready for whatever came next. Something was percolating, and when it bubbled up to the top, I would be ready. Somehow, family and career were intertwined in my preparation. I had always wanted a career combined with the normalcy of traditional life as I had known it in my own childhood, and it was happening with Sara.

Work and family were spiritually intertwined and physically on top of each other. We liked living in the centre of town, and the fact that the Colonnade was on University of Toronto land made the rent more reasonable (I never understood why but gladly accepted). So when a three-bedroom suite became available at the Colonnade, we moved up. The kids had a room, we had a room and the third room was an office-cum-den. As soon as the kids got bigger, which they did day by day, I was ousted from the den. I still needed office space, and we still liked where we lived. Time to expand again. It dawned on us that we seldom sat on the balcony, and when we barbecued out there we got into trouble with the neighbours, the building superintendent and sometimes even the fire department, so we decided to enclose the balcony to create an office. Now the kids occupied two rooms, we had our room and I had my office.

But daily the need for more space grew. My life, whether I acknowledged it or not, was not just my career. My life was Sara, and my life was these two children, Tobaron and Adam. Their personalities needed to emerge too. No matter how overbearing mine might be, they were not going to be stopped.

One night I heard Tobaron's tiny feet padding along the floor in the hall. I got out of bed and followed her into the living room. Unnoticed, I watched as she walked to the window and gazed out into the night. Standing there in her flowered nightgown and long, gorgeous locks, she looked like an angel. She was mesmerized by something, something that was as much inside her as it was outside the windows in the night. I in turn was mesmerized by her wide-eyed focus. I stayed hidden from her sight as she seemed almost otherworldly, and I didn't want to intrude. Finally, she turned and I watched her walk back to her room and get into bed with a little smile of satisfaction on her face. I don't know what it meant, or whether it was just my reading of her behaviour, but I found it deeply satisfying, a bit awesome even, to see her personality emerging—this little girl becoming her own person.

I remember one evening at the dining-room table a few years

later, when we lived in our first house. It was during *King of Kensington* by then, and Tobaron was eight years old. I leaned over to her as Sara and the housekeeper were serving the four of us supper, and I started to sing a song to Tobaron that was popular when I was a kid: "There's my girl, take a look at her, she belongs to me." I was being loving, and for sure I was being cute, perhaps too cute to suit her precociousness. She looked up at me and said, "Daddy, I belong to me!" Sara and I looked at each other with pride as well as amusement, wondering, "Where did she learn that?"

She didn't learn it from us. Maybe it was the times? But no, we thought she was too young to be absorbing ideas and attitudes from the emerging feminist movement and the general drive towards self-realization. But bravo! Who cared where it came from? Here was a little person who had come into the world as all of us do, regardless of what is learned later, with her own personality and character. When I heard her say that to me at the age of eight, I thought back to the incident in our apartment when she was just two years old, fascinated by, and unafraid of, the night.

Back then, while we were still in the Colonnade before Adam was born, Tobaron shared her room with our first nanny, Debbie Fast. We needed a nanny because Sara had decided to go back to work. She got a job as a court reporter—among her special skills must be included the ability to take verbatim shorthand as fast as lawyers, judges, plaintiffs, defendants and witnesses can talk—sometimes all at once.

Debbie was a nineteen-year-old Mennonite girl from Steinbach, Manitoba. She was at Bible college for part of the day, so between Sara and Debbie, and including some of my time as well, we coordinated schedules to care for Tobaron. Many accommodations were made—including accepting Debbie's wish to say grace every night before dinner. Why not? It was lovely, touching and sometimes inspirational, as the wording was improvised every night. A Christian ritual that became our ritual because the words didn't run counter to our beliefs, as far as we were concerned, and even served to remind us of how lucky we were and how thankful we should be.

One night Ted Allan and I worked right up until dinner so we invited him to join us. Sara and Debbie served steaming bowls of chicken soup. Very appetizing, but we were waiting for Debbie to say grace, as had become our custom. Ted, however, was already into the soup; indeed, he was all over it, with one arm around the bowl as though protecting it and the other rapidly ladling the soup into his mouth. We sat quietly. I was amused, but Sara and Debbie probably felt a little awkward, anticipating even more embarrassment. Debbie awaited our instruction. The only sounds were coming from Ted and his soup. Suddenly Ted became aware of this. He paused and looked up, questioningly, as if to say, "Why don't you start?" I nodded to Debbie. But first she said to Ted, "Do you mind if I pray?"

He promptly replied, "Do you mind if I don't?" and then, as though not missing a stroke, he continued with his soup. Debbie calmly said grace for herself and for us.

A few minutes later, Ted said to Debbie, "I used to have faith like that, but Stalin let me down."

Debbie, who has always been generous in her thanks to us for helping to broaden her outlook, wrote these words to us some years later: "It was beyond my comprehension how anyone could possibly confuse God with Stalin, but when I saw a documentary on Ted and realized the connection he had with Communism and his fight against fascism, the faith comparison became much more clear."

This fervour of Ted's was perfect for me and for our work together on *Them Damn Canadians*. It helped to fuel a vision I had of the behaviour of the two central characters based on conscience and morality. Our efforts resulted in a film script called *Joe and the Boy*.

Joe and the Boy is a story about a man who reluctantly agrees to take his seemingly delicate thirteen-year-old nephew on a trip to drum up prospects for the family's mule-train business, which is being eclipsed by real trains—the locomotives spreading across the

West. It becomes a two-year odyssey as the two travel together throughout the Western states and Prairie provinces, the boy learning all the while from his rugged uncle, who is the epitome of the Wild West troubleshooter and scout. Joe cares so little for his nephew, at least in the beginning, that he doesn't even learn his name, he just calls him "Boy." They come across lots of danger and lots of fun, nefarious wolfers, Indian wars, whorehouses, saloons and gunfights. Fiction flirts with fact as many of the people they encounter are real historical personalities, and finally fact and fiction coincide at the hanging of Uncle Joe's friend Louis Riel. The boy grows into a man as a result of his experiences and adventures with his uncle. The uncle, the reluctant teacher, begins to rely on the boy, who in the end is man enough to save his uncle's life.

This turned into a marvellous screenplay with great potential. I would attribute most of our success in writing the screenplay to James McNamee's enchanting novel, which immediately draws the reader in, so that you want to ride along with Joe and the boy. His story and characterizations, his sense of fun, truth and adventure, gave us at once a foundation, guidance and liftoff. In fact, the script garnered a lot of attention, but in 1972–1973 the great genre of the Western had temporarily played itself out. John Wayne and Clint Eastwood were wearing suits and ties. *Bashert*? Unfortunately, fate is fickle, but fate has fun with us in its twists and turns. This script proved to be very important in the development of my career nonetheless. The whole trip of writing it through to trying to package it was a wonderful episode in my life.

The emotional, egotistical fights with Ted Allan during the writing of *Joe and the Boy* were frequent and explosive, but always ended in "hugging and kissing" and then loftily attributing our differences to the "creative struggle." During some of these creative confrontations, Sara, who had never heard such passion in the workplace, worried that we would come to blows. I would yell something like, "Leave your Commie Jewish family out of this story about Joe

Campbell, a goyishe cowboy!" Ted would fire back, "Take my name off the script!" And I would counter, "Put that in writing!"

So Sara would start to cook something. The aroma drew Ted and me from the dining-room table, where we were working, into the kitchen to sample whatever she was creating. The one time I remember most clearly, it was potato latkes. We hovered around her in the kitchen and ate them as they came off the frying pan, and quickly forgot, or at least put into perspective, whatever it was we were arguing about.

On another night Ted and I were very much in concert about a certain issue, or should I say a fascinating phenomenon, that I'd heard of but never encountered before: a pregnant woman's cravings. Sara suddenly had to have root beer. I said, "Sure, honey. I'll go downstairs and get you some." There was a convenience store on the ground floor. I came back up with some cans of Hires root beer. No, it had to be A&W root beer! At that time there was only one A&W in Toronto that I knew of, and it was near the airport. The Colonnade is downtown, about three-quarters of an hour's drive away. "Aw, honey, please. This is just as good." No. It had to be A&W! I didn't have a car, and it was raining.

Ted said, "Come on. I'll drive you out to the airport." Ted's car was what in Los Angeles would be called "transportation." It took more than an hour to get to the airport. As we chugged out there, I wondered whatever happened to the fabled craving for ice cream and pickles. After more than two hours we returned with what I hoped would satisfy Sara's craving: a huge jug of A&W root beer.

"Here it is, honey!"

"Oh, thanks," she said sweetly, "but I don't want it any more."

At moments like this, it was good to remember her kindness with the latkes.

With the scripts for *John and the Missus* and *Joe and the Boy*, I was now equipped with two properties that made the joint venture with my accountant partner worthwhile. The thing to do now was get a star to express interest and then perhaps the other elements would fall into place. Although George C. Scott turned it down, *John and the Missus* had attracted the interest of Colleen Dewhurst and Robert Shaw, who had just made a big impact in *The Sting* and *Jaws*. But the package, perhaps because of my lack of a track record as a producer/director, wasn't raising enough interest from the distributors. Still, there was life and hope in it.

Joe and the Boy had attracted the attention of David Dortort, whom I met while we were both scouting locations to shoot Westerns in Alberta. He was the producer of two of the most successful television Western series ever, *Bonanza* and *High Chaparral*. That represented about twenty years of TV episodes. He loved episodic TV, because of residuals: "You make money while you sleep!" As successful as he was, he was still a TV producer, not a film producer, and with me in the package, more clout was needed. He got the script to Ted Post, who had just directed Clint Eastwood in *Hang 'em High*, a very successful Western. Dortort tried to get them both to commit to the project.

Although Eastwood apparently liked the script, he felt his character should rescue Louis Riel. When it was pointed out to him that this was Canadian history, and that Riel was indeed hanged, Eastwood's rejoinder was, "I know what my audience expects of me." There was something to be learned here, something about market orientation; after all, history has proven Mr. Eastwood to be an astute filmmaker. Dortort suggested I rewrite to accommodate him. Well, I wasn't about to change history, but I did like the challenge of fiction intertwining with fact and coming within inches of changing it—an entertaining device, as I said earlier, if it works. I rewrote the scene so that Uncle Joe makes a valiant but desperate attempt to rescue Riel. Although Post and Eastwood, I'm told, liked the rewrites, they decided against the Western genre altogether, opting instead to repeat his Dirty Harry role in *Magnum Force*.

I don't think Eastwood did another Western for some years. But friendships flourished. Ted Post and I, in particular, got along very well, and later on, as a result of this, we worked together, and remain good friends to this day.

The firm in which my partner in the joint venture was a senior partner was, and still is, a major international accounting firm. He found out that one of his partners in the Los Angeles branch of the firm represented Lorne Greene. (Lorne had of course starred in David Dortort's *Bonanza*.) We sent him the script of *Joe and the Boy* by inter-office memo. He was impressed and wanted to meet me. At the same time, I was able to get both scripts, through an assistant director friend of mine, to Lee Marvin. Lee expressed interest in both and also wanted to meet, but not until he finished the project he was currently working on, which was the American Film Theatre production of Eugene O'Neill's *The Iceman Cometh*, with Lee playing the coveted role of Hickey. He said he was "monosyllabic" vis-à-vis "taking meetings" while making a movie, and so we should meet when he finished. I would wait.

I arranged both meetings for the same trip. This was good, because there wasn't enough money in my company for two trips; I needed all the money for script development. I flew economy class, but I didn't have enough money to rent a car or stay at a posh hotel or eat in trendy restaurants (which is, after all, part of the business). Neither lack of fancy food nor the inability to stay at a happening place was a big problem; but being without transportation rendered me almost useless in Los Angeles.

I stayed with long-time friend and fellow Canadian actor Stephen Young. He was glad to put me up. One thing about actors, they usually come to one another's aid. But Stephen couldn't lend me his car because he needed it himself. So when Lorne Greene's secretary called to invite me to join Lorne for lunch at the Universal commissary the next day, I was stuck for transportation. I started out early in the morning, hitchhiking and taking public transportation. This was unheard of in LA, especially for a producer with two potentially big-time projects under his arm. It felt strangely contradictory to be bumming lifts while carrying, I felt, the two hottest properties in Hollywood. Regardless, I made it there in time for our lunch meeting.

It was exciting for me. I had never been to a studio commissary before. I'd only heard about them, probably in movie-magazine hype. Still, for me, the "commissary" was an exotic word. I was soon to find out that it's simply a cafeteria by another name to lend it importance. What occupied my mind as I got closer to my destination was that Lorne Greene was interested in the leading role in *Joe and the Boy* and I thought he was too old; instead, I wanted him for the boy's father (Joe's brother), a much smaller part, but a terrific cameo. Well, I would try to convince him that my plan and goal was to get stars of his calibre and stature for the many outstanding cameos in the script, so that he would be in good company.

I guess I wasn't successful in winning him over with the cameo argument. He wasn't offended, but he did seem more interested in which important directors and producers were "taking meetings" or "doing lunch" at tables adjacent to us. We each had scrambled eggs and a glass of wine—a light lunch and, fortunately, a light bill, because when the check was propped between the salt and pepper shakers, Lorne just kept on looking around the room at who was having lunch and wondering what deals were being talked about, seldom glancing back at our table. I couldn't tell whether he was genuinely preoccupied with stargazing or whether he was just trying to avoid the bill. He certainly wasn't making a move for it. I thought, "But *he* invited *me* to lunch!" After a few more minutes of stewing, I decided I'd better pick up the tab. I was more amused than put off, because I knew this was an anecdote I would savour for long time.

Out of fairness to Lorne, I must add that when we later became friendly and worked together, he certainly reciprocated. However, at the time we lunched over my film projects at the Universal Studio commissary, we weren't a pair of friends or co-workers; I was the producer and he was the actor. I was the potential employer, he the potential employee. And as Sara said when I told her the story, if you're going to be the producer, you better be able to pay the shot.

I had a script conference with David Dortort on *Joe and the Boy* at his Tudor home, hidden at the end of a long, winding drive up some wooded hills in Bel Air—spectacular and spooky. After all, the previous owner had been Basil Rathbone, who had starred for years as Sherlock Holmes. You almost had to be a sleuth to find the place, it was so carefully hidden. At one point during our meeting I had to go to the washroom. When I came back, instead of resuming the meeting right away, I asked if we could take a break while I phoned my wife. I got Sara on the phone, back home in Toronto, and I said, "I just used this guy's john. He's got gold-plated faucets over the sink that are worth more than our whole house!"

I was always quick to tell Sara, in person or over the phone, what was happening in Hollywood, what and whom I saw. Since my voluntary departure in the mid-sixties, I thought that I was no longer in awe of Hollywood, but truthfully I could still be like a kid in a candy store, my face pressed against the window looking in. For instance, there was the time years later that I met Sammy Davis Jr. This was when I was doing *Cagney and Lacey*, and I was a guest at his house for dinner. It was a small dinner party of about eight, so he and I had a chance to talk quite a bit on a one-to-one basis, and we got along well. I wanted to share this with Sara. It must have been 2 a.m. in Toronto, but I phoned home. Sara usually got furious when I did that, because she would have difficulty falling asleep again. But as soon as she answered, I put Sammy on the phone, and from asleep she became aglow. She knew right away that this was no imitation; this was the real thing. And sometime after that, still during the making of *Cagney and Lacey*, Sammy invited us for dinner because he loved to cook and wanted to cook for Sara.

Lee Marvin finished working on the low-budget production of *The Iceman Cometh*. I stress the low budget, because, before I could meet with Lee, I had to talk with his agent, Myer Mishkin, who was very concerned about budgets. All the stars who appeared in American Film Theater productions worked for a fraction of their normal fee (I had heard it was as little as $25,000) for the rare opportunity to perform one of the great roles from classic American theatre on film. Mishkin, who was getting paid 10 percent of very little, needed Marvin to get back up into the high six or seven figures as quickly as possible. So he said to me, "Look, kid, forget this. I know Lee likes the script! I know he likes you, but it's not gonna happen."

"Why not?" I asked.

"Because when I'm talking to you, I'm talking to some hick kid from Canada, and what kind of commission am I looking at—10 percent of what? I'm looking at 10 percent of 'if come maybe,' that's what I'm lookin' at! I can't let Lee do this."

Lee had to support and go along with his agent of (at that time) over twenty years' standing. There was loyalty between them. But there was also respect between Lee and me. He liked both *Joe and the Boy* and *John and the Missus*, so he very considerately said to me, "I can't say no to you just like that. Please let's talk about it over dinner." And he invited me to have dinner with just him and his wife at their home in Malibu Colony.

That's about a forty-five-minute drive from Hollywood. I explained my situation, expecting that I would, as a result, have to pass on the invitation. To my surprise, this elicited even more thoughtfulness from Mr. Marvin. He offered to come all the way in to Hollywood, pick me up and drive me all the way out to Malibu Colony. Stephen's house was on Palm Street or Palm Drive, something like that. Lee agreed to pick me up on the corner of the street. I did not know at the time that there are several streets with similar names in that area where Hollywood borders Beverly Hills. I stood there waiting and waiting, thinking that maybe I was dealing with some "movie star" who didn't mind standing me up or coming very late. The fact was that this dear man had gone to every "Palm Drive" on the map before he finally got to me.

It was fairly common knowledge then that Lee Marvin was a heavy drinker. I realized as our dinner progressed that he had had only two drinks during the entire evening. It impressed me a great deal that he would take such care to stay sober, particularly, I thought, in order to be an attentive host. I found this big lug of a tough-guy movie star to be a very sensitive man. The meal was simple, meat and potatoes, that his wife cooked. It was nicer than going out. After dinner he handed me the Oscar he had won for *Cat Ballou* (the closest I would probably ever get to one), and later we walked on the beach. He talked animatedly about both properties, even excitedly about certain scenes, like an actor does when he can taste a role. I was proud, as though there had already been some achievement.

When it came time to go home, I felt that I couldn't ask him to take me all the way back into town, but he insisted. As we were driving back, he said to me, "I know you are going to make it. I don't know how you are going to make it, because I don't know how anyone makes it. No one does. There is no pattern for success. It's an individual thing. You'll make it your own way."

I already knew that about making it. I had my own understanding of those words. But what he said, and the fact that he said it at all, meant a lot to me at that moment, perhaps because, although I had developed two good properties and taken them this far, it seemed pretty clear that I was not going to succeed in making either of them into a film. Maybe it was just a kind thing to say to a colleague who was struggling, but the very fact that someone so well established would say such encouraging words has stayed with me ever since.

Although I would like to have remembered Lee Marvin as the star of my film, I still remember him with respect, not only as an actor, but as a true mensch and a gentleman.

My option on Gordon Pinsent's script ran out and the property reverted to him. Some years later he made a film of *John and the Missus*. I still own *Joe and the Boy*. It's a wonderful script, but it was never made. Mind you, it rewarded me and my career in other ways.

CHAPTER 19

Kensington, By Way of Rosedale

Our first house. It had to happen. With my office in the enclosed balcony, the personal and professional in my life were, if anything, toppling over each other. Even with Tobaron going out to nursery school every day, our living quarters were too cramped. My office space was regularly invaded, and wherever else I took my work in that apartment, I was in someone's way. Still, if it were up to me, we'd probably be living there even now. It took Sara's instigation and encouragement to move us onward and upward.

We found a dream of a house on Roxborough Street East. Immediatcly to the east of Yonge in midtown Toronto is the fashionable enclave known as Rosedale, often thought of as upper-crust WASP. But we moved into an area that was becoming quite yuppie—I even bought a Volvo. Ours was the first house east of Yonge Street: we just made it! I would often joke that we were one of the first families of Rosedale, but in fact our new house was just beside the railroad tracks, albeit on the right side of them. We were very near the Rosedale subway station, and all day long we would hear the rumble of the subway trains accentuated every few minutes by a screeching halt as though the cars were sliding with huge cleats into second base. Within moments, the steel wheels would again build up to speed as the train barrelled out of the station. We would look at each other and I would say, as though in reference to some distant sound, "Did you hear that?"

"Hear what?" Sara would lie.

"No, I didn't hear it either," I would pretend to agree. "Hardly noticed it."

We were determined to love our dream house, because it was a gorgeous Georgian townhouse with its own little courtyard, entered through an imposing gate. There was a dog run alongside the house (we would soon get a dog), and a patioed backyard. We had a splendid master bedroom, and each of the kids had a room. As well, there was a large recreation room downstairs, adjacent to which was a bedroom for a full-time nanny, and there seemed to be bathrooms everywhere. It was not a huge house (when I was interviewed some years later on the *fifth estate,* they referred to it as "modest"), but the living room and dining room were spacious, and that was great because we loved to entertain. There was a little room off the living room that became my office.

So, with what was left over from my inheritance plus some help from Sara's dad and whatever savings we had, we put together enough for a down payment of almost a third of the purchase price. In the fall of 1973, we moved in. Onward and upward.

We had many great parties in that house, for ourselves, for our friends and for the kids. Birthday parties. Hanukkah parties. Seder services. Polling parties for candidates who interested us. Dinner parties. Theme parties. Actually, we started all that partying back in the Colonnade with theme parties. For example, we had fish-and-chip parties, with the food wrapped in British newspapers, in honour of visiting British friends.

Another of my favourites was our Academy Awards party, which we started because we seemed to be the only ones in our group of friends, all of us in the early stages of our careers, who had a colour television set. Each of the guests, all of whom were in the TV and film industries, would bring a bottle of wine in exchange for a scorecard, resulting in a pot for the winner of approximately fifty bottles of wine. We had that many guests, even in our apartment, and two or three rented TV sets in addition to our own, strategically placed around the apartment so all could see the Oscars. Whoever scored closest to the actual results in Los Angeles went home with a wine cellar.

Of course the most special parties of all were the birthday parties. Sara would always bake the cake herself, and it never failed to lovingly reflect whatever either of the children was fascinated by at the time. One year, for instance, Adam loved the zoo more than anything else, so Sara sculpted and decorated the cake to look like a lion. Tobaron was delighted by butterflies, so Sara delighted her with a cake shaped and coloured like a monarch butterfly.

Sara spent as much as she could of the first few years of our children's lives at home. (Her court reporting was on a part-time basis.) She wanted them to smell cookies baking when they walked in the door. And her culinary skills were remarkable—and delicious. The kids didn't like salad, so she invented CN Tower salad, which consisted of long stalks of celery and carrots standing on end, held together by a round slice of apple jammed onto the stalks, with a slice of orange on top of that and a little cherry tomato fitted on top of the fruit. Tobaron and Adam were each presented with a miniature CN Tower on their plates. Me too.

As well as cooking and caring for us, Sara also sang to us; she still does. She had trained for the opera when she was younger, and even sang professionally. When asked to corroborate this, she'll quickly clarify, "But just in the chorus." At home, however, I was treated to her solos. Once, when we were still in the apartment, I came in and heard her singing "Un bel dì" from Puccini's *Madame Butterfly*. It was in our smallest apartment, the first one. I stood quietly and listened, enraptured. She stopped suddenly, feeling the presence of someone, and came running out of the bedroom. "Did you hear me singing?" She was shy about it.

"No, I didn't hear a thing."

"Yes you did!"

"Yes I did, and I loved it—please don't stop."

Often I had to coax, but I would eventually succeed. It was easier when it was for the benefit of the kids. I used to love to listen to her singing "Teddy Bear's Picnic."

A few years later, during *King of Kensington*, when there were many requests for my participation in community and charity functions, I had the honour of being a co-host on the first Variety Club of Ontario telethon. There were only a few Canadian entertainers with high profiles, and we were all continually being asked to help attract attention to worthwhile causes—people such as Don Harron and his talented wife, Catherine McKinnon, Barbara Hamilton, Bruno Gerussi and Pierre Berton. I was flattered to be amongst them. I co-hosted with Monty Hall and Don Harron, and helped Bev Oda, Global TV's producer of the show, to assemble the talent for it. That annual telethon is in high demand now—that is, a lot of performers want to appear on it—but for that first one we had difficulty finding enough talented people to fill the whole twenty-four hours. So I came home from a production meeting a couple of days before the show and said to Sara, "You're singing on the Variety Club telethon."

She said, "Are you kidding? I haven't sung professionally in years!"

But I convinced her. I'm sure it was more because of the importance of the purpose than because of the beautiful new outfit I promised to buy her to wear on the show. What a trooper! I was so proud. Paraphrasing a line from the song "There's No Business Like Show Business," she joked, "and the next day they hung a star on my dressing-room door!" She had just one quick rehearsal, a few hours before showtime. Although she was nervous, she overcame it, and her voice was beautiful—as beautiful as she looked in a new blue ensemble matched by the blue of her eyes. She sang, without irony (I think), "What I Did for Love."

Public service was not uncommon in our lives; we were both

brought up to consider it an integral part of life. At around the time we moved into our house, a terrific idea for a series of public service messages for the Toronto Recycling Action Committee (TRAC) was brought to me by Ed Cowan, who was a public relations and advertising executive, a creative guy with a lot of vitality and genuine caring for the community. I would act in the spots, and direct and co-produce with Ed. They were to be scripted by Marion Waldman, a funny and very clever writer. These public service messages were intended to make people more aware of their responsibility for our urban environment and ecology. They supported the TRAC recycling program, a precursor to Toronto's Blue Box program.

I played a garbage collector, a kind of citified Will Rogers, who talks to the camera on a one-to-one basis, expressing homespun humour and philosophy. As I went about my work, I would discuss topics such as grocery shopping, pointing out overpackaging of products; conserving and composting; waste disposal and recycling. Each spot ended with the slogan "Bundle up for Wednesday," which was at that time Toronto's collection day for newspapers. The commercials were award-winning (again the prestigious Clio) for me and for all of us. They served their purpose while being entertaining and catchy, and we were all very proud of them. They were also, in a way, though I didn't know it at the time, a precursor to *King of Kensington*.

First came another movie. This was an offer from an American producer, Harold Sobel. It was an encouraging and timely surprise, because Revenue Canada's tax loopholes were closing, and the private sector, without fiscal incentives and protection, was getting gun-shy. As a result, there were many good film directors doing whatever episodic TV they could get because there were so few feature film assignments to be had. People were hungry for work. As a matter of fact, while I was in the producer's office in New York City finalizing negotiations, he was getting phone calls from established film directors in Toronto, trying to get him to change his mind in favour of them. For some reason, though, he decided upon me, perhaps because he sensed how important it was to me to make a successful film.

Now, success has to be assessed within a context, namely, in this instance, the film I was contracted to make. It was *My Pleasure Is My Business,* it starred Xaviera Hollander (the woman known as the Happy Hooker) and its purpose was to make money. It was to be made as inexpensively as possible and targeted to the market for the biggest return it could bring. The budget was to be $300,000—small even in 1973–1974, but today probably the lunch budget on most pictures. Its schedule was to be twenty days—short for a feature film. There was no deceiving myself about silk purses. My effort, in spite of logistics and the material provided, would be directed towards making something playable. This goal was achieved. The film came in on schedule and on budget, that I know for a fact, and turned out to be marketable, grossing I was told approximately $15 million.

Xaviera Hollander, who had, as I understood it, been expelled from the United States but allowed entry into Canada, feared that if she left Canada, she would not be allowed to return. So the producer, who would rather have made the film in Germany, settled on Canada. The producer preferred Germany because German actors were more comfortable with pornographic content in filmmaking. Although it still contained some ingredients to satisfy the voyeur, shooting *My Pleasure Is My Business* in Canada resulted in a film that was softer, essentially non-pornographic.

Nevertheless, I'd be lying if I denied that it hurt when I was criticized for associating with a notorious prostitute. This, as well as disparagement of the film, caused some embarrassment. But what the hell? What else should I have expected? I *was* associated with her; we were, after all, working on the same project, and we all knew what we were making. So, if I disregarded the critical comments, didn't take myself too seriously but stayed focused on the purpose, on the fun to be created onscreen despite the constraints and overall challenges of the project, I would came away in my own eyes a winner.

Xaviera played a character called Gabriella, who is deported from the US for being "too sexy." She is refused entry into all countries except the principality of Gestalt, whose corrupt government accepts her presence in an attempt to take the heat off its shady activities by drawing attention to her "immorality." Needless to say, the government's attempts fail and the culprits are brought to justice, while Gabriella, after lampooning corrupt politics, investigative reporting, undercover detectives and international spies, emerges more popular than ever. Sex is here to stay!

I surrounded her with some of Canada's most talented and award-winning actors, such as Colin Fox, George Sperdakos, Jackie Burroughs, Henry Ramer, Jayne Eastwood, Monica Parker and many others, all of whom by virtue of their presence assisted her performance (not to mention the acting lessons I was giving her from shot to shot). Similarly, the crew was excellent, led by director of photography Harry Makin, with whom I'd worked at the CBC and whose feature film career I'd helped launch with *The Crowd Inside*.

With all that skill assembled in cast and crew, it was possible for me to meet the challenge of a tight schedule and small budget and still get the most fun and substance out of the material. For example, the script called for a chase sequence. The page merely said two words, "The Chase," nothing else—the implication being, "The rest is up to you, Mr. Director." The producer was hoping for cars; what he got was a comic caper with mopeds.

There was a party scene with little more description than the chase sequence—just "The Party." A page of film script generally represents approximately sixty seconds of film time. The description of the party was less than an eighth of a page, yet we improvised a fifteen-minute sequence of sexy send-up in two days of shooting. The camera, like a peeping Tom, floated through the bacchanalian bash, an orgy of kinky comedy and phallic fun. The party-goers were all *femmes fantastiques*, handsome hunks and wonderful weirdos, in costumes that were alternately bizarre or scanty. Extras and bit players would appear in the beginning of a shot masquerading in one outfit and then step out of the frame only to reappear as another character in another costume in the back end of the shot. Finally, everyone followed Hollander, all ending up naked in the pool—except Jackie Burroughs, who, perhaps wisely, chose to camouflage herself in the character of an old granny, jumping into the pool fully clothed.

The result was a satirical sexploitation film that would not have been rated Restricted if it had starred someone else. But with Ms. Hollander in the lead, it got an R rating, and this suited the producer's strategy because it specified the market he was targeting, although in truth, because it was more romp than rump, I don't think it fulfilled that market's expectations.

The making of this film was excellent practice for me, but the selling of it was a new and valuable learning experience. The producer and I had got along well. He appreciated my control, direction and leadership over the project, and particularly my guidance, creatively and logistically, of its star through the maze of a filmmaking schedule. He offered me a bonus of $5,000 in exchange for guiding her through the promotion campaign prior to the opening in Toronto. I had never done that before, but this producer had good instincts, and I needed the bonus, which brought my remuneration to a grand total of $15,000. With little work available, that was better than a kick in the ass. My work on the film reaffirmed in my own eyes my expertise with budget and schedule (in contrast to *The Crowd Inside*), as well as my creative resourcefulness with available material. Therefore, I wanted the picture to make money for the producer and his investors; if it didn't, the experience was incomplete.

In spite of many people proclaiming their distaste for the Hollander phenomenon, we nevertheless encountered curiosity everywhere we turned. People wanted to see the film. We drummed up even more interest through the press, radio and television interviews, plus ads and promos. I gave Hollander a theme that suited her and her film persona: "Between and amongst consenting adults there are no perversions, only different versions." This springboarded each of the interviews into fun and parlayed them all into promotion paradise. I learned how important the curiosity factor is in enticing an audience. With Hollander, of course, there was built-in curiosity, whereas in other situations you have to create the curiosity factor.

Toronto has always been one of the major movie-going centres in North America, so the box-office returns in Toronto after the first week were a barometer for sales across the continent. The producer, who was his own distributor, said to me that if I got him a big first week in Toronto, he didn't care about the reviews or the second or third week; he would be able to rack up sales to theatre chains and circuits throughout the United States, Canada and then worldwide—and that's what happened! The second and third weeks did dwindle, but the first week was a big enough gross to encourage sales everywhere he marketed the film.

Of course there was just as much horny humour in the anecdotes surrounding the making of the film as there was in the film itself. Before we started, I had a meeting with Xaviera, during which I generally stressed the importance of discipline and focus, for her own sake as well—she was, after all, the star and part-owner of the film. I pointed out to her that if we came in over budget and had to use contingency funds, it would eat into her salary and points. I don't know if that was true, but it was a good incentive for her to work hard and not screw around. (A deliberate choice of words.) "No screwing around," she agreed. I wanted her to learn her lines the night before, show up for work on time, and be present, prompt and attentive throughout the day. If she did, there would also be the time and opportunity for me to coach her in acting and dialogue delivery, within the context of directing and constructing a scene. If she would apply herself as I wanted her to, I would help her to look good on the screen.

We had an understanding. She took the advice, the warning and my offer to heart, and learned quickly, so much so that she actually thought she was becoming a good actress. This delusion could be problematic. When George Sperdakos's scenes started, we were already two weeks into the schedule. On his first day, believing herself to be that much more experienced than he was, she generously offered him a suggestion on how he should play a certain moment. George's response became a catchphrase on the set. He stopped her from saying any more with, "Hey, I don't tell you how to fuck. You don't tell me how to act."

A couple of weeks after our first pre-production meeting (during which she'd agreed to "no screwing around"), Xaviera and I participated in another meeting, this one called by the associate producer and the writer. The four of us sat around a lunch table in a crowded restaurant, Xaviera opposite me. During the course of the discussion, I felt something gently rubbing my crotch. I looked at the other three, and none of them skipped a beat during the businesslike conversation. I glanced down and caught the flash of fiery red toenails. Looking up, I met Xaviera's eyes, silently, mischievously smiling at me, as the other two talked seriously. I said, "Xaviera, I thought we had an understanding!"

"Oh, Al," she winked, "just a little toejob!"

This brought an abrupt finish to the meeting, which was typical of my studious efforts to avoid anything that didn't pertain directly to the filmmaking, earning me the reputation on the set, as far as Monica Parker was concerned, of being a square. Monica played Gabriella's Freudian shrink with a comic German accent, and of course she was just as funny on the screen as she is in real life. Monica has kidded me about *My Pleasure Is My Business* on many occasions since then. She claims that I was unbelievably unaware of what was going on after hours, and even during filming. "You're such a square."

On the contrary, I was well aware of what was going on, and none of it concerned me unless it had a negative impact on the work. I never lost sight of the purpose for which I was hired: to make it for small and sell it for big. The result was that the producer wanted to hire me again!

He had two films scheduled to go, this time in foreign production centres more conducive to exploitation. One was to be called *Whose Child Am I?* (to be shot in a Scandinavian country, if I recall) about test-tube babies, and the other speaks for itself: *Massacre at Central High*. It was good to be offered work, but what was I going to do, make a career out of schlock? On the other hand, there are more than a few celebrated and successful mainstream directors whose careers got their start as they built from one exploitation film to another, finally graduating into mainstream films and even artistry.

While I was deliberating, Perry Rosemond came to my house for a meeting. He had a concept for a television series, a sitcom to be called *King of Kensington*. He had just come back, at John Hirsch's request, from successful work in Los Angeles. The friendship between Perry and John went all the way back to when they were both starting out in Winnipeg. John was now head of television drama at the CBC, and Perry had been working extensively in comedy and variety in LA. There had been a few unsuccessful attempts at sitcom here in Canada. John felt we were lagging behind the States and England, and that it was time for us to have a sitcom that worked. He believed that Perry was the man to make that happen, and Perry in turn was glad to come home and give it his best shot.

Interesting that Perry and John were from Winnipeg—a city of humour and hospitality. Both are means of generating warmth during those long winters of so-called "dry cold." When it came time for the hot comic talents of Winnipeg to get their work produced professionally, it was either travel 1,500 miles east to the CBC studios in Toronto or travel approximately the same distance southwest to the studios of networks in LA. And when, during the first twenty years of CBC TV production, these comic talents were given a colder reception in Toronto than the climate they left in Winnipeg, they found it was just as easy for them to travel the other way, to LA.

The programmers and producers at the CBC in Toronto, apart from a few exceptions like *Wayne and Shuster*, favoured drama over comedy. Drama was considered "meaningful," comedy was frivolous. In those days, the airwaves emanating from the CBC gave you the feeling that we were like some Scandinavian country, with wind and mood blowing through most of our shows. In LA, on the other hand, there was comedy—and it was coming from Winnipeg-inspired writers and producers. Comedy like *The Smothers Brothers Show* and *Sonny and Cher*. Comedy which I'm told a lot of alumni of St. John's Tech in Winnipeg could recognize from skits performed back in their high school days.

Perry was concerned that there was at that time (1974) only a "short list" of talent here in Canada for writing and directing comedy. This was of course before SCTV and the treasure trove of talent for comedy that would be discovered all over Canada in the coming years. So, at the time of this meeting, Perry asked me to read the "bible" on which *King of Kensington* was to be based, plus the pilot script that he had written, with a view to my either writing or directing on the series. After reading the material, we would meet again to talk.

Chapter 20

Where Do I Sign?

"Funny," I said to Perry, "This reads and feels like something I should be playing."

"Funny you should mention that...," was his smiling response, like "gotcha!" It's what he had in mind to begin with. But he didn't make me an offer at that point; first he wanted a screen test. I wasn't exactly offended by this, just a little perturbed by what seemed to me an unnecessary procedure when he already knew I was right for the part. Still, he felt that as a producer he could require a screen test. I don't think he was power-tripping, Perry's not that kind of guy, but I felt it was unnecessary—and so we were at an impasse.

Perry chose another actor to play the part of Larry King for the pilot of *King of Kensington*. This I think was against John Hirsch's wishes, but John felt he had to support his producer's policies. The person chosen was an accomplished actor, but the chemistry between him and the character wasn't right. Complete, accurate and comfortable chemistry between character and actor is ideal casting in any medium, but in television, a close-up medium, a medium of familiarity, it's not only ideal, it's essential. The problem with the casting was partly to blame for a pilot episode that wasn't entirely successful. Still, everyone at the CBC felt the pilot was good enough to go to series—but with recasting.

In the meantime, I had guest-starred in an episode of a cop series the CBC was doing at the time called *Sidestreet*. It starred Donnelly Rhodes and Jonathan Welsh. *Sidestreet* was a show with a twist, at least compared to most US shows: community-conscious cops who tried to communicate with the suspected "perps" (perpetrators of a crime). Whereas the American TV cops mostly shoot first and talk later, on *Sidestreet* it was the other way around.

A season later I directed one of the episodes, because the first one, the one I'd acted in, had turned out so well. So well, in fact, that John Hirsch was able to use a clip from it to show to Perry Rosemond. This way, although I didn't screen test for *King*, Perry got to look at footage of me in something current. Like a modern King Solomon, John Hirsch ensured that both parties had their conditions met; we were all happy and could move ahead.

Needless to say the offer to do thirteen episodes of *King of Kensington* knocked the other offer I'd received—to direct another exploitation film—out of the running. And I was glad of that. But I chose *King* for many reasons. The character of King was an ordinary guy, an Everyman—someone I could relate to, someone I could play. Indeed, as in my philosophy of acting, he was someone I could "be."

I liked what King believed in, in terms of family, neighbourhood and country. He had foibles and failings, but he had conscience and character too. He had street smarts but he could be outsmarted. He was cockey, but he had the confidence to be vulnerable. He was loyal and could always be counted on. He was funny, even able to find humour in the headlines. Most of all, there was love in his life, particularly in the give and take between him and his wife, ultimately and excellently cast with one of the cleverest actors I've ever worked with, Fiona Reid.

I also felt, as John Hirsch and Perry Rosemond did, and indeed the two brilliant writer-producers, Jack Humphrey and Louis del Grande did as well, that our country's entertainment scene needed a successful sitcom, a show that would reflect the country back to itself.

I knew that if this show was a success, it would bring together so much in my life that I was dedicated to. I felt that the show as a whole was a perfect vehicle for the ensemble and for me in particular to strike a chord with the Canadian audience: a show which would not concern itself with what we are not, but rather would focus on what and who we are.

I was delighted when the business affairs department of the CBC asked me to sign a contract, but puzzled by their approach. They were embarrassed, as I saw it, because even though they were in the business of television, they had a snobbish attitude towards it, at least towards the entertainment side of it. This may have been inadvertant, but it was there. They virtually apologized for asking for a three-year commitment, but explained that they had learned it was important to sign an actor for three years just in case the series took off. They had signed John Vernon for only one year at a time on *Wojeck*, for example, and when that series burst into success—as did, simultaneously, Vernon's career—he wasn't available when the numbers indicated they could go ahead with a third year. No Vernon, no star, no show, no third year. But this kind of success doesn't happen often, so I was actually told, as though to reassure me, that I should go ahead and sign for three years, but not to worry, because after the first thirteen episodes I probably wouldn't have to do any more.

I said, "If I do this, it won't be for just thirteen weeks, it won't even be for just three years. It will be for five full years. I intend to do this, so give me the contract. Where do I sign!?"

CHAPTER 21

A Commoner's Kingdom

The next five years were a feast. The initial critical response to *King of Kensington* was mostly positive, even some raves. We made a big impact on the public, something no English Canadian sitcom had ever managed to do before. After some struggle in the ivory towers of the Kremlin (as the CBC executive offices were then known), we emerged, guided by the inspired and tenacious John Hirsch, with an order for another twenty-two episodes.

Perhaps it was the show's unexpected freshness, its unabashed cockiness, or maybe the ingenuous friendliness of it that caused Canadian audiences, in the beginning, to see it as just another successful American sitcom, like the others they watched every week. I was amazed when people on the street would approach me during the first thirteen episodes of *King* in 1975 and say, "We love your show. Enjoy your visit to Canada!" It was as though its success meant it couldn't be Canadian. But the concept, situations and content were Canadian. The actors, writers, producers and directors were Canadian. No, we were a genuinely Canadian show.

Of course the genre of the sitcom had been developed by the Americans. But what difference does that make? Is an opera composed in North America, such as *Louis Riel* or *Porgy and Bess,* any less an opera because it's not European? We were a Canadian show, and I was proud of that. As indeed the network and the Canadian public and even the media mavens soon were too.

As a matter of fact, in the beginning, when we taped on a Friday night and aired the following Monday, we tried to weave in specific references to current events and issues. This changed when we became aware that topicality hurt our chances for reruns (even within Canada) and foreign sales. So without diminishing the Canadian content and personality of the show – maintaining honest references to who we were—the issues became more universal, like alcoholism, adultery, racism, feminism, multiculturalism, national unity, immigration, homelessness, homosexuality, crime and rehabilitation, and so on. We dealt with all the contemporary issues, which may account, at least in part, for our success in both foreign sales and healthy reruns in Canada even today, over twenty-five years later.

The one time that we deviated from "honest references to who we were" was when (over my objections) the writers used the term "district attorney" rather than "Crown prosecutor" because they felt the latter was cumbersome and the former was funny. (Really—that was the argument!) I don't know why I gave in, perhaps because I was sensitive to the growing perception that I was difficult to work with, that I had a temper. But the public by that time had so embraced us as a Canadian show—this episode was probably in the third year—and so identified me with the show that all the negative mail that resulted from using the American term was addressed to me, as though I was personally responsible.

I was determined to make this show a hit, and I knew that morale was a key ingredient. We were dealing with CBC crews who got paid whether we were a hit or not. If we got cancelled, they'd just be moved over to another show, unlike what I was to encounter years later on *Cagney and Lacey*, when the crew's jobs depended on the success of the show. Amongst the tasks I gave myself was to make the crew care whether we succeeded or not. In order to do this I took it upon myself to create a bond with them, in addition to simply kibitzing (which I would do anyway). I would buy a gift on any occasion that came up: a birth in someone's family or if someone was away sick, or got over the sickness and was welcomed back, whatever. Sara would often remind me of the Lorne Greene lunch bill that I had to pick up because I was the producer, and she would point out that in this instance I was *not* the producer. Still, I led the way, perhaps to the producers' liking, perhaps not. I would also buy gifts of flowers or wine for the guest star each week, and oftentimes for the rest of the cast.

Picture my reaction, then, when one day I received a memo from the producers saying, in effect, that I needed to be nicer to my co-workers, particularly the guests. I went ballistic. I charged up three flights of stairs to the producers' offices and demanded to know who'd authorized that memo. They all cowered behind their desks, proclaiming innocence and trying to shift the blame. I said that until someone owned up and apologized to me, I wasn't coming out of my dressing room. I was in almost every scene, so if I didn't come out to work, no work was going to get done.

Hours passed; production time was being wasted. I waited in my dressing room. Finally there was a knock on my door, and when I opened it, there was John Hirsch with a bouquet of roses for me. Solomon-like John Hirsch! Handing me the roses, he said, "Al, please come back to work. What do they know about the emotions of an artist? They're not like you and me, they don't understand. Please come back to work!" He apologized on their behalf. So I got my apology and they saved face. I never learned who the culprit was, but because of John I didn't care and went back to work.

If I was driven, I make no apology for it, even though it could sometimes result in terrific outbursts of temper (like my dad's). After all, I thought, opportunity may knock more than once, but who knows how many times more than once?

My temper is described in anecdotes by colleagues like Ron Singer, a dear friend under whose aegis I later became an adjunct professor of theatre at York University. Ron tells the story of guesting on an episode of *King*. From Monday's rehearsals through to Thursday (the first taping day), according to Ron, I kept requesting some rewriting of the script, but my requests were ignored until after the writer/producers viewed the first taping. On Friday, with only a few hours left before final taping, I was presented with rewrites for about two-thirds of the script. That's a lot of new memorizing to do in a couple of hours. Ron says I was so livid that I physically knocked over the set. I honestly don't remember that, but if it's true—and I have no reason to doubt Ron—I must have been in some advanced state of righteous rage. I do remember the apologetic and sheepish behaviour of the writers, and the hurried study of the revised script. I improvised a great deal—which was an exciting challenge, because I could improvise within a speech or dialogue but always had to hit the right cue for another actor or for a camera-cut (there were four cameras).

If these were examples of "professional" temper, there were also instances of "personal" temper at home. The kids were growing up and we were trying to see to their needs; at the same time, Sara and I were still finding our way. We had all the pressures of a young family, compounded by the pressures at work. I was rehearsing all week, taping three shows at the end of the week, participating (welcomed or not) over the weekend with the editing of the taped shows, and prepping of the next script over that same weekend. On top of all this, there was PR work all week, particularly in whatever time was left on the weekends. It was like living in a pressure cooker. But I was determined to make a hit show in a country that seemed resigned to not having hit shows.

I had to make it work, the family and the career. That wasn't always understood by others, at least not the same way I understood it. I knew that each of us in our family of four had his or her own needs and that I as father and husband should strive to understand. I also wanted my family to understand the task I'd set myself, a task that if achieved, benefited us all. That understanding, both ways, was ultimately achieved under Sara's leadership and mine, but there was lots of tension along the way. And sometimes explosions. Thank God I always directed my anger towards walls or doors and never hit anyone. But even better would have been to ask myself, Where is the humour?

It must've been difficult sometimes to tell from my behaviour that I was making a comedy. Fortunately, Sara never lost her own sense of humour. One time when I lost my temper at home, I swung my fist in the direction of the kitchen door. When it connected, thankfully my knuckles weren't broken, but the door was; there was a big crack in it. I was embarrassed, and I was also concerned about the cost of replacing the door. As I went to work I guiltily asked Sara if she would hang a picture over the crack in the door, so that no one would see it and we wouldn't have to buy a new door. When I got back from work there was an empty frame hanging on the door, enclosing the crack with an inscription at the bottom right-hand corner of the "picture" that read, "Rage, 1977."

From its inception I was determined to achieve more than one purpose with this show. By combining good production with good promotion, I hoped we would create not only a successful sitcom but also an image Canadians could identify with and be proud of. That was my twofold purpose in doing *King of Kensington*.

First of all, of course, the show had to entertain, and as sitcom is a popular art form, it would have to attract a popular audience, that is, a large audience. Its numbers needed to be comparable to those of other successful sitcoms. *All in the Family*, for example, averaged about 3 million Canadian viewers per week. So, even if the show was good, if it didn't reach a large audience, then I felt its purpose would be unfulfilled. To reach those large numbers, it wasn't enough to be Canadian; you had to be good. (A paraphrase of an apocryphal story: There was a time when many of the talented filmmakers in Hollywood came from Hungary. One day the Gabor sisters arrived, at which time the word went out that it was not enough to be Hungarian, you also had to be good!) And it wasn't enough to be good, you had to let the audience know that you're good. You had to promote.

There was, of course, nothing on film or tape with which to promote the show in advance of its air dates, because no shows had yet been taped. Most shows nowadays have a few episodes "in the can" from which clips can be taken for promos, but we were promoting a show that didn't exist yet. I was sent out on the road, from coast to coast, for a two-week period to drum up attention and create curiosity in the upcoming production and scheduling of *King of Kensington*.

I was accompanied by the CBC's publicist, Maureen O'Donnell. We visited every city across the country in which there was a CBC owned and operated station, which meant every major centre in every province, starting from St. John's in the East and finishing in Vancouver and Victoria in the West. Besides local TV and radio interviews, we did newspapers and magazines as well, and there were lots of photo opportunities. We made promos with local CBC crews for the regional markets. I usually improvised the spots, man-in-the-street fashion, at a local marketplace, like Jean Talon Marché in Montreal, or in front of a popular restaurant, like Kelekis in the north end of Winnipeg or The Bagel in Toronto (affectionately known by its regulars, including me, as the Dirty Bagel). In all cases the locations chosen for filming and photo ops were multicultural in character.

It was such a good feeling, when the series took hold and I was stopped in the street by a Canadian from South Asia and thanked for "representing us on TV"—this in spite of the fact that, out of 111 shows, only one dealt specifically with South Asians. I believe it was the overall flavour of the show the man was referring to when he said "representing us," that is, all the "others" of our population whose origins are neither French nor English.

I was pretty good on one-to-ones with the camera (not unlike the public service messages I'd done for TRAC), especially when the character was a new guy I liked a lot. Of course, part of the process of creating a character is to take a liking to him. Sometimes that's a problem; it certainly wasn't in the case of Larry King. (This, by the way, was long before the advent of CNN's King of Talk.) The promos were spontaneous, fresh, direct and engaging, and with them and the cross-country tour we began to build our connection with the Canadian TV audience.

I learned a lot about cultivating relationships with the media from Maureen O'Donnell. Etiquette and strategy. I found myself following Maureen's lead of writing thank-you notes as we departed from one PR stop and before prepping for the next, as we flew from city to city. We were mostly well received across the country, even in Quebec, where I scored well with the English-language media, and surprisingly, *pas mal* with the French.

As I see it, the problem has never been the means of communication so much as the will to communicate. If that will isn't there on both sides, then language skills won't make much of a difference. But I found that if the will is there, the struggle to communicate is always appreciated. Often people in Quebec seemed to recognize and appreciate that I had the will and the desire to communicate—to listen as well as to speak. A few years later a columnist for *Le Soleil* in Quebec City said he believed that our show had some following amongst French Canadians because my character was "unsnobbish."

On the other hand, confident command of language made no difference if there was no interest in meeting us. One Vancouver television journalist preferred sailing to keeping an appointment for an interview with me. In retrospect, if I had had the opportunity to go sailing instead of meeting with him, I too would probably have gone sailing, but I would at least have given him notice first. Oh, well, I rationalized, I'll get him next time, certainly before I'm through my three years. For the most part the media we met across the country were very receptive. They were engaged by my enthusiasm and energy, generating curiosity and anticipation amongst their readers, viewers and listeners about the debut of *King of Kensington*.

It was an exciting tour for me, launching an important venture in the business I love, in the country I love. But for excitement and love, the highlight came at the end of the tour, when I arrived back home.

Maureen O'Donnell was not only a savvy PR person but also a beautiful one. Sara thought that no matter how professionally behaved we were, the tour still involved my spending a lot of time with a sexy-looking lady. She reasoned she was going to have to do something spectacular to top that. Accordingly, Sara planned an intimate supper for the two of us upon my return: Russian blini with caviar and all the trimmings, and a chilled bottle of Charles Heidsieck champagne (a sentimental favourite of mine). Sara was still luxuriating in a bubble bath as my plane was making its final approach for landing. She was interrupted while drying off by the honking of the taxi she'd called to take her to the airport (we didn't own a car yet). Panic: what to wear? She had to choose quickly or she could be driving out to the airport as I was driven home by CBC transport. How about this? No, that. She had to hurry or we'd miss each other. Oh, to heck with it. None of them. Reminding herself that "Brevity is the soul of wit," she stepped into a pair of high heels, put on a trench coat and arrived at the airport just in time.

I was so pleased to see her. She looked fantastic in that short trench coat, which came down to just above her knees. We got my luggage, hailed a cab and then, as I followed her into the back of it, I caught a glimpse of just how fantastic she looked. I gasped, "Sara, you've got nothing on under that raincoat!"

I followed her delightedly into the house, and the blini, caviar and champagne all tasted even better for breakfast the next morning. I always used to say that as great a cook as Sara is, I really married her for her breakfasts.

Rehearsals—telling the story, building the characters. Where is the humour? Where is the love? Now add some more questions. Where is truth? What is formula? What is freshness? Is keeping a promise every week and giving an audience what it wants to see "predictability"? Are jokes what comedy is all about? Is character also what comedy is about? Is character more important than jokes? Are lines intended just for laughs forgettable after they're spoken? Are laughs that are remembered based on something deeper than just words on a page? Is studying emulating? Is emulating imitating? What is style? Is it inherent to the concept itself, or to be found in the performing of it? Is style the man himself? Are we trying to tell too much and solve too much in 22 1/2 minutes? But should we settle for surface and silly?

We had a lot of exploring and studying and learning to do. Like Perry Rosemond used to say, we were doing our homework on the air. Actually, we were doing our homework all week, creating our show and studying others that had aspects worth learning from—like *M*A*S*H* for irreverence, *The Mary Tyler Moore Show* for pacing, *Barney Miller* for shot composition, and my favourite, *All in the Family*, for truth, irony and even poignant storytelling within the context of comedy. Ultimately, though, we had to find and create our own thing.

When casting was completed we were "peopled" with performers of skill and warmth, people our viewers looked forward to seeing every week. Fiona Reid, who played my wife, Cathy, was gifted and skilful beyond her years. Helene Winston, as my mother, was a trouper with panache and style to match her well-honed comedy skills. And talk about experience in comedy: Bobby Vinci, my taxicab-driving best friend on the show, brought years of clowning to his character as well as ready-made loyalty and fondness from the huge Italian community in Toronto and across the country. He soon won over the rest of the audience, as did the other regulars, the handsome hunk Ardon Bess, who played my buddy Nestor the "Jestor," the postman, and John Dee, a kind of Santa's elf named Max, who worked in the variety store for me and my family, as well as overseeing the club where my neighbourhood friends and I hung out. The sum total of the casting created a group of characters who, in a Capraesque way, reaffirmed good old-fashioned values, even as we grappled with society's ever-changing attitudes. I thought of King as a character with one foot securely in yesteryear but with the courage and curiosity to let the other foot test the waters of today and tomorrow.

Within the first half-dozen episodes we found ourselves gravitating towards the kind of comedy that was to distinguish our show at its best: comedy drama, not sitcom. Sitcom, to me, was just what it sounds like: the cast sits down and makes jokes. I preferred movement, emotion, purpose and theme. Jokes, of course, but not jokes for the sake of jokes; rather, jokes resulting from character and plot. I much preferred the impetus arising from three-dimensional characters behaving and interacting and thereby creating situations, or conversely, a situation might be dumped upon the characters, causing them to react and interact, and thereby thrusting us forward. In either case there is action, and the characters propel that action.

There were in a sense two attitudes towards comedy on our show, each expressed by two pairs of writer/producers; Perry's task as executive producer was to try to blend the two attitudes. On the one hand there was a commitment to a minimum of, let's say, five jokes per page regardless of whether they were organic to a character or situation; and, on the other hand, there was comedy resulting from character. Fortunately, the latter approach won out. Most of us were inclined that way, and I was pretty vocal about it, along with certain of the writers. I didn't want to invest my life for three years or more in a show whose comedy was flip and superficial. When Perry, as he had always intended, prepared to leave the show after the first year, asked me whom I preferred to write and produce the second year; my choice was the two producers whose approach coincided with mine. They were the second pair of producers, Jack Humphrey and Louis del Grande. It's important to note, however that it was the first pair of producers (Aubrey Tadman and Garry Ferrier, along with Bob McMullen) who wrote the catchy theme song for *King of Kensington*:

"When he walks down the street, he smiles at everyone, everyone that he meets calls him King of Kensington."

Comedy that went to and came from the core of each character was what, in my opinion, allowed *King of Kensington* to find an audience from coast to coast. Through three-dimensional characters we were able to touch a universal chord. You have to be universal to reach across Canada's immense geography with its internal divides, its regionalism, racism and differences of language, accent and custom. Storytelling that's local results in an appeal that's local. That's parochialism. Storytelling that's based on the truth of particularism, especially personalized particularism, results in a truth that's universal.

The concept of particularism goes to the inner being of an individual: those ingredients of personality, character, physical and psychological traits, the history and background that are particular to that individual. It means those specific characteristics, physicalities and influences that describe his or her body and being, that comprise the essence and totality of that person. That is particularism.

At the core of King's character was a human condition to which we can all relate: contradiction. This contradiction did not lead to hypocrisy—he had too much integrity for that—but to confusion. This caused the audience to care for the character, to want him to work it out while simultaneously laughing at whatever predicament he found himself in that week. In a way, the audience is laughing at itself; we all recognize ourselves, or someone we know, in a similar predicament.

King orders a pizza and says, "Give me double cheese, double pepperoni, double sausage and some salami. Oh, what the hell, double everything—and oh, by the way, don't forget a diet Coke."

Because of community conscience, King decides to donate blood in a local Red Cross drive—but he's squeamish. Still, he has to set an example, so he decides to go through with it, and while he's trying to muster up the courage Cathy and others prop him up to prevent him from keeling over in a faint.

King counsels a friend whose honeymoon was a disaster because he was a virgin and didn't know what to do. As a result of King's advice, the friend's marriage is suddenly fantastic, and just as suddenly King finds himself all bottled up in the same predicament that this friend was in. Cathy, of course, wants to discuss the problem; King is reluctant. Finally he blurts out that as a result of all the textbook reading he did to help his friend, he's like a pianist who can't play because he's thinking about his fingers too much.

"When's the last time you played the piano?" she asks.

"No, you don't understand; that was just an analogy."

She says, "Forget about your fingers, your piano and your analogies, and come over here and kiss me," and of course we all know they're going to make music. That episode was called "The Joy of Sex."

With all the hugging and kissing between Larry and Cathy, I used to feel I was doing something for the morale of anybody in the audience who didn't fit the Hollywood stereotype of the romantic hero. After all, in a good romantic relationship any man, every man, can feel like a leading man. Cathy and Larry had a good romantic relationship. I assure you, between Fiona Reid and me there was only respect and camaraderie, just as with the rest of the cast of hard-working colleagues. As Larry King, however, I was always horny for Cathy King. Sara understood that. When asked how she felt when she saw me kissing Cathy King, she'd say, "That's not Al, that's Larry King."

In some episodes there were laughter and tears in the same moment, as when King, in anticipation of fatherhood, starts buying hockey equipment for his son-to-be, and then finds out that there are fertility problems between him and Cathy. Also, it's pointed out to him that if they were to have a child, it might be a girl. When he gets home from buying a pink snowsuit, he's informed that the infertility is not because of Cathy, and it's now his turn to see doctors. No way! He swaggers about nervously. Finally he reluctantly undergoes a medical examination. When he comes home, in a moment of solitude he holds the pink snowsuit and fights back tears. Then he describes to Cathy, in what must have been a TV first, that the doctor gave him a sterilized plastic container and showed him into a little room, where he did something he hadn't done since he was a teenager. Result? A kind of a high—a sperm count of 15,000. Unfortunately, you need at least 35,000, so the count was in fact too low. "Fertility for Two" and "The Joy of Sex," both written by Louis del Grande and Jack Humphrey, were the kind of shows that got us international sales.

I think the classic example of contradiction within the character of King was when his mother decides to go out on a date. Now King the son is all of a sudden behaving like a father, insisting that she be home before midnight. Of course she does not come home before midnight. King is pacing. She finally shows up at 2 a.m.; actually, she floats in at 2 a.m. King is alarmed by her behaviour, scared by it. He hides in a corner to watch as she says good night to her date. But she doesn't just *say* good night, she *kisses* him good night. King is shocked, stunned. The look on his face is of a child betrayed. King has not only been the grown son but also carried on like a father to his mother, and now suddenly reverts to an infant in an intense Oedipal reaction. Fan letters from around the world testified to the universal nature—and universal humour—of this situation.

With the universal appeal necessary to reach an audience from coast to coast in Canada (in the second, third and fourth years we averaged upwards of 1.75 million viewers a week, sometimes hovering around 2 million), we knew we could reach beyond our borders as well. After the first nine episodes, *King* was sold to commercial stations in the United States. This was, if not a first, then at least something rare at that time. Many shows produced at the CBC sold to non-commercial markets (that's almost a giveaway) like the Public Broadcasting System, but *King* sold commercially into syndicated markets in the US without having the ideal prerequisite, that is, pre-sales to foreign markets. This was an in-house CBC production that sold worldwide.

The impression I got from the purchasers, a New York agency called Dancer Fitzgerald Sample, with whose representatives I spent some time doing PR in the States, was that the CBC's foreign sales department was not aggressive. Indeed, our show sold not so much because the vendor was selling but because the purchaser was buying. To paraphrase further, the Dancer Fitzgerald Sample agent who did the deal, Heather Regan, who was just twenty-eight at the time, told me she had never dealt with so many "left arms at one time" as when dealing with the CBC.

Unlike other shows in US syndication at that time, such as *The Brady Bunch*, *I Love Lucy* or *Eight Is Enough*, we didn't come straight from US network success. For shows like that, promotion isn't necessary, which is just as well because syndicated shows have little budget for PR. Our show, however, needed whatever PR could be mustered. Some money was found between CBC and the syndicators, and in the summer of 1977, when the show aired in the Los Angeles market on KCOP-TV, I went down to do interviews and promotion. As I was not known in the US, they needed a hook, so one of the first interviews was done behind the counter of Barney's Beanery. No longer a showbiz watering hole, it had become a biker hangout. Still, it was a victory and lots of fun for me, because I was able to show Sara where and how I had worked a dozen years earlier.

I was advised by friends in the industry to spend the summer in LA because I was appearing in my own show every week and getting some good attention in the city that was and still is the centre for the TV and film industries. It's an "in your face" business; I had a weekly calling card going for me on KCOP, a popular local station, assuming I was on hand to "take meetings" as the show was being aired. I was considering it, leaning towards it, but as I was deliberating I got a phone call in the spring of 1977 from John Roberts. John was Secretary of State for Citizenship and Culture in Pierre Trudeau's cabinet.

(John and I had been classmates at the University of Toronto Law School, and were considered our class's two most famous dropouts.) Would I take a trip across Canada, in June, to talk to Canadians about unity, finishing up in Ottawa for the July 1 celebrations, which I would co-host with Jean Gascon and Bruno Gerussi? I was invited to take my family along on the trip to help convey the image of unity.

What an opportunity for me and my family to see our country! And what an opportunity for me to serve my country. As ambitious as I was in my career, of the two opportunities presented, I knew that a higher purpose would be served by the cross-Canada trip culminating in Canada Day. That makes me sound holier than thou to some, salt of the earth to others, so I never talked publicly at the time about why I chose to tour Canada rather than seek opportunities in LA. I certainly didn't want to contend with the skepticism of the Canadian press (who, ironically, were generally anti-American nationalists). But I meant it and still do: I felt honoured and privileged. Besides, my instincts knew that opportunity stateside would knock again, as it had before.

It was a memorable trip for me and my family. Mind you, while it was, I'm sure, beneficial for Adam and Tobaron, the travel was also hard on them. To be continually on display is an unnatural situation for kids. Perhaps I didn't appreciate it enough then, but in retrospect I can see that it was no fun for them to be stared at all the time. They were a little unsure of how to deal with or respond to "Hey look, it's the King's son" or "That's the King's daughter." Kids, I should have realized, prefer being like everyone else rather than standing out. Also, it wasn't easy for them to have to share their daddy. One time, while carrying Adam in my arms, I was talking with a bunch of enthusiastic kids in a schoolyard in Gananoque, when Adam covered my mouth to prevent me from talking to them. God love him. Still, Sara and I always expected exemplary behaviour from them, and that's mostly what we got, at least in public.

"Canada, I want to shake your hand" was the theme of the tours taken by me and my family, and by others, such as Bruno Gerussi and Pierre Berton, in different parts of the country. We travelled in a Winnebago; the first leg was up the coast of British Columbia from English tea at the Empress Hotel in Victoria to our first spectacular Japanese meal of culinary acrobatics, highlighted by juggling steak carvers, in Nanaimo. This time Vancouver was more receptive. Why not? Canada Day is every Canadian's birthday. In Alberta we had an inspirational visit to the Stoney Indian Reserve near Morley. This was the one time the kids didn't behave well in public. They got into a sibling scrap, bopping each other. Sara was mortified. I was alternately embarrassed and infuriated, more concerned, I'm sure, about the image we were presenting than about the naturalness of the kids' behaviour. The Native kids on the reserve, now that I think back, seemed to know about naturalness better than I, as they hardly took notice of Adam and Tobaron's behaviour.

On the way up to the reserve from Calgary, I stopped at a grocery store to buy some bread and honey. At a council meeting in the huge teepee-shaped, wood-and-log main lodge of the reserve, gifts were exchanged. I said to our host, Chief John Snow, that in my religion, on the eve of a new year, we dip bread into honey, and I did this as I was speaking, and then passed some to him and wished him a sweet year on this the eve of his birthday and mine, Canada's birthday. Then Tobaron and Adam (now exemplary!) went about the room, giving pieces of honey-dipped bread to the other chiefs, elders, women and children.

Chief Snow said to me that "the Mountain" (a reference to Mount Sinai) has "significance in my religion too," and presented me with a book he had just written called *These Mountains Are Our Sacred Places*. He drew my attention to a passage that combines the teachings handed down from his ancestors with the Scriptures. His image is of people living together in harmony, as in a forest, where trees and shrubs and tiny plants grow in a harmony of variety. "Why is the forest beautiful?" he asks. Because the "diversity of plants and trees makes a beautiful forest." These words and thoughts I've carried with me ever since.

In Portage la Prairie, Manitoba, we participated in a celebration at a traditional wooden open-air grandstand, so old that they had only wooden outhouses. Four-and-a-half-year-old Adam had to go to the john. "Good timing," I said, "so do I." At least the grandstand was wide open, surrounded by fresh air; but the outhouse was small, enclosed and stuffy. Suffocating. Adam gasped, then stood tall, but still barely high enough to pee into the hole. As our streams criss-crossed, I tried to joke: "Look, we're having a sword fight."

Adam said, "Yes. And I'm going to win."

"What do you mean?" I scoffed. "How are you going to win against me?"

"Because I'm getting out of here first," he said, as he finished, tucked himself in and ran out, the squeaking hinged door banging shut, leaving me standing there a distant second.

Adam was the star of the show when we were in Quebec City. Tobaron and Sara went for a calèche ride through the city streets while Adam accompanied me to a TV studio for an interview. I had already braved my way through one in French, so this one in English would be a relaxed affair; I didn't mind having Adam along. Mind you, though it wasn't difficult, it was still important; this was the 6 p.m. local news hour. Adam got bored with whatever he was given to occupy himself with and just walked onto the set during our live interview. The interviewer didn't seem to mind. Neither did I at first. Adam sat on my knee, quietly for a little while, but then he became fascinated by the Lavalier microphone pinned to my lapel and began playing with it, thereby affecting and finally interrupting the Q & A of the interview. The interviewer tried to capture Adam's interest by directing questions to him. He asked Adam if he liked *King of Kensington*. Adam said no. What did he like? Adam answered, "Captain Kirk."

"Oh well," I said, "at least he's another Canadian."

Then the interviewer asked if Adam was assigned a job on our travels. I said yes, he was like a barker drawing attention to the Canadian flags we were passing around. Adam heard the word "barker" and thought I was talking about our dog, Puff. So he started barking like a dog. This was a lot of fun for him and apparently funny for everyone else in the studio. Ruff, ruff and woof, woof! He persisted in this as he climbed all over me for the duration of what seemed like an endless interview. Perhaps it seemed endless to the viewers as well. But the next morning, as we toured the charming streets of Quebec City, the member of the Waxman family who was getting all the attention was Adam.

We then proceeded, again via Winnebago, in a roundabout route so that we could visit some Ontario cities and towns before arriving July 1 in Ottawa for all-day partying followed by the live TV show at night in front of the Peace Tower.

Canada Day. The capital beckons. The Hill invites. What an exciting day. Drums and cymbals, blasts of brass, flag waving and fanfares. Riding with my family in an open car in parades at midday through streets crowded with people waving and cheering. Rehearsals during the afternoon for a *King of Kensington* sketch that evening. Excitement builds. Reviewing material for the portions of the show that I would be hosting. People have been gathering on the lawns of Parliament Hill all day. As evening approaches, an audience is accumulating, ultimately more than 100,000 people. An awesome sight. Somehow more thrilling than knowing that 3 million people will be watching the show on TV. Nervous excitement. The evening is suddenly here, but it looks like rain!

The skies open up and showers rain down. Umbrellas snap open. The huge crowd is now a shining sea of umbrellas. It looks like they might disperse. Some on the outskirts are already scurrying for cover. Long-legged John Hirsch is frantic, running about backstage in a panic. How can we hold on to this audience? Will the rain stop in time? What can we do? The singers wouldn't sing without their electronic equipment, which was generally integral to their acts. Dancers couldn't dance on the slippery stage. Speakers, caught up in the mounting excitement, were well on their way to inebriation and therefore no safer on the stage than dancers with their feet sliding out from under them. Others, with no change of costume or wardrobe, wouldn't risk soaking their crisp sartorial style. What to do?

I thought to myself, if only I could sing! I wouldn't depend on electronic gadgetry to project my voice, or long-stemmed dancing beauties to buoy up my talent. I would just belt it out. I'd always remembered the story about Al Jolson's reaction to a technical problem that threatened to cancel his radio performance one night. Undaunted, he said, "Open the windows and I'll sing loud!" I thought to myself, if Jolson were here, he'd sing the rain back up into the sky.

I didn't know what I was going to do, but I assured John Hirsch that we would not lose that audience, and then I proceeded carefully, under my umbrella, across that huge, empty—and slippery—stage. It seemed nearly the size of a football field. With each measured step on that wet and windswept stage I looked out at the immense gathering of people, who I felt sure also wanted the rain to stop, also wanted the show to go on! When I got to the apron of the stage, two things crossed my mind, and both had to do with power. First, is this what the Pope feels like when he looks out at the crowds in St. Peter's Square? Second, I remembered hearing once that the way to stop a brawl or a riot in a crowded gathering—like, let's say, a sporting event at Maple Leaf Gardens—was to play the national anthem. People would stop what they were doing and stand at attention. But I had no band, just me.

By this time I was thoroughly drenched. My rented tux was soggy and baggy, my umbrella had turned inside out and I was hanging on to it for fear of it flying away into the sky. I stood alone on the apron of that enormous stage looking like a chubby Charlie Chaplin with my umbrella in the wind and rain. And then I began to sing, as loud as I could, "O Canada."

Very few people heard, I'm sure, but some did and sang with me. At first it was just the people in the front rows, but happily, they were soon joined by people in the next few rows after them. Serendipity! It was as though little waves of "O Canada" were surfacing here and there across the densely populated lawns of Parliament Hill. Coincidentally, inexplicably, the rain began to weaken. Serendipity? Or the magic of show business? Perhaps those in front wanted to brave the rain in order not to lose their places close to the stage, perhaps those in the middle couldn't move because they were packed in from both sides, and perhaps those on the outskirts began to return because the rain was in fact subsiding. Lucky break? For sure! But also a belief in the basic rule of show business: The show must go on!

After all, I'm the guy who taped episodes of *King* when my throat was so sore and my voice so low I was told by the doctor to write notes rather than speak, or with a temperature so high I was under doctor's orders to stay in bed. No understudies, no insurance policies in our budget. The show always had to go on. And that night on Parliament Hill the rain stopped, the audience did not leave, and the show went on. Serendipity, yes. And sparkling entertainment that soared like the colourful balloons that were released into a night of fantastic fireworks, flashing and flaring from over the stage and across the glittering sky.

At the end of it all, I hope we helped, even in a small way, to serve the purpose for which we were asked to travel across Canada. I was asked to tour again and host again for the next two years after that. Indeed, in the following years I would host the celebrations in Ontario's Queen's Park in the afternoon and then fly to Ottawa to host the show from Parliament Hill in the evening.

I was doing everything I wanted to do: acting, directing and working for the community across the country on behalf of charities I wanted to help and causes I believed in. Everything was coming together in my life—my family, my interests, my profession. I was making a living from acting and directing, and giving back, as my mother had taught me, through community and charity work, to the country that was giving to me. I was in my early forties. It didn't happen overnight. It took a long time to happen, but it was happening, and it would go on happening for a long time.

In the hiatus period between production schedules of *King of Kensington,* I was acting in feature films and directing TV, no longer drawn to the theatre (except as audience), more fascinated now by the immediacy of radio and television. In fact, I used to feel then that if I had been ten years younger, or started out ten years later, I'd be in TV or radio journalism. So when Don Harron went on vacation for a week and a replacement host was needed for CBC Radio's *Morningside* (this was before the Peter Gzowski era) and they offered it to me, I quickly said yes. Suddenly I was immersed in the captivating world of "now." Everything I was dealing with was happening live for three hours every morning of the week. Mind you, I don't know if I could have kept the pace up much longer than a week, because I'm a slow reader and I forced myself to read cover to cover the book being promoted by each author I interviewed (there were three or four of them), in amongst all the news items that we covered.

I also directed an episode of CBC's police series *Sidestreet.* It was a lot of fun directing wonderful actors like the stars of that series, Donnelly Rhodes and Jonathan Welsh, as well as the guest star, Larry Dane. But what was most memorable about that show for me was all the hockey scenes I shot, because the show was about a teenaged hockey player—talented but tough, and teetering on the brink of breaking the law—played by Geraint Wyn Davies.

The players we used for the hockey scrimmages were from a team of sixteen-year-olds called the Seneca Nationals. We had the whole team skating for us that day for background action, and for (as it turned out) some first-unit shooting as well. Geraint Wyn Davies is, of course, a very good actor, and a surprisingly good skater too, but there was a blond-haired kid on the Seneca Nationals who was a phenomenal skater, so he doubled for Geraint even in some first-unit shooting that had no dialogue. At one point I began to demonstrate to this kid how to throw a mean and dirty body check, and then I said, "Why am I showing you? You're the hockey player. You show me."

He said simply (in reference to dirty checking), "I don't do that, sir, I just play hockey."

Later I had him skate the length of the ice through and around all the players, who were trying any means to stop him, including sliding in front of him to protect their goal, so that he had to jump over the players and two cameras, one on top of the other (one long lens, one wide-angle) with his skates almost going into the lenses. An exciting pair of shots.

At the end of the day I assembled all the players to thank them. I was so impressed with all of them that I was curious and had to ask, "Which one of you will make it to the NHL?"

Without any hint of envy, they all pointed to the young player I had chosen to double for Geraint and said, almost in unison, "Gretz will!"

Whenever I see Wayne Gretzky now, he always reminds me jokingly, "You once paid me $100 to skate for a whole day!"

The charities I was involved with at that time were mostly for kids, such as Big Brothers and the Variety Club. Joining the Variety Club was like reaching a plateau for me. It meant achieving a level of accomplishment and acceptance in show business. I remember as a kid, whenever I read or heard about major show business stars or personalities, they seemed always to find time to work for Variety. And of course the word "variety," perhaps because of *Variety*, the show business trade paper, meant show business itself. I had always hoped that someday I would achieve the industry endorsement of acceptance into the Variety Club. I later learned that you don't have to be a star to be in Variety; you don't even have to be directly in show business. It makes no difference what business you are in or how high up the ladder you have progressed—you just have to care about wanting to do something to help kids. I'm still a member of Variety and proud to be.

By the time we reached the third year of *King*, we had honed the magic combination of good production paralleled with good promotion. We were on the air, including reruns, almost every week of the year, playing all over Canada, as well as in many markets in the US, Europe, Australia, Southeast Asia, Africa, the Middle East and the Far East.

In the States I was invited to be a presenter at awards shows, such as the Miss New York State beauty pageant and the National Association of Television Program Executives convention in Florida, as well as events in other states where *King* played. In Canada, I toured, sometimes with family, sometimes on my own, but as a result I had the good fortune of seeing most of our country. Our ratings were high, our numbers were high—comparable to the American hits like *All in the Family*. It was clear, as I had said when I signed the original contract three years earlier, that we would do more than three years. At least two more. Time to renegotiate.

CHAPTER 22

The Road Broadens

Catherine McCartney was my agent at the time. Still is. I guess she officially became my agent in 1975 when she negotiated the original *King of Kensington* deal, although we've never had anything in writing. She'd represented me on an ad hoc basis for a few years before 1975, mostly in commercials, but it didn't become official or exclusive until *King*. Neither of us is sure, but we know that as of this writing the agent-client relationship between us is at least twenty-five years old. Almost as long as I've been married. Sara says she doesn't mind that there are two women in my life, as long as the other one only gets a commission and she gets all the rest.

When it came time to renegotiate my contract with the CBC, we were aware that I was in a favourable position to seize and even create opportunities. To make the most of this required a sophistication in deal making that to my knowledge no agent in Canada at that time possessed, owing simply to lack of experience in that particular area. Catherine recognized this and was receptive to the idea of guidance from someone who had been around this specific block before, indeed someone who had perhaps invented the block. Perry Rosemond recommended his friend, the second-in-command at the powerful Brillstein Company in Los Angeles, Sandy Wernick.

I invited Sandy to Toronto with first-class airfare, and put him up in a suite at the Sutton Place, almost kitty-corner from the executive offices of the CBC, which were located at College and Bay at that time. Sandy, ever resourceful and a master of brinkmanship, negotiated the substance of the deal, leaving Catherine to dot i's and cross t's. He subsequently stayed in touch with Catherine and me, and was available to advise and steer us, and specifically for Catherine to use in a "good cop/bad cop" sort of way in dealings with the CBC. This set-up worked really well for us, right from Sandy's first negotiations.

Across the bargaining table from Sandy was the new head of CBC drama. Not John Hirsch, who had departed by that time. Cultured, confident, worldly and very tall, John Hirsch had espoused an American-style of entrepreneurialism; he also had the physical advantage of being able to look down on whomever he was confronting. The new head, John Kennedy, had considerable experience as well, but mainly within the confines of CBC bureaucracy. Now he found himself on new and unfamiliar ground, face to face and eyeball to eyeball with cool, confident Sandy, a man who might look like a beach bum but who manoeuvred more like a chess expert.

Sandy apparently started the negotiations by establishing that both he, my manager, and the CBC, my producer, needed Al to be happy in order for all concerned to get the best out of Al. What could we do together to make Al happy? Part of Sandy's strategy was to create a positive mood and a sense of working together for our mutual benefit. The end result was that I became the highest-paid freelancer contracted to the CBC at the time. The new agreement included a number of development deals for the duration of the contract, in which the CBC had to buy at least three concepts that I would put forward and then pay for their development; in return, they had the right to pursue or reject the projects. The deal also included directing commitments to me as well as acting assignments apart from *King of Kensington*. This was a first for the CBC, and I don't know that they made very many comprehensive deals like that again.

When I asked Sandy what I owed him (fearing the traditional

whack of 15 percent right off the top), he said, "Nothing. I only want what you're going to make down here [in the US] after *King*." Thus a relationship began that has lasted for many years. Since I returned to Canada after *Cagney and Lacey* he is no longer my manager, but we're still good friends.

There were many changes in *King of Kensington* as we approached the fourth year. The writers were feeling limited by the repetition of some of the regulars, and so Larry's three friends, Duke, Nestor and Max, were not renewed in order to make way for more story opportunities with a variety of new guests every week. Helene Winston's character, Larry's mother, would now run the store with Larry, and she would find a companion, the old Jewish druggist in the neighbourhood, to be played by Peter Boretski. Although I had become sentimental about King's three friends, all these changes made sense and could be taken in stride. The change that made a substantial impact on the show was, of course, Fiona Reid's departure.

Our relationship was a little rough in the beginning. I can't remember whether she told me this herself or whether I heard it second-hand, but she said about me in the first year that she had never encountered an ego as big as mine and that she was afraid I was going to eat her up. By the second year, she said, although my ego hadn't diminished, she realized that no one in the company was more dedicated than me to creating space for all the egos in the cast. When Fiona left at the end of the third year we were, and had been for some time, on the best of terms.

Fiona Reid was excellent as Cathy King. She was attractive and funny. She was feminine and feminist, strong and believable. Her pacing and timing were crisp. And just as King was identifiable to a lot of men in the audience, Cathy was a character that a lot of women could relate to, particularly in her need for self-expression. More than that, the marriage between Cathy and Larry was a relationship the audience believed in and cared about. So it was not without consternation and even a sense of betrayal that some members of the audi-

1987. With Sharon Gless, on the cover of *TV Guide* in the U.S.

Throughout the 80's. A limo waiting to drive me from home to the airport for a flight back to work in L.A.

1984. Sharon Gless, me, Sara and Tyne Daly at the Shaare Zedek dinner.

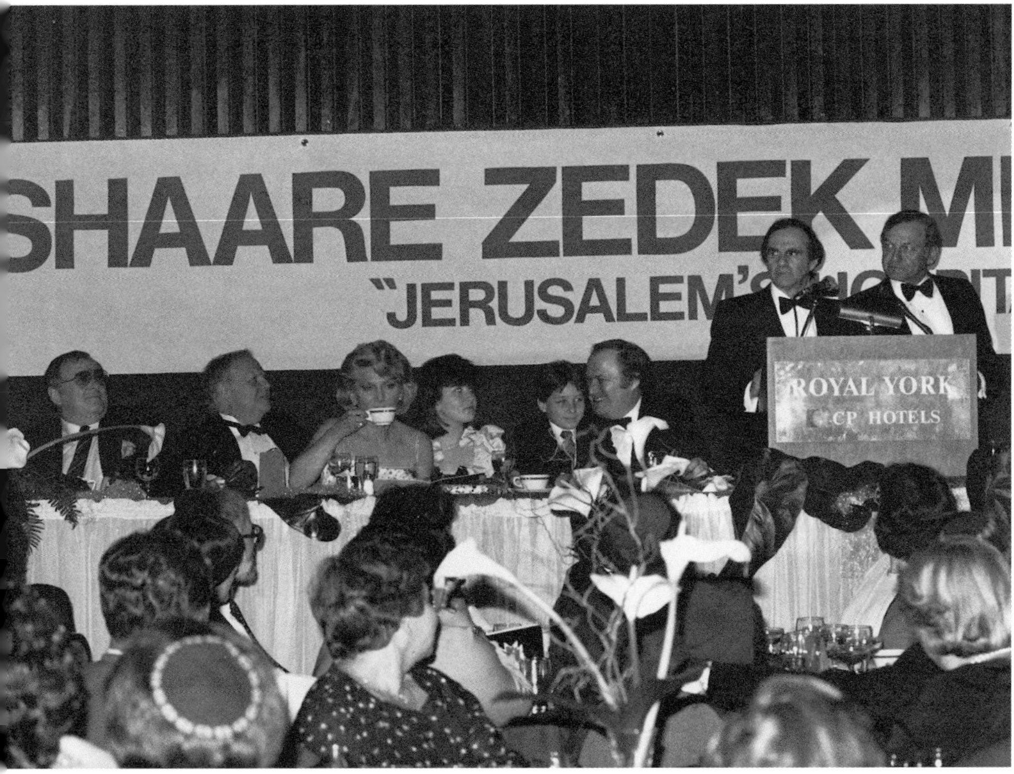

1984. Johnny Wayne and Frank Shuster roasting me at the Shaare Zedek dinner.

Toronto Star Newspapers Ltd.

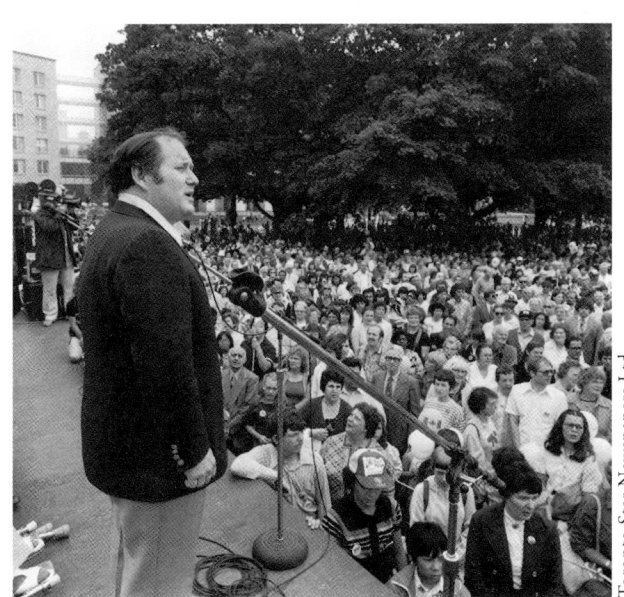

1978. The singing of "O Canada" as I hosted Canada Day celebrations at Queen's Park on July 1st.

1985. Three generations of laughter: Adam and me, with Sara's father at Adam's bar mitzvah rehearsal.

1990. Tobaron, Sara and Adam at a party at the Canadian consul general's residence in Los Angeles. Like my dad, as always, I was at work.

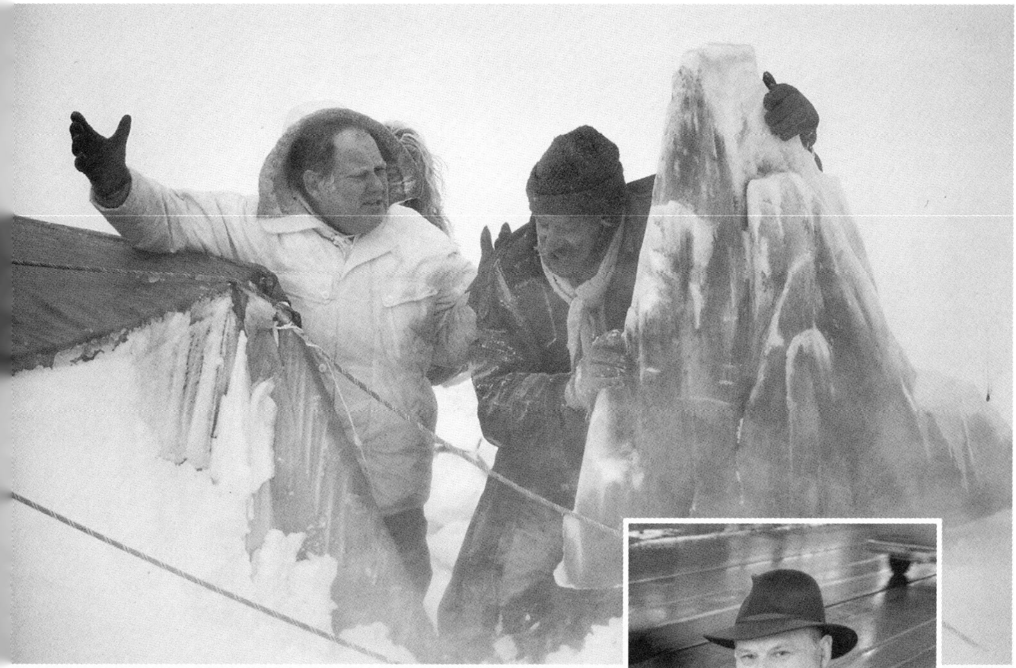

1992. Donald Sutherland and me, improvising a scene in a blizzard at the foot of Cerro Torre for *Scream of Stone*.

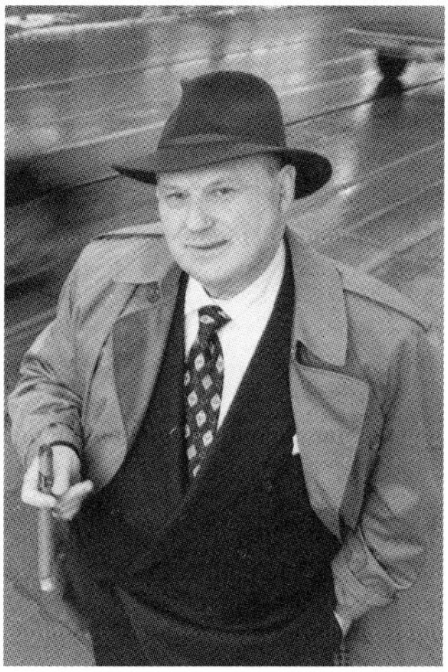

Mouthpiece for the mob. In 1996 I played John Gotti's lawyer in the HBO film *Gotti*.

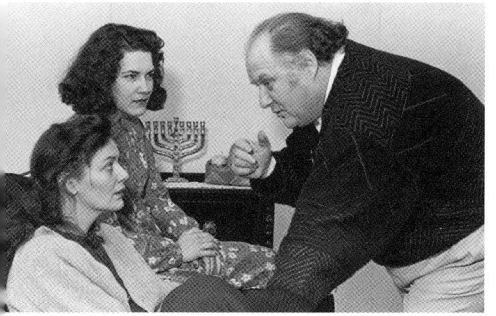

1994. Directing Shannon Lawson and Sharon Bernbaum, the two sisters in *A Shayna Maidel*.

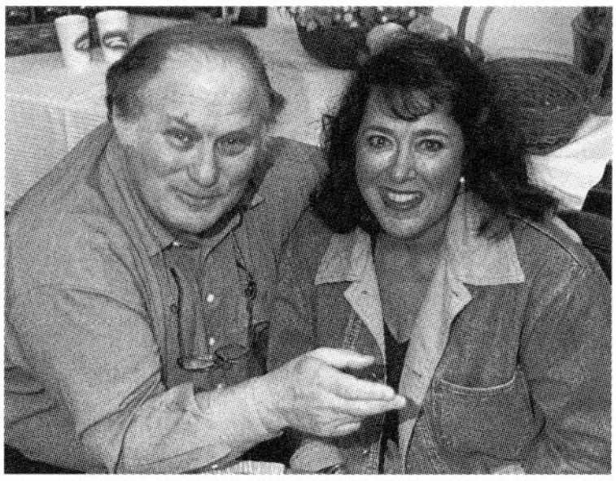

Tom Sandler Photography

1995. A meeting with Janese Kane, the producer of *Sight Unseen* and *A Shayna Maidel*.

1995. The cast and crew of the CBC's *Net Worth*, posing like a cup-winning hockey team.

1995. Whoopie Goldberg and me being directed by Norman Jewison for a scene in *Bogus*.

1999. Patricia Idlette and me in Neil Simon's *Proposals* at the Royal Alexandra Theatre.

1997. Martha Henry and me, as Linda and Willy Loman, in the Stratford Festival Production of *Death of a Salesman*.

1997. Cover of the program for *Death of a Salesman* at Stratford's Avon Theatre.

ence saw Larry and Cathy's marriage fail. In fact, one viewer wrote that she wouldn't watch *King of Kensington* again because we had flown in the face of the values the show had espoused; as far as she was concerned, having Cathy walk out on Larry "in search of herself" was downright insulting. The viewer asked why we didn't just state the facts, that Ms. Reid's contract was up and, rather than renew, she wanted to work in the theatre.

The episode in which Cathy leaves Larry captured what was happening in many marriages across the country. Most people considered it a heartbreaking, yet still funny, episode. Frankly, I thought the writers did a superb job, and had great insight in using what Fiona was feeling herself—not unlike Tyne Daly's character on *Cagney and Lacey* becoming pregnant when Tyne was pregnant, or my character on *Cagney and Lacey* having heart problems and others on that show struggling with alcoholism. These are instances of a perceptive use of fact to create artistic truth and the universality that results from particularism.

Fiona left television and went on to achieve great success in the theatre. We almost worked together on the stage in a production of *Born Yesterday* at the St. Lawrence Centre for the Arts, in Toronto, but my schedule on *Cagney and Lacey* wouldn't allow it. We did, however, work together very briefly, more than twenty years after Cathy departed, in a wonderful film for the CBC called *The Sue Rodriguez Story*. It would be nice to work with her again.

In the fourth year King had a girlfriend, played by Rosemary Radcliffe. Rosemary had a Second City background and a lot of TV series comedy experience. Her character was sweet, funny and vulnerable, making for a comic yet warm and romantic relationship with King. And of course, as the writers preferred, there were many guest appearances, characters from King's past and new relationships in the present. The result was that the show's high numbers were sustained and even grew during the fourth year.

For me personally the numbers were still higher than that, as I did what was virtually a second series in 1978–1979. The CBC's variety department had purchased film footage of international circus acts and placed me, playing a kind of ringmaster, in front of the footage, surrounded by local kids, popcorn in hand and seated on bleachers, in Studio 7 on Mutual Street. When it was cut together, it looked like me, the kids and the filmed acts from all over the world were under the same big top. It was called *Circus International with Al Waxman*. It was a clever, inexpensive way to make entertaining programming. There were seven episodes, and they appeared as part of a series called Super Specials, alternating with specials featuring performers such as Anne Murray and Wayne and Shuster. Good company. As my seven episodes were spaced out over the year, it was like I had a second series going.

The CBC apparently paid very little money for the fantastic circus footage, which was a good thing because they had very little money with which to produce the show. I was probably the most expensive item on the budget, and after the seven shows were made there was little left for publicity. (There was a CBC publicity department with its own budget, but whether they allocated something for *Circus International* was another matter.) I knew when the first episode was scheduled to air, and I looked in *TV Guide* the week before, just to check out the blurbs; all I saw for its designated time slot the next Saturday night was "TBA," to be announced. Was I ever pissed off! The schedulers apparently missed *TV Guide*'s five-week deadline, and there was no money for any other promotion. It was like throwing a show out on its own, into the darkness. Well, there was no way I was going to let it float out there in no man's land.

I think it behooves us as professionals to have the respect for our work to get out and promote it. This was true even then, before today's explosion of stations, networks and programs available at the flick of the remote control. I say "even then" because, although we weren't completely inundated yet, there were already many networks and stations available throughout North America, plus our own networks and stations—not to mention all the other things a person can do in the evening besides watch TV. Indeed, promotion is not a question of bravado but rather of humility in the face of daunting competition.

I phoned the CBC's PR department Monday morning and asked two questions: 1. Do you have a long-distance telephone charge number? 2. Could I use it to make some phone calls across the country? Happily, I got an affirmative answer to both questions. I started phoning TV columnists across the country, first in the East, where it was already later in the morning, and working my way to the West, where it was of course three hours earlier. I didn't know what to expect. They might have hung up on me, saying, "You've got some nerve!" or they might want to talk and listen. It was worth finding out. From St. John's to Victoria, at every newspaper or radio station I could connect with, they were pleased to hear me talk about a show I was proud of. The personal contact was appreciated. All the networking that we'd started four years earlier, on that personal appearance tour for *King of Kensington,* paid off. The result was that the show was written about or spoken about right across Canada during the few days left before its otherwise unheralded air date. The audience for the first *Circus International* numbered 1.9 million viewers. The six remaining shows averaged over 2 million viewers each, with one of them getting an audience of 2.6 million and beating out the rival network's Canada–Russia hockey game.

Too often we used to hear that we don't have the publicity machinery and the budgets they have in the States, so how can we compete for attention? Yes, organization and money are important, but they're useless without two ingredients that don't cost anything at all: attitude and energy. With resourcefulness and commitment it's possible to make up for some of the money and machinery that are missing. A few years later Saul Rubinek and I did the same telephone blitz for a five-part radio series of Mordecai Richler's *Joshua Then and Now,* in which we co-starred, again with successful results.

It was during this heady period that I was asked to be the subject of a piece for the CBC's current affairs show, *the fifth estate*. This was an honour for an actor, and to my knowledge a rare one; at that time in Canada, entertainers were seldom considered worthy subjects for shows like *the fifth estate*. It happens more often today, and certainly there are many more forums now. I thought it would be interesting to explore the difficulty of creating a popular star for the purposes of making a television show succeed, and to that end show the process of achieving stardom in a market that had been thought of as apathetic. (I'd learned that the country was in fact hungry for homegrown stars; it was the professional communicators who were apathetic.) For me, stardom wasn't about ego; it was an aspect of professionalism and a necessary component in the process of making a successful Canadian show for a Canadian audience. Therefore, I thought it newsworthy. Was I naive? Maybe. But they came to me, and I thought they were interested in entertainment news.

The journalists to whom the piece was assigned would rather have had a hard news item, not what they considered a "puff piece." They seemed determined to take a negative slant in order to make it newsworthy, as though controversy were an end in itself. The host, Adrienne Clarkson, said (whether she wrote the words or not I don't know, but she certainly spoke them) that I was no more talented than anybody else, it's just that I had a lot more drive than other Canadian actors. The piece made "drive" sound so crass, as though entrepreneurialism could not be part of talent; they made "drive" sound un-Canadian. Furthermore, it was clearly suggested that my commitment to Canadian unity was for ulterior motives. (Ironically, Denis Harvey, in charge of English-language television at that time, had told me that he thought of me as Canada's ambassador to Canada.) It hurt me that anyone should think my love for my country was anything but genuine.

In the end, it didn't matter; whether it was seventeen minutes of praise or of criticism, the reaction in the street was "Wow, you were on *the fifth estate!*" "Congratulations!" "You were the subject of a piece on Canada's *60 Minutes!*" "Fantastic!" Apparently, it made no difference what was said; the important thing was that I'd been profiled on Canadian TV's most prestigious newsmagazine. Perhaps the medium really *is* the message. Still, I appreciated it when the following week's episode of *the fifth estate* included letters from viewers praising my work and criticizing the piece for casting doubts on my talent and the sincerity of my motives.

I moved forward, continuing on all fronts that interested me: acting, directing and community work. It was as though my path was now defined. I could see my future laid out straight ahead, waiting only for me to clear the way so I could proceed.

On the occasion of Israel's thirtieth anniversary, in May 1978, I was asked to host the Montreal Jewish community's celebration in honour of Israel, to be held at the Montreal Forum. They had been negotiating with Barbra Streisand, but her fee (reportedly $65,000 at that time) and other demands were proving difficult if not prohibitive. I was asked what my fee would be; I said I just wanted expenses to cover travelling with Sara and the kids and our nanny, as well as a fee for my writer, but that I personally wouldn't take money for charity work. This was not exactly charity, but frankly, what interested me most was the opportunity to stand up in front of an audience of twenty thousand people, including many provincial and federal politicians, TV cameras and newspaper journalists, and particularly my two kids, and express how I felt about being a Canadian nationalist and at the same time dedicated to the state of Israel. I would be able to say how these were not conflicting loyalties; that I had energy and love enough for both. My feelings for Israel, an expression of my Jewish heritage, were facilitated by my freedom as a Canadian. My giving to Israel did not diminish the Canadian in me, rather, as a Canadian Jew, it enhanced my Canadianism. I said all this, and it was greeted with cheers and ovations.

The cheering actually started when I got up to speak and uttered my first few words: "Bonsoir, mesdames et messieurs." The place erupted with surprise at my French. There were a lot of politicians present, amongst them Prime Minister Trudeau, Marc Lalonde, Monique Bégin and Claude Ryan—but no René Lévesque. He sent a representative. Mr. Lévesque may have been genuinely unable to attend, but the joke going around that night was that he was miffed at the organizers for hiring a Jew from Ontario to host the event rather than a Jew from Quebec. So when there was such delight at my first French words, I continued, "Oui, je parle français, parce que je suis canadien, et donc je parle les deux langues officielles du Canada: Franzoyzish und Yiddish!" Then I poked fun at the politicians present—and absent—finishing with my own appreciation for the opportunity to be humorous at their expense, saying that amongst the rights we Canadians cherish, rights that are fundamental to us as Canadians, is the right to be irreverent. Mr. Trudeau applauded when I said that.

I'd met Pierre Trudeau before, particularly at functions such as Canada Day celebrations, but those moments were brief and *en passant* because there were always many people milling about. This night was the first time we actually got into an extended conversation. He had recently separated from his wife, Margaret, and in spite of his time-consuming job as prime minister, he was taking on the daunting responsibility of single parenting. So the talk to begin with was mostly about the difficulty of travelling with children. I remember being so impressed with his genuine commitment to caring for his boys. So it was doubly shocking and heartbreaking to hear, at the time of this writing, of the loss of his son Michel. A tragedy for the young man, his brothers, his mother and father: pain that no parent should ever have to endure.

My daughter, Tobaron, eight years old in 1978, presented Mr. Trudeau with a colouring book made by her class at Rosedale Public School for his young sons. Whenever we have met since then, he always asks how my children are doing. In 1988, when Tobaron was a student at McGill, he made time in his busy schedule to take her out to lunch to talk about her studies. When I asked her afterwards if I came up in the conversation, she answered, "No, we talked mostly about T.S. Eliot."

In 1979 I was again asked to tour Canada prior to the Canada Day celebrations, which I would host in the afternoon at Queen's Park and in the evening on Parliament Hill. What I had learned from earlier travels across Canada, and what was being reinforced every time I travelled, was a feeling that Canada, if personified, loved all Canadians but needed this love to be reciprocated by individual Canadians. I decided to write a love song. Now, this takes a talent I don't have, so I got hold of my friend Skip Prokop, a talented musician formerly in the band Lighthouse, and he agreed to collaborate; indeed, he happily took over and ran with it. My only contribution was the concept and co-writing of the lyrics. "Gotta Hear You Say It Too" was released and played across the country in medium rotation on middle-of-the-road stations. It was not a hit, but it did get played, as one of its refrains goes, "from Beacon Hill through Parliament Hill to Signal Hill."

We wrote the song for fun, but it made me aware of how lucrative the music business can be. Consider that we were played only about half a dozen times a week on half a dozen stations across the country, and I still got a cheque from BMI (the royalty collectors for songwriters) of a few thousand dollars every quarter for at least a year. If I got this much, can you imagine what, let's say, the Bee Gees were collecting at that time for "Stayin' Alive," which was a big hit then, playing probably half a dozen times every hour on every radio station in the free world? Astonishing? Yes, but I found it amusing, and was delighted with my cheques.

I was determined to have a sense of balance in my community and charity work. For every Jewish or Israeli cause, like the United Jewish Appeal, B'nai Brith or Israel Bonds, I would dedicate an equal amount of time and effort to, let's say, the United Way (for which I narrated a short film), Big Brothers, the Variety Club or the Canadian Cancer Society. I was always glad to help out, because there was the joy of giving and also an immediate reciprocation. For example, there was the time I was asked to go to Corner Brook, Newfoundland, to help raise funds to rebuild a local arena that had burnt down. Once again, they wanted to know my fee. My answer was, "Instead of a fee, do you have a deal with the airline?" They said yes, so I asked if I could bring my wife and children, and they were glad to do this. My kids had fun for a few days in Newfoundland, and even attended class in the local school. Of course Sara and I had a good time too. We always made friends in the course of our charitable work. They put us up in Grand Falls House, a mansion owned then by Abitibi-Price, and even presented us with a painting of the view from the window of our room in that house. Grand Falls House hosted VIPs in the days when the airport in Gander, Newfoundland, was where flights to and from Europe connected or refuelled. When Sara and I signed the guest book, we noticed the signatures of politicians such as Nikita Khrushchev and movie stars such as Marlene Dietrich.

On another occasion, Sara and I attended a function in Summerside, Prince Edward Island, and were guests of honour at a luncheon being held in a high-school gymnasium. There were about five hundred people there, and it seemed like they were all called Mackenzie or MacGregor or MacIntosh. While we were waiting for the luncheon to start I leaned over to Sara and whispered, "We've got to be the only two Jews in this room." Sara leaned back and whispered to me, "On the island." At that moment a gentleman came over and said they were all set to begin, and he wondered if I would like to say grace. I was flattered, but something possessed me. (I don't know why, because I have no problem with words like "For these gifts we are about to receive."). I felt I could only say grace in the language of my faith and told him so. He said, "We would be honoured." I stood up and gave the blessing over the bread in Hebrew, and then Sara stood up and translated it into English.

The Road Broadens

I know there is a distance to go yet, but I like to think of how far we have come, not just as Jews in Canada but as Canadians. I think of specific events over the past century, like my old uncle Moishe Fuchs's only memory of pre–World War I Canada being "Punch you in the mouth, you fucking Jew!" or the pre–World War II days of "none is too many" in reference to Jewish immigrants, or the post–World War II days of the late 1940s, when I was refused the captaincy of my hockey team because I was Jewish, or the years after that when I wished my name was Watkins rather than Waxman. Then came the emergence of the state of Israel, and with it the romantic fervour, the pride and fun in being Jewish. By the 1960s I was able to look into the eyes of powerful Hollywood agents and say, "No, I will not change my name. I'm an Al Waxman! That's what I am!" A sense of self that proudly included both religion and nationality. And now, in 1978, I could stand up in a room full of Canadians, five hundred of them, none of them Jews, and be welcomed to say the Jewish grace before the meal that we Canadians were about to share. Yes, we have come some distance. Yes, we are on the right road.

CHAPTER 23

The Party's Over, but the Feast Goes On

"You've taken an orchid and turned it into an onion!" That's what I said to Jack Humphrey in the fifth year of *King of Kensington,* and my words brought a rueful smile to his face. He understood exactly what I meant. He didn't disagree, but after four years I think his creative juices had to flow in other directions, and he didn't own the show; Perry Rosemond and the CBC did. He wanted his own show, and that's where he was ultimately headed.

During the summer hiatus between the fourth and fifth years, the show seemed to go off course. I can't, in all honesty, say that this happened without my knowledge, because Jack was too honourable a gentleman not to have consulted me, but I don't remember whatever conversations we might have had about it. This is probably because I was so involved in making other shows (four theatrical movies that year, plus the CBC-TV movie *The Winnings of Frankie Walls* that summer), touring the country making speeches for the CBC (to the Canadian Association of Broadcasters in Jasper, or an assembly of Catholic schools in Saskatoon, or Kiwanis or Rotary or Canadian Legion halls anywhere from Halifax to Lloydminster).

I was also commited to doing charity work, primarily for the

Canadian Cancer Society at this time. I became honorary campaign chairman of the Society in 1979 for two years. The word "honorary" had no meaning for me; I threw myself into it. As well as making public service messages for TV and radio, I gave fundraising speeches across the country. I also took time to familiarize myself with the progress being made in cancer research and in the care and treatment of patients and their families so that I'd know what I was talking about.

That same year, Terry Fox burst onto the scene. As he ran his one-legged hopping marathon across Canada, that valiant young man did more to unite the country than any unity program emanating from Ottawa. It seemed that he was linking the nation, city by city, as he started his quest on the shores of Newfoundland with a view to finishing up in Coquitlam, British Columbia. Quite apart from the huge contribution he made for cancer research and medical science in general, the example of his sheer will and heart, together with his athletic prowess and perseverance was an enormous boost to the morale and spirit of the country. An inspiration.

It was obvious to me and to others, I'm sure, that the personal story of Terry Fox's dedication, courage, tragedy and legacy would make a fantastic film. But I felt it incumbent upon me to steer clear of that project, because in my position as campaign chairman it might look opportunistic and fraught with ulterior motives if I pursued it. Yet a film about Terry Fox had to be made. It was the kind of story Canadians needed to hear and see. Too often in our history, in the established broadcasting and filmmaking institutions, the emphasis has been on fact (that is, news and documentaries) rather than on fiction. Canadians have certainly done it well, but culture, I believe, grows more out of fiction than fact—that is, storytelling. Here was a chance to marry fact and fiction, an opportunity seized by Robert Cooper (formerly CBC's on-air ombudsman and then a successful film producer in Canada and the US), who was quick and resourceful enough to make it happen. Even though I wasn't involved, I'm glad that I was able to be of some assistance to Cooper with relevant information and introductions in the formative stages of *The Terry Fox Story*.

In the fall of 1979, when I started back on the fifth year of the series, a reorientation was necessary, as King now worked in the local community centre rather than the variety store, there was yet another new woman in his life, not to mention a different rendition of the theme song. This is not to suggest that the new actress wasn't terrific, or that the new version of the song wasn't good, or that the community centre wasn't a plausible setting for a show like this, but all these changes, and there were more, added up, in my opinion, to too many fundamental changes from the original concept. A successful long-running series needs elements both of constancy and of change. That is, predictability (in this case, not a bad word), something the audience can count on, plus the freshness of change. For example, the producers of *Cagney and Lacey* tenaciously hung on to the concept of a two-female buddy cop show. This provided a constancy at the core of the show, while changes came about in personal relationships, personnel in the precinct and the flow of storylines.

Turning an orchid into an onion is perhaps a comical turn of phrase, but it's also funny-peculiar in its convoluted imagery. The phrase of course connotes the ruination of something, but the irony of it, in this instance, is that onions are one of the key ingredients in that aromatic casserole called Kensington Market. Instead, the show in its fifth year had been sidetracked back towards sliced white bread.

Still, to say "ruination" isn't exactly fair. There were some good people involved in the fifth year, especially the very talented Jayne Eastwood, whose earthy, wisecracking style of comedy could poke fun at King and puncture his balloon. Her character was a good foil for him, and a rewarding romantic relationship for both characters was the result. Nevertheless, the show did veer onto a different course than the one promised to the audience. If I lost interest, well, I still managed to "get it up," as we say in the business, every week because

The Party's Over, but the Feast Goes On

I'm a pro. Some members of the audience lost interest and did not come back, as reflected in the numbers for the fifth year. We dropped from approximately 2 million in the fourth year to 1.25 million in the fifth, sometimes falling as low as 1.1 million. Those numbers are, especially in terms of today's barometers, very high; nevertheless, it was a drop of about three-quarters of a million viewers.

I thought the writing was on the wall. Still, Peter Herrndorf, who ran the English-language television network at that time, said to me that I could have two more years if I wanted them. But I felt we'd accomplished what we set out to do, and I'd personally achieved the two aims I had for *King*. Two more years? No. I felt sated. I had my feast in five years; I didn't need seven. Time for new kingdoms. Furthermore, if I wanted to continue, although I was not the producer, it might have meant somehow working in that capacity, as a new team of writers and actors would have to be assembled. This was not my bailiwick, nor was it in my best interest. No, the timing was good. It was better to go out while the numbers were still respectable and people would then ask "Why?" rather than "Why not?"

Still, there were highlights for me in the fifth year, perhaps the most memorable being an episode called "King to Pawn 4," when our show was complemented by the performance of Lou Jacobi, one of Canada's greatest and funniest actors. He has often phoned me over the years in Los Angeles or Toronto from his home in New York, and he'll start the conversation by saying, "Hello Al! This is Jew Lacobi," and then proceed to do twenty minutes of jokes like the stand-up comic he used to be in his younger years.

The real glitter of that star-filled episode was the performance of eight-year-old Tobaron Waxman. Toby, as she was more often called then, came to me one day and said all the kids at school were always asking her why she'd never been on *King of Kensington*. I said to her, "Toby, what are you really saying to me? Do you want to be on an episode of *King*?"

"Well, not a lot. Just one," she replied hopefully.

I explained to her that it was not that simple. "You can't get on the show just because of your dad. You have to audition. And before you even get an audition, you have to be interviewed by the producer."

"What's an interview?"

"Oh, the producer asks you some questions to see whether you can be relied on as an actor."

"Oh," she said, a little worried. "Will he ask me anything in mathematics?"

One day during rehearsal I saw a darling little girl walk on the set with a script under her arm. I did a double take—it was Toby.

I called dear Jack Humphrey and demanded to know why and how. I told him he didn't have to do this for me, and that if it didn't work out it was on his head. He assured me that she had read some lines to him from the script and she made him laugh, and so she got the part. She was indeed good. For me, "King to Pawn 4" is one of the most memorable episodes among the one hundred and eleven.

We had many guest stars that year, and over the five years, who furthered our show and whose careers were in turn, I hope, furthered by our show. John Candy was in a number of episodes, and Eugene Levy did a couple, as did Dave Thomas. Harvey Atkin showed up every now and then. The great Jane Mallett graced our show. Eddie Shack was one of our first guests. Andrea Martin was superb. So was a very young Mike Myers, who still persists in calling me Mr. Waxman. (He has shown a clip from that episode of *King* on David Letterman.) Also terrific were Joe Flaherty, Saul Rubinek, Helen Shaver, Monica Parker, Lally Cadeau, Patricia Collins, Marilyn Lightstone, Tony Rosato, Mimi Kuzik, Ken James, Gale Garnett, Jan Rubes and Billy Van. Some very talented writers and directors got and gave valuable experience too. Writers such as Suzette Couture and Anna Sandor did a few—and Ken Finkleman wrote a hilarious script. In the third year of *Cagney and Lacey* the head writer, a woman named Liz Coe, told me she and I had worked together before: she had successfully submitted scripts to *King of Kensington* from New York. So too had other Hollywood hotshots, like Carmen Finestra, who would later write for some of the highest-rated sitcoms. Of course there were many talented directors, among them Sheldon Larry, with whom I've done a couple of very good movies since *King*, most notably *The Sue Rodriguez Story*.

I have at times been critical of the CBC in this book, but I'm not without appreciation for the Corporation. Anyway, how can you be critical of something as monolithic as the CBC? Comments, positive or negative, have to be directed at individuals, particularly in middle and upper management rather than in the remote realm of executive royalty. It's the people who actually make and plan programming who are responsible for it. On that level there were people who frustrated me, but there were and are also people to whom I shall forever be grateful, like that great man of theatre and entertainment, John Hirsch, or broadcasters in whose pulse beat the best of intentions for the airwaves of Canada, like Knowlton Nash, Peter Herrndorf and Denis Harvey. But if the letters CBC are to be used as a matter of convenience, then I can express gratitude for the lovely farewell letter the CBC sent me via a half-hour on their popular talk show at that time, *Take Thirty*. It was produced by Eva Czigler (who later became Eva Czigler Herrndorf) and hosted by Hana Gartner. Hana interviewed me and my family—Sara and Toby (eight years old at the time) and little Adam (six years old)—and showed genuine interest and curiosity in us, in my career, in all my activities and my efforts to make things happen. She covered the full run of *King of Kensington* and poked fun at my propensity for PR when I plugged the upcoming *Winnings of Frankie Walls*. That half-hour was like a valentine from the CBC, coming off the TV screen right to me.

I will always be able to get passionate, critical, loving and utterly mushy about the CBC. We grew up together. Indeed, we were born about the same time. The CBC provided me and many of my colleagues with incredible opportunities to develop and advance, to make mistakes and still continue, and I believe it can be said that the

CBC caused greatness to happen more often than it screwed up; great radio for sure, and in television from the golden age of the fifties and early sixties and oftentimes over the years up to the present. There have always been golden moments at the CBC. As well, it can be said that from its inception up until the eighties the CBC was the glue that held our country together. Now, happily, they are finally seeing themselves in an adjusted role because there is a huge fabric of broadcasting communications out there, of which the CBC is only a single thread, but still one of the most central and important of them all. Its role is to offer, as it is now doing (and as other networks and stations are emulating to some degree), a completely Canadian option. To succeed in this, the CBC needs to be run by someone with a public-sector heart and a private-sector head.

The Winnings of Frankie Walls, which aired in 1980, would be my last appearance on camera for the CBC for approximately a decade. It was a triumphant way to complete a chapter of my life. This performance on the anthology series *For the Record* was a portrayal of an unskilled labourer who finds himself automated out of his job. Like my father, Frankie Walls believes that a man who doesn't work is a bum. He now has to struggle to regain self-respect and to make ends meet. He flounders, even considers robbery, but finally is guided into the difficult task, for a man in his forties with little education, of retraining, in hopes of getting a job. It won me an ACTRA award, the Earle Gray Award, named for one of the great early actors of Canada (and a prestigious pioneer of the Alliance of Canadian Cinema, Television and Radio Artists). The Earle Gray Award is now presented by the Academy of Canadian Cinema and Television for recognition of a body of work, but it was then given by ACTRA for a single performance. This was my second ACTRA award; I won my first in 1976 for Best Performance in a Continuing Role for *King of Kensington*.

The feast was over; but I knew it would not be followed by famine. (Did I ever look it?)

Chapter 24

A Winning Streak

"The King Is Dead. Long Live the King!" was the caption printed over my picture on the cover of *Starweek* magazine in the first week of March 1980. This was not the first time I'd been on the cover of *Starweek*, nor would it be the last. By this time I had been featured in almost every magazine in the country. Being on the cover of *TV Guide* three times during the 1970s and '80s was especially important because of its circulation of approximately 3 million in Canada.

With all the magazine covers and articles, newspaper articles and pictures, TV profiles and interviews, telethons for Sick Children's Hospital or the Variety Club or muscular dystrophy, plus the regular impacts of TV series and reruns, specials, TV movies and films, it seemed as though I was popping up everywhere. My attitude was that there was no such thing as overexposure, the rationale being that I was helping to promote the shows I was in and raising the profile of worthy causes. Indeed, the higher my own profile, the more requests I received from charities. This wasn't always appreciated as either professionalism or altruism; it looked to some as though I had ulterior motives. I'd be less than honest if I didn't admit that there was some element of self-promotion involved and that I did enjoy the activities and the perks.

It *seemed* as though I was at every opening in town, even if I wasn't there. At times I was written about as being at an opening when in fact I had been at home, which is where, more often than not, I preferred to be. So it stung a little when some smartass, trying to sound clever, would write about "the ubiquitous Al Waxman," who would show up, as another wrote, at "the opening of an envelope." However, if you're going to be in public life, a sense of humour is essential, and that kind of thing can be relegated to yesterday's news.

The irony about invitations to openings was that in the past, when I couldn't afford to buy tickets, I was never offered complimentary seats, but when I finally could afford to buy my own, I didn't have to do so. Sometimes certain shows or events needed the presence of well-known people in order to get launched, and in those days, when there weren't nearly as many high-profile Canadian shows or Canadian performers as there are today, my being there was a way of helping. I actually felt, on occasion, that it was my duty to show up at a certain event. And you wouldn't dare leave at intermission, as I did once for good reason, because this was noticed and written about as a negative comment on the event. After that I always stayed right through the evening no matter how unbearable I thought it was. Small price to pay. Celebrity, I believe, comes with responsibility as well as privileges. Anyway, we were having a great time.

I say "we" because Sara, who likes the public spotlight much less than I do, was starting to get attention in the media in her own right. By this time Sara's first book was out, a best-seller called *The King's Wife's Cookbook*, and she was in the *Toronto Star* every day with an innovative column, read probably by everyone going home from work and trying to plan a quick and inexpensive supper. Using the information published under "Best Buys of the Week" at all the supermarkets, Sara would come up with creative and budget-conscious recipes for "Supper in a Hurry." The name "Waxman" was getting a lot of media attention.

My attention was focused, as always, mainly on my work—acting, directing and trying to develop programming. By this time Louis

Malle's highly acclaimed *Atlantic City* had come out. In it I played a comic character who was running an endless poker game throughout the film and needed cocaine to sustain the energy of the players. In every scene in which I appeared I was buying cocaine from Burt Lancaster and Kate Reid. When the film earned Malle an Academy Award nomination, I congratulated him, and he responded by saying he wished there was a category for Best Ensemble, because our cast would then be nominated. It made me feel proud because, aside from Burt and Susan Sarandon, the entire cast was Canadian.

Louis Malle had chosen me without an audition, presumably from seeing *King of Kensington* footage. I didn't meet him till I arrived on the set. My scenes were filmed on weekends to accommodate my *King of Kensington* schedule of Monday to Friday. After working late Friday night I would get the first flight to Montreal on Saturday morning, where we would film my scenes at the Windsor Hotel. When I got started in the morning I felt like I was trying to fit a square peg in a round hole. Pardon the cliché, but it's the most apt description of my work until I warmed up later in the morning. At the end of the first day Burt Lancaster said to me, "You're like a fine racehorse. You start slow, but you finish first."

Also at this time, Eric Till's feature film *Wild Horse Hank* was released. It was a Western shot in Pincher Creek, Alberta, with, would you believe, citified me playing a cowboy. This was the same year that *The Winnings of Frankie Walls* aired on the CBC. Each of these films showed me with a different look and characterization, and all were different from *King of Kensington*. The added profile that went with the increased work helped raise my price. Still, I always had to hustle; work didn't just fall into my lap, ever. Between Catherine McCartney and me, we'd find out what was happening and what was going to happen and we'd go after it. Occasionally "it" would be going after me at the same time.

I got offered a part in a film called *Tulips*, to be shot in Montreal. It starred Gabe Kaplan and Bernadette Peters, and was produced by the late Harold Greenberg. I played Gabe's older brother. It was a comedy about a guy and a girl on their separate attempts at suicide. Finally, but reluctantly as far as the guy was concerned (he would have preferred to do it on his own), they make a mutual attempt—not succeeding, but instead falling in love.

Harold Greenberg was a man I am awfully glad to have met and worked with. Our relationship started back during *The Crowd Inside*; he owned the lab and post-production house that serviced that film. We had become friends and, like many Canadians, particularly in the film business, I appreciated his contribution, through film and television and community work, to his home province of Quebec within a larger commitment to Canada and the film industry nationwide.

He had a great sense of humour. He generously provided me with a limo for the Montreal opening of *The Crowd Inside* which, while not exactly a hearse, was rented from a funeral home. The reviews justified his premonition. I, in turn, would joke that it was a joy to know somebody fatter than me and he could therefore count on me to stand by him any time! I remember one time when we happened to be on the same flight from Montreal to Toronto. He was sitting a couple of rows ahead of me with a huge brown bag on his lap. He was munching away, and I asked him what he was eating. He offered me a bagel. They were warm and fresh and delicious. "Good?" he asked me.

"Very good," I agreed.

"Montreal bagels," he said with jolly pride. "Better than Toronto's, aren't they!"

"No way!" I challenged.

"What? You eat my bagels and then insult them?" He started throwing bagels at me, pelting me with them. I caught them and fired them back at him. We had a bagel fight, high in the sky, much to the enjoyment of the surrounding passengers, who not only had a laugh but a more delicious trip than they normally would.

Yes, he was a proud Montrealer, Quebecker and Canadian. I often use the name Greenberg in arguments with Québécois colleagues in the film business, who are separatists and of the *pure laine* persuasion. I maintain that Greenberg, a dedicated Canadian who created so much opportunity and employment in the province of Quebec, and who expanded beyond Quebec but never abandoned it, was no less a Quebecker because his name was Greenberg than if his name had been Bouchard or Parizeau.

Tulips ran into production problems and needed to be partially reshot. Because I had hit it off so well with both Gabe and Bernadette, Harold asked me to direct the reshoots and additional shoots. As I didn't direct the whole film, I didn't want a director's credit. Instead, in addition to my acting credit, I was named as "creative consultant." More important than any credit was the experience and fun of another feature film, the continuation of friendship with the Greenbergs and their company, Astral Films—new work experience and new friendships, particularly with the beautiful and multitalented Bernadette Peters.

From comedy to drama. I directed, for producer Mike McManus at TVOntario, a touching and complex story about an ethical question that, as the film says, won't go away. It was about abortion, and it was called, appropriately enough, *The Moral Question.* Starring Pat Hamilton, Ken Pogue and Ron Singer, it was filled with courtroom and hospital drama. I shot one medical procedure with such attention to detail that I wasn't aware of how accurate, risky and realistic it would ultimately look when cut together. This was of course something I wanted to achieve on film, but it wasn't until I finished the final edit that I was reminded by its chilling effect on me of how squeamish I am.

I became quite friendly with Mike McManus, who in addition to producing and writing also did in-depth profiles as an on-air host. He did a five-part interview with me and two other subjects, intercutting amongst the three of us. The other two were renowned actor-director Douglas Campbell and Ontario provincial cabinet member (at that time) Bette Stephenson. I don't know how he arrived at the three of us, but it was, in all three cases and in its entirety, a probing, intelligent and sensitive interview, driven by genuine curiosity and aptly titled "Journeys in Time."

Keeping with the subject of genuine curiosity and attention to detail, I was also interviewed many times in those days by Brian Linehan. He would joke that if he assembled them all there would be at least a five-part miniseries for Citytv. For one of them, just for the fun of it, I bought a sport jacket from Lou Myles, where Brian also shopped. Unbeknownst to him until we started to tape, I came on the show wearing the exact same outfit he was wearing. He wasn't thrown—taller and slimmer, he looked better in it than I did—and we went on to have another half-hour of lively conversation.

One of my most important half-hours on Citytv at that time was a show I did with Patrick Watson called *Titans*. It was the leadoff episode of a series of one-on-one confrontational discussions in which Patrick interviews historical personalities. I played Louis B. Mayer. I took the role, as I believe I take all my roles, very seriously. I thoroughly researched the character, reading everything I could get my hands on about him, looking at stills and studying film footage of him, as well as flying down to Los Angeles and visiting the MGM lot to interview old-timers, such as a janitor, who remembered him from personal experience. It turned out to be an excellent half-hour. It was a show Patrick was proud of, and so was I. It kicked off *Titans* in a very positive way, and soon benefited my career as well.

At the same time, under the deal that Sandy Wernick had negotiated for me with the CBC, I was developing pilot scripts for new series for me to star in. Since the beginning of the deal in the fourth year of *King of Kensington*, of the many ideas that had been explored, two had emerged as having real potential. One was called *Joe Mack, Agent-at-Law* and the other, *Ethnic Squad*. Either one would have been good for me to star in. Both generated some excitement and were initially considered by the network to be promising.

Joe Mack, Agent-at-Law was about a character who, without being a lawyer, practised law within certain prescribed limits. He couldn't be a lawyer because he had been convicted of a crime and had done time. In prison, however, he studied law and helped out fellow inmates. When he was released, he opened a storefront office, and started a practice as an "agent-at-law"—a phenomenon that exists in Canadian law—to help provide service to those for whom lawyers are too expensive or somehow intimidating. He was a friend to street people, people who felt disenfranchised.

It was a good idea from a concept by Len Wise, a practising lawyer, comedy writer and wannabe scriptwriter. The pilot script wasn't bad; it was written by Steven Alix, who had some experience in and around feature film scripting and production, and then rewritten by the late Jim Burt, who had read and analyzed scripts for the CFDC (and also for me) and who later became an executive at the CBC in charge of long-form development and production. The main obstacle to its progress was the cost factor. I had assembled a lot of writing and producing talent like a vanguard for this project. Instead of moving it forward, however, this impressive producership, albeit enticing, proved to be such a financial burden that it paralyzed the project. I can't remember all the personnel, but I know they included, as well as the writers already mentioned, Jack Humphrey and Perry Rosemond as executive producers, Ralph Thomas, who had created, produced and directed many episodes of the CBC's journalistic drama series *For the Record*, and finally, myself. Everybody cost money and would cost more money. This scared the head of drama and, out of fairness to him and to the CBC, I acknowledge that the project was overweight with "above-the-line" costs. Still, it was a shame that we couldn't find a way around that, because it would have been, in my opinion, an entertaining show about an aspect of the law found only in Canada.

Ethnic Squad was a concept from George Allan, who had done some wonderful writing on *King of Kensington*, both comedic and dramatic. It was based on an actual squad in the Metropolitan Toronto Police Force at that time called the "Ethnic Squad." I don't know if it exists today, twenty years later, because ideally, the whole police force is an ethnic squad, but there was need for it at that time. It comprised a group of men and women representative of the different racial and religious elements in our community, as well as the many ethnic and cultural backgrounds that exist in Toronto, all serving under a captain, to be played by me. It was (pardon the pun) a colourful group, buoyant with personality and brimming with policing talent and the desire to be sympathetic to people of all persuasions in the city.

I was really hot on this one. Unfortunately, the pilot script scared the head of drama, perhaps it was the pimp whose race could make for sensitivity among some viewers. As well, the last name of a mobster could be problematic with other viewers. The head of drama actually said to me, "If we do this right, we'll offend somebody every week. I'm afraid of this." I don't know why he couldn't be persuaded by the truth of what's going on out on the street, that ultimately there is a sense of balance, that there are good guys who are this colour or that and mobsters with names of every ethnic background. If you don't like the first script, you don't throw away the idea but commission another script, because good ideas don't happen every Monday and Thursday (to employ a direct translation of a Yiddish aphorism). But in this case the script, the idea and the project were aborted. That was too bad, because if we had done it, the way I saw it, we would have had a quality show that would have predated the likes of NBC's *Hill Street Blues*, CBS's *Cagney and Lacey* and ABC's *Miami Vice*, all three amongst the biggest hits of the eighties.

My salary for five years of *King of Kensington* didn't equal one year of my *Cagney and Lacey* salary, and remuneration for *Ethnic Squad* would certainly have been more in the order of my *King of Kensington* paycheque. Frankly, though, as much as *Cagney and Lacey* turned out to be a fantastic experience for me, I would have preferred doing *Eth-*

nic Squad. I would have preferred a Canadian show that sets a trend rather than following in the footsteps of the US.

Both those ideas (*Joe Mack* and *Ethnic Squad*) were better than most that come along, but to make something happen in this business takes courage and vision plus perseverance, power and passion, not to mention luck and timing. The players involved—perhaps that includes me too—didn't possess, at this juncture and in this combination, all those prerequisite ingredients that make for success.

The CBC fortuitously offered me an episode of their anthology series *For the Record* to direct. It was called, appropriately enough, "Cop" and it starred Larry Dane. It was the story of a cop whose integrity is called into question. Under intense personal and professional pressure he succumbs to suicide, or as they would say, "eating the barrel." It got Larry a Best Performance by an Actor nomination and placed me solidly on a path of real and rewarding research (that is, going out with cops on the beat), because as it turned out I was going to be doing cop shows for most of the next decade.

I always remember, in my studies of philosophy at the University of Western Ontario and particularly the course in logic, discussions on causality: all the factors that make up a cause, which in turn results in an effect. It's always refreshing for me when theory actually works in practice. That, strangely enough, is one of the first things I think of in connection with *Cagney and Lacey:* a confluence of circumstances that catapulted my career.

King of Kensington had been playing in some important markets across the United States and had thereby given me some profile and, more importantly, drawn the attention of certain casting directors, like those at CBS. *Cagney and Lacey* was a Movie of the Week that CBS planned to shoot up in Canada because of the favourable exchange rate. The dollar was then, in 1981, in the low eighties or high seventies. I remember American producers saying that if it ever got up to 85 cents they'd be "outta here" because the benefit wouldn't be enough to cover the inconvenience, and it was a real possibility then that it could get up to 85 cents. Think of the enticement today, in the late 1990s, with our dollar worth less than 70 cents; no wonder there are film crews everywhere.

A factor that made *Cagney and Lacey* more interesting for me was that, as a Movie of the Week, it would possibly be considered, depending on the degree of its success, as a "backdoor" pilot; that is to say, if the ratings were high enough, it wouldn't just be a one-off but rather a leadoff into a series. Deirdre Bowen, the Canadian casting director on this project, had formerly been an assistant casting director on *King*. She was very much on my side, and she came to a mutual understanding with my agent, Catherine McCartney, that the potential for me in doing this Movie of the Week more than justified what would be less salary than usual. The producers were looking to benefit not only from the exchange rate but also from smaller salaries in Canada. The director of the piece was to be Ted Post. Teddy, with whom I had worked so well ten years earlier on the never-to-be-produced script based on *Them Damn Canadians Hanged Louis Riel*, wanted me to be in *Cagney and Lacey* because he said it would create for me in the US what I had in Canada; even though the part wasn't that big in the pilot, it could be expanded in the series.

I was all for it. Konstantin Stanislavsky taught that there are no small parts, only small actors, but that, with all due respect, is bullshit. There are indeed small parts. What determines my decision making then and now is, can I make it interesting? All factors seemed to point to the answer yes, except one: the executive producer, Barney Rosenzweig. Television, as opposed to feature film, is a producer's medium. Even with a highly regarded director like Ted Post, the producer is the power in TV, and Barney said, "Who is this guy Waxman? I've got a guy in New York I want for the part." Ted prevailed upon him to look at a show of mine that was on the air that night.

The next day I was at a celebrity charity tennis tournament. At that time I was taking tennis pretty seriously, and all I could think of was that I was playing against Wayne Gretzky (this was the first time he ever played, and he still beat me). Suddenly a guy whom I had never seen before came over. I thought he was going to ask for an autograph, and I didn't want to be rude, although I didn't want my concentration interrupted either. When he reached out his hand and introduced himself, he said, "I'm Barney Rosenzweig, and I'm your boss."

I'm thinking to myself, who's this smartass, and I said, "You're my what?"

"Your boss."

"How's that?"

"When I was a kid I was a press agent at MGM. I saw your performance of Louis B. Mayer last night and you scared the hell out of me."

"So?"

"So I'm the producer of *Cagney and Lacey* and I want you in it."

So I lost the tennis match to Wayne Gretzky that day! So Barney Rosenzweig, who plays tennis every day of his life, went on to win the whole damn tournament! So what? As far as I was concerned, in terms of the larger game of my life and career, I was on a winning streak!

CHAPTER 25

Long-Distance Love

There had been many male buddy shows, such as *Starsky and Hutch* on TV and *Butch Cassidy and the Sundance Kid* in the movies, but never, in either medium, a female buddy show. The producers, Barney Rosenzweig and Barbara Corday, his wife then, and co-writer and co-producer Barbara Avedon had been trying since as far back as the Butch Cassidy film to realize this concept in a feature film, and subsequently as a Movie of the Week. They had been trying for around six years, and finally, history was about to be made. And I was going to be part of it.

This would be the second time for me. The first, *King*, was in 1975. It was very exciting to have been part of history-making TV in Canada, history-making because *King* was the first successful sitcom in English Canada (there had been *The Plouffe Family* out of Quebec) and because *King* was largely based on multicultural relationships, a combination—successful sitcom and multiculturalism—that had never happened before in all of Canadian TV, English or French. Now, in 1981, I was going to be part of a show whose formula, a buddy relationship starring two women, was a first in American and ultimately worldwide TV.

The impact of this backdoor pilot was greatly enhanced by the casting of Loretta Swit (very popular because of *M*A*S*H*), and an impressive acting talent, Tyne Daly (who got the part when a more popular TV star turned it down rather than take second billing to Swit). Tyne was fairly new, to me and to most people, in comparison with Swit, although everyone seemed to remember her from her performance in *The Enforcer*, a Clint Eastwood film.

There were possibly two parts available for me: Tyne's, that is Lacey's, husband, or the sergeant in the squad. The way the pilot script was written, it looked like the husband might not last beyond the pilot, and it appeared possible that the character of the sergeant could probably be melded with the captain of the squad into a single character for the series, a squad lieutenant. Mind you, the husband was later reworked and recast with the high-energy acting of the wonderful Johnny Karlen. But I was happy to have Sgt. Samuels in the pilot with the belief that the character would become Lt. Samuels in the series, with hopefully third-star billing after the characters of Cagney and Lacey.

First, the Movie of the Week had to score as a backdoor pilot. It was a good script, based on a good concept, telling a good cop story and set in a good sociological situation (crime perpetrators masquerading as Orthodox Jews in New York's diamond trade, with thievery and ultimately murder—but happily, the producers weren't afraid that any ethnic group would be offended). It was well cast and well directed. Nevertheless, all of these virtues might not have been sufficient without one crucial addition to the package—namely the star's (Loretta Swit's) TVQ. Those letters denote the measurement of popularity and want-to-seeability of a TV star. Loretta Swit had nine years of super success *on M*A*S*H*. Loretta Swit had super-high TVQ.

Cagney and Lacey got a 45-percent share of the TV viewing audience. That was high, very high, even in 1981–1982. Today it's unheard of: all three networks together (NBC, ABC and CBS) barely compile much more than a 45 share. That number was momentous, and so was the impact of the show. *C & L* was on its way to becoming a series.

The playwright in the sky, as I've said before, has a peculiar sense of timing. Sara and I had just bought a new house. Over the years, whenever we moved, I always managed to be on location or have an asthma attack. In either case Sara would be stuck with the laborious and possibly even traumatic task of moving from one house to another. This move was likely to be particularly difficult because, although the reason we moved was that we needed just one more room, the house we bought had about eight more rooms. (It had eighteen rooms; we knocked out a couple of walls to enlarge some of them, but there were still fifteen or sixteen.)

Why did we need all that space? We didn't. But this huge manor (as it was sometimes described in the media) in lower Forest Hill Village represented an important achievement for me. Ever since I was a kid, it was something I'd aspired to and needed to accomplish with my own means. It was a tough time, though, because we had to sell our Rosedale house, as a result of the real estate market collapsing over a weekend in 1981, for about 40 percent less than we asked. Otherwise, I would have been the owner of two houses at a time when mortgage rates were sky-high, over 20 percent. (Thank God I'd paid off the first one. When the final payment was made, we stuck the mortgage contract in the barbecue. Our supper that night tasted terrific!) Still, I was in over my head from the get-go.

Fortunately, I got *Cagney and Lacey* (perhaps the playwright in the sky's timing is perfect after all), with a high US salary and an exchange rate in my favour; and fortunately for me, though perhaps unfortunately for Sara, almost the day after we moved into Forest Hill Road, I had to go to Los Angeles to start filming the first episodes. The only thing I could do to protect my wife and children, my hearth and home, was to install an elaborate security system—and start commuting.

It was either commute or move us all down to California. Why not, my friends asked. It's not such a bad life. But the original order from CBS was for a limited number of episodes, six I think, and who knew if we would get picked up? My family enjoyed such a beautiful life in Toronto, Sara had a great job (although she said she could type anywhere) and the kids went to good schools. I was afraid to give up what we had built in Toronto. There was fear, but there was something else. I loved Toronto. I felt I had contributed to the growth of the city. It was my city. I had no intention of leaving. Sure, I could relocate for a time and still be a Canadian, but at this juncture I decided to commute. I never even changed my clocks; I just added or subtracted three hours. I used to say some guys take a bus to work, I take a plane. I would fly back and forth about four times a month. There were even articles about me in the Los Angeles press; one headline read: "Talk About Commuting!"

It was tough for me to be away from home then because Canada had become a different place in the eighties than it had been years earlier. There was a lot happening here. Many actors who'd left for greener pastures in earlier years would not have done so if Canada had been what it was to become by the eighties. Indeed, some were returning. There was now work to be had, especially since the emergence and recognition of Canadian storytelling and storytelling about Canadians, and most importantly, since private-sector production began to flourish in film and particularly in TV. This came with the new maturity in the Canadian film and TV industry, as evidenced by alliances and international co-productions rather than individuals working (and floundering) on their own, as in the sixties and seventies.

Cagney and Lacey was difficult for me in the beginning. My salary was not as large as it would become with the advent of pickups and renewals; therefore I didn't, at first, commute as much as I would be able to later on. I was lonely without Sara and the kids and the lifestyle I had developed in Toronto. Never mind; I would throw myself into my work. But I was no longer the star of the show, I was no longer in control. That was hard to swallow. (On *King*, I wasn't contractually in control either, but when the producers came up against me they didn't always have the control they liked to think they had. In LA, particularly in TV, the producers could be iron-fisted.) At best I was the third star, so my part in some episodes wasn't that big, and the work, as a result, wasn't always as time-consuming or fulfilling as I would have liked. But there was an upside: working with dynamic and talented people, being accepted as their peer, being recognized as possessing the universality of talent, and working in an atmosphere and on a project of great potential. As well, I had of course made lots of friends over the years in this business, and many of them were now in Hollywood.

As it turned out, neither the loneliness of missing my family nor the unfamiliar (for me) task of jockeying for artistic and career positioning in each of the storylines was going to be a problem—for long. After the first six we were not exactly cancelled, but the network put us on the proverbial back burner. Frankly, this, particularly the indefiniteness of it, was more frightening than loneliness or fighting for artistic life. It's worse not to be able to fight at all. It was frustrating and damn disappointing to be put into abeyance.

The difference between the first six episodes and the very successful pilot was, I think, to some degree in the writing, and certainly some of the directing wasn't as good as Ted Post's. Mostly, though, the difference was in the casting. When the pilot scored so big, CBS wanted to go to series right away, but one of the essential factors bringing on that high rating was Loretta Swit as Cagney—and she would not be available, because of her commitment to the tenth year of *M*A*S*H*, for at least another year. CBS did not want to wait. They preferred instead (*M*A*S*H* was also a CBS show) to proceed with other casting for the part of Cagney.

The woman who was cast to replace Swit as Cagney was a very talented actor, just as talented as Swit, but again there was the question of chemistry, not only between the woman and the part, but particularly between the woman and her partner, Lacey. The woman whom they cast, unlike Loretta Swit, was dark-haired, almost as dark as

Tyne. That obviously was not a substantive issue—hair can be dyed—but I cite that as being symbolic of the insufficient difference in look and feel between the two characters to make for a complementary chemistry.

CBS, however, in spite of the not-impressive-enough numbers for the first six episodes, felt that there was still something worth trying for in the concept of *Cagney and Lacey*. The producers were asked to recast Cagney in another attempt to find the right combination. With casting that the network would approve of, there would be an order for an additional seven episodes, making a total of thirteen to date. The producers went about their search for another Cagney and I went back to Toronto in the interim to be with my family and enjoy our new home—and to seek employment. I had mortgage payments again. Fortunately, a German shepherd came to my aid. The dog was the star of a show called, in some foreign markets such as Israel, *A Friend in Need*. Here in Canada and in the US it was called *The Littlest Hobo*. During the downtime of *C & L* (and I wasn't 100 percent certain it would start up again) I had the good fortune to do, amongst other work, five episodes of *Hobo*; two I acted in and three I directed.

In 1982 the part of Cagney was recast with the wonderful Sharon Gless. Barney Rosenzweig claimed he had always wanted Sharon in the first place. Well, he got her, and we were all the luckier for it. Back in LA, doing the first of the next seven episodes, I noticed that Sharon looked nervous, as though detached from the rest of us, who were already fitting into our roles. This was, I think, the third time she had replaced the star of an established series, as though she were making a career, she joked, out of replacing rather than creating. I went over to her and said, "You're not a guest here, you know; this is your show. We're all here because of you, and I thank you for that." That started a warm friendship that continues, I'm happy to say, to this day.

Cagney and Lacey did, of course, take off, but not without further experimentation. It was as though the next seven episodes were seven pilots, each a possible direction for the series to take. Each episode had an A plot and a B plot (the subplot); the A story was generally a crime story while the B story was a relationship story that intertwined with the A story. I was in all the episodes, but one in particular featured me very strongly. The B story involved my character and his teenaged son, who was almost estranged from me because he lived not with me but with his mother, my ex-wife. The boy gets arrested for a minor infraction and is kept overnight in one of the precinct's holding cells. Being the lieutenant of the precinct, I could have released him, but as painful as it was for me I didn't want him to think he could get around the law. In a gut-wrenching scene, I tried to explain to him why he had to stay overnight.

This episode was well received across the country, positive reviews for the show and for me. It was now clear that my character would be a presence in each episode, sometimes bigger, sometimes smaller, but always necessary, maybe even pivotal, to the crime story and perhaps one or more of the subplots. This was enough for me, because when the series was sailing securely, this situation would allow me sufficient room and time, if given the opportunity, to take on the additional responsibility of directing. Something I really wanted.

There were many episodes over the succeeding years (1982 to 1988) in which Lt. Samuels had, and caused, emotions that ran up and down the scales of comedy and drama. I again remember Nathan Cohen's instructive words, that a character, in order to be interesting, has to go through change, a metamorphosis. Samuels went from resisting and resenting women in his squad, preferring that they should instead be school crossing guards, to reluctant acceptance, then full acceptance. Because he was a cop's cop through and through and therefore recognized good police work, no matter who was performing it, his attitude eventually graduated to respect, albeit grudging, and then all-out respect and finally respect and fondness, like a mother hen guarding and caring for the squad, which he was happy to say included, right at the top, Cagney and Lacey. Just as a character in a play goes through change in three acts, Samuels's attitude evolved and matured over 125 episodes, like a 125-act play. In a sense he was like a lot of the male population in our TV audience with respect to attitude towards female co-workers. I was proud of the character of Samuels and felt he was important, not just as a pivotal character in most of the dramatic situations from week to week, but also, in a way, as a representative of the changing male attitude towards women.

Fortunately for me, the writing of my character coincided with my own attitude about his development (most good producers try to write the character for the actor, that is, adapt the character to the actor who plays him or her). Despite the so-called iron-fisted policy of Hollywood TV producers, the various writers/producers over the years welcomed discussions and input regarding my character's development—wonderful writers like Peter Lefcourt, Liz Coe, Jonathan Estrin, Shelley List, Terry Louise Fisher (later the co-creator with Stephen Bochco of *L.A. Law*), Steve Brown, Allison Hock and Joe Viola. All of these writers were bright, sensitive and well informed on many subjects, and blessed with humour, not to mention their skill and talent as dramatists. Everything flourished under the creative guidance of that superb and savvy producer, Barney Rosenzweig. In all cases, and particularly with Joe Viola and Barney, the friendships lasted and even deepened. As a matter of fact, after *Cagney and Lacey*, because of my successful direction of episodes he had written or supervised, Joe Viola hired me to direct on a series he was producing for Aaron Spelling called *Heartbeat*, starring Kate Mulgrew. And I was very appreciative when, years later, during the run of *Death of a Salesman* at the Stratford Festival, Barney and Sharon Gless (they got married after the run of *C & L*) flew up from Florida, where they now live, just to see my performance of Willy Loman in that great play and in that great theatre.

I said above that Samuels looked after his squad like a mother hen. This was in fact a criterion of the New York Police Department in measuring the effectiveness of a lieutenant. It's also what the lieutenants of the New York Police Department said about me and my portrayal of a police lieutenant when they awarded me membership in the NYPD as an honorary lieutenant. The ceremony was covered by CNN, and the next day I received patches from police departments across the continent. The Metro Toronto Police even went one better than the NYPD and made me an honorary Chief of Detectives, and a year later an honorary Chief of Police. In both cases the badges are real. Awfully tempting to use. But it's bad enough to be accused of impersonating an officer by a TV critic; it would be a lot worse if you got caught doing it by a cop. Like Spencer Tracy said about acting, "It's OK as long as you don't get caught doing it!" To avoid the temptation I had the two real badges framed. They hang on my wall alongside the honorary lieutenant's shield from the NYPD.

These marks of approval for my acting, including being part of an Emmy Award–winning show, were matched by a couple of awards for my directing on *Cagney and Lacey*. Along with others in our company, I received the Luminous Award from the American Women in Film for an episode called "DWI" (drinking while under the influence). For another episode I directed, I received, together with colleagues in key functions in the show, the Nancy S. Reynolds Award, which is an industry acknowledgement for depicting sexual themes in a "relevant and responsible" manner. That episode was called "Button Button" and it dealt with AIDS. There were two storylines: one involved the fear and rumours resulting from a school kid apparently getting AIDS from a blood transfusion, and the scare that spreads throughout the school; the other, a more comedic thread, involved two adults, Cagney and a new friend, in the awkward but sensitive discussion of precautions they should each be taking for safe sex.

My artistic life and professional reputation flourished through *Cagney and Lacey*, as both an actor and a director, and my personal profile kept pace, with fan mail coming to me from all the countries in which *C & L* played. This attention was fuelled not only by the impact of weekly performances, but also by my guest appearances and interviews, nationally and internationally, on talk shows like *Regis & Kathie Lee* or *The Oprah Winfrey Show*, and in newspapers and magazines like the Canadian and US *TV Guide*.

I don't know if the latter would have happened if Sharon Gless hadn't agreed to appear on the cover with me. Although the lead article was on me alone, there was concern that my TVQ wasn't high enough to carry the cover on my own. It certainly would be strengthened by additionnal star support—but it might cost that star a single cover further down the road. Sharon's talent, that is, her ability to live on the screen as though she was born to it, was surpassed only by her generosity. When asked by the editors, she said that she would be glad to be on the cover with me. With a circulation of 3 million in Canada alone—it was probably about ten times that in the US—*TV Guide* was a powerful PR tool.

I received many offers for work during the hiatus period between production schedules. Sometimes, because of time constraints, I had to opt out of important projects. Two that I was quite sorry about were a feature film, *Once Upon a Time in America*, and a cable film, *Between Friends*. In both cases scheduling would have conflicted with my prior legal commitment and loyalty to *Cagney and Lacey*. Losing work because you're working makes the loss less painful, but still you regret missing the opportunity of working with great people.

I didn't often audition any more, but I was glad to audition for *Once Upon a Time in America* because it involved participating in an improvisation with Robert De Niro, who was to star in the film. Working with him, even briefly, was a reward in itself. The part was that of a Jewish gangster. The auditions were held in New York, where there must have been thousands of actors who would have been right for the part. When I flew into town I was so confident that I actually said to Sara, "When I arrive in New York all those other actors are going to be out of luck." Well, in some ways I was right. I certainly enjoyed improvising with De Niro, and was flattered that

Sergio Leone's writing staff, all Gucci-shoed, with Italian sausage in one hand and a pencil in the other, were taking down verbatim the lines I was improvising. Sergio Leone, who apparently didn't understand English, nevertheless did respond to my improv with an offer of a part. I don't know whether I passed the audition, though, because I was not offered the part of the Jewish gangster but, apparently because of my blue eyes, the part of an Irish cop. Unfortunately, I couldn't do it because of schedule conflict.

The other film starred Elizabeth Taylor and Carol Burnett. I was approached for the part of Liz Taylor's husband. The producers asked me how I felt about her. I said, "Are you kidding? I've been fantasizing about her since *National Velvet*!" But again, a schedule conflict prevented me from pursuing the part. As with De Niro, to have worked with Elizabeth Taylor would have been reward in itself. She has always been a great beauty, an actor of quality and one of the great movie stars of all time.

PBS was able to accommodate my hiatus period and provided me with virtually another television series. They purchased fifty-two episodes of CBC's prestigious series *For the Record*, one of which I had directed (*Cop*) and another I had starred in (*The Winnings of Frankie Walls*). They wanted a Canadian with an American profile to host the show. I bookended each episode and interwove it with narration. The series was called *Moments in Time with Al Waxman* and my work was filmed for PBS at the CBC studios at home in Toronto.

While I considered Toronto my home, I had a family back there that was functioning like a one-parent family with a dad who had visiting privileges. I tried to make my presence felt by phoning and visiting as often as I could. Being there by telephone wasn't as good as really being there, but it was the next best thing, and to some extent it served us well. I was a long-distance sounding board for Sara; she would read me her columns over the phone before she submitted them. Tobaron would test her accent and accuracy as she practised

Long-Distance Love

her French vocabulary with me on the phone. Once, when I couldn't help Adam with a math problem over the phone, even though I had to be at work the next day, I flew home by red-eye to help him solve the problem, then flew back with three hours on my side to get me to work on time. I didn't do that ever again, not because of the financial and physical cost but because the math problems soon got to be too difficult. That damn New Math!

The kids had to learn to deal not only with math but with the unwanted attention that arose from having a public figure for a father. Like "My dad's a brain surgeon, yours is just an actor. How come he's in *Who's Who in America* and my dad's not? My dad's much more important." Or "Your dad's fat." Or "How does your mom like it when your dad kisses another woman on TV?" But I'm proud of Adam and Tobaron; they eventually got past any hurts and handled it well. They were proud of me, as Tobaron once wrote in a Father's Day poem:

> To our Father, an ever-rising star,
> whom we think of when you are far away,
> working harder with each passing day
> to reach higher heights and fulfill your dreams—
> you really kick ass!—Whatever that means.
> This is our card, a message to say
> we do love and respect you.
> Yes, even when we dare disobey.
> For words of wisdom, words of kindness,
> and for treasured words of open-mindedness,
> we thank you.
> So, from Adam, Toby and your loving wife Sara—
> Enjoy your today and your every tomarra.

On another occasion Tobaron courageously confronted a teacher in front of the whole class after he said of my career something like,

"Your dad's just lucky." Tobaron, scared, nevertheless stood up and said firmly, "My dad has worked hard for everything he's got."

They were proud too of their mother's strength and example as she essentially built her career to combat loneliness, and wound up being recognized both in Canada and internationally as a respected food writer and restaurant critic. I missed them; but I guess because they were always on my mind, in a way they were always with me—as though I carried a piece of home around with me.

I certainly tried to bring something of home to LA every Christmastime. Our cast was extremely generous with one another, and some of us were very imaginative in our generosity. I tried every year to bring a Canadian Christmas to the entire company of *Cagney and Lacey*. The first attempt was successful, with a bottle of Canadian Club for each person in the entire company of executives, administrators, writers, producers, directors, cast and crew, totalling about 130 people. (When Hiram Walker Limited heard of my Canadian Christmas in California, I got a case of their Charles Heidsieck champagne as a gift!)

In succeeding years, with bigger salaries at each pickup, I got more inventive. One year I decided to give a gift of Sara's book *Back Roads and Country Cooking*, about the foods of Ontario. That was nice, I thought, but not nice enough, because they would surmise that I got a deal from my wife's publisher. I had to add to it. What goes with a book of food? A bottle of wine! But Canadian wine? Was that, as was generally thought in the mid-eighties, a contradiction in terms? I was probably amongst those who thought that way. Fortunately, I had recently met Donald Ziraldo, head of Inniskillin Wines in Niagara-on-the-Lake, and they produced a wonderful wine that I enjoyed and was proud to give as a gift. It was a red wine, Maréchal Foch. Inniskillin sent me 132 bottles of it, all the way from Toronto to California. Two broke. Serendipity: I needed exactly 130. I put a bottle alongside the book in each of 130 colourful Christmas bags, and it made for a very happy Canadian Christmas for a lot of Californians.

As a matter of fact, many of them asked where they could get this wine. Why are you Canadians hiding it from us? Can we find it in a rare-wine shop? Nice to hear that from Californians, who have some of the best wines in the world right in their own backyards.

As much as I loved California wines and working in California, the head office of commercial and creative possibility, and as much as I loved working, in particular, with the cast and company of a great show, I still loved my own backyard best.

Chapter 26

A Mansion of Love

I loved our new house in Forest Hill, we all did. Even our dog, Puff, a miniature poodle, loved it. (When we got him, Tobaron said, "He looks like a ball of fluff, let's call him Puff.") It was an old house, built in 1909, with many add-ons over the first half of the century. Old is lovely—but costly. For starters, the purchase price was more than we could afford. Then it seemed like every week we were pouring more and more money into it, doing repairs and renovations. Some parts we were actually rebuilding, that is, modernizing but always with respect for the sensibility of the original design. It was worth it for us. Glorious, creative comfort.

We turned one area of the second floor into an apartment for Sara's widowed father (her mother had died at Christmastime in 1988), so that he could have his privacy and still be with the family when he chose to. I liked that, because he was a darling man, although set in his attitudes (perhaps a right that comes with age), a funny old curmudgeon and a real joy for the few years he was with us. It was good for Adam and Tobaron to have a grandfather so close, something I never had.

I remembered his prediction that I'd never be a millionaire; now I could gently prove him wrong. And it happened the way I wanted it to—my wealth had grown as a by-product of my primary goal, that is, good work. But he had also said that I was "too honest," so perhaps I should acknowledge that by this time, about fifteen years later, the dollar was worth only about half what it was when he made that prediction.

As always, no matter where we lived, it was because of Sara's exquisite taste that our home was so loved and so lived in—whether it was the living room with its antique fireplace framed by ornate woodwork and panelling, or our bedroom with its huge Jacuzzi surrounded by mirrored walls. Of course the kitchen was big enough to film a cooking show in it, which happened on occasion. The dining room could seat twenty for dinner, and it often did; we loved to entertain. Our third floor, which I seldom saw, was for our housekeeper and any guests we might have. The basement had a huge octopus of a furnace in it, but there was room enough to build a playroom for the kids and a gymnasium (after a fashion). I did less exercising than I should have and spent more time watching Adam do countless chin-ups. I used to love to watch him do that. It was, dare I say it, a kind of *nachis* for me. (In my most physically fit times, when I was a bouncer at the Village Gate in New York and in my best shape ever, I still erred towards pear-shaped and could do only a few chin-ups, whereas Adam was and is V-shaped and can literally do scores of them.) Just as the limo would come to pick me up to take me to the airport, Adam would say, because he knew I loved to watch, "Come on, Dad, we've got a few minutes, I'll show you some chin-ups." I hated to leave. I think my heart broke a little every time I did.

Perhaps it was the best of both worlds, a captain's paradise—or should I say a lieutenant's paradise. As well as the cast and company of *Cagney and Lacey* (we were all very supportive of each other, and many of us are still in contact), over the years I'd made lots of friends in the business in Canada, New York, London and Los Angeles, many of whom were now in LA. In addition, so much of my charity and community work, although mainly in Canada, was very international in nature and reach, particularly Variety, and also the Shaare Zedek Hospital in Jerusalem. There were of course branches of the Shaare Zedek in the US, as well as Canada, and the Friends of Shaare Zedek in LA knew of my involvement with this very special hospital's supporters in Toronto.

Rabbi Monson, as I mentioned earlier, had been so thoughtful during my mother's shiva that I had vowed to do something for him if he ever asked. He asked Sara and me to speak on behalf of the Shaare Zedek Hospital, that is, to do public service messages directed towards the Jewish community in Canada. This was a happy coincidence, because my brother, Benny, who was now internationally recognized as a physician and teacher, had lectured there; so by helping out the Shaare Zedek, I could show both my appreciation to Rabbi Monson and my respect for my brother.

In 1982–1983 Rabbi Monson and the Shaare Zedek asked Sara and me to be the honourees at its next biennial official function, a dinner to be held in 1984. The tickets would be $500 each. I wanted to know more about the hospital if we were going to undertake that much of a commitment. For a few public service announcements and an occasional public appearance at large parties or gatherings, it was enough for me that my brother spoke well of the hospital, but now I had to see more, and see it for myself. For example, I wanted to know whether the attitude there was unconditionally welcoming and caring for all who needed medical help and attention, even though the hospital was administered by Orthodox Jews and its practising and teaching nurses and doctors were mostly, if not all, Orthodox Jews.

Sara and I went to Jerusalem to visit the Shaare Zedek Hospital and learn more about the work that was being done there. I was inspired by what I saw with my own eyes. Shaare Zedek literally means "gates of righteousness (or duty)." All who need medical help are welcome, whether they are Orthodox Jews or not, whether they are Christian or Muslim, Israeli or Arab. It's taken for granted in

Canada that a hospital would not turn away anyone who needed medical attention, but in that region, at that time, this openness could not be counted on. I was struck by the sight of Arab families in the corridors, standing outside the patients' rooms, who were overcome with fear when they saw me approaching, perhaps thinking I was some authority figure. We noticed that they were immediately comforted and reassured by nurses and orderlies. Shaare Zedek is known as "the hospital with a heart," and everything we saw there proved the truth of that reputation.

I came away from my visit with a theme for my speech, and it was based on something I saw with my own eyes. When a baby cries, the doctors and nurses of the Shaare Zedek are not concerned with its colour, its religion or its nationality; they are concerned only that a baby is crying—and they immediately care for that baby. Again, it was good fortune and coincidence that my brother, who was an obstetrician and gynecologist, had begun to focus on prenatal and perinatal medicine.

The evening honouring us resulted in the creation at the Shaare Zedek Hospital of the Sara and Al Waxman Center for Maternal and Fetal Medicine. Truth be told, although there is indeed a centre there in our name—at least that's what it says on a big plaque at the entrance to the centre—there are many plaques with variations on the same theme, like a plaque denoting, let's say, mother and child medicine, and yet another with yet another but similar designation. I thought, Plaque-land, at least according to my dentist, was the inside of my mouth, or as I was soon to learn from my cardiologist, the inside of my arteries. Still, these plaques in the corridors of the Shaare Zedek Hospital each serve an honourable purpose: they bear witness to the hospital's continuing need and success in both medical care and research.

One mustn't deceive oneself about the word "honour." The honourees for one of these dinners are indeed being honoured, but they are chosen as well for their ability to be a catalyst in the community for the raising of funds. This often means the honourees are in a position to "paper" the room with their own donations and purchasing of tickets, as well as by selling many on the basis of favours that can be called in. That may sound cynical, but the purpose to be achieved is the higher concern and the honouree is, after all, genuinely being celebrated by the community.

In our case, we were not financial heavy hitters. Sure, I had begun to make a substantial income by this time, but I did not have the depth of wealth to sell out the room (the Canadian Room at the Royal York Hotel, seating approximately 1,200 people). Nevertheless, the room was sold out, and it was done on the basis of popularity and reputation. We did not have to make a donation, sell a ticket or twist an arm; rather, we lent our name, our time and our talent. I'm sure, however, that the volunteers and staff of the Friends of the Shaare Zedek Hospital had to work hard to make sure the tickets were sold. I was humbled not only by the hospital itself but also by the purpose of the event, that is, the fundraising and contributing that people were willing to do on our behalf. It caused me to look closely at the word "honour," as evidenced by words I spoke during the speech I gave that night:

> The great acting teacher Konstantin Stanislavsky taught his students, and through his writings taught many students of acting throughout the world, including myself, that an actor "should not love himself in the art but rather he should love the art in himself." It's a nice distinction and I believe it applies as well to charity or philanthropy or to the Hebrew word *tzedakah*, or as we understand it in practical terms, giving. That is, the giver should not love himself in the act of giving, but rather the act of giving in himself.
>
> As an actor, if one becomes what is thought of as successful, that is, if one acquires the outward trappings of success—a bigger house, bigger car, limousines, tuxedos, opening nights, tribute

dinners, fame, etc.—one has all the more reason to continually remind oneself that it is "the art in oneself that should be loved, not oneself in the art."

Similarly, it is easy to confuse oneself about the act of giving and being honoured for the act of giving. So Sara and I thank you deeply for tonight, but we believe that in honouring us you truly honour the act of giving in yourselves. In effect we all pay tribute tonight to *tzedakah* and perhaps thereby, and only thereby, we are all honoured.

The evening was a tremendous success for the Shaare Zedek and a momentous event in our lives, a time Sara and I will never forget. We arranged for Sara's father to say the blessing over the bread. He was nervous in the spotlight with 1,200 people waiting to say "amen," but he was adorable. Sara and I made speeches. The great Canadian opera star Maureen Forrester sang "O Canada" magnificently, and the cantor of our synagogue, Ben Maissner, who himself could be an opera star, sang the "Hatikvah" (which is not only the Israeli national anthem but, as its meaning is "the hope," the national anthem of the Jewish people as well, as it was before 1948 and continues to be now). Eddie Greenspan was a witty and eloquent master of ceremonies, and the speakers he introduced included John Hirsch, a towering and amusing presence of artistic integrity, and Johnny Wayne and Frank Shuster, who normally declined such invitations but in our case generously made an exception (they were hilarious). I was proud that the head table included Sharon Gless and Tyne Daly, who were both funny and profoundly flattering. A memorable evening for all.

It was so successful that the Shaare Zedek counted on me to make their fundraising dinner a reality two years later, in 1986, when they honoured Canadian show business, again a star-studded and successful night, and two years after that, in 1988, at which time I corralled Eddie Greenspan into being the honouree, with me as his MC. This was another huge success for the Shaare Zedek, with the funds raised earmarked for a medical target determined by Eddie and Susie Greenspan—both generous friends, both worldly and sophisticated yet down-to-earth likeable.

Sharon Gless, when invited to come to Toronto in 1984, responded instantaneously with, "They're honouring you up there? I'll be there!" And Tyne too immediately joined in. They both added lustre to the evening with their beauty and vivacity. Also adding glamour from Hollywood was the talented singer-songwriter, Carol Connors, whom I befriended on the production of *Tulips*. She wrote a couple of songs for the film that never got the attention they deserved because the film was not a hit. But our friendship was. Carol had written (and probably still writes) many hit songs, starting with her first when she was just a teenager in the 1950s in a group called the Teddy Bears, with whom she co-wrote "To Know, Know, Know Him, Is to Love, Love, Love Him." On the occasion of our dinner she reworded that song especially for Sara and me, and sang it for the great enjoyment of all who were there, especially those who remembered the original.

Very important for me that night was the presence of my brother, Benny. When he spoke, he joked about "swelling," which in his line of business, obstetrics, usually meant something other than what it did that night. He said that at that moment it meant pride, swelling with pride—in me.

It must have been around this time that Benny and I had the chess game that I referred to in the first chapter of this book, when we were discussing how and from whom we each learned to play chess. I'm not exactly sure when it was, but I distinctly remember the content of our conversation, which also included "What would you do if you had it to do over again?" Benny said he would be doing what I was doing. I couldn't get over that. When my brother Benny wrote an article, it was published in medical journals around the world. More importantly as far as Sara was concerned, what greater accolade for an obstetrician than to be published in *Vogue* magazine as Benny was. I would joke about him having enough initials after his name to print a whole new name. And yet he would rather be doing what I was doing?! I asked him why, then, when he'd been so talented on the piano as a child, hadn't he pursued his first love—music? His answer: "I never had your balls!"

Chapter 27

Bicoastal Paradise

A lieutenant's paradise indeed. Fun and work, and my work was fun too—either in Toronto or on the West Coast. I went home three or four times a month. I was encouraged to fly first class because my accountant said we needed the expense. The air travel was mostly me coming home to Toronto, but sometimes, particularly when I was directing an episode and couldn't free up the time to come home, Sara would fly down to be with me. My apartment in Westwood was big enough to accommodate the kids too, particularly at Christmas and New Year's, or Thanksgiving or spring break, at which time we would also include a few days at La Costa, a spa near San Diego, or an equally luxurious resort in Palm Springs. We chose those places because, if I had to hurry back to work, they were only a ninety-mile drive from the *Cagney and Lacey* studio.

That was the only downside to my bicoastal ball—a constant eye on the clock and the ensuing rush back to work. I was determined, even if I was coming from three thousand miles away, never to be late for work. This denoted professionalism, yes, but also a preoccupation with controlling things over which I had no control. For example, during the winter months there was always a potential weather problem, so I was double and triple booked, first with Air Canada, which I found to be the most cautious (preferable), and then with American

Airlines and United Airlines, both of which, in my experience, would be a little more daring in troubled weather. I was always looking at the clock, checking the weather reports and reviewing the airline schedules.

Just as I was determined to be professional, I was equally determined not to be an absentee father, not to be just a father by phone or a dad with visiting privileges. All that determination caused some pretty frantic and obsessive behaviour, which no doubt undermined my so-called quality time with my family, not to mention the toll the tension took on my physical health, as I was soon to find out. It probably caused strain on Sara and the kids too. There is an uneasiness inherent in continual whirlwind visits. I don't think I was unaware of it, as I used to joke that they heaved a sigh of relief every time I returned to Los Angeles because now they could relax again.

When I was at home there was always a lot of ground to cover in a short period of time. Tobaron's use of language was, from a very early age, precise, deliberate and thoughtful. She once said to me, when I wanted her to get on with whatever she was talking to me about, that I didn't really want to have a talk with her; I really only had time, she said, for a report—"journalism, not conversation." That stung, but I had to respect the wit and wisdom of her observation, so I tried to find more time for them while at the same time getting my own things done. For example, I helped Adam deliver his flyers. He started a company when he was hardly a teenager, called Canadian Flyers Inc. He would go to small business establishments in Forest Hill Village and offer to deliver their advertising flyers for less than the post office charged. I would drive him to the corner of each street, and he would get out and deliver the flyers up and down the street, then we'd drive to the next one. I enjoyed watching him run—like a deer. Mostly, though, I forced myself to sit in the car and study my lines, which I would have to know for filming in the next day or two back in Los Angeles. Always enjoying, always working, always on the go.

It's easy to see all this now—the tension, the push and pull—but what I saw then was, above all, the satisfaction I sought at home and the adventure I experienced in LA. There's no question that LA has always had an aura of possibility; of dreams to be realized. Ever since I was a kid Hollywood has had that lustre and lure for me. But I wasn't a kid any more; I was in my mid-forties, and I was able (most of the time) to focus through the glare and the enticement of the lights. They would kid me sometimes on *Cagney and Lacey* that I had been "rescued from stardom in Canada"—a joke that was not without some perception. But from my perspective, even with the success I enjoyed in LA, the feeling was growing that potential was to be found in sense of self, and this took priority over place. I was able to see that Toronto wasn't dead-ended as compared with LA. Rather, it's up to the individual and depends on his or her attitude; for some, even the land of possibility can be dead-ended. It took living for a while in LA, together with a growing belief in myself, to realize that the aura of possibility exists within the individual, who has it in his vision no matter where he lives in the world.

I remember having breakfast one morning at the counter in the legendary Schwab's Drugstore, when a guy I had worked with in New York showed up. He was broke and out of work, and his wife had thrown him out, and would let him see his kids only if he did five bundles of laundry on the weekends. I bought him breakfast. He told me he was "tapped"—Las Vegas language for broke; he had no more "chips in his pocket"—a Las Vegas metaphor for life force. He said of me that I would always be able to reach into my pocket and find more chips. I believe that life force has nothing to do with place; it has to do with the person. I believe he's right that no matter how close I get to being tapped, I will always be able to reach in a little farther and find more chips to pull out.

Sara used to say of me, way back during *King of Kensington* (particularly when people would ask, "If you're so good, why aren't you in Hollywood?"), that I went to Hollywood every day and came home for supper every night. That's the confidence she had in me. She also had confidence in herself. When her girlfriends cautioned her against my going on my own to LA, land of starlets, she said to me, "What I don't know doesn't hurt me, but I'm not worried, because I know you; and knowing you, I'll see it on your face when you're coming around the corner!"

Sex for me was and still is a four-letter word—Sara.

Nobody else? Well, I'd be lying if I said the thought never crossed my mind, but it's complicated when you're working around the clock. A *Cagney and Lacey* shoot day as an actor was a minimum of twelve hours, sometimes as much as fifteen hours; as a director, because of prep and homework and viewing dailies, it was fifteen hours at a minimum. No, straying wasn't worth the trouble, particularly when the attraction was so strong and positive at home.

Still, there were weekends when I didn't come home. At times like that there were always parties, generally "see and be seen" events, a fun way to do business—and that's what it was for me. Indeed, most people go to these gatherings because they provide an opportunity for contacts, and of course there are paparazzi and columnists covering the goings-on, offering the possibility of being written about in the trades, which everybody in Hollywood reads over breakfast. My preference was to go home, but if I had to stay in LA on a weekend I'd usually be invited to these events, as indeed was Sara when she was in town. The invitations came from my publicist or our dear friend Carol Connors, who, like my publicist, always seemed to have a party or a benefit or a charity or social event of some sort to go to at any given moment. Good to have a well-connected publicist as well as a very popular friend.

I wasn't always very savvy in my dealings with the media. I once got a call from the *Globe*, who wanted to interview me. If it was anything Canadian, I wanted to cooperate. I gave them my Toronto home phone number. They called and we talked, but we couldn't meet because the caller was in Vancouver. "Oh," I thought, "of course they're a national newspaper, so they've got a Vancouver office." They then called me in LA, still from Vancouver, and tried to arrange a meeting in LA, but I was leaving for Toronto. "Call me there," I said, "and we'll get together." They wanted to set up a photo session. "OK," I said, "but you don't need to, you must have enough pictures of me on file. If you don't, the *Sun* or the *Star* would be very cooperative, I'm sure." They called me when I was in Toronto, but they were in Boca Raton. Why there? I thought to myself, "They probably have an office there too, because there are so many Canadians visiting during the winter."

Finally the caller said to me, "You really don't know what this is about, do you?" It suddenly dawned on me that he was not from the *Globe and Mail* but from the tabloid called the *Globe*!

"No," I said, "I don't. What's this about?"

He actually said, and this is almost verbatim, "About nothing, because I can't find any dirt on you unless I make it up, and after having gotten to know you a bit, I don't want to do that to you!" As a result the piece was no longer about me (I'm glad to say), but instead a rather innocuous article, probably boring for *Globe* readers, about the men of *Cagney and Lacey* and their respective spouses. I'm proud to say that when I was written about in the *National Enquirer* it too was without titillation and probably one of the least interesting pieces in the history of yellow journalism.

When I stayed weekends in LA it was because I was scheduled for Friday and Monday filming. On Sunday nights I would usually go to Hugh Hefner's mansion, where there was a limited guest list, but thanks to Carol Connors I was always on it. I would pull up to the entrance. The gate was always closed. There was a huge boulder beside it with a tiny, almost indiscernible hole in it, from which a camera would eye you and a voice would question you. After you identified yourself and the boulder verified it and checked that you were on the guest list, you gained entry.

Of course there were some fantastic-looking females there, right off the pages and centrefolds of *Playboy* magazine. Their only competition were the colourful, fine-feathered, long-stemmed rare birds in Hefner's private zoo. And "Hef" was an excellent host as he, pipe-smoking and always silk-pyjama-clad, showed a guest through his incredible miniature zoo. The sights didn't stop there. Also present were old movie stars like Cornel Wilde, or young movie stars I'd worked with or studied with, like James Caan, and famous athletes, as well as highly respected directors, like Richard Brooks (no one sat in his chair when the movie was shown). This brings me to the real reason I went there on the occasional Sunday night: to see a screening of a first-run, not-yet-released movie. Every seat was as well placed and as comfortable as Mr. Brooks'—and equally surrounded by popcorn, candies and a continuous flow of any beverage you could want. Of course the dinner served to the thirty or so guests prior to the screening was sumptuous. After the movie I would get home early to prepare for the Monday morning shoot.

I alternated my Sunday screening venues. Some Sunday nights I would avail myself of the more intimate hospitality of Sammy and Altavese Davis. Their dinner parties were for only about six or eight. They were smaller, less sparkling but more radiant, mostly because of the presence of Sammy Davis Jr.'s enormous talent, which extended to cooking the dinner. His guests were people like Ricardo Montalban, Steve Lawrence and Eydie Gormé, Carol Connors and me—and Sara too when she was in town. (Sammy was actually nervous about Sara's critical response to his culinary efforts.) Again there would be a first-run movie, just eight people in a spacious but still cozy living room that had, like Hefner's, a theatre-sized screen in it.

I couldn't get over the size of Sammy Davis, so slim and tiny, not much bigger, I thought, than the king-sized cigarettes he smoked. The first Sunday night I was a guest at his house I had to leave earlier than the rest, because of an 8 a.m. call the next morning for which I'd have to get up at 6 a.m. When he saw me to the door I turned to him, not fawning like a groupie or star-struck like a kid, but truly in awe of all the talent that was generated from that little body, that instrument of art. I thought of all the movies and shows I had seen him in over the years, since the early days of TV in the fifties, all the way back to the Eddie Cantor shows for *The Colgate Comedy Hour* and the Ed Sullivan telecasts, when he performed as part of the Will Masters Trio. I said to him as I thanked him for his hospitality that I wanted to thank him too for his talent, and that I thought he was the tallest talent I had ever seen in my life. He came over and hugged me when I said that, genuinely moved, almost as though he needed to hear it.

It was a moment that demonstrated for me the common ingredient I believe to be at the very core of any talent, big or small, accomplished or struggling. Talent is at once both a means and an end. It's composed not only of positivism and magic but also of insecurity, which seems to be required as a hurdle to be overcome in order to achieve an affirmation of self. It's like courage being impossible without the accompanying presence of fear to be conquered.

I'm glad I said thank you to him because I had vowed years earlier that I would always express my appreciation to any talent I admired, that I would never miss the opportunity of doing so—because I did once. When I was eleven years old, in 1946, I was at Maple Leaf Stadium, which used to be down at the waterfront at the foot of Bathurst Street, to see a baseball game between the Toronto Maple Leafs and the Montreal Royals, both Triple A ball clubs, both farm teams of major league clubs, the Leafs for the Philadelphia Athletics and the Royals for the Brooklyn Dodgers. Montreal had a second baseman who was black, the only black man on the field. But that wasn't something I took any notice of. All I know is that I saw in that man, whose name was of course Jackie Robinson, one of the most talented baseball players ever. He'd provided me with one of the best afternoons of entertainment I had ever had.

Years later, when I was living in New York and commuting sometimes to my brother's house in the Washington area, I noticed on the shuttle back to New York a black man who looked old and tired and unhappy, sitting bent over. There was whispered recognition from other passengers. It was Jackie Robinson. I wanted to go over and tell him what a memorable and exciting afternoon of entertainment he had given me so many years before. Maybe it would've made him feel better. But no, I chickened out. I was shy. He's probably thinking about something and would prefer not to be intruded upon, I rationalized. Hell, the worst that could have happened is that he might have said, "Don't bother me." But I doubt that. He probably would have said thanks in return. A short time after that Jackie Robinson died. I've always been sorry that I didn't thank him when I had the chance. Since then I've never missed the opportunity to compliment talented people on their talent.

For all the fun I was having in Los Angeles and all my productivity career-wise in that city, my preference was to fly home and be with Sara and the kids. This was against the advice of managers and agents, who said it was necessary to fraternize in order to get nominations and drum up more work. Happily, the crew of *Cagney and Lacey* respected me for my dedication to home and family. They'd say, "Hurry up, we've got to finish this shot so Al can catch the red-eye and go home to his family." The red-eye: that's a habit I'm glad I no longer have. Those flights and hours and time-zone changes can take a toll on one's health. At that time, though, I would fly many more thousands of miles to be with my family, as I did when I joined Sara and Tobaron in the south of France in the middle of shooting an episode of *C & L*.

When an episode started on a Thursday it would finish seven shooting days later, on the following Friday. I was scheduled in this instance for the first two days of the shoot only; so barring any rewrites or additions and the necessary shooting that would entail, I was through until the first day of the next episode, two Mondays later.

Tobaron was in summer school in Cap-Ferrat studying French, and Sara had gone to visit her. I decided to join them if I could manage it. When I finished shooting on the Friday, after getting clearance from the producers, I flew the next day and night and day all the way from LA to the south of France to spend five days with Sara and Tobaron. My bicoastal ball danced across a couple of more coasts! This was reckless (in terms of stress and strain) and expensive, but fun. Once over there, Sara and I had some time with Toby, and that was a joy, but she was, after all, at school, so Sara and I had some time together in romantic Beaulieu-sur-Mer, a very different experience than when we were in Cannes in 1970 as kids, young and broke, with my first feature, *The Crowd Inside*. It was fun then because we were young and could handle being broke. Sara and I had actually hand-delivered little mimeographed handbills for my film to all the hotels along the Croissette, just the way kids would do to promote a high-school dance, while overhead flew painted blimps and airplanes pulling banners, and everywhere in that over-the-top atmosphere, neon in your face. Now it was fun for different reasons. Now the only roughing it would be slow room service.

One afternoon we drove to Monte Carlo. Sara wanted to shop. I have no patience for shopping, but if I bring a script along so that I can study while Sara shops, it's OK. It's particularly reassuring for me that Sara enjoys the pastime of shopping more than the act of purchasing. Besides, she promised she wasn't going to buy anything, she just wanted to look, and while she was doing that I would memorize my lines for the next show.

It was hot and sticky, so it was very pleasant to walk into the air-conditioned Christian Dior showroom—although perhaps not pleasant for the proprietors when they saw me, in what had become on the drive from Beaulieu a very sweaty T-shirt. Indeed, I must have been a rather unpleasant sight, so they chose to ignore us. That was unfair to Sara, who looked crisp and clean but had the misfortune to enter the establishment with me and so was also ignored. This pissed me off.

As I tried to get a sales clerk to give her some attention, I noticed a white mink coat that looked about Sara's size. I got their attention. I blurted out (without looking at the price tag), "I want that for my wife." Sara was as surprised as they were. Everyone in the room, clientele and clerks alike, stopped what they were doing to watch. As hot as I looked and as hot as I felt, I coolly added, like a throwaway, "See if it fits her!" It did, as though it was made for her—like a dream, a vision in white. Perfect. I loved it on her. So did she. So did everyone in the shop. When I saw the price I silently gulped but acted blasé! I went the distance with my role. I nonchalantly indicated to the clerks with a wave of my hand to wrap it up. There was no longer any concern about my T-shirt; they were now giving me gifts of shirts and ties.

I had planned, a couple of months down the road, to buy Sara a wonderful anniversary gift. I said, "Do you mind getting your anniversary gift a little early?" She silently shook her head no. She was thrilled. After all, she had intended, and indeed promised, not to buy anything at all, and yet she was coming away with this most exquisite gift. I love to see her wearing it—even now, all these years later. It's still as beautiful as a white Christmas—a peculiar image for me to use, I know, but a perfect description of the coat.

Sara and I did a lot of travelling courtesy of *Cagney and Lacey*—not necessarily paid for by CBS or Orion (the production company) but certainly facilitated by them. I received many invitations because of my *C & L* connections. I was the TV-star guest of 4-H Clubs in West Virginia, or the TV-cop-star guest of Crime Stoppers where it originated in Albuquerque and Santa Fe, or a guest marshal of the Calgary Stampede parade. Sara and I were guest celebrities at the Kentucky Derby; guests of CBS at network-affiliate meetings in LA, New York and San Francisco; Orion's guests at the National Association of Television Program Executives convention in New Orleans; and of course, guests at the annual Emmy Awards and People's Choice Awards in LA.

In Canada, I was doing guest appearances on TV shows and some guest directing. There was also teaching, which I did first at community colleges and finally at York University in the mid-1980s, as an adjunct professor of theatre—a way to give back for the good luck I enjoyed and a way as well to stay fresh. My remuneration was a small honorarium; much more appreciated, and even coveted, was a parking space. There was also continuing dedication by both Sara and me to our respective and mutual charity endeavours.

Of course two of the most important events for us in the eighties were bat and bar mitzvahs. We had a song composed for Toby's bat mitzvah in 1983 that was so touching, beautiful and full of fun that we used a variation of it for Adam's bar mitzvah in 1985. It was written by Joey Miller and Steve Witkin and sung at each event by Sara and our two nieces, Essie and Davey Guttman's daughters, Lisa and Randi. As each of the singers was originally from Winnipeg, the trio called themselves Three Girls from the Peg. The song included, in each case, a specific verse that was a witty introduction of each friend or relative lighting a candle on the bar mitzvah cake. In between each verse was the following refrain, sung first by the trio; as the song progressed and the cake flickered more, they were ultimately joined by everyone there, until the whole room was singing:

> Take a little walk with me,
> And with every candle you will see,
> With each new flame that glows,
> The brighter the memory.

We visited Tobaron in Europe each summer, Cap-Ferrat for a couple of years, Siena one summer and Oxford another—at which time we were all guests of our High Commissioner in London, Roy McMurtry, for Canada Day festivities celebrated with the Queen Mother on the grounds of Buckingham Palace. While I enjoyed these European jaunts, my most enjoyable visits were to Camp Arowhon in Algonquin Park, where seeing Adam paddle a canoe was like watching poetry in motion. I loved going up there every summer during the eighties.

If I couldn't go to Algonquin Park as often as I would have liked, I at least made every effort to get home in time to say goodbye to Adam before he went up to summer camp. One summer my efforts included willing the plane I was in to fly faster so I could get to Adam before he left the house. When I couldn't make that happen, I instructed the limo driver at the airport to drive directly to the bus depot so I could say goodbye to Adam before he boarded the bus. When we arrived just as the bus was pulling away onto the highway, I ordered the driver, "Follow that bus!" The bus couldn't legally stop on the highway, but as we drove neck and neck, as though in a chase (which I guess it really was), we finally, successfully, after about a forty-mile detour for me and my limo, communicated to the bus driver that he should pull over at the upcoming service centre. Adam and I hugged and kissed as all his friends and the bus driver and the limo driver cheered, but perhaps they also wondered (as I did) which of us was the bigger kid.

The 1980s were rich for me, eventful. I was continually honing my craft as an actor and director through 125 episodes of *Cagney and Lacey*, plus all the other shows and films I acted in or directed, and now as a teacher too, and always I was trying to develop screenplays. This was also when Sara authored the best-seller *Backroads and Country Cooking*. The book's launch took place on a commercial jet, circling over the regions of Ontario whose cooking was profiled in the book. While Sara's career as a food journalist and writer was burgeoning, her beautiful body stayed in shape despite all the fantastic food.

The 1980s was a time of acquisition. Although often thought of as the greed decade, those years rewarded me with the riches of travel and the rewards of friendship and the texture of added culture through the artistic, professional and philanthropic work we were both doing. Certainly the latter, philanthropy or *tzedakah*, helped put our lives in balance so that the Me Decade was for us also the We Decade. Being a regular on two TV shows, with reruns playing almost every day and a new episode once a week in most TV markets in most countries around the world, as well as all the interviews and guest appearances I did on talk shows in both Canada and the US, was bringing me a lot of attention. My secretary in Toronto was regularly preparing letters as well as photos to be signed by me in response to requests from fans in Canada, the United States, Australia and Europe.

It was at this time that I met Robin Leach. That might have happened through my publicist, or perhaps Carol Connors or perhaps Hans Gerhard, a good friend of ours who ran the hotel then frequented by stars visiting Toronto, the Sutton Place. Leach used to stay there. Anyway, however it happened, he and I met, and he invited me to be a guest on his show, *Lifestyles of the Rich and Famous*. Frankly, although this would be a huge PR coup, I was a little uncomfortable with the idea, perhaps even with the philosophy of the show, so I said to Robin, "It doesn't make sense. Why would you want me on your show? I'm not that rich and I'm not that famous. It's not what I'm about."

He said to me sincerely, "Yes, you *are* rich. You're rich in friendship, and that's wealth too. That would be the perspective your episode would take."

He invited the kids on. Adam thought it might be fun, but we, including him, decided against it when Toby declined. She was always strong in her opinions, and she thought the show was "tacky." Sara and I respected her for that, and so, believe it or not, did Robin Leach. Robin also respected me and Sara and kept his promise about the perspective the episode would take. We became good friends as a result. There was no Sultan-of-Brunei-ism about our episode. It really focused on Sara and me and our life together more than on material things. It was as though—and I've always believed this to be true—our fortune was and is the fidelity between us, and our home was and is the happiness between us. Indeed, as in my mother and father's little apartment on Spadina Avenue, our mansion was and is our family. As for fame, well, I always thought my mother and father were the king and queen; perhaps our kids thought of us as pretty royal too.

CHAPTER 28

Adjustments: Arterial and Attitudinal

Bubbles burst, balloons pop—maybe even explode. Life, which had appeared hardy, was really quite fragile. I always acted as though I was invincible. At the same time, because my father died so young of a heart attack, I silently feared, even accepted, that inevitability in my own life. That expectation was greatly diminished, swept under some psychological rug, when my brother took the hit, as it were, for both of us. I felt as if I needn't worry about it any more. After all, I was always physically the stronger of the two of us. Stress and tension? These were part of the ride. And because the ride was so busy, so bursting with activity, there was no time to stop for exercise. Obesity, I told myself, was only a problem of vanity, not of health—and vanity, I rationalized, was a waste of time.

Benny had his heart attack in 1976, at the age of forty-five—the same as our father. Benny kept our date with destiny. Fortunately, the attack wasn't massive; Benny didn't even need surgery. But his lifestyle had to change. Not long afterwards I got a phone call from his wife, Shirley, tearful, saying that Benny had left her. Why? She didn't know, and I certainly didn't. I phoned Benny immediately, to give him my support, frankly, and to find out the truth. When he

Adjustments: Arterial and Attitudinal

verified what Shirley had told me, I suddenly articulated a thought that may have lain dormant in my subconscious over the years, unexpressed. I asked him, without any preliminaries, "Is it because you're a homosexual?" He answered simply, "Yes."

I wasn't taken aback. Although the subject had never come up before, it was something that I now realized had always existed in the subtext of our lives. It was as if I had always known.

Adjustment. In my chosen field, that is, the arts, homosexuality was nothing new. I had worked with and become very fond of quite a number of people over the years who were gay. It had never been a problem, but it had never been this close to home.

Adjustment. Benny had obviously made a necessary change in order to free himself from what must have been a life cloaked in tension and lies. He removed the facade of normalcy in order to live normally. Adjustment was necessary for me too. What does "normal" mean? I had never regarded homosexuality as normal—but dare I consider my brother any less so-called normal than me? Homosexuality that close to home was something to be ashamed of—but I was so proud of my brother. If I wanted to get biblical, homosexuality was an abomination, something to hate—but I loved my brother.

A change in my outlook was necessary, but when it's been natural for you to think a certain way for approximately half a century, change is indeed difficult. I remember once coming into the kitchen and watching my mother, who was doing the dishes, separating the meat dishes from the dairy dishes, as required by kosher law, thereby giving herself more work to do. She smiled at me because she knew what I was thinking. She said to me, "If I were a young girl starting out today I would not have two sets of dishes; I would not do this."

So I said to her, "Then why are you doing it?"

She answered with pleasant resignation, "When you've been doing something for fifty years, it's hard to change."

Although the subject was different, I think that simple answer was a mouthful of understanding from a woman with no formal education but blessed with the accumulation of great wisdom. It would take me time; and Benny, God bless him, understood this, because my slow adjustment caused no resentment in him towards me. We continued to love and respect each other.

I finished that first phone conversation with him by asking, with reference to the then still relatively new phenomenon called AIDS, "Do I have to worry about you, Benny, with regard to that?" I couldn't even name it, just like when cancer used to be called "the Big C." He said, "No, I'm not a fool." I wasn't secure in his answer because I knew that, even though he was a doctor who should know better, he was going to go at life with a vengeance, as if he had lots of time to make up for.

Adjustment. The air that fills up the balloon is ultimately the same air that causes it to burst or float away. You've got to do what you do in order to live, but at the same time, what you do can diminish your life or even threaten your very existence. You can't take life for granted. The breath of life sustains the balloon, but adjustments are sometimes needed: new air might have to be breathed in to prevent deflation, too much air and the balloon might explode. For me, well, as in the case of Ec. 20, I didn't always learn the first time around.

As life and career were expanding during the 1980s, seeds were being sown for a contraction. In about 1983, when I was not yet fifty, on an afternoon in Toronto before an evening flight back to Los Angeles, I suddenly got what I thought was intense heartburn. I wondered whether it might be more than that, because I'd never known such penetrating or spreading pain from a heartburn. I lay down for a while, until it subsided, and then went off to the airport and back to LA. My brother was in LA that night, and he reassured me that it was only heartburn and gave me some chewing gum intended to give relief by causing me to burp. The only relief and reassurance I got was from my brother's presence. After he left I went to bed, but I slept only fitfully. I woke up in the early hours of the morning with the

Adjustments: Arterial and Attitudinal

same pain I had had in Toronto the afternoon before. Never before had I woken up from pain. It was still dark out. I couldn't be comfortable anywhere, standing, walking around or sitting, least of all in bed, so I got dressed and started my drive to work.

I held on to the steering wheel more firmly than ever before because, while I wasn't ready to acknowledge anything serious, I recalled hearing about heart attack victims losing control of the wheel while driving, resulting in car crashes and catastrophes. When I was approaching the exit for Cedars-Sinai Hospital, I thought maybe I should check in and find out what this was all about, but I was afraid of what I might discover. I was about to direct an episode of *Cagney and Lacey* as well as play a major role in it; I didn't want to be thought of as an insurance risk. This is, as I've said before, a nervous business. Having a heart problem, being an insurance risk, could have dangerous implications for my career. Who was nervous? The business or me? I was so obsessed with work that, ironically, I never thought of the dangerous implications for my life of ignoring my body's warning signals. I just drove past the turnoff for Cedars-Sinai and continued on to the studio.

When I arrived it was still very early. There was no one there except the woman in charge of props. She and I used to kid around a lot. When I asked her to help me to my dressing room, she said, "You're coming on pretty early in the morning, aren't you?" Then she noticed that I wasn't kidding; there was perspiration on my temples, I was pale and I needed help getting to my room. When I lay down on the bed she said, "You better watch out, there's a flu going around."

Although I wouldn't acknowledge it, I knew what it was. "No," I said, "this is not the flu."

Not very intelligent of me, but this time I was lucky. A little later in the morning I got up and went to work, immersed myself in it, lost myself in it, and as a result directed an episode that won an award. The incident was completely past tense and forgotten about.

As the song goes, I just let the good times roll. And the times rolled around about a year later to Adam's bar mitzvah. Just a few days before what turned out to be a magnificent celebration, Adam, running along a corridor in school, collided *à la* Keystone Kops with one of his mates running down the intersecting corridor. Adam sustained a broken nose, but it was not badly dislocated. Our close friend Brian Hands, an ear, nose and throat specialist, said he could have it looking like new for what would be a much-photographed bar mitzvah party in a couple of days. However, he said he would fix it only if I promised to look after a dislocation that was much worse as far as he was concerned—he pointed at my protruding stomach. I hated seeing doctors, but if that was to be the condition for fixing Adam's nose, then I agreed to let Brian make an appointment for me.

The upshot: it was determined that I had indeed had a heart attack just prior to that directing assignment a year earlier, and I was now given a regimen of diet and exercise to follow—which I didn't. Had I been given it immediately after the scare, I might have followed it, and even then probably for just a while; for me, when there's no fear (of ill health), there's no respect for the rules. I just continued acting, directing, doing all the activities that interested me, all the bon-vivanting I could do, as though life were a banquet.

I certainly had enough examples in life to encourage more prudent behaviour, starting with my own family. Now there were some of my colleagues too. In April 1987, Jack Humphrey died of complications including heart problems. I came back to Canada to attend his funeral as one of the pallbearers. I always admired Jack, not just as a skilled, gifted and very intelligent writer and producer of comedy shows, but perhaps even more as a man who triumphed over the demons of addiction and went on to be a leader of, and example for, others. Not a week went by that he wasn't attending and speaking at AA meetings, wherever he was in the world. It was said of Jack that he could find an AA meeting in the desert. He was a man who had really got it together in his life, personally and professionally. I was thinking of him as I was getting dressed to go to the church, and I was also thinking of another very funny man who also died of a heart attack that day or the day before: Dick Shawn, a comedian whose range went from Vegas to TV talk shows to movies and Broadway. I had met Dick only the month before at a party in Los Angeles. As I was leaving for the church I said to Sara, "Dick, a very funny man, just died, and Jack, a very funny man, just died. You know death comes in threes in show business; I wonder who's next?"

Sara said, with a little smile, "Don't worry. You're not that funny!"

When I got to the church I told that to Louis Del Grande and he cracked up laughing. He had been a much closer friend to Jack and his wife, Liz, and said, "I'm going to tell that to Liz." I was concerned that it was not the right time or place, but he was confident. And he was right: Liz laughed out loud, and she assured me that Jack was probably laughing too.

I will never forget the eulogy that day, delivered by Jack's good friend Peter Trueman. Peter had been, and maybe still was at that time, the news anchor for the Global TV network. He had been with Jack the day before and gave us the feeling that a lot of what he was saying in the eulogy had been directed, if not actually authored, by Jack. It was very much in Peter's own words, however, when he said of Jack, with the authority, compassion and insight that marked his newscasts, that the day before, Jack had given him the impression of a man sitting with his bags packed in the departure lounge, awaiting his flight out.

Yes, Jack was a man who had got it together, and that image has come to mind during the writing of this book, in 1998–1999, as I prepped and performed the role of Burt Hines in Neil Simon's *Proposals* at the Manitoba Theatre Centre and then at the Royal Alexandra Theatre in Toronto. Burt Hines is a man who knows that his final departure is imminent. Now, before it's too late, he wants to put his house in order.

Later in the spring of 1987, I was told that, because I had not made the lifestyle adjustments that were necessary, my arteries had followed the natural laws and the result was plaque-land in my arteries, passages that needed to be unclogged or replaced. The latter course was prescribed, because the narrowing of the arteries had gone too far for the simpler procedure of angioplasty, that is, inflating them like a balloon. I was informed that heart bypass surgery was required.

My brother wanted to participate in this decision, so he came up from Washington to consult with the Toronto doctors. This was a source of some comfort for me. It would be an understatement to say that I was not keen on the idea and wanted to delay it as long as possible. Couldn't we do it next year? I asked. The cardiovascular surgeon argued that, according to his reading of my angiogram, I wouldn't be here next year (and I thought I was the dramatist!). He agreed to three months, and they all concurred. Then they tried to advise me on proper health habits over the next three months: diet, gentle exercise like walking, and control of the stress in my life. The latter prompted a fascinating and, from my perspective, comical discussion amongst the four doctors present. Benny said, "Stress? Have you seen him in that show he does? He's in a rage every week."

"But it's only *simulated* rage," one of the local doctors countered.

All of a sudden they became TV critics. It got even funnier as they seemed to forget I was even there and went around in circles, both physically and academically, conducting an almost Talmudic argument, posing a question in the singsong fashion of rabbis that only my life and art could answer: "Does simulated rage cause the same stress on the system as real rage?"

Barney Rosenzweig thoughtfully offered to put the company through the mental gymnastics of block shooting, that is, filming in succession my scenes from a number of different episodes, out of sequence and in one location. That way, I would miss as few episodes as possible, and the storylines wouldn't lose continuity during the three months of my recuperation. In three months I could have lost as many as nine episodes. As it was, I lost only four, one of which I was to have directed, which meant I lost five paycheques instead of ten. It could have been a lot worse. Barney told me that this was the best arrangement of block shooting he could do, that I would have to be written out of four episodes (my character was to be in hospital, recuperating from surgery), and that he was sorry I was going to lose all that money.

I said to him, "Thank you for doing this much. I'll still be making more than I was ever promised in life. How much money does a man need to make before he's got more money than he needs to live on?" I told him that I was most thankful for the opportunity to work right up till the day I would check into the hospital. That meant my mind would be occupied and I wouldn't have time to worry about the surgery.

I was scared. I wanted to be a good patient, not for appearances' sake but for my own sake, so that things would go better during and after the surgery. I relaxed with the aid of massage on the set (there was a masseuse always present for $1 a minute) and with mantras the masseuse designed for me, with some input from me. I eased myself to sleep at night with cassettes of music made from the soothing sound of ocean waves against the shore. I eventually realized that two other means of combatting fear are a sense of humour and a focus on other people. It dawned on me that while I would be in the careful and skilful hands of excellent doctors and nurses, Sara would be sitting by herself in a waiting room for four or five hours until she would be told (we hoped) something like, "Everything's OK."

Before I came back to Toronto, I went into a chic shop in the Rodeo Drive district of Beverly Hills and bought Sara a stunning necklace made of crystal, a work of art. I gave her this gift just as I was about to go into the surgery, but the only art she was interested in was the work the doctors were about to do. I don't think she's ever worn that necklace.

For comedy, I rehearsed a line to say to the doctors when I came out of the anaesthetic. When all those green blobs came into focus and I could make out which was my surgeon, I said to him, "Bernie, how come with all these beautiful nurses you got here, you sent a guy in last night to give me an enema?" I thought that would be at least a little bit funny, but Bernie Goldman, the doctor of dramatic statements I referred to earlier, had a sense of comedy as well, and certainly more wit than me. He responded mercilessly, "Al, you'll never know how good you made that guy feel!" There I was, only minutes after life-or-death surgery, laughing so hard that I feared my just-stapled-together chest would bust open.

My recuperation went well because there were always friends visiting and building my morale. Johnny Wayne came and made me laugh so hard that I again feared for my stapled chest, and so did many others in the business, in person or via the phone. The entire company of *Cagney and Lacey* took turns phoning. As well, I heard from Sammy and Altavese Davis and Carol Connors. The room was overflowing with gifts and flowers, which we shared with hospital staff and other patients on the floor. My non-show-business friends were of course just as caring and often at least as funny, such as Seymour Weinstein, my diamond-in-the-rough friend who lent me money to get into this business in the first place. He would make me laugh just as much as any pro in the business. As a matter of fact he and I still talk almost daily, with a view to making each other laugh for at least a moment. I learned from dear Lou Jacobi that laughter is one of the best medicines available.

Above all, Sara was there. She took the first steps alongside me in the centre hall of our house and then accompanied me as I graduated out into the garden, and finally around the block. She was there, too, for the delicate task of tending to an infection in my incision. They say hospitals are the best place to get an infection, and I was proof of that—the only bad luck in my procedure. They had to open the neatly stitched incision, clean it out and let it heal naturally rather than sew it up again. At first, a nurse came to the house to do the daily cleaning and rebandaging of the incision, then towards the end of the healing (which took approximately ten weeks and coincided with my recuperation), Sara took over.

As I was always lying on my back during the daily treatment, I never saw the rehealed incision till the process was over. I must digress for a moment. I had been given a turquoise-coloured track suit by the *C & L* costume department. Sara thought it was ugly and hated to see me wearing it. She used to say, "You don't exactly go unnoticed as it is, let alone wearing turquoise!" Well, I finally stood in front of the mirror unbandaged with the newly and naturally healed incision, which looks like a large blotch on my chest, and I exclaimed, "What an ugly scar! That is the ugliest scar in the world!"

Sara, standing by, said, "I agree. On the scale of ugliness it ranks second only to your turquoise track suit!"

I became an official spokesperson for the Ontario Heart and Stroke Foundation, doing commercials for them, writing letters to their subscribers and potential donors, making public appearances and giving speeches whenever I could. As well as advising about preventive measures such as diet, exercise, not smoking and stress management, I urged people to care for and share time with post-surgery patients who may not have the same support system of family and friends as I was so fortunate to have. I have often volunteered my time to visit with recuperating patients or encourage those in the pre-op stage. And as for doctors in the audience, when I spoke I assured them I wasn't sorry for being given such an ugly scar from the surgery, because along with it, as it's so sensitive to the touch, I got a brand new erogenous zone!

My health was good. I was thankful to the playwright in the sky—but as always, he persists in doing it his way. No contrivances or coincidences this time, just irony and a terrible foreboding, for it was around this time that we learned what I had feared would happen one day, that my brother Benny was sick. It was now approximately a decade since that phone call when he "came out" to me. Just as I couldn't mention the words "heart attack," he wouldn't acknowledge at that time, at least not to me, the word "AIDS." As a doctor he had access to the best and the latest in information, medicine and drugs, so he reassured us that all the right steps and treatments were being taken. I wanted to believe that, but I feared the worst, the inevitable.

CHAPTER 29

A Frame Freezes, but the Film Advances

When I returned to Los Angeles it was with my obesity decreased and my exercise regimen increased. I walked three miles or one hour a day and went at my work, both acting and directing, with the same energy I had always given it. My mood was up and optimistic, but the mood on the set was not—at least with regard to a seventh year. It was clear that this, the sixth year, would be the last.

A tough break for me, losing that amount of money (which would have been even more in the seventh year), because I was still trying to bench-press a mighty mortgage off my chest. Too bad, another year would have done it; but the playwright in the sky said the curtain was coming down on *Cagney and Lacey*. The network was not keen on it, but they probably could have been convinced to keep the show for one more year if the spirit had been there amongst the principals of *C & L*. It wasn't. And frankly, it had reached the point where I often wondered whether I'd watch the show if I weren't in it. It had become, in my opinion, too much like a soap opera, with too much emphasis on the personal lives of the two women (which, ironically, is what had made it special in the first place). It might have taken a different turn, one that I would have preferred, under the new producership that was proposed for the seventh year, but we'll never know.

As for the weight on my chest, it seemed almost futile to try to remove it, although I didn't want to be squashed under it. I was always advised, and I think well advised, that the best investment for me was to reduce debt. However, I no sooner paid down the mortgage than I would simultaneously engage in an activity that increased debt. Someone who was making the kind of money I made in the 1980s (close to seven figures a year), if they had any financial savvy, would have been far richer than I was. It was as though I was paying down the past in order to secure the future, but along the way I overloaded the present, so that I was soon again having to pay down the past in order to secure the future. Talk about financial circles!

My life was illustrating a story I once heard Uncle Moishe, my mother's brother, tell to one of his grandchildren who had asked him to explain the difference between depression and inflation. He said, in an accent sweetly reminiscent of my mother's, that when he came to Canada during the Depression he would walk by Shopsy's window and see a sandwich there piled high with corned beef. He was tempted. His mouth was watering, but it cost ten cents, and he didn't have ten cents so he didn't buy it. Nowadays, in the eighties, the days of inflation, Uncle Moishe said, you walk by Shopsy's window and you can still see a delicious-looking sandwich piled high with corned beef. You're hungry and you want it, but now it costs $5 and again you haven't got the money. This time, though, so what? You're hungry, you want it, you buy it! My interpretation of this is not only the thirties versus the eighties, not only depression as opposed to inflation, but pre-plastic in contrast to post-plastic. Now, if you don't have the money, you pull out a credit card.

The debt load notwithstanding, our lifestyle was fantastic, and as for rainy days, I've always said I loved the rain. We spent a lot of money on travel for the four of us, which was always rewarding; we accumulated some treasured possessions; but mostly we seemed to be endlessly pouring money into our eighty-year-old house. In the late 1980s, we started pouring it outside the house as well, changing the facade and undertaking extensive landscaping, a job that was meant to take a few months and cost a lot of money. It wound up taking about a year and costing a lot more than a lot of money. In the meantime the front of the house looked like the trenches of World War I. When it was finally finished, before the end of the decade, it gave us great joy—and helped to increase the value of our house, according to real estate agents who were anxious to sell it. This knowledge gave me a sense of security, a "hedge against disaster" (I had learned that in Ec. 20), like a fallback position against which my debt seemed minor.

At the beginning of the 1990s, the economy began to turn topsy-turvy, something apparently not even the pundits, let alone I, could have foreseen, and the value of money changed. The market price of the house plummeted: if it had gone on the block then it would have fetched only about half of what it had been worth a couple of years earlier. This fact, combined with my substantial drop in income because *Cagney and Lacey* was not renewed, suddenly turned the mortgage from minor into major.

The hurdles of high debt never really hindered my forward run even if the speed of that run was reduced by half. My income was still considerably more than the magic number I'd given myself about thirty years earlier, at which time someone whose business acumen I respected said to me, "As long as you're making $2,000 a week, you'll be OK. You are, aren't you?" I said, "Yes, of course." I think I lied. But that concept served as a bottom-line goal for me from that time on, and it's never changed: as long as I'm earning at least six figures a year I'm doing OK. I didn't care how high up in the six figures it got—and it got very high during the 1980s—or whether it was just over the mark; as long as I cleared six figures I reckoned I'd make it through the year.

I never had a balance sheet, columns of ins and outs, never budgeted, but was always aware of my means, trying to live within them while testing how far I could push them. I just liked living and hated debt, so I paid things off in lump sums rather than by plan, and for thirty years somehow cleared my bottom-line goal. Not since Barney's Beanery in the early sixties have I had to supplement my income with a job-job like driving a cab or waiting on tables. And although making insufficient money to support the lifestyle we'd grown used to had now become a very real possibility, I continued to clear my bottom-line goal doing exactly what I wanted—acting and directing. But I was starting to be reminded of a phrase I had used earlier in my life: what if it all turns to "rat shit" next year?

That possibility did not get in the way of my commitment to community work, resulting in my once again being recognized for these efforts. In 1989 the B'nai Brith, which means "children of the covenant," presented me with their Humanitarian Award. The B'nai Brith is a leading human rights organization both nationally and internationally. I was honoured to be associated with them. I wanted all the guests in the huge ballroom at the Sheraton Centre in Toronto, some 1,500 people, to feel like humanitarians. They all were. They each donated a substantial amount of money to help further the good works of the B'nai Brith and specifically to create the Sara and Al Waxman Audio and Visual Library in their League for Human Rights Building. Just as when the Shaare Zedek honoured me and I shared the word "honour," so too at the B'nai Brith dinner I wanted to share the words "humanitarian" and "harmony" (the theme for the evening).

The symbol in the logo for the B'nai Brith is a menorah—a candelabrum with seven branches. We decided to use our bat and bar mitzvah music once more. Again the team of Joey Miller and Steve Witkin wrote beautiful lyrics to introduce each of the candle lighters; and the refrain on this occasion became:

Take a little walk with me,
And with every candle you will see,

> The brighter the candle glows,
> The brighter the harmony.

Each of the candles symbolized an important theme in my life: family and tradition, friendship, community, charity, justice and human rights, profession and the future.

Sara, my uncle Moishe Glass (my late mother's only living brother, at that time eighty-five years old) and Sara's father lit the first candle. The second, friendship, was lit by Art Clairman, Seymour Weinstein and George Sperdakos. The third, community, was lit by impresario Garth Drabinsky, ambassador Allan Gotlieb and producer/distributor and broadcaster Harold Greenberg, each of whom had been honoured by the B'nai Brith for their community work. The fourth, charity, was lit by Reg Bovaird of the Variety Club, Nancy Tsai for a wealth of work she had done and probably still does, particularly in cancer research, and John Kim Bell, symphony conductor and founder and leader of the Canadian Native Arts Foundation. The fifth candle, justice and human rights, was lit by judge and legal scholar Allan Linden, illustrious lawyer Eddie Greenspan, journalist, activist, author and B'nai Brith Woman of the Year June Callwood and former Ontario ombudsman Dan Hill Sr. For the sixth candle, profession, it was a joy for me to have my colleagues, co-workers and friends Catherine McCartney (who was central to the production of that fantastic musical number, which everyone in the room seemed to be part of by now), Fiona Reid, Harvey Atkin and Marty Kove. And lastly, I *kvelled* with the seventh candle, the future, lit by Tobaron and Adam Waxman.

The singing (and dancing) of each verse and refrain was done by the talented and generous Michael Burgess, Denis Simpson, Louise Pitre and Liberty Silver, and the script was narrated by the man with a gift from God in his *gorgle* (throat), Henry Ramer. Knowlton Nash, both dignified and comedic, was the master of ceremonies. The lieutenant-governor of Ontario, the Honourable Lincoln Alexander, was in attendance, as well as many people from the three levels of government, show business and the film industry. It was a marvellous and memorable night for me and my family—but it wasn't perfect. Benny wasn't there. He had died nine days earlier.

A short time before Benny died I arranged for each of our family to visit him in Washington. Tobaron went on her own; so did Adam. Sara and I went together. We visited with him in his apartment. He now lived at the Watergate, although he had by this time remarried Shirley (I think as a tax protection for her and the family). He had some gay friends there, who formed a strong support system for him. We had some small talk, some laughs and some lunch, all of us together. Benny said he felt strong and was determined to see Tyne Daly in *Gypsy* when it came through Washington, and to visit her backstage. Then one of his friends said it was time for him to go to the hospital for his treatment. We went downstairs together, and Sara and I said that we would get a cab after he left. He got into the back seat of the car and, just as it was pulling away, he turned and looked back at me through the rear window and mouthed the words, "I love you." I never saw him again.

I think of him often. That image of him mouthing those words to me, his face framed in the rear window of that car, has stayed with me ever since, like a freeze-frame in my mind.

Fifty-eight years old. Still so much to live, still so much to give.

These thoughts occupied my mind as Adam, Tobaron, Sara and I flew down to be with Shirley and my nephew and nieces. The whole extended family was there, and many friends came to pay their respects. I was so distraught, so within my thoughts of Benny, that I don't actually remember where the funeral was held—in the Baltimore area or Virginia. I do remember it was the first time that I was at a family funeral when the fields were not covered with snow.

Life and death form a completeness, a oneness that is forever, and forever is any time and all the time; it is winter and it is summer, it is fields of snow and it is fields of green. It is grey skies and it is sunshine. It is eternity, like my mother and father are, and now my brother too. My mind's eye could only see Benny in the car window mouthing the words "I love you." And I loved him, as I loved my mother and father.

I listened to the eulogies from his colleagues and friends—professors, doctors, students, all with words of wisdom, respect and love, ranging from wit to tears, and all portraying him as a champion of social and medical causes. But all the while the ear of my soul heard only the music of Benny at the piano, the music that gave pleasure and pride to my mother and father, and inspiration to me. As I continued to listen to the eulogies I saw the fingers my mother had told me about, fingers of his youth playing along the wall as though it were a piano, fingers I never in fact saw in my life until I was old enough to see him mature into marvellous talent, fingers feeling the keys now slowly, gently, playfully, now with flowing feeling, gracefully, dreamlike, now flying over the keys, intensely, forcefully, now thundering, pounding, as wells of natural talent exploded skyward into magnificent music—now suddenly, abruptly, too soon, spent. It would have been good to hear more, both musical and medical, but now it was muted, and finally and forever I saw and still see that freeze-frame of my brother, Benny, in the rear window of that car pulling away, as he was smiling at me, silently saying "I love you."

CHAPTER 30

From *Persona Non Grata* to Patagonia

Back in Canada after *Cagney and Lacey*, I was getting good roles in TV and film that took me across the country and back and forth between Los Angeles and Toronto. But I started to veer more towards directing.

This double activity, acting and directing, proved to be gratifying but not without some difficulties. Most people in this fast-moving and nervous business need to pigeonhole you, for reasons of expediency, so that you are conveniently categorized in their minds. They don't want the complications of a hyphenated talent, which is what I guess I was and still am. I was, however, never famous enough to rise above these complications as Danny DeVito did or Mel Gibson or Robert Redford or Warren Beatty, all great talents who, if they decide to direct, can direct. For me it was a struggle to be accepted as a director. Certain people, usually other directors, preferred not to think of me as working in their field, and most people, even those with nothing to lose but time, like some casting directors, tended to think "Oh, he's directing now, not acting any more," or producers would think, "He's acting now, probably not interested in directing again." Compound this with the fact that I was also teaching and it's as though I deliberately made the hill ahead of me steeper. Nevertheless, I kept climbing, because I wanted to get to the top of my hill—the hill I chose to climb.

The hill is a very significant image for me for another reason. As I've said before, I love to watch my son, Adam, run. You wouldn't think he's my son, no fat at all on him, he's like wire and muscle. His workouts include long jogs ending with a run up a hill. When in Toronto he chooses the reservoir at Spadina and St. Clair—two hills, one straight up from the other, each at an incline of what looks to me like forty-five degrees. He charges up the first hill, runs along the flat road separating the two, then charges up the second hill. He does this four or five times, while I sit in the car, alternating between watching him and studying a script. He still runs like a deer, and still brings such a smile to my face.

So, while busily climbing my own hills and criss-crossing the country for acting and directing gigs, all worthwhile activities I felt, there now came a new and equally welcome trip—an invitation for Sara and me to a dinner with Derek Burney, our ambassador to the United States at that time. We'd been invited to embassy dinners before, but this time I sensed it was a kind of audition—which I think Sara and I passed. There were maybe half a dozen tables with about six people at each, and I was seated at the head table. Alongside me were our ambassador and Jack Valenti, the charming but infamous (as far as Canadian filmmakers are concerned) lobbyist for the US film producers and distributors. Sara was seated at a table with David Brinkley and other heavies, such as Judge William Webster, then head of the CIA.

During conversation with Valenti, while I agreed that you can't legislate people into theatres and that a film or show needs to have "its own legs," I nevertheless maintained that every culture has the duty to protect its own right of expression, not to the extent of closing itself off from the world but sufficient to keep itself vibrant for its own sake and for the sake of it neighbours and the rest of the world.

Indeed, I suggested that he may find the United States will need to do the same someday, and that arguably it already does.

After dinner, I introduced Valenti to Sara, and she pursued a lively discussion with him, as she was then the vice chair of the Ontario Film Review Board. She argued that each jurisdiction has the right to determine its own standards of classification for feature films, rather than simply accept the ratings that would otherwise be imposed by the film producers he represents.

Back to my hill. For the first time in about fifteen years I was not looking at a regular paycheque, yet I still had to make sufficient income to maintain our lifestyle. At the same time I never lost sight of the fact that this business deals with a product that is for me an art form, one that I am continuously trying to learn more about and get better at. This attitude sometimes proved counterproductive for me, particularly in episodic TV, where producers are often looking for an assembly-line approach. At least one producer was critical of my way, one of individuality as opposed to conformity with the pattern of a particular series. Perhaps they were right, and certainly my professional responsibility was to achieve their purpose. Nevertheless, no matter how hungry I was, I would not betray my own conscience. I've heard it said that you can measure a man's integrity by how hungry he is. Well, I certainly was hungry, but I wasn't desperate.

An example of the perils of integrity came in a casting session for a TV episode I was about to direct. Approval of an actor was made by me and the American producers, but theirs was on the condition that I monitor the actor's Canadian accent; they didn't want to hear "aboot" instead of "about." This would have made sense if the character had been an American, but I said that with this tight shooting schedule I didn't have the time to devote to that aspect of one actor's performance, particularly when it really wasn't a problem as far as I or the story was concerned. They, however, felt it would be a problem for American audiences. "Why is it a problem?" I asked. "It's a Canadian story."

"But," they argued, "we're selling this to American audiences."

"It's being shot in Toronto," I countered. "The city is not being used for Chicago or New York, it's being used for Toronto. If it weren't, then that would be a different story. In this show Toronto is Toronto!"

They were starting to steam. "We don't care!" They tried to contain themselves. "It's what we want you to do. We have artistic control."

I too was adamant and getting impatient. "In the story it says we're in Toronto. It says so right in the script you've OK'd, with your artistic control. You want to monitor the actor's 'aboots,' then you come on the set and do it yourselves. I'll be too busy making you a good episode!" Which I did, but after completion my contract was not renewed.

A similar situation, but with a different ending, came in a casting session on *Cagney and Lacey* in 1983. It was before the first episode I directed. I thought it would be wise for me to observe, from inception through to completion, the work of the person considered to be our best director. He was not only the director who gave our show its look, he was also one of the busiest directors in Hollywood. It was said of him that he had "oil wells in his mailbox" because there were so many residual cheques arriving all the time. I was excited about watching him; I knew I would learn something about the craft of directing series television.

In the casting session the writers and producers were sitting around this director and his assistant, both of whom were at a desk in the centre of the room. I sat off in one corner. Barney's spy (that's how we all thought of her) was seated in the opposite corner. A number of actors had just auditioned for the same role. They were all good, but when the last of them, a short man, left, the director, very sure of himself, said, "That's the one I want. The last one. The short one, because I see this character as short."

Suddenly a voice from the corner, the spy, said, "Really? Barney saw him as tall."

To which the exemplary director responded without missing a beat, "Sure, tall is good too!"

Laughable? Certainly not something I respected. But perhaps there was an aspect of his behaviour I ought to have considered. Maybe he was smart enough to size up which fights are worth fighting; maybe he had oil wells in his mailbox because he could tell the difference between the battle and the war. Maybe. But while making a living is important for me, in my aspirations oil wells do not outrank truth and integrity.

This cost me. Around this time I was interviewed on a CBC talk show and was asked to comment on a then popular CBC TV show. I tried to avoid answering, but finally responded with some critical comments on a general level, not mean-spirited or directed at anyone in particular. I fully expected the interviewer to engage me in some discussion on this, but we moved on to other subjects. Later I got a call from a CBC executive expressing the anger that CBC brass felt towards me, an attitude that lasted for quite a while. Indeed, when a producer for whom I had done some successful directing was packaging a show to present to the CBC, he thought he would strengthen the package by saying, after he secured my agreement, that I would be the director of the project. He was cautioned that the addition of my name to the package would in fact weaken the project. Why? He was told that I was *persona non grata* at the CBC. Well, that was comical. And what a change!—to have once been considered the CBC's ambassador to Canada and now to be *persona non grata*. I wasn't about to make apologies. I wasn't above criticism; why should they be? I'd rather have my truth and integrity, even if it cost me oil wells.

Nor do oil wells outrank the loyalty I feel towards other actors I work with. I'm not talking about criticism, I'm talking about morale, particularly in the artistic process. While directing an episode of a police series in Toronto, I was watching dailies with some members of the company, including the producer, who had been quite a fan of my work. Suddenly the producer blurted out a complaint at having to watch yet another angle on a multicovered scene—something to be expected with six or seven speaking characters, TV being a close-up medium. The producer said something like, "Is there more of this? It's boring to watch." Well, dailies can be tedious, but the producer should have known better. It was mean, and I didn't like the actors having to hear this. I told the producer to stay out of my sight and off the set. Well, the producer never came on the set again and I was never hired again, in spite of making a very good episode for them. The ramifications spread far, as this company produced many shows during the eighties. Overreacted, underemployed.

Truth and integrity. I feel richer with them than without. Years later, in 1998, when Norman Jewison, one of the great gentlemen of cinema and Canadian culture, offered me a part in his film *Lazarus and the Hurricane*, I couldn't do it because, although the scenes for this cameo role were to be shot over just two days, they were inconveniently scheduled, coming just eight days after I opened at the Manitoba Theatre Centre in Neil Simon's *Proposals*. My agent wanted me to accept the offer: it was a Jewison film, and my scenes were going to be one on one with Denzel Washington. It was too important to miss. "I can't," I said. "I really want to, but I can't let down the morale of the cast and company of *Proposals*—a prior commitment."

She said, "I can get you out legally for the three or four days" (shoot and travel).

I said, "No. I can't let down the company. Norman will understand that. I would work for him for nothing, so please let him know that the reason I'm declining has nothing to do with him, his show or the money; it has to do with my commitment to the morale of my fellow cast members."

Norman's office phoned back to say they would reschedule to accommodate my returning to Toronto for the run at the Royal Alexandra Theatre. Norman is a mensch. My integrity was intact and so was his, because he got the casting he wanted. In fact, we both got what we wanted.

Truth and integrity. Perhaps they are overworked words—I don't care. To me they are a natural and integral part of being an artist, and worth reiterating. The artist diminishes himself if he cops out to any degree on either of them. I never did, and one of the results was a reputation that, on occasion, caused producers to warn me against confrontation before we started work, as though to let me know from the get-go who was boss. They did it by way of a question: "What will happen if we disagree, if we cross swords?" I would sincerely, innocently wonder at the need for such a conversation, because I only cared to do good work, for my sake and theirs. Apparently, though, I was getting that kind of reputation. One producer, in a dispute with me, acknowledged, as though capitulating, "OK, you're right!" then added, "But do you have to be so right?!"

In the meantime, in spite of alienating some producers in both the private and public sectors, in both the United States and Canada, I seemed to retain enough credibility and respect as a member of the cinema and TV industries to be invited, and ultimately elected by the membership, to be the chairperson of the Academy of Canadian Cinema and Television in 1988 and to be re-elected each term until 1992. And even though as an artist I felt I could speak my mind and express my thoughts and feelings directly and sometimes even at the price of diplomacy, someone in Ottawa, apparently, still thought that I would be a good candidate for a diplomatic posting. Come to think of it, in that specific field I would, if I had to, choose a different hat to wear, one more appropriate to the requirements of diplomacy.

It was at this time that Prime Minister Brian Mulroney asked me to be Canada's consul-general in Los Angeles. Derek Burney was still our ambassador to the United States; this occurred not long after the dinner described earlier. My territory of responsibility would include southern California, Hawaii, Nevada and part of Arizona. I was profoundly flattered. This for me was an honour. I had earlier given thought to politics, having been tempted by requests from each of the three parties to run at both the provincial and federal levels. I thought (and still do think) that serving your country, in either an elected or an appointed position, is a high calling. This opportunity was something that I very much welcomed and appreciated. The offer came while I was shooting a feature film in Toronto called *White Light*, which starred Marty Kove and Martha Henry. The playwright in the sky was again creating coincidences, with absolutely no regard for my sense of timing. Still, I was given a while to think about it.

Upon completion of shooting and before getting into post-production I accepted an offer to act in a Werner Herzog film with Donald Sutherland called *Scream of Stone* (also known in other territories as *Cri de roche* and *Schrei aus Stein*). It was to be shot on location down in Patagonia, near Tierra del Fuego at the southern tip of Argentina. I was initially inclined not to accept because my mind was preoccupied with *White Light*, but while driving with Sara to Woodbine racetrack for a charity function I got a call in the car. Tobaron was excited—she'd just been on the phone from Munich. The caller had been Donald Sutherland (who, she said, sounds like a nice man) and the film director was Werner Herzog, "my favourite director. You should do it, Dad." Well, my three weeks down in Argentina would coincide with the editor's first cut of *White Light*, so I decided, as is ideal, that the editor should carry out that work without me peering over his shoulder, and then I'd come back after some distance and detachment with a fresh mind—which would be good for both the film and the decision-making process regarding the diplomatic posting.

Herzog, considered a visionary and a cinematic purist, would often wait for the light of day to be exactly as he envisioned it before shooting a scene, which gave me lots of time to think in the cool wind on the "negative" desert of Patagonia. The ground was red like the sand of Prince Edward Island beaches, but hard, so it was nice to walk on, not like rock but not shifting sand either. Perfect for a stroll, particularly with that refreshing wind blowing crisp and clear—conditions conducive to lucid thinking.

I would often walk with Donald Sutherland. Sometimes we would see the huge wingspan of a condor or an eagle flying above. Before Donald and I took one of our many walks I noticed that he had a laptop computer, which he seemed to use a lot. I asked if he was writing something. He said he was writing a diary, that it would be good to have, and he suggested that I should do the same, possibly working towards an autobiography. I said that would be the furthest thing from my mind but I might that particular day write a diary. We then borrowed a pickup truck from the company rather than take our usual walk. When we had driven out a few miles onto the desert we got a call to come back to shoot. Somehow, as Donald attempted to turn back on this narrow road, he stalled and couldn't restart. Then I tried. I got it going, but again, in the process of turning, it stalled, and stayed stalled. It wouldn't turn over, so these two gringos had to wait shamefacedly for one of the locals to come to our rescue. At the end of the day we compared diaries. In Donald's version I had screwed up the vehicle and caused the stall; in my version he was the culprit. So, if this story makes it into *his* autobiography one day, we will be able to compare the selectivity of our respective memories.

On another day, when we were walking back to our cabins—five or six new wooden structures constructed especially for the members of the cast—we saw that one of them was on fire. (They had someone, literally called a fireman, who stoked the brick fireplaces to keep the cabins warm for our return.) The closer we got the more certain we were that it was either Donald's or mine, and then I clearly saw that it was mine, or rather had been mine. The cabin was burnt to the ground; all that remained standing was the brick fireplace. Everything I had was burnt to a crisp, gone. When I searched the charred remains I noticed something shining through all that blackness beneath my feet. It was a silver oval cowboy belt buckle that Seymour Weinstein had lent me. Nothing else was spared. Clothes, books, identification, luggage, medicine, important papers, even the diary I had started—all were gone.

There was only one phone in the whole area, an ancient thing that you had to wind up like a barrel organ. I decided to call home, acutely aware that Sara might get frightened, because my heart specialist had cautioned against my going up to such high elevations. He had told me, "I wouldn't if I were you." I said there was no way I was going to give up the company of such talented people or the excitement of such an exotic location. When I finally reached Sara she could hardly hear me on that primitive phone, some 13,000 kilometres from Toronto. She didn't believe me when I said I was OK, so I kept shouting "There's nothing wrong!" Finally I convinced her that my only problem was that I was "wearing my change of underwear."

Between Sara sending me some essentials and the company buying me the rest, I was sufficiently equipped till the end of the shoot. I had very little to bring home, and no luggage to bring it in—just a white plastic garbage bag on which Donald printed "Roots," a reference to the store, no doubt.

We were helicoptered every day from our base camp up to a glacier surrounding the mountain location. The mountain is called Cerro Torre, which is beside the more famous Mount Fitzroy. Cerro Torre goes straight up into the air, with hardly any incline, like a super-high grain elevator made of ice. The story of *Scream of Stone* is about a competition between a traditional mountain climber (an Italian) and a young renegade climber (a German) in their quests to prove the superiority of their respective mountain-climbing philosophies and, in the process, to best Cerro Torre. Being a Werner Herzog film, nature is a character, and of course Cerro Torre wins over both as the young climber falls to his death and the older one makes it to the top, promptly goes mad and stays there alone on the top of the frozen nothingness. Needless to say, I didn't play either of the climbers; I was an American TV producer filming the event.

At one point the whole company was caught at the foot of Cerro Torre in the midst of a blizzard that was becoming progressively more blinding. The blizzard was only at the high altitude, not down at base camp, but the helicopter pilot refused to fly up because it was too risky. The choice: climb down the mountain or remain up there till the weather cleared. Sutherland and I decided to climb down. I figured, what the hell, it's downhill and I like walking (the one exercise I continued religiously after my heart surgery). We soon found, however, that with each step we sunk waist deep into the thick snow. It was a long way down and it took many minutes to achieve only a few steps.

When the helicopter radioed that it would chance one flight before the blizzard made vision impossible, Sutherland, his makeup assistant, the French actress Mathilda May and I crammed in with the pilot. The question was, who was opting for the more dangerous course—those who flew out or those who remained? Our tiny helicopter was buffeted by the winds as we tried to fly through a corridor of mountains. While we were bounced and belted about, we feared for those who remained on the glacier at the foot of Cerro Torre. Meanwhile they were praying that we wouldn't be smacked into the side of a mountain, which from their perspective looked close to happening until they finally, frighteningly, lost sight of us as we vanished into the whiteness. Any fear we might have had was channelled into concern for one of our group who was sick the whole way down. Frankly, I was excited by the danger of our journey. We flew suddenly into a clearing, the sun blazing on us as we approached base camp. You would never have believed that these two weather conditions could exist so close to each other. The helicopter pilot refused to go back up, and the others remained under Herzog's direction as he led the way down the mountain, which if I remember correctly was a trek of about twelve hours, with some stragglers (I would have been one of them) taking closer to twenty hours.

Herzog has a reputation for dangerous circumstances attending his films, but he is a risk taker intellectually and philosophically too. I enjoyed talking to him between shots. We would discuss politics, poetry and philosophy, and of course our different approaches to the writing of film scripts. He was excited by my ability to improvise within character, and said he preferred what I came up with to what he had written, at least within individual scenes; as for the overview, he preferred his way. Donald and I, for example, did an improvisation that made the point of a scene with a spontaneity that can only be captured on film. Werner was disappointed that the wind and snow which had rocked through rehearsal subsided during the take. We suggested that he print it anyway; in post-production, he could mix wind onto the soundtrack and with the snow all around us, albeit not blowing, we would appear to be in the midst of a storm. He didn't buy that but agreed to print it. Then we did another take for "safety." This time the improv was awkward and rough—but the weather was rougher. Blinding snow filled the lens, and Werner saw what he wanted.

Like most North Americans, my approach is to begin with a realistic story, whereas Werner's inspiration came from a single powerful image or a vision, like two men climbing up either side of a dangerous mountain. Then he built a story around that vision in order to realize it on film. It's like I've said of method acting: whatever method works is the best method.

CHAPTER 31

And Master of None?

I returned to Toronto from the distance of Patagonia with new perspective and went about finishing *White Light*. While I was away I had also been able to consider the question of the consul-general posting. I wrote a letter to the prime minister, thanking him for the high compliment but regretfully declining his offer. The press had gotten wind of the offer, but I refused requests for interviews until the Prime Minister's Office had received my letter. Then I agreed to discuss my decision with a columnist for the *Toronto Sun*, Michele Mandel. She accurately described my dilemma with these words:

> The part calls for much more than hosting glittering parties for Tinsel Town celebrities. Responsible for a territory that includes southern California, Arizona and Las Vegas, he would oversee political and economic affairs, trade and industrial development, tourism, public affairs, immigration ... leaving no time for acting—or directing.

She then quoted me:

> "If I took it on, it would be with the view to doing it 100 percent, and there was the dilemma ... You can't do it halfway. You have to do it all the way or you don't do it."

Essentially, I was not prepared to close one chapter of my life and start a new one; not prepared to end my career and begin again. It was so tempting, though, and as a team, Sara and I would have been so good at it that part of me hoped one day things might be different.

In the meantime I was finishing up *White Light* and anticipating another feature film, *Diamond Fleece*. It would be produced by Alan Landsburg, who was also the producer of *Maggie's Secret*, a very successful film (an after-school special) I had directed a few years before for CBS. *Maggie's Secret* was amongst the best directing work I had done up to that time, and I'm very proud of it to this day. It's a story about alcohol and family abuse and its direct effect on a teenage girl called Maggie, played by Joanna Vanicola. It won me a Scott Newman Award (1990), named for Paul Newman's son (a victim of drug abuse) and given for shows with integrity on the subject of drug and/or alcohol abuse. The award is presented as part of the Daytime Emmy celebrations. I received a nomination for directing and Joanne won an Emmy for acting. Equally wonderful in the film were Mimi Kuzik, who had been a guest years before on *King of Kensington* and at the time of *Maggie's Secret* was a regular on *Hill Street Blues*; Joseph Bottoms (of a very respected family of American actors); and Jaimz Woolvett. Jaimz later starred (and this picture helped him get the part) in his own series, the pilot of which I directed.

Maggie's Secret achieved high ratings and rave reviews, and was successful for all involved. *White Light* did not turn out as well, either as a film or for me personally. The story had great potential to engage and entertain, blending fantasy and reality. For this to work, there has to be a skilful reconciliation of the two, which wasn't evident in our script. I don't blame the writer so much as myself. I wasn't able to help him on this, nor to convey to him how the logistical difficulties in having too many location changes (almost as many location changes as shooting days) would prove costly and draining. The story involved mystery and a kind of odyssey, as the lead character (played by my *Cagney and Lacey* buddy Martin Kove) goes from place to place, through twists and turns, in his quest for a woman he thinks he loves, whom he only met in the six or seven seconds' duration of a near-death experience. We don't find out till the end of the film whether or not the woman exists.

It was a tough production schedule on a small budget. It was ambitious, working against difficult odds, but worth the try, and I went at it like an addict. At the end of the process one of the actors in the cast, Bruce Boa, a good friend in both Londons (Ontario and England, where he had worked on *Secret of the World* with me) and a successfully recovering alcoholic, said that I had reminded him of a "man on the bottle," as far as food was concerned, that I couldn't have done the inordinate amount of work involved without constant eating. I had by this time gained back all the weight I had lost a couple of years earlier, after my heart bypass surgery. The weight gain started with and continued throughout the preparation and making of this film. Bruce said he wanted to stop me for the sake of my life, but that he knew I had to finish the film for the sake of my life. It hurt my health; I was now as heavy as I had ever been. It perhaps hurt my directing career as well, at least in feature films. *White Light* was released in 1991 and the criticism it received was aimed mainly at the script, and I think unfairly at some of the acting. The most perceptive criticism levelled at me was that it was more of a TV film than a theatrical film, and indeed it sold and played well on late-night television.

Fortunately, soon after *White Light* and regardless of its fate, I had another film to direct that had been in the works for some time, although not as long as these things sometimes take, Alan Landsburg being very experienced at what he does. Landsburg, after the success of *Maggie's Secret* in 1989, began the process of packaging a new film called *Diamond Fleece*, with me as director. As is usually the case, along the way it went from one network to another, and even to feature film before being packaged and ready to go in 1991–1992, with USA Cable as the network and Landsburg's company co-producing with Harold Greenberg's company, Astral Films.

And Master of None?

The story again involved reality blended with a kind of fantasy. It was a tender love story interwoven with a caper plot about a diamond heist. A sophisticated thief, who is a recent ex-convict, and a woman who owns and runs a Dickensian bookstore fall in love. He is well read and loves books as she does, and she is beautiful but with her guard up for fear of revealing how fragile and vulnerable she is. As the story unfolds, her guard slowly but surely drops. He is a dashing American whose modus operandi in executing his complicated but clever plan for stealing a super-protected super-diamond includes posing as an eighty-five-year-old diamond cutter from Antwerp. Of course there's a cop involved, who is really behind the whole thing, outfoxing everyone as the story climaxes, only to outfox himself at the very end. In the meantime the woman is smitten by both the handsome young thief and the flirtatiously cherubic old man—who are, in fact, the same person. He, of course, in love with her, is in a dilemma of conscience.

Kate Nelligan played the woman and Brian Dennehy the cop, while the young thief was played by British actor Ben Cross. This time I had no trouble as director in meeting the challenge of the lead character's accents (Belgian and American) because it had to do with the truth of character and locale. Other experience was brought to bear here was well, as some of the financial backing dropped out in the week prior to shooting and the only way we could proceed was to tighten the shooting schedule, eliminate contingencies and overtime, and reduce some salaries. Fortunately, the logistics were controllable and I was well prepared. The result was a feature-length film made in seventeen days. It turned out well, and if circumstances had been less constrained it might have turned out even better. Nevertheless, I still felt quite good about it, and it resulted in other work coming my way a little farther down the road.

In the letter I had written to the prime minister turning down the diplomatic posting, I stressed my belief in service to one's country and suggested that, while I might one day welcome such an appointment, there were in the meantime other ways in which to serve. I claimed (accurately, I think) that I was doing just that right here at home by my involvement in charity and community work, including the acting seminars I was giving at York University, and above all by my role as chair of the Academy of Canadian Cinema and Television. Through my work in this position I felt I was not only doing the job I was expected to do for the Academy but was ultimately serving the country as well, through the efforts the Academy was making to popularize the Canadian entertainment industries.

I was by this time well into my second term as chairperson of the ACCT, a job I took very much to heart, from 1989 through 1992. The Academy was and I hope still is one of the (all-too-few) national entities within which east and west, French and English, can be reconciled to one purpose, in this case the celebration and promotion of film and TV production throughout the country, leading to a self-sustaining film and television industry from coast to coast, or as I used to say in many of my speeches, "d'un océan à l'autre."

My approach was, with the Academy, to help raise the profile of Canadian programming, performers and personalities through the philosophy of oneness of family. This isn't unrealistic, because artists love each other when they create together. I've worked all day long with Quebeckers who are separatists, and at the end of the day, in spite of our respective political views, we still hugged each other and wanted to hold on to what we have in common—our work, our art. Even in a sixty-second spot I acted in once for the legendary director Claude Jutra, because we both cared so much about achieving excellence together, the day ended with a commercial we were both proud of, and we punctuated our achievement with a triumphant embrace. I had seen this often in actors who have the courage of artists, that is, respect for the universality of art, both in themselves and in others, so there is a common bond uniting disparate practitioners of the art. I've seen this when I worked with American actors in Los Angeles or New York, British actors in London, Czech actors in Prague or Israeli actors in Elat; with South African actors, black and white, in Pretoria; and certainly east and west, French and English, here in Canada.

When I was much younger in this industry I used to envy French Canadian filmmakers their raison d'être, their apparent courage. It seemed they had something to say, particularly about themselves. As I got more experienced and worked in many places around the world and across Canada I began to see that a lot of the people in the entertainment industry in Quebec took a stand for separation, not because of the courage of artists, but more from a fear of losing the status quo, their local popularity with a supportive audience. By closing off this miniature Utopia from the outside influence of universality, by protecting their autonomy, what results is not the fresh air of internationalism or ideas that transcend borders, but suffocating parochialism.

We in Canada ought to understand each other better. Canada vis-à-vis the rest of the continent is not unlike Quebec vis-à-vis the rest of Canada. Despite our differences, we are so alike. We have in common our pursuit of self-realization in the face of the overwhelming influence of our neighbours. To reach this goal we need some protectionism, but that opens up the very real possibility of total protectionism, thereby being destroyed not by our neighbours but by our own parochialism.

Sometimes I wonder what the point is in repeatedly asking someone to dance with you if they just don't want to dance. Then I say to myself, hey, we came to this party together, we're going to leave together. Let's face it, like it or not we are each other's dance partner, so why not find the right music to satisfy each other's dance steps? That may be difficult to do, but in the end worth the effort because the likelihood is that neither of us can do a successful solo. Floating on its own in a sea of English, without constitutional protection for its culture and character, Quebec would become like Louisiana, sooner rather than later. As well, the other regions of Canada, if any kind of separation were to occur, would also flounder.

I don't know why we can't convey to Quebeckers Canada's belief and pride in the Quebec identity, in the specificity of who Quebeckers are, for their sake and for Canada's. For too long this message was not felt, let alone conveyed.

Similarly with our western contingent. For too long, during the formative years of the industry when most of the work was in Toronto, it seemed that there was no communication with our western colleagues; it was as though the actors in British Columbia were distant cousins. That was wrong. Geographic distance should not have prevented our sensing the immediacy of family. So when film and TV activity burgeoned in British Columbia in the last decade or so, the BC members of the Canadian acting community said: "What's this 'we' business? You never made us feel that we were part of the 'we,' so now we're branching off and forming our own thing." That temporary rupture in ACTRA in the early nineties (still not completely healed) was very distressing to me. Here was a situation where language was not the problem; rather, the will to communicate, which is more fundamental than the language of communication, was absent when it was needed.

I travelled the country often on private business, like film or TV jobs in Winnipeg or Vancouver, or family functions in Calgary or festivals across the country, so the Academy wasn't stuck with travel and accommodation bills—only entertainment expenses, because wherever I went I would invite the entire local membership out for breakfast or lunch on behalf of the Academy. Gab sessions and get-togethers. We would discuss what was going on in the industry in all parts of the country, so that no matter where a member of the industry was, he or she could feel a part of the whole. Whatever visits I had with any chapter resulted in communiqués being sent immediately to all the other chapters across the country. Similarly, correspondence was shared as much as possible, and input was welcomed from any and all. I felt that this inclusiveness was another way, along with nationally televised celebrations, to promote the oneness of the Canadian industry to the Academy members and to our Canadian marketplace. I know that many of the western members appreciated my efforts; they told me that during my term they felt like they were part of what was going on. I also know that when I was cautioned against saying "un océan à l'autre" in a speech to the Québécois membership, I said it anyway and they applauded.

I understand and share the love of home, as well as the assertion of self. I believe that both are part of the foundation on which art is built, and that inherent within the commitment to Canada are the best safeguards for this foundation, whether the art comes from the Maritimes, Quebec, Ontario, the Prairies or British Columbia. Our commitment to this nation allows for and encourages self-identity in any part of the country, while welcoming work from other parts of the country and from abroad. Art, no matter where it comes from, if it is to inspire, must not be parochial or designed solely for local consumption; rather, it should be based on the particularism of roots, roots that aspire to grow and branch out, transcending borders and reaching shared heights.

In addition to traversing the country I had the good fortune to travel abroad on behalf of the Academy. On the occasion of the tenth anniversary of the Canadian Academy, the British Academy of Film and Television Arts (BAFTA) wanted to honour us. We were invited by them to London and then to Paris for the French version of the Oscars, called the Césars.

In London, I did many interviews on TV, in the press and on radio, in my capacity as chair of the Academy. We, that is the Academy, benefitted PR-wise from the fact that *Cagney and Lacey* was still a hit show over there. As a matter of fact, outside my hotel one day I was arrested by two female bobbies, one blonde and one brunette, who were both real cops but also the co-presidents of the British *C & L* fan club. Joke or not, a picture of me handcuffed showed up in some of the daily tabloids. They took me to Scotland Yard, where I was welcomed and given gifts and tours—altogether a joy! One of the interviews I did on BBC radio was with Denys

Arcand, a Quebec filmmaker in whom all of Canada takes pride. His film *Jesus of Montreal* was shown at BAFTA's theatre, to an audience that praised it highly, as part of the celebration and as a tribute to Canadian filmmaking. Afterwards there was a dinner given for us in the elegant dining room of the Piccadilly Meridien hotel, where we were staying.

The host, technically, of BAFTA's dinner for us was my British counterpart, Sir Richard Attenborough. I didn't know that I was going to be asked to speak; as a matter of fact, I had been assured that I wasn't going to be asked. This was reminiscent of the time Sara and I, in our first house in Rosedale, gave a polling party for Donald Macdonald, the Liberal candidate in our riding. I only agreed on the condition that I wouldn't be asked to speak. Of course, when the party was in progress and it came time for Donald to speak, I was expected to say a few words of introduction. This was in the early seventies, a couple of years before *King of Kensington*, and I had no experience with public speaking. I had nothing prepared and I was frightened. I got up and merely said, "Ladies and gentleman, Mr. Donald Macdonald." Well, over the years, I had acquired a lot of experience in public speaking, even extemporaneous public speaking, and I had become, I think, good at it, and actually enjoyed it. Nevertheless, I was not expecting to speak on the night of the BAFTA dinner.

Suddenly, after Sir Richard's warm and welcoming wit, someone stood up who looked like he stepped off the label of a bottle of Beefeater gin; either he was from Malabar costume house or his day job was guarding the Tower of London. Besides his colourful costume he had what looked to me like a spear or sceptre, some ceremonial rod that was royally ornate. He began pounding it on the floor and then, like a town crier, announced after a "Hear ye, hear ye" that the chairman of the Academy of Canadian Cinema, Mr. Al Waxman, was now going to speak. Holy shit! As I walked up to the microphone I had no idea what I was going to say, but the applause indicated an expectation of some words of wit. First off I thanked BAFTA for this honour and their hospitality, and Sir Richard for his kind words. After I said, "Sir Richard," I repeated it with a question mark: "Sir Richard?" Then I looked squarely at him and said, "Can I call you Dickie?"

He said, "Only if you call me Dickie Darling."

I said, "Hey, I'm Canadian. We only go so far—it'll just have to be Dickie!"

Canada's High Commissioner to London was invited to the dinner as well, and what a wonderful coincidence—our High Commissioner at the time was Donald Macdonald. This was fortunate for me because, after I spoke some words about our Academy and our industry, I then had, because of Donald's presence, something else to talk about. Improving upon the brevity of that earlier introduction, I invited Donald to speak and used the phrase "tall talent" for the second time in my life. The first time was figuratively about Sammy Davis; the second time was that night, and it was both a figurative and a factual description of the six-foot five-inch Donald Macdonald.

The next day it was off to Paris, where I felt their television celebration of film excellence was nowhere near the level of professionalism regularly achieved by the Oscars or even our own much lower budgeted Genies and Geminis. Indeed, I thought they could take a lesson from us. The truth is that awards shows are always going to have, regardless of the popularity of the performers and personalities, parts that are entertaining and parts that are not so entertaining, no matter where or how glamorously they are produced. I remember sitting at the Emmys one year when the show felt like it was never going to end, and the look on everyone's face indicated that they felt the same way. Boring! I noticed a Canadian journalist sitting nearby and sent him a note that probably gave him his only laugh of the night. It said, "See? You don't have to be Canadian to be boring!" These shows are difficult but necessary, and they are effective as instruments of PR not only for performers and productions but also for cultural and national identity. And we do ours quite well.

Sara and I were invited about a year later to a luncheon during a week-long presentation of British films in Washington, DC. The luncheon at the Library of Congress, hosted by BAFTA, was in honour of British film and under the patronage of Queen Elizabeth and Prince Philip, both of whom were present. Prior to the luncheon the royal couple were guided by Sir Richard Attenborough through the human corridor of guests and they stopped here and there for introductions. When they reached us, Sir Richard, or Dickie, stopped and introduced the chairperson of the Canadian Academy, Mr. Al Waxman, and his wife, Sara, to Her Majesty and His Royal Highness.

It was only fitting that I should finally be introduced to the Queen and Prince Philip, because I missed just such an opportunity during the *King of Kensington* days when we were invited by Prime Minister Trudeau to a concert given in their honour at the National Gallery in Ottawa. After the concert we were informed that at any moment the Queen and Prince Philip would come through the hall we were in, for a walkabout. I didn't know that Her Majesty is as much a stickler for time as I am, and I figured, this is going to take a lot longer than a few minutes. There was a bar about twenty or thirty feet away from us, giving out free drinks. "Sara," I said, "while we're waiting I'll get you a drink."

She said, "I don't want one."

I thought she wasn't aware of the facts, so I said, "Honey, it's for free, I'll get you one."

She said, "No thanks, I really don't want one."

So I said, "It's OK, you stay here, I'll be right back with drinks." I thought I would be right back because there was hardly anyone standing between us and the bar. After the bartender gave me my two drinks I turned around, one in each hand, to return to Sara, but my path was suddenly blocked by a swarm of posh people. The guests were packed in like sardines in evening gowns and tuxedos. I held the drinks high so they wouldn't be jostled and spilled, but I couldn't move an inch forward. Over the shoulders and through all the heads in front of me I saw Sara where I had left her. I held up the drinks and shouted, "Honey, I've got the drinks." She didn't hear me, though; she was talking to the Queen.

I stood there with the drinks, unable for a few minutes to get to her. When I finally did, I asked forlornly, "Did she ask about me?"

"No," Sara said, enjoying her answer. "Her Majesty said there were a lot of people here tonight; did I know how many? I said yes, 2,800. And she said, you're so exact, how do you know? And I told her I read it in the *Globe and Mail*."

"Oh," I said. "Well, do you want a drink?"

"No. I told you. No thanks."

The last trip I took on behalf of the Academy, before my term as chairperson was up in 1992, was as part of a team of members of the Canadian television and film industry to a China–Canada conference on TV and film in Beijing. When co-production treaties are in the back of people's minds, particularly in China, you have to think in terms of building blocks, layer upon layer, over time. After all, it's been said in China that it's still too early to determine the impact of the French Revolution on Chinese history. In the meantime, awareness raising goes on and perhaps liaisons happen. I did a lot of listening, and when I did speak it was about the organization I was representing and its function in the Canadian film industry. When I got back to Canada I reported comprehensively to members of the Academy.

In terms of personal enrichment it was very satisfying and educational, like all travel. The Great Hall of the People, the Forbidden City and the Great Wall of China. The images of young heroes who fought for democracy and freedom in Tiananmen Square were still fresh in our minds, but we were asked not to talk about this. The subject did, however, sneak into our conversations because our interpreters were generally young and receptive; however, we were careful, because we didn't want to get them into trouble. As well, we visited their movie and TV studios, theatre and Chinese opera. All this was squeezed in between meetings on top of meetings and speech after speech; after all, we were there for a conference. A TV news crew covered some of the events that we participated in, and the item was seen on that night's news—by 600 or 700 million people!

I did bring back one unpleasant memory. At one of the luncheons early in the trip, as soon as we sat down, about four delegates from the contingent of Chinese hosts came to our table, each smoking a cigarette (they all seem to chain-smoke) and each with a shot glass of rice wine in his hand. One of them made a speech. It was translated into English. Then I responded in English. It was translated into Chinese. Then we all said something that sounded like "Gambei!" (Chinese for "cheers") and promptly knocked back our wine. No sooner did I sit down than another group of chain-smoking Chinese bureaucrats came to the table and started the same procedure of Chinese speech and English translation, English response and Chinese translation, "Gambei!" and knock 'em back. This happened at least two more times, without any opportunity to start eating lunch.

Our ambassador came over to me and commended me for the way I was handling these little, but apparently important, formalities. He said something like, "Good. They like you."

I said, "They're not going to like me for much more of this. I've already had at least four shots of that rice wine without any food in my stomach yet, so I don't think it would be wise to try to get them to like me any more!"

The food looked fantastic—sumptuous, colourful, wonderfully aromatic. There was an interesting sculptured stone hotpot, the contents of which were appetizing-looking chunks of meat on bone, sort of like spareribs. I'm a sucker for spareribs. I asked, "What's that?" I was assured that I would like it and was encouraged to try it. "You like," I was told, "you like." But what is it? All they would say was, "You like." So I, with skilful use of my chopsticks, lifted a piece to my mouth, and as I began to crunch I was told by one of my Canadian colleagues, a filmmaker from Vancouver who had earlier in his life been a zoologist, that what I was eating was dog! "Not just dog," he said, "but puppy!"

"Don't they know we don't eat dog? Weren't they informed?" I asked the attaché from our embassy. "Why are we so concerned about whether they like us or not? Isn't it a two-way street? Shouldn't the reverse also be considered? Shouldn't they be a little bit concerned about whether I like them? If I invite you to dinner, I'll find out first what you like and what you don't like, what you're allergic to. If you don't eat fish, I won't cook fish!"

"But," I was anxiously told in an attempt to appease me, "They are trying to impress you, to please you. This is the specialty of the house!"

Interesting diplomatic dilemma. I wonder what kind of diplomat I would have been. From that point on I requested and got the accompaniment of my interpreter, who was with me for all the meetings and also sat by me at all the luncheons and dinners thereafter.

When I got back to Toronto, I picked up our beautiful little poodle, who was, no matter how clichéd it sounds, like one of the family. I hugged him and said, "Puff, I didn't know, I'm so sorry, I had no idea. But that one time was the last. It never happened again!"

Puff was a bilingual French poodle; he understood Yiddish. As a matter of fact Puff and I understood each other a lot. For example, when I picked up his leash to take him for a walk, he'd hop about four steps up the staircase so I wouldn't have to bend down over my big stomach to fumble my fingers around his neck; I just reached through the banisters and snapped the leash onto his collar.

He was a miniature poodle, a little dog in a very big house. We needed either a bigger dog or a smaller house. I wonder if Puff felt the way I was starting to feel about the house. I never saw more than a third of it. Maybe I needed something smaller; I certainly didn't want myself to be any bigger. Smaller would also be wiser for the sake of my physical and financial health. But the direction I took, of course, was to seek more work. There I would find solution and solace. Work, I thought, was the only answer—but it never just fell into my lap.

I called a friend of mine who was the co-executive producer of a series being made in Toronto about teenagers and asked if I could direct an episode. He was receptive and encouraging, but when he called me back after checking with the other executive producer, the real decision maker on things creative, he was no longer enthusiastic. Almost apologetically he explained that because it was a story about young people they wanted a young director. My mouth dropped—and out came something about my having directed an award-winning show about a teenage girl, *Maggie's Secret*, which was highly acclaimed, well reviewed and full of teenagers.

"Oh, we know you're talented, Al," he reassured me, "but it's about young people." He sounded uncomfortable. "We've got a young cast and a young crew. We want a young director."

"What do I have to do? Rip my jeans at the knees and let my hair grow into a ponytail?" (which happened to be a distinctive feature of his otherwise bald appearance).

"Sorry, Al."

I asked rhetorically, "Isn't the work itself the ultimate reference?"

It seemed not.

So here I am in my mid-fifties, apparently on the wrong side of middle age, and add to that the wrong side of passion—that is, the kind of heat I thought was integral to what I was, part of my talent. Suddenly, it appeared, that heat had become part of Waxman's problem. I was almost committed to directing a sensitive story about a woman; most of the decision makers approved, but one heard that I had a temper—and so, because of the one veto, they all passed. I suggested that they look at *Diamond Fleece*, in which the woman, who is quite delicate, like an open wound, is, according to reviewers, directed very sensitively. Makes no difference: they heard from a reliable source that I had a temper. Not a lot of John Hirsches out there any more.

Again, when I was considered to direct a film involving children, they heard that my language could be rough sometimes. Well, that made me laugh. I wasn't going to deny that that had happened on occasion, but I am also a thinking individual; why not give me credit for being considerate? Do I have the intelligence, the sensitivity and the talent for the job? That's the question they should pay heed to, I suggested, not hand-me-down gossip. Look at my award-winning episode of *Cagney and Lacey*, which involved children afflicted with AIDS in a public school. No way. They heard I had a temper and that my language could be salty. What a nervous business!

So after four or five years post *C & L* of constant activity—sometimes achievement, sometimes just scrambling for it, sometimes rewarding, sometimes not, lifestyle always up, income not necessarily so—suddenly I noticed that my weight was as high as it had ever been (it was as though I was too busy to see what was right there), my health at the brink of danger again, my debt load dramatic. What a double burden to be carrying. And just as suddenly it seemed my phone calls were, uncharacteristically, not always being returned. Requests I made for work were being turned down more than accepted. I had trouble believing this. And now throw into this malicious mix, my age becoming a problem, and memories that can't be lived down, memories of temper and colourful (or off-colour) language. Others, it seemed, had begun to doubt my ability or reliability, and worst of all there were the beginnings of self-doubt for the first time in years.

Talent, at least in me, is a fragile phenomenon. Was I any good? And what was I good at? Acting? Directing? Writing and producing? I was still always consulting and doctoring on film scripts in development. Would I ever actually develop my own film project? And what about politics and diplomacy? And teaching? Community work and leadership in philanthropic and professional associations? And what about my responsibilities to my family? As father? As husband? Was I apportioning my time well? Were my priorities in order? Did my wife think so? Did my kids think so? What did my colleagues think? What did I think? What? Talk about the crowd inside. What was I? Was I a jack of all trades and a master of none?

CHAPTER 32

Bottom of the Barrel

My best thinking happened while I was working—no matter what I was working on, no matter what I was thinking about. So some of the difficult questions plaguing me were becoming harder to deal with as requests for my acting and directing services in television and films became less frequent.

Why was this happening? Overexposure? I had always believed that popularity was worth the risk, but maybe I had crossed the line into overexposure. This, plus an influx of new talent, particularly in directing. Whatever the reason, I had less of the two satisfactions that I always sought in work: the intrinsic joy of the work itself and the financial reward. More and more, the work that I was getting less and less of offered only limited financial reward and even less intrinsic joy: a lose-lose situation. I often felt that the work I was doing was *drek*, inane filler, an intrusion on my life. It tried my patience. With each job I would be confronted by my own conscience and would ask myself whether I was a hypocrite or a hooker. The simple answer was that I had to make a living, and each job lasted only a few days.

No matter what the job was, I always tried to encourage myself in the doing of it with the approach I had learned and practised over the years. I would ask myself: what am I doing, why am I doing it now, and how will I achieve it? Two other key questions follow: where is the love, where is the humour? (The philosophy behind these two questions had guided me for years; now, as I was teaching and consulting the writings of other teachers, I found these principles well articulated in Michael Shurtleff's book, *Audition*.)

Next I would ask: what lesson can I learn today, what new insight can I benefit from? Or, also worthwhile, will I find something already learned expressed in a new or different way today? The whole point of this exercise is to avoid becoming a hack. It got harder to do, but as long as I reminded myself of these questions there was the chance of some sanity, some satisfaction.

It seemed that there was more of this in teaching. This activity was not only fulfilling for me because of the opportunity to give back, not only cause for optimism at a time when I seemed close to becoming jaded, but also refreshing because, in the process of illuminating for young, searching minds (and their unadulterated ambitions and appetites), I found that purity and genuineness were there for me too. Sharing ideas, energies, knowledge and experience was a two-way street. If I gave the students belief in themselves and in this process, then I received something in return: renewed belief.

At York University for a period of ten years from the mid-1980s to the mid-90s, I was an adjunct professor, lecturing and teaching scene and character analysis. This happened only a half dozen times a year, on an ad hoc basis—whenever they called, if I was available, I would go up. At the same time I was asked by a group of professionals to lead a workshop, in a rented space downtown, on a weekly basis. This has evolved over the years, with people leaving and later coming back, and new people joining and then moving on to be replaced by others. It's held on Monday nights, the traditionally "dark" night of the off-Broadway or alternative theatre. Conceptually, I always treated it as a workout. I'm happy to say that even at this writing, Al's Gym, as it came to be called, continues to meet whenever I can schedule it.

It's a sanctuary, my acting class. It's private and personal, just like the rehearsal process for a play or film—it's an actor preparing his or her instrument for the rigours of real life, learning to take the ideals from the academic atmosphere out into the practicality of professionalism. We start off with exercises, limbering up, mainly vocalizing. Then we have what I call networking: we inform one another about what we know that's going on in the workplace, and we discuss our professional endeavours of the past week and the week coming up with a view to analyzing and assessing the way things were or might be done. Then we probe and explore scene and character, through improvisation, various acting exercises and scene presentation. Sometimes actors do scenes they never get a chance to do in the professional world, or scenes they've done but want to do better. In either case the object of the work is to expand and enrich the acting instrument. It is my hope to help them become more self-reliant and resourceful actors. To that end I bring all of the experience, training, studying and reading I have done into the workshop. Nevertheless, I still approach it as a fellow student—perhaps with thirty or forty years more to share but still, happily, one of them. I would never abandon my own need for mentoring even when I am mentoring others.

I am delighted to say that, over the years, many actors, writers and directors who have been part of my class have gone on to work professionally in the theatre and in film or TV, some quite successfully. I'm sure they would have done so no matter whom they had studied with, but as I was at least one of their teachers it gives me some pride and satisfaction to have been a light along their way.

In 1992 an idea for a new project was brought to me. Unlike some of the episodic television I had been doing, this was intriguing and refreshing. Developed by Gary Blye, a solid production manager and line producer, it was a reality-based series to be called *Missing Treasures*, about the search for missing children. The children might have been kidnapped by a family member (as 85 percent of them were) or by strangers, or they might have disappeared for other reasons, like kids who run away and end up living on the streets. The show, with me hosting, included dramatic re-enactments, resulting from thorough research, of how the young person, to the best of our knowledge, "went missing" (a peculiar phrase, but it is what's used). There were interviews with witnesses, family members and police, as well as community care workers from children's aid organizations and places like hospices and hostels; computer-enhanced photos to show how the child would look today if the kidnapping had happened years earlier; dialogue with international sources such as foreign police and Interpol; and finally, regular updates. I narrated throughout. The show, according to police records, helped to locate children and reunite them with their families in three cases, and in all episodes we succeeded in raising awareness and in educating kids in particular.

It was comparable to a few very popular reality-based shows coming out of the States at that time (1992–1994), but we were careful not to indulge in sensationalism or exploitation. Indeed, because some of the cases ended tragically, it was important for us to be scrupulously careful in our wording and our purpose. The show wasn't designed just to entertain or get good ratings. *Missing Treasures* was a style of TV I had never been involved with before. I had done comedy and drama, half-hours, hours and long form, film and tape, live and pre-recorded, but I had never done reality-based TV. Also, I had been on every network except Global (apart from telethons and interviews) and this was to be on Global. Most exciting for me, this series used the medium to reach the audience in a way that no other medium or genre could. You could engage viewers, connect with them, incorporate them into the process and into the case, so that they felt as though they were sleuthing and contributing to the puzzling out of a problem. This was so good for me, at a time when I felt TV was becoming like muzak, insulating and numbing rather than connecting. The only danger was the temptation to cross the line from responsible reporting, storytelling and re-enactment into exploitation; but I had a good governor in my head, which saved us from doing that. And the others on the creative team were with me in my concern and efforts to stay on the right side of that line.

We were greatly aided by the Metropolitan Toronto Police Department. I think they would have helped us regardless, but when they saw our pilot they were enthusiastic. Moreover, we ultimately met the chief's request regarding my wardrobe. For the pilot I wore grey flannels and a blue blazer (always my favourite outfit). Over the breast pocket of this particular blazer there happened to be a distinctive silver and gold threaded Scotland Yard crest; the crest was a memento of my visit to their headquarters with the two London cops who were the co-presidents of the British *Cagney and Lacey* fan club. When Chief David Boothby saw the pilot, he said, "I'll give you all kinds of co-operation from our files and help you access the OPP, RCMP, FBI and whomever you want to reach, providing Waxman wears the Metro Toronto Police Force crest on his jacket instead of Scotland Yard's." Resourceful producer that Gary Blye is, a new blazer was purchased for me with the Metro Toronto Police crest sewn onto its breast pocket, and *Missing Treasures* turned out to be another successful TV series—my fifth. It reunited me with *King of Kensington* executive producer Perry Rosemond, who directed many of the early episodes of *Missing Treasures*. I did some directing myself, as well as assisting in the story editing and co-executive producing. It lasted about two and a half years of weekly half-hour shows, and won the Worldfest Houston Gold Award for public affairs programs in both 1992 and the year after. As in the case of *Cagney and Lacey*, if I had gone one more year I might have overcome the obstacle of mounting debt. Tantalizingly close, and then out of reach.

At the time it was apparent that there were only two ways to get past the financial problems I faced: make more money or sell the house. The latter made some sense because Sara's father, who needed professional care, was now living in a nursing home and Tobaron and Adam were either away at school or moving out on their own. I was beginning to feel as though I'd actually become the image I'd had of myself years earlier, a tiny person running around in a house full of empty rooms. Well, the rooms weren't empty, but I felt empty and tiny. Still, selling the house somehow signified defeat for me. My house symbolized a permanence in the land I loved, an accomplishment, a fortress shielding my vulnerability from the world's penetrating eyes.

I preferred to make more money, an approach contrary to what I started out to do in this career, certainly an approach contrary to the first premises which acting classes were ideally always reminding me of. I crossed a line—a line I had drawn defining purpose and integrity. I don't know when I crossed that line, because it was as though I didn't know I had. But I did know that making money was becoming increasingly difficult; doors seemed to be shut everywhere I turned.

Around this time I was offered a play to direct by producer Janese Kane, a friend of many years earlier who always loved the theatre but left it to become successful in business and was now working her way back into theatre. The fee for this directing assignment would be minor, but worse than that, I couldn't get past the title of the play: *A Shayna Maidel*. It sounded like a Catskill Mountain comedy. But Janese very patiently said, "You read it when you find the time, and then we'll talk about it."

So what was I doing instead? Some acting in and directorial consulting on martial arts films, which were slapped together on tiny budgets. I didn't know what I was doing, but I needed the money and I needed the work. Certainly the people I was working with knew what they were doing in this particular genre. When the writer, who was glad to have me doing his material, saw me struggling with it—resisting going over the top yet knowing what I was doing wasn't enough—he came up to me and whispered in my ear, "Mr. Waxman, in a martial arts film, less is not more, more is more." Like I said, there's something to be learned on a set every day.

Continued effort to get work. Against Catherine McCartney's advice, I decided to go directly to the heads of companies, many of whom I had grown up with in this business. Indeed, some of us had helped the business itself to grow up. I decided to ask for work. Catherine felt I would be lowering myself, losing face and in the long run hurting myself, because my image was one of strength and confidence, and this would, she felt, make me appear weak. Catherine would have preferred that I bite the bullet and sell the house, not beg! I didn't see it as begging. As I've always believed, if work is dignity, then any effort made to get work is by definition dignified. So I made the effort. Catherine may have been right, however, because all I got was patronizing reassurance from one producer, sympathetic incredulity from another, barely hidden glee from yet another. But there was an enthusiastic welcome from one, which unfortunately soon changed to exasperated impatience as I persisted in phoning to build on his enthusiasm—embarrassing, but I couldn't help myself. I guess I panicked.

For the first time in years I was desperate. I encountered studied indifference from someone whom I'd helped at the beginning of his career; I naively thought we were like family, I guess. (This served me well as an emotional recall a few years later when, as Willy Loman in *Death of a Salesman*, I'm fired by a young man whom I deluded myself into thinking was like family.) I resembled a kid who forgets to hold his guard up in a contact sport and never ceases to be hurt and amazed when he inevitably gets injured. Like the hockey goalie I once was, I kept insisting that I can take a hit, that I've got shoulders big enough to bear the load. But it hurt all the same.

The end result of these efforts was only one offer, from a producer who was a little more receptive than the others, to do some second-unit directing on a series. I had directed some episodes of this series quite successfully a couple of years earlier, but this is all he had to offer me now—and this offer was available only because another director turned it down. I needed the money, so I took the assignment and was glad to. Once they had me, I noticed I was being given more of the first-unit shooting, although I was being paid and credited only for the second-unit shooting. I decided against a credit. The important thing was to be directing again, exercising muscles that needed to be exercised.

Another series offered me two gigs after I hounded them—one, acting, and the other, directing. I was happy about that, because in addition to the work and the money, the location was fantastic—Elat, at the bottom tip of Israel.

I had been to most parts of Israel but never to Elat. This was going to be exciting, plus there would be visits with family who could come down to Elat to see me, and before I returned I would visit with friends at the Shaare Zedek Hospital in Jerusalem.

Somewhat unexpectedly, the work turned out to be fun. The Israeli crew was surprisingly good. Some of them had worked with Norman Jewison when he made *Jesus Christ Superstar* in Israel. They were not only expert but had a sense of humour too as they went about their work. The director of photography, for example, was also doing his own camera operating, and when he lined up the first shot he didn't give me a word cue, like "camera set" or "camera ready," which I had grown to expect after so many years of directing in the US and Canada. This was not the procedure in Israel. So he waited while I waited. Everyone waited. Finally, still bent over the camera, he took his eye off the eyepiece and turned his head towards me and said, "Noo?" which is Yiddish for "Well?" I then shouted "Action!"

Later that night we were about to do explosion scenes right beside the Jordanian border, near where David Lean had shot his famous approach to Aqaba in *Lawrence of Arabia*. I was concerned about the closeness of the Jordanians to the huge special effects we were about to set off and asked the producers, "Have the neighbours been told that we're lighting firecrackers tonight? Tell them they're invited to the party if they'd like, because we're not making any big statement here, just a little picture."

This show's regular stars were consistently skilful and stylish, but with each succeeding change in producership, the show was becoming something less than it had been before. Still, when the son of the previous producer offered me a couple of episodes to direct in its third year, I was glad to accept—I needed the work, and again, the location, South Africa, was a big lure.

Sara would accompany me. We would spend at least two weeks there, including a safari, before I started work, at which time Sara would return to Toronto. We had earlier met the South African High Commissioner to Canada in Ottawa and were now good friends. He offered to help arrange a marvellous itinerary for us, starting from the bottom, Cape Town, then over to Paarl, the wine country, and back to Cape Town to take the Blue Train (South Africa's version of the Orient Express) overnight to Johannesburg. Then we'd have a couple of days in Sun City in Bophuthatswana. All together, it promised to be an awesome experience that would, if I kept things in perspective, make the gig worth it.

On the way to South Africa, Sara and I took a recess from the long flight, stopping in London to see Sharon Gless performing in the West End. Barney was there too. Sharon was wonderful in the difficult two-handed play (only two actors) *Misery*, and the four of us had a splendid visit together before Sara and I continued on to Cape Town.

Before committing to the trip I had spoken with Barbara McDougall, our minister of external affairs, and asked her about Canadian policy towards South Africa and whether I'd be breaking any rules. On the contrary, she told me; although from government to government there were still official sanctions, they encouraged travel and the exchange of social, cultural and business activities amongst individuals. She said that if I spoke to their actors' union and answered questions on how we in Canada do things, I would be contributing something worthwhile. The South African High Commissioner happily complied when I asked that members of the black theatre community be included at some small dinner parties that were being given for Sara and me in Cape Town and Johannesburg.

Amongst the guests at one of the parties was a man named Mbongeni Ngema, one of the stars of the South African film *Sarafina!* He was accompanied by some of the members of his acting company. I was then invited by him to attend rehearsals of a new play he was producing and directing in Johannesburg and to participate in discussions with the company.

At one of the dinners in a sprawling modern house whose dining room was open to the sky, the huge square dining table had on it a centrepiece (itself the size of a normal dining table) of colourful South African plants, fruits and vegetables. Sara was sitting beside an elderly white gentleman who looked on in disbelief at the sight of blacks at the same table. Assuming she would be sympathetic to his incredulity, he quietly said to Sara that he never expected to see this in his lifetime. Sara, without disrespect (because of his age) chided him, remarking that times were changing and that he must try and keep up with the times. He didn't disagree but remained in a state of bewilderment.

Our fantastic journey culminated in a safari at Sabi Sabi in Kruger National Park, where we came face to face with skyscraper-high giraffes (I had no idea how tall they are), spectacular birds—so beautiful—and hippos, who are so ugly, no matter how much they clean themselves in the rivers. There were lions that sort of lazed about until they smelled the food they were hungry for, lumbering elephants making thundering sounds, and rhinos crashing through the woods as they tried to avoid our Land Rover. They could just as easily have charged at us as away from us, and more than once I fearfully wondered why they didn't. We were flirting with danger, but within the protection of an armed guide and a ranger who was riding shotgun. Even the comical-looking baboons that loped by were not to be befriended, we were cautioned, because of teeth that made them as dangerous as any animal we encountered. A gorgeous group of impalas swept elegantly by us. Our ranger asked me if I thought the impalas were beautiful. I said yes.

"How many do you think there are out there?"

"I don't know, how many?"

He said, "About thirty. Tomorrow there will be twenty-nine."

"Why?" I asked.

"Because tonight the lions have to eat."

That gave me pause.

Later that evening we saw a pride of lions, all females, form a kind of vanguard. They had an unspoken instant communication with each other, radar-like. The leader knew who she was, and the others fell into formation behind her, all poised for action. With singular speed and accuracy, they crossed a meadow and disappeared into the woods. We then heard an animal screaming in terror, followed by bones crunching. There was one less impala that night.

Back at base camp, when we were served a big barbecue buffet, the first item on the rustic but inviting table was sausage—impala sausage. Coincidence, but it made me think. Are we all part of the jungle? Where do I fit into the chain?

The next day, our Land Rover halted suddenly on the dirt road and we were told to sit absolutely still, not get out of the vehicle for a better view or stand up for an improved camera angle, as we were confronting, from a distance of just twenty to thirty feet, two lions lying in a thicket. According to the two experts guiding us, these lions were about to mate. The one that looked like the MGM logo made a sudden move. (By the way, I found out why he is called the King of the Jungle—he gets laid about thirty times each weekend, then rests the remainder of the week as female lions find his food and feed him.) I liked to think of the male lion as Louis B. Mayer. Louis B. lifted his powerful paw and placed it playfully (foreplay, I think) on the back of his missus. She let out a growl as if to say that *she* should be on the MGM logo, and he, very unkinglike, withdrew his paw in quick retreat. I said to Sara, "I think she's got a headache." Whatever the reason, it was apparent he was not going to get any satisfaction now. I began to hope that he wasn't partial to kosher meat. Happily, the ranger stealthily backed our Rover out and took off.

This whole trip was a thrilling experience, which I guess made up for the quality of work I was about to do on the two shows I was contracted to direct in Pretoria. Not only were they poorly scripted and in terms of supporting players inadequately cast (in an assembly-line process, the director doesn't do the casting), but these hour-long shows, which would normally, in other production centres, be done in seven days or so, were being shot in four days for the first unit and the same four days for the second unit. (I suppose the producer could argue that this made it an eight-day shoot.) The second unit comprised two minimal crews, one doing bigger stunts with planes and copters and cars and motorbikes, while the other did stunts like fights, all coincident with me and my reduced crew shooting the cast in first-unit storytelling sequences. My work played second fiddle to the young producer's preoccupation with the more fun stuff—stunts and fights and planes buzzing and bikes and cars crashing. Storytelling was apparently not what it was about. But no matter how spectacular the stunts, they don't have the same significance without storytelling and character development giving them a reason for being. You have to care for someone or nothing is at stake, regardless of how dangerous the stunts.

Oftentimes when I was about to shoot, my actors weren't available because they were off on the second unit. Normally, I enjoy the challenge of puzzling out the logistics of such a shoot, but the story, whatever it was, was being sacrificed to effects and schedule. The stupidity of the situation was becoming as oppressive as the heat: December and January, over 40° at the height of the South African summer, plus the hot lights on the set. Fighting lack of time, lack of air, lack of story, lack of consistent cast and, worst of all, my own lack of interest, I suddenly lost my will to continue and totally blanked. The young producer, like the lion leading the vanguard, took control as I stood by, watching numbly. I remember noticing, out of the corner of my eye, the star's look of surprise at my inaction. I would normally have had too much power and pride to allow this to happen, but I simply didn't care any more.

Later that night I realized that this experience was telling me something important, if I'd only listen. I mean, I was the guy who always cared so much, as though it were the most important thing in the world—even about continuity in a commercial for sausages! If you didn't care, you weren't any good. But this stuff wasn't worth caring about. No, maybe it was my work that wasn't worth caring about, the work I was doing. Still, I chose to do it and should not have thought of it as "bottom of the barrel"—this was unfair and counterproductive. I realize now that I was really being judgmental about myself, perhaps it was just me who was at the bottom of the barrel. I should have remembered to ask myself "Where is the humour?" It's all about taking the work seriously, not taking yourself seriously. But when you hit the low that I hit at that time, you lose all perspective, and the only thing you take seriously is the self-questioning: "Am I any good?"

CHAPTER 33

A New Perspective

I wasn't inclined to, but because my plate was empty and I had time on my hands I finally read Barbara Lebow's *A Shayna Maidel*. How fortunate for me that Janese Kane was patient and had the courage of her convictions. She had been cautioned to get another director, but she trusted her instincts. I was very taken with the script. In fact, I loved it—a very moving story, with well-delineated characters in a beautifully structured piece. The story is rooted in the involuntary separation of siblings during the Depression of the 1930s. One sister remained in Poland with her mother while the other went to America with her father. They intended, as many immigrants did, to reunite as soon as funds were sufficient, but their separation was prolonged by the Depression and made all the more tragic by World War II. Finally, as adults, the sisters, now virtually strangers, meet in New York.

I could personally relate to this story. I had to become that involved in a story to breathe life into it, my life. As I said in the director's notes provided in each program:

> During the first few years after World War II, when I was in my early teens, my family responded to the need for accommodation to be provided for what were then called Displaced Persons. We

had room in our house, and so at any given time there would be at least one and sometimes as many as four young men who had survived the concentration camps staying with us. We became as close as family.

As I got to know each of them, their fears, their nightmares, their hopes, I couldn't help but think, "What would I have done over there? How would I have managed? How would I have survived, and how would I deal with the struggles, realities and dreams they were now facing, thrust into new, foreign and strange circumstances?"

Apparently, these same questions struck Barbara Lebow at approximately the same time I was thinking them. Years later, she explored and probed these thoughts until they became insights in her keen mind, resulting in the creation of this excellent play.

The characterizations and relationships Barbara Lebow arrived at carried her and her Holocaust-related themes into the timeless and timely, indeed classic, dramatic structure of the family coping with so-called, in contemporary terms, dysfunctionalism. In spite of the weighty backdrop of the Holocaust, the Depression before it, and the threat of assimilation after it, the foreground story of *A Shayna Maidel* is really about a father and his two daughters confronting and perhaps overcoming obstacles in the path of becoming a functional family... certainly an issue of the '90s and again one I can personally relate to.

Despite my earlier preconceptions, I now wanted very much to do *A Shayna Maidel*. Here was a chunk of life worth biting into.

The play was to be produced and presented for a one-month run at the Studio Theatre of the Ford Centre for the Performing Arts. This is a wonderfully intimate space, which was perfectly suited for our production. Unfortunately, a two-hundred-seat house could only pay a small amount of money, and I intended to put a lot of time into it, with about two months of study and pre-rehearsal preparation and casting, followed by another month of rehearsal, plus sticking with the company after the play opened as a sort of morale-sustaining companion if needed. That would be at least three or four months of work, so Janese's generously high salary for a production of this size became in fact the lowest salary I'd received in decades. However, the richness of the material and the high purpose of the production, together with the loving and dedicated actors who would be giving life to the characters, promised and indeed proved this to be the most artistically rewarding experience I had had in years.

What a remarkable change from the cardboard cut-out characters, artificially structured stories and assembly-line TV episodes that I had been directing over the past few years. I had been looking in the wrong place for the answer to the question, "Am I any good?" and I knew I would not go back there again. Where I was working now was where art could be achieved, where answers could be found. This is what it had been all about for me, and would again be. The work itself—heaven is in the work itself. I was back in the theatre for the first time in over twenty-five years, but not to the exclusion of film and television if the right work came along.

I still wanted to direct film and I wanted to find the same answers in film that I knew I could find in the theatre. Regardless of the medium, the answers are to be found in the material, the purpose of the project, the people involved in it—in the work itself. Happily, the same opportunity came in film just before *A Shayna Maidel*, in the form of a minute, a glorious minute. This was not a commercial but a minute filled with potential for integrity, again because of the subject matter—and the hoped-for marriage between subject matter and filmmaker. It was one of the very classy series of Heritage Minutes, most of them produced and written by Patrick Watson. I think as a result of his visiting Kate Nelligan on the set of *Diamond Fleece* (probably to discuss her Heritage Minute performance as Emily Murphy, Canada's first woman judge) and having therefore had the opportunity to watch me work as a director (he already knew my work as an actor through my *Titans* episode as Louis B. Mayer), he offered me one of the Minutes to direct. The subject was to be Marshall McLuhan. Some of the Heritage Minutes were superb pieces of film work, with fantastic photography. More important than that, they achieved, not only with look and feel but especially with content, the purpose for which they were made: to illuminate a piece of Canadian history and/or a Canadian historical personality.

Again, the salary, when you consider two days of filming, was substantial, but spread out over a month of prep and a couple of weeks of post-production it was not what I had been used to getting when I was directing or acting in film. But so what? I didn't care about that when I could care about the material like I hadn't in a long time.

As I had met Marshall McLuhan only once, I needed to do a lot of research. I put as much study into these sixty seconds as is normally put into a ninety-minute feature film, with a view to achieving as much in the minute as can be achieved in the longer form. It took me a month to read a substantial part of his writings and much that was written about him; to visit and study the space in his house in Toronto's Wychwood Park and his offices at the University of Toronto, where he conducted his famous seminars; to interview regulars who had attended those weekly sessions, as well as former students of his English classes, his colleagues and members of his family. During this process, among the many people I met through print and face to face was Bob Logan, one of Marshall's last partners in his work at U of T, who was most helpful to me. He and I have since become friends. (Bob, by the way—talk about a McLuhan turn of phrase—teaches a course called The Poetry of Physics at U of T.)

It was a fascinating challenge to understand and communicate the life work of a person in any amount of time, let alone a minute. As I said subsequent to making that minute, in an article co-written with Logan for *McLuhan Studies*, a journal published by Eric McLuhan (Marshall's son):

One minute is not enough to tell anyone's life story, let alone someone like Marshall McLuhan. But the essence of a person can be captured through a keen glimpse into his character. And, in the making of this Heritage Minute, an interesting parallel of juxtapositions within the subject's life and my life became evident to me.

It is quintessentially McLuhanesque to compress two extremes, as Marshall does with his concept of the "Global Village"... And it is just as essentially cinematic to compress a lifetime into a few shots... I had to compress McLuhan's life work into a minute; and it required a life's work in filmmaking to express the minute. So, two lifetimes, the subject's and the filmmaker's, compress into one moment.

What I learned from his students and colleagues is that Marshall, with his use of dramatic one-liners, shock, paradox and humour expressed from his deep roots in the oral tradition of repartee, was an intellectual turn-on. I too was turned on, particularly by his aphorisms, which led me to understand and recognize some fundamental truths: image-breaking phrases such as "print changed the shape of the world"; phrases that I had lived, like "cash is the poor man's credit card" and "you don't read newspapers, you get into them, like a warm bath"; and thought-provoking phrases, especially for someone making his living in TV, like "the content is the audience" and "TV sucks the brain right out of the skull." And of course the mind-bending concept, the one remembered perhaps even more than Global Village: "The medium is the message."

The key, the "keen glimpse into character," was discovered as a result of research. I could thereby make the moment, which had no physical action in it but just intellectual content and dialogue, hum with energy and swiftness—through showing the philosopher, the poet, the teacher actively projecting his mind, whether he was pacing or stretched out on his couch; showing his passion for ideas and the reactions they stirred and stimulated; and showing all this suffused with his mischievous sense of humour. Normally you would need a couple of hours to tell the story of such a scholar, but it became not only an exacting but also a fitting challenge to dramatize the discovery of the concept that "the medium is the message." Logan called the result an "electronic monument." For both the subject and the filmmaker it was a monumental moment.

Like the Heritage Minute, the production *of A Shayna Maidel* rejuvenated me, restored the purpose in me for which it all began, my raison d'être. The theatre at the Ford Centre is apparently an out-of-the-way place for some to get to; nevertheless, as a result of the critical response and word of mouth, each of the performances was well attended, sometimes even sold out. The reviews in all the papers and other media, such as radio, were satisfying to the soul. The acting and the production as well as the play were praised. It was a personal triumph for Harvey Atkin (a *Cagney and Lacey* colleague), a known, experienced and skilled voice-over and TV actor, in his first stage appearance. Similarly successful was the incandescent and Dora Award–nominated performance of Shannon Lawson, an actor of Irish and French Canadian descent who found within herself the inspiration to become a believable Polish-Jewish heroine. The entire cast, I'm proud to say, became their roles. There was an honesty on stage that invited the audience to become a part of the artistic truth of the evening.

I will always remember this show fondly. Certainly, I'm reminded of it every day when I look at my watch. It was a gift from the producer, Janese Kane, with an inscription to express her appreciation of what was for her too an important artistic achievement. This was the first time I owned and wore a watch since being separated from the watch left me by my father almost fifty years earlier. I had been given another one when I was fourteen years old, about five years after my father's death, by my mother and stepfather when they returned from their honeymoon trip to Europe. It was an expensive Swiss watch and a generous gesture on their part, but I wasn't ready to accept something that would have relegated my father's watch, existent or non-existent, to the past. I asked Jack to hold on to it for me till the hockey season was over, for fear, I said, of losing it in the locker room—and I never asked for it back. Now, forty-nine years later, this new watch represented not a timepiece (I still ask other people for the time) so much as a reminder of *A Shayna Maidel* and, because of my willingness to wear it, a turning point in my life. One could say, "Hey, come on, it's just a watch," but that's not what I am.

In the meantime we had finally sold our house and bought a new one. As my career bottomed out prior to the Heritage Minute and *A Shayna Maidel*, the value of my house was bottoming out too; it finally sold for half of what it was valued at before the recession of the early 1990s. That was reality. However, the price of a new house was less too. Still, it hurt, just like when the career was at a low. But reality, if addressed realistically, can result in maturity, and that's finally what happened as we put into perspective the value of money and the value of life, and removed the albatross that the house had become. We were able to look at it and say that, over the thirteen years we lived there, we had experienced great joy in our lives in such a lovely home. I remember some prospective purchasers who toured the house commenting on what a "loving" house it was—but now it was time to move on.

When Sara and I became the only inhabitants of the big house in Forest Hill, I used to complain that I saw only a third of it. Although we did not specifically look for fractions, the new house, in Rosedale, is literally one-third the size of the Forest Hill house. Again thanks to Sara's exquisite taste and resourcefulness, the new house is like a jewel box, a music box. As soon as you enter the house the feeling is one of elegance and music. And love would be felt here too. I'm lucky to live here. It's small, compared to what we had before, but big enough to house both the kids if they visit at the same time. And of course Sara and I each have our offices in the house, so we have a completeness in our home and are still rooted in a piece of land in the city and country we love.

This little house, not unlike the little theatrical production in the little theatre, was to be the start of something big in our lives. I could feel the upswing. I was working in films as an actor and doing a kind of work that was new to me—voice acting, that is, voice-overs for TV and radio commercials as well as animated films, and narration. Sara's career was in full bloom too. She was writing for two major newspapers and two major magazines, and other prestigious writing assignments came up regularly, giving her a life with at least ten deadlines a month. Between the two of us we were earning substantially more than the magic number.

There was always a resourcefulness and strength in Sara, as she stood by me. Although she once joked that I didn't have any sides, all curves, she was and is forever by my side. She's always had courage and talent. When she graduated from high school it was at a time when girls were supposed to be secretaries or grade-school teachers until they got married. She had the brains and the determination to go on and do whatever she wanted. She wasn't daunted by the unknown. I've always said I wish she'd become a movie producer; I'd never be out of work. When she did decide to go back to work after tending to the kids (her choice) for their first few years, it was in journalism, a field in which she had no formal training but an active appetite for reading books, newspapers and magazines. She just had a feeling for it, and now she's often a guest lecturer at schools of journalism. This ability to take on the unknown while standing by her partner in life was learned from her parents, who were now gone.

Sara's father died in 1994. Her mother had died in 1988. Annie Shapiro's death was expected, as her health had been diminishing for some time due to Alzheimer's disease. She was a dear and pretty lady, who in spite of her diminutive size was strong of spirit and mind.

When she was younger she must have been strong of body too. She gave birth to Lorne, their only son, when she was forty-six. To look after a family and farm with the kind of facilities they had, or didn't have, in rural Manitoba circa 1939 must have been tough. (I always remember Tyne Daly's reaction to Annie Shapiro. Tyne said, when she met her at the Shaare Zedek dinner for Sara and me, that she felt riveted by the strength that emanated from Sara's mother.) As well as being poor they faced harsh weather conditions and anti-Semitic neighbours, and there were just the three of them (until Lorne came along)—a tiny mother with her two tiny little girls, all as delicate as doilies but strong too. Perhaps they were made strong by the circumstances they faced while waiting and preparing for the return of the only male (at that time) in the family, as he travelled about dealing in grain and cattle. Sadly, in her later years that vitality deteriorated as Alzheimer's increasingly took over.

In the case of Sara's father, even when he was in his eighties there was always something strong and alert about him. He had a charming sense of humour and was physically lively, so I got to know him a lot better than I did Sara's mother, and so did the kids. One is inspired by those who come before us, who paved the way and showed us the "how" of things—and in the case of Mendel Shapiro, *how* his physical strength was matched by a gentle love for his three children and his extended family; and *how* he had a concern for them all until the end. He was an example for his whole family, an example for me, as were his eighty-five years of courage to always move on, to keep going.

Once ensconced in our new house I considered another project brought to me by Janese Kane. We decided on a play called *Sight Unseen* by Donald Margulies. I liked the play a lot because it was again something to which I could personally relate. The protagonist, coincidentally named Waxman, is an artist in search of what it was that motivated him to achieve the success he enjoys, as he is now commissioned to do paintings "sight unseen." The predicament he is

A New Perspective

in, and the process he needs to pursue, were familiar aspects of my life too, as I wrote in the director's program notes:

> Jonathan Waxman and I have more in common than our last name—that is merely coincidence. Or maybe serendipity. More substantive identification is in our Jewishness, our heritage, our ambition and our passion for our respective artistic endeavours.
>
> We meet Jonathan at a time and place most of us can identify with or at least understand. I certainly can relate to it. It is just after his father died and not long before he himself is about to become a father to a son. He feels abandoned by, yet loyal to, his past and unsure of his future. Although he is thought of as a visionary, his talent and integrity are undergoing uncomfortably close and challenging scrutiny. He needs to rediscover first purposes and to re-examine the direction of his life's journey.
>
> In his search he comes in contact with the other three characters of this play, all of whom are catalyzed by him as all four characters are caught in the crucible of their mutual interaction.
>
> In the beginning it is impossible for any of us to see what's ahead, yet our vision is so clear. Years later, after we have seen so much, our vision is perhaps not so clear. I believe each of us, regardless of age, ethnic, cultural or religious origins, no matter what our profession or occupation, arrives at a juncture when and where we need to go back and see again that which we never saw before.

It was a play that, while engaging, was perhaps too cerebral and convoluted to grab the audience in the way *A Shayna Maidel* had. That production viscerally touched the audience and held it in suspense, with the story unfolding in a more straight-ahead fashion—something the audiences attracted to this theatre needed. However, *Sight Unseen* was a successful production too, receiving respectable reviews. For me personally, because of the content and the commitment I made, it was an artistic achievement.

Before starting rehearsals I was offered an episode of a TV series to direct. This series was a cut above the episodic TV I had been directing. It was *Lonesome Dove*, a show from Calgary. The offer and the fact it came from out west were both important to me, as a director and as a Canadian. As I said earlier, I had been vocal about the psychological and political distance filmmakers from east and west were putting between themselves. A kind of parochialism. I didn't think it was beneficial for any region of the country not to think of itself and all regions as part of one whole entity. And, of course, the money offered for a much shorter schedule was about five times what I was to be paid for directing *Sight Unseen*. Although these predicaments are often understood and contracts forgiven by sympathetic theatrical producers, I had already made a commitment, and it was not only a contractual one but a moral one as well, to a specific producer with whom I had become very good friends. Even more fundamental was the commitment I had made to myself, a commitment to artistic endeavour and to truth. The truth was that the work was more important than the money, and as for the offer to direct filmed TV, something I still wanted to do, it was good just to be asked because this reaffirmed my reputation as a director. My priorities and goals were again in the right order. The work and the quality of work came first, and a living would be made as a result. I threw myself into the protagonist's search for meaning in *Sight Unseen*, which coincided with my own search. It was a worthwhile effort.

While I was directing *Sight Unseen*, I was offered a job, hosting a series. I had hosted before; as a matter of fact this would be my fourth series as host (after *Circus International* for CBC, *Moments in Time* for PBS and *Missing Treasures* for Global). The subject was new to me, however: wine and cheese. The show, my sixth TV series, was to be called *Simply Wine and Cheese*, hosted by Al Waxman, the English version of a Quebec series, *Vin et Fromage*. An advantageous thing for me was that the series of thirty-five episodes would be done in a few weekends over the four seasons, totalling less than a month's work, for which I would get paid exactly my magic number, quite apart from everything else I would do over the year. And the people involved were interesting and well informed, not only on the subject of wine, which I wasn't, or the subject of cheese, which I wasn't—although I like them both—but also about politics, Canadian and Québécois (most of them were separatists). We argued all day long, but drank the props all day long too. Wine transcends borders. By the end of the day we had not come any closer politically, but physically we would be hugging each other. I used to infuriate the producer by telling him he was the most Canadian person I knew. Indeed, we travelled Canada together. We filmed in Quebec's Eastern Townships, had press parties and wine and cheese tastings in Ottawa and Toronto, conducted interviews in Niagara-on-the-Lake with wine producers there and went to Banff Springs to meet wine producers who came to the annual food and wine festivals held there.

Wine is as old as history and as welcome as the future, but what interested me most was meeting and researching the wine producers. They were, as a rule, Renaissance men, powered by passion—passion for all that they did, like skiing down dangerous slopes, flying planes, driving fast cars. They were intellectually curious and active. Some wrote books as well as managed huge businesses; all lived international lives, and all had love in their lives, love of their land, love for the arts and joie de vivre. And oh, by the way, they produced wine. The wine producers were more intriguing to me than their wine, except when the wine itself was an expression of the winemaker.

Well, I never skiied down dangerous slopes—the only inclines in my life were the psychological hills I was trying to climb. And when I flew in a plane, I was just a passenger. But there was love, appetite, curiosity and risk in my life too. As for a Renaissance man, I don't know. But I was always engaged in a number of different and wide-ranging pursuits. I could relate to the passionate and principled dedication of these winemakers in both their professional and personal lives. I had the taste again for all that I was doing and could do. I had pride again, as the passion that was rekindled by the Heritage Minute and the theatrical productions I had directed set in motion a sense of renewed purpose in my life, a new perspective.

Chapter 34

The Playwright in the Sky

In 1995, I was sent a script from the CBC for my consideration. It was called *Net Worth*. This wasn't an offer, merely an expression of interest on their part, with a view to finding out my availability. After *Frankie Walls* and the final episodes of *King of Kensington*, both in 1980, I had acted only twice for the CBC—in the late '80s in *Street Legal* and in the early '90s in *Scales of Justice*. It was time. More importantly, this was from Bernie Zuckerman, a producer with an impressive list of credits and a man of taste, integrity and solid commitment to serious and indigenous subjects. He made TV drama something to again be proud of, and he chose his projects and his people well. I wanted to be one of those people.

His director was to be Jerry Ciccoritti. The word "hip" has of course become clichéd, but the one time I believe it's clear of cliché is when it's used to describe Jerry —a bright and "cool" filmmaker. He was hot and deservedly so, and I wanted to work with him.

Net Worth was a strong script about the first attempt, back in the 1950s, by the National Hockey League players to form a union. The effort was spearheaded by Ted Lindsay, captain of the Detroit Red Wings, and foiled by, among others, Jack Adams, the general manager of the Red Wings. I was being considered for the part of Jack Adams in this story of an important chapter in Canadian-American relations, in Canadian sport and culture and in the Canadian labour movement. I wanted this part, in this story.

Their interest in me was weakened to some extent by the fear that when I came on the screen the Canadian TV audience would say, "Oh, there's Al Waxman," rather than believe that I was Jack Adams. It looked like I was going to have to be my own iconoclast. I don't remember auditioning, but in effect perhaps I did. The first meeting I had with Bernie and Jerry went well, but then I didn't hear anything. So I studied the material, working specifically on one scene, with a view to plumbing the depths of the character. I urged Catherine McCartney to get me a second meeting, which she succeeded in doing, this time with Jerry alone. The two of us really got into the script, and then the meeting expanded to include the rest of the producing and casting team. I felt the role was of paramount importance for me to do, for their sakes as well as mine. When I left the meeting I had a gut feeling we had all succeeded, but of course I wouldn't know till I got the phone call. Soon after, while I was accompanying Sara at a food and wine festival in Monterey, California, Catherine called our hotel and asked for Jack Adams.

When I returned home I virtually moved into the Hockey Hall of Fame in downtown Toronto for a few weeks of intensive research. To become Jack Adams, I needed to absorb the psychology of this childless but devoted Catholic husband who considered the team his family; I had to understand the emotionalism of obsessive dedication and feel the physical feistiness of a fighter.

When I lived in Forest Hill, I was a neighbour of Red Kelly, the great defenceman on that Detroit team. Red said to me that he didn't remember the story as Ted Lindsay, his former teammate and our technical adviser, did, but he said, as did Ted, that I "sure nailed Jack Adams!" That was high praise for me, as I apparently succeeded—according to those who remembered the man and those who reviewed the show—in creating the character of Jack Adams for *Net Worth*.

Soon after *Net Worth*, I got another opportunity to do interesting research into a real-life character. I was cast in the HBO film *Gotti*. HBO was still headed by Robert Cooper, which may have helped, but I think it was my performance as Jack Adams that got this role for me. I was to play Bruce Cutler, the New York lawyer who successfully defended John Gotti three times, earning Gotti (played by Armand Assante) the nickname "The Teflon Don"; none of the charges stuck. Whereas in the case of Adams, who was deceased, I was restricted to studying film of him and reading everything written on him, as I had done years before with Louis B. Mayer, in this instance there was an interesting difference. Cutler was alive, and I could therefore interview him personally as well as study film and read material on him. I sought to achieve the interesting contradiction of a man who swaggers with the solid strength of a winning wrestler, particularly in court, yet is at the same time in awe of Gotti, whose self-confidence Cutler admitted overwhelmed him.

Apparently my characterization of Cutler was good enough for me to suddenly gain entry into a celebrated restaurant called Rao's in East Harlem (owned by one of the New York cast members). Normally, you have to book months ahead. Cutler and many people who know him frequent this fascinating place, of which it is said that if you're lucky enough to get a table, you can be sitting beside a governor or a godfather. More than one person approached me at Rao's to congratulate me on my performance. The film was very successful for all involved, and now I can get a good table at Rao's.

Net Worth had aired to high praise not only from TV critics on the entertainment pages but from columnists on the sports pages, political pages and front pages of the newspapers, as well as from TV and radio commentators. It looked as though I and others on the show would be strong contenders for Gemini awards, a pleasant and gratifying feeling, and one that would happen, I'm thankful to say, a number of times over the next couple of years. But why now? Why not earlier, or why ever at all? Inexplicable. Or maybe not. Maybe the playwright in the sky does, after all, know the story he's writing and the one he's got me acting in. Maybe what seems happenstance, structureless, falls into a design and even a plan and a purpose. Maybe he knows when it works and when it's right, and maybe he even considers if and when it deserves to be recognized.

One day in August 1996, I got a phone call followed by correspondence informing me of an award of a different type that I was to receive. This was nothing to do with acting per se, although mention of my acting career would be included. I was to be named to the Order of Ontario. The ceremony was a splendid affair marked by prestigious protocol yet individual attention, as much a party as a procession. Pride and jubilation. A proclamation was read as each inductee was named—a unique combination, in each case, of the public and personal side of the recipient. Mine started with the words, "Few Ontarians have achieved such a high level of international acclaim and remained as deeply committed to their home community and fellow citizens," and finished by referring to me, on behalf of "Ontarians and all Canadians," as "one of our national treasures."

Speaking of matters national and provincial, public and personal, I had by this time, although still active in the Academy of Canadian Cinema and Television as immediate past chair, accepted invitations onto other cultural and community boards, such as the board of the Stratford Festival. I cautioned them that I was not an arm-twister of a fundraiser, and was reassured that that was not the reason they invited me onto the board. They wanted the PR possibilities I might create, and they wanted someone on the board from the field of arts and entertainment as a kind of sounding board for Richard Monette, the company's artistic director.

The conversations with Richard over the period that I was on the board (1993–1995) gravitated, more by chance than by design, to the possibility of my directing at Stratford. Certain plays were discussed, and when *Death of a Salesman* was mentioned I said, "No, that one I would rather act in." Richard agreed, and the summer of 1996 was our goal. However, schedules and casting, the mixing and matching of actors over a number of productions in a repertory company, present a difficult logistical challenge and caused the plan to be delayed to the summer of 1997. This was okay with me, because I wanted the extra time to lose weight and get into shape, so that I could physically carry the workload and the emotional strain of playing Willy Loman for three hours each night. It's funny, but the continuing threat of serious health problems from excess weight was not as convincing a motivation for me as the immediate promise of creating artistic life. *Death of a Salesman* turned out to be the most effective incentive I've ever had for losing and keeping off a substantial amount of weight.

In the meantime I was suddenly getting interesting offers for both acting and directing. The acting included a number of films. Among them was a small role in a film called *Bogus*, directed by Norman Jewison, which for me was memorable because, although I had only two scenes, one with Whoopi Goldberg and the other with Gérard Depardieu, it was an opportunity to work with Norman, a man I've long held in high regard and am very fond of; his commitment to the art of film, to culture and to Canada is worthy of emulation. Another small part, this time in a movie called *Critical Care*, was memorable for me because of the people involved in the project, notably Sidney Lumet, a pillar of cinematic and theatrical talent. It was worth it just to witness his skill and energy. What I remember most about this septuagenarian was his unbelievable speed—always wearing tennis shoes.

Then came a TV movie, *The Rescuers*, with a director whose work and writing I admired, Peter Bogdanovich. Peter has, in my eyes, a special status as a filmmaker. He combines the historian's love and knowledge of the art and craft of filmmaking, particularly through his respect for and relationship with many of the great filmmakers, with the natural result of all his study, the student's sincere search for his own expression. He is a student in the best sense of the word, like I hope I am; that is, even though he's arrived as a professional and practised filmmaker, he remains committed to the never-ending process of learning.

The Rescuers is a sensitive film about Christians who helped Jews during the Holocaust. It starred Elizabeth Perkins, and I had a substantial supporting role as an erudite Jewish doctor. It was produced for Barbra Streisand's company by Jeff Freilich. Jeff is a producer whom it was a joy to work with. It was well reviewed for all of us, and resulted in my doing in the next couple of years terrific roles in two more films with Peter and Jeff.

During this same period I was offered a play to direct. I'm sure this was because of *A Shayna Maidel* and *Sight Unseen*. The offer came from Daniel Kerzner, a bright young producer, to direct Neil Simon's *Lost in Yonkers*, a play about family dynamics both funny and poignant—this writer's trademark. It would be produced at a theatre just as much out of the way as the Ford Centre but in a different direction: the Atlantis Theatre at Ontario Place. I don't want to say that this is Neil Simon's best play because a couple of years down the road I would be in preparation for the lead role in another of Mr. Simon's plays, *Proposals* (also about family). In 1996, however, *Proposals* hadn't yet received, to my knowledge, its first production; I hadn't even heard of it. So perhaps I can say that at that time, *Lost in Yonkers* was considered Simon's best play, and I was going to throw myself into it as deeply as a "best play" deserves.

While acting in movies and prepping to direct *Lost in Yonkers*, one day towards the end of November 1996 there was a courier knocking at our front door. He presented me with a confidential letter, from the governor general's office in Ottawa. It was from the secretary to the governor general, informing me that I was to be appointed a Member of the Order of Canada, and they in turn would "appreciate being informed as soon as possible whether you are willing to accept this honour." Willing? Are you kidding?! This was the pinnacle for me, the Oscar, the highest I could have hoped for. What a surprise! What great elation for me, for Sara, for Tobaron and Adam, for all of us. Although they limit the number of guests you can take, I wanted those closest to me to be part of the event. The rest of my family would be there in my heart. I thought of my mother, of my father and of my brother, and I cried to myself. There was a rush of pride up my whole body, a rush of warmth as I felt the presence of those departed loved ones. I thought of where we had come from and what was left of us, and I was determined to bring my family of four. That was all I had; there were no more Waxmans in Canada in my immediate family. The governor general's office kindly agreed.

An evening again of pomp and splendour, of personal satisfaction and public pride. Because it came so soon after the Order of Ontario (which I will always cherish), the ceremony was perhaps not as singular as it might otherwise have been. Nevertheless, this was the Order of Canada, and it was enormously special to dine in and tour historic Rideau Hall, and to share the glow of the event with no less than Frank Shuster, the three members of the band Rush, and people who may have had less public profile but were nevertheless at the top of their respective fields, endeavours and accomplishments. That is perhaps what was most awesome, to be included in the company of high achievers, to be recognized and honoured with, among others, a paleontologist from Alberta, a scientist from BC who commutes from his university teaching post to NASA headquarters, and a lovely lady who dedicated herself to creating, without financial assistance, a library for indigent kids who might otherwise be illiterate. Yes, I thought as we departed Ottawa the next day, most memorable for me would always be the august company I was in, and my family past and present were with me in that moment—and that moment will be with me forever.

Back to planning the production of *Lost in Yonkers*. I had to make it reach out beyond the venue it was in, which was inaccessible not only in terms of city geography but even from the parking lot, with steep stairs on either side of a long bridge. Also, the theatre itself had a peculiar structure, with a wedge-like protrusion thrusting from the back of the orchestra towards the stage, almost splitting the audience into two halves. On top of all this, the stage was wide and shallow. I welcomed the challenge. First I shared memories with the set designer, of railroad flats, long and narrow, that I'd lived in in New York, which would be appropriate for the financial status of the family in the play. Then I got the sound designer to put together a track of World War II pop music and had it playing for an hour prior to curtain from the box office, across the bridge and up the stairs to the theatre, to put the audience "In the Mood" (Glenn Miller was of course included). Lastly and most importantly, the excellent cast was staged, despite the challenging design of the theatre, so that all the audience could see everything and everyone as the characters developed fully and honestly, and the story unfolded with a truth the audience could feel a part of.

Lost in Yonkers opened to rave reviews, even from the critic most theatre people feared and dreaded. I won't quote the reviews, but I will again quote from the director's program notes, where I articulate the thought fundamental to making it all happen: "For me, whether acting or directing, I have to find something in the work, or find some way in which to make the work, personal." And I did. Family, functional or dysfunctional (two buzzwords that cancel each other out in any family as far as I'm concerned), is something that I, and I think all of us, can relate to.

It was a good feeling on opening night, watching *Lost in Yonkers*—good because of the excellent acting I was watching, good because I had lost enough weight to wear a navy blue suit that was twenty years old (it was made for me to wear in a General Motors commercial that aired only once, during the 1977 Super Bowl) and good because I had pinned onto the lapel of that suit my Order of Canada.

I also wore that Order of Canada pin in the lapel of my tuxedo when I went up, two years after *Net Worth* originally aired to collect a 1997 Gemini award for my performance as Jack Adams. That was on March 2, my birthday. What a gift! Sometimes the playwright in the sky is so kind and has such fun with us!

CHAPTER 35

Conversation with My Dad

I first studied *Death of a Salesman* at the University of Western Ontario in 1956, when the nearby Stratford Festival was still in a tent. I was a fan of Stratford as early as that, and I was smitten by *Death of a Salesman* from that time. The strongest image of the play in my memory was Willy Loman with his arms around his sons, more like a buddy or a big brother than a dad, praising them as his two Adonises. Those words may not be exact, but the image is, and particularly my memory of Willy's preoccupation with teaching his handsome sons the relative importance of personality over schooling, his emphasis on misplaced values, on the surface over the substantive. I was struck by these alternatives and identified with being caught between them. I knew the path I should follow and always tried to pursue it; still, sometimes I felt drawn, with wishful thinking, towards the power of personality.

At approximately the same time as I was studying Miller, I had other lasting encounters with literature. As I have mentioned in this book, one of my guiding principles came from Robert Browning's "Andrea del Sarto," encapsulated in the lines, "Ah, but a man's reach should exceed his grasp, / Or what's a heaven for?" Heaven for me was on the substantive side, in the work itself. Still, I felt that Miller struck a chord in me and in anyone who was ever drawn towards the dream of success and the material trappings that accompany it. As an actor I may have wanted to play Biff when I was younger, but I think I always knew that one day I would play Willy Loman.

I started studying the role and learning the lines months before going to Stratford. My head, as we say in the business, was into Willy Loman. Ironically, as soon as I arrived in Stratford I was offered a role in a major international film. The producer of it had approached me with a part during the *Cagney and Lacey* days, and I'd turned him down then. This time it was tempting, and so was the money. Furthermore, the director of *Salesman*, Diana LeBlanc (herself an actor and a very understanding friend), said that she would rearrange our rehearsal schedule to accommodate the few days the film would require. But despite the importance of the film and its producer, and the kindness of Diana LeBlanc, I said no. I passed on the movie because I didn't want to shift focus to accommodate another character; Willy was the one I intended to live with over the next eight months. Moreover, I was scared. I hadn't been on a theatrical stage since *Dodo Bird* in 1966, thirty-one years before; I had to zero in on the play I was about to do. Thirty-one years since the last time: thirty-one years of working with a microphone hanging over my head, or hidden by a prop on a desk, or wired into my jacket; thirty-one years of working in the intimacy of close-ups and two-shots. How could I keep that intimacy and yet project it to a theatre audience? And this was not a small theatre like the ones in which I had directed the three plays, where I emphasized to each of those casts that film truth could be maintained and still projected in those small houses. How could I project the truth as I saw it—naturalistic, film truth—unmiked, into a major-sized house? Yes, I was scared.

It was good that I was scared, because it helped me to have respect and discipline. I took advantage of all the training that Stratford had to offer, practising and honing and sharpening the instrument (me)—particularly in voice classes. Not a day went by during the weeks of rehearsal that my name wasn't on the bulletin board bearing the schedule of individual voice classes. I was working on the three things Stanislavsky said an actor needs most: voice, voice and voice. As I used to tell my students, the soundman on *Cagney and Lacey*, whom I seem to recall winning an Emmy almost every year for his efforts, often came to work wearing a T-shirt that read, "A good actor is a loud one!"

I threw myself into it, and it felt good; it was at once as invigorating as a complete physical workout, as intellectually stimulating as a McLuhan seminar, and as relaxing and comforting as a warm bath. I loved working and preparing and concentrating, leaving no room in my mind for fear. All my time and effort were targeted on the character and story I was engaged in.

This, I realize, had again become the most important thing for me: storytelling. That's what it was always about for me in the field of entertainment and show business, but at some point, early on, although engrossed in the same process and purpose, I became more focused on what was happening *now*; that's why TV and film became the media of storytelling that I preferred. They are the media of now, telling stories but with a subject and content of now, beating with a pulse of now. That's still a major attraction for me, but over the years a lot of TV, and certainly the TV jobs I was getting in the late 1980s and early '90s, had lost its impact, its importance and especially the vitality of now. It was becoming Muzak, product filler, not unlike the commercials it was a conveyance for; indeed, sometimes the commercials had more artistic merit and entertainment value. I came to realize that storytelling, if it couldn't always be found on TV, could still be found in theatre; that's what the theatre has always been about. Not that it isn't still offered on TV and in film. They are all—theatre, film, radio and television—interesting challenges and worthwhile venues for storytelling. No one of them is valued, as far as I'm concerned, over the others; what is valued is the story, regardless of the medium. The play is still the thing. That's what the three plays I had directed prior to coming to Stratford had reminded me of.

Now it was time for me to act on the stage again, and this was the place, because I've always believed I wouldn't be complete as a Canadian actor without playing Stratford. What a way and what a place for me to prove something to myself: one of the great parts, in one of the great plays, in one of the great theatres. That was daunting, but once I embarked I could only function as though undaunted. Like it or not, I would find out very soon if I measured up. Morale was high and the mood was conducive to good work, because the time, the timing, the place, the part, the character, my character, his age, my age—all a perfect coming together. As indeed was the whole cast, who were mostly seasoned and respected Stratford regulars. They were all supportive, particularly Martha Henry (who played Willy's wife, Linda); she is not only one of the most gifted and skilful actors I've ever worked with, she is also one of the most hospitable and sharing artists I have ever known. They were all there beside me—but they'd all been there before. There was no competition, only co-operation. But would I measure up? Some people in the press wondered that. So, yes, it was daunting, because although I would be finding out something essentially for myself, it would be in the most public way possible. As a Toronto critic said in the press, I was "coming back in a vehicle with a higher profile than the Pope Mobile." Certainly my commitment was sufficient, but if more belief in self was needed it came, as though *bashert*, in the form of this note from my son:

Dear Dad,
I don't know if you're nervous or not, but I want you to know how proud I am of you, and how much I admire how hard you've worked for this. I've never seen someone work so hard, for so long, under so much pressure, and pull it off so well—in work and in health—the way you have. You've got a lot of guts, and I can't tell you how impressed I am with you. You're the greatest man I've ever known, and I love you! Good luck tomorrow!
    Love, Adam

A missive intending love and support, but achieving, serendipitously, more, as I was radiant with the distinction between my relationship with Adam and Willy's with Biff. I was so moved. I was proud of my son. I held back my tears, but my inspiration soared.

In the process of studying Willy, I found a great deal of myself, because I was looking into myself for Willy. Of course there was some external research and investigation, such as what New York was like in those days, and Boston, what impact the Depression would have had on him, and World War II. The profession of travelling salesman was a thing of the past, so I couldn't go out and do what Willy did, the way I had worked in a factory for Frankie Walls, immersed myself in the Hockey Hall of Fame for Jack Adams, interviewed the real guy for Bruce Cutler, or gone out on the beat for Lt. Bert Samuels. Even in the case of Larry King, I was able to revisit Kensington Market, and hang out in variety and convenience stores. With Willy Loman there was mostly myself as the place from which to build a character. As it turned out, there was much in our respective backgrounds that made for mutual genesis.

There was sameness and similarity. I could believe that, for the sake of "building a character" (another Stanislavsky phrase, indeed the title of his second book). And this suited my approach to the character, which unlike my first impression of the play had more to do with the emotional and psychological aspects of his personal life than with the sociological characteristics of his professional life; more to do with his personal dream than with the American Dream. Willy's father abandoned him when he was three; my father died when I was nine. Willy had an older brother, who could have been a father figure for him but instead walked out on him; I too had an older brother, who might have been a father figure for me but wasn't. Both our brothers were named Ben. Willy felt cheated and deprived; although in my case no individual could be blamed, in a way I too felt cheated and deprived. So, in searching into my own life, finding similarity on the one hand and significant distinctions on the other, I discovered keys to understanding and building character.

Then came opening night. I was revved up; first sitting by myself, sinking into myself, then pacing slowly in the wings, ready to make my entrance, just as soon as the haunting theme music starts to signal my fatigued walk forward, my two valises weighing me down, but with the actor's energy in me ready to start the play. Eight o'clock, and instead of the theme music a phone call from front of house: "It will be a few minutes until the audience is in their seats." Pacing, concentrating on the images in my mind that trigger emotions and thoughts, concentrating on what happened to cause me to drive home. Why am I coming home? What am I going to do here? What do I want here? Linda? Near collisions on the road, and certainly collisions of thought in my mind. Why did I abort the trip? My mind wanders off the road and I almost kill a kid. Confusion. We're about to go, the audience is in their seats, but now they're standing as I hear, not the theme music, but "O Canada." Oh no, I had forgotten about that. Another minute of interruptus. In the meantime don't lose it, redouble concentration, relive my aching and tired back from sitting so many hours in that uncomfortable car. Now, finally, the flute plays; it seeps instantly into my soul, I am almost home, then my cue, and I, hunched over, struggling, a sample case in each hand, return … home.

The show that night was, in my opinion, not nearly as good as it would become, but still the opening night reviews were raves. In Toronto, where the three papers usually split or are unanimously negative, they were all positive. One of the papers even remarked on that. There were raves, for the most part, right across the country, as well as in the international press. I won't quote them except for one, the headline of the *Calgary Herald* review: "Waxman's Willy a splendid thing." Sara said, "Oh, now the whole world knows!"

It must have been good to get that critical response, but the production got so much better as the season progressed. I likened it to buying a new pair of gloves in December: they're good, they fit, they look good, they're the colour you want, but two months down the road they're really going to fit your hands so much better than on opening night! Although the reviews couldn't have been more positive, I almost wished, if only for academic curiosity, that the critics would come again. I certainly worked on the script every day as though each new performance was a new opening night. Each performance was another opportunity to feel not only the tactile connection between me and the other actors on stage, but also a palpable connection between me and the audience like you can't get in any other performance medium. Although not recorded for posterity on film, I personally will remember forever the artistic rush throughout my entire being during the three-hour experience, building to the climax of each performance in the catharsis of exhilaration spent—in what only Willy Loman thinks of as a triumphant finish to his life.

I was often asked if I was exhausted after the three hours of performance. My answer was always no. Because I was playing a man who was near death at the start of the show, I felt exhausted at the beginning, not the end. On the contrary, after that nightly standing ovation, I was energized.

As a result of my premise, my approach to the work, the work itself, I *was*, I believe, Willy Loman—with at least one significant difference. Although I loved Willy and would never judge him while playing him, he was, nevertheless, a loser, and I knew I was a winner.

During the run of the show I was often asked by the management to give a short talk to patrons, followed by a question and answer for about fifteen to thirty minutes. I was glad to do this, particularly when the group was made up of students. The questions generally had to do with interpretation, comparison to other plays, comparison of theatre to film or TV. These sessions were always delightful for me, sharing ideas with, communicating knowledge to and maybe even illuminating some things for those attending.

At one of these Q & A sessions, the revelation was for me. That day, after pointing out the similarities between the beginnings of Willy's life and mine, I explained that the thrust or action or intention (as we say in acting class) of both Willy and me, whether either of us was aware of it or not, was a search for authority or maturity (in a sense, the successful achievement of the American Dream would have been that), or the search for an adult figure in our lives, specifically our respective fathers. Following a lively discussion, there was applause and people were about to depart, when one of the students shot his hand up in the air for one last question. "Sure," I said. "Go ahead."

He asked me, "Are you still looking for your father?"

Wow... a thought from out of nowhere, like this kid was a messenger. This brought a smile to my face and then, after a second—I don't know where I was looking, probably at the student who asked the question—but I suddenly saw myself totally, completely, as though for a moment I was the only person there, and I felt very much at home with myself. I was about to respond when he asked more: "Do you still need to talk to him?" I answered, and it was the first time I ever thought these words: "No. I don't have to. I would like to, but I don't have to."

It was such a good, clear, wonderful feeling. Of course! That was my feeling: of course! As though my whole being was saying that to myself. Purity, as I telescoped my memory through all the years, and in an instant could see it all right back to the beginning. The snow that covered the ground in the cemetery on that morning years ago when I was a nine-year-old who wanted my father back, pure white; but it was the white of dense snow, like a cloud you couldn't see through. Now the ground was illuminated by sunlight, the light of knowledge processed through living experience, distilled deep enough in understanding that words are unnecessary, filtered into perception so that articulation of that knowledge is just the look on your face, because you can see. Now the ground was covered in sunlight and I could see the lay of the land, pure daylight, such clarity of vision that I could see openly all the way back to the beginning and right up through to today, and could look confidently into the future. And in the future I could see the oneness—not completeness, never that, because I'll always keep going. I could see continuation.

A year and a half after my run in *Death of a Salesman*, at the time of this writing, I was again presented with the Earle Grey Award by the Academy of Canadian Cinema and Television, this time for a body of work. The first line of my acceptance speech, if I can borrow from the future, is the last line of this book:

If you think it's been pretty good so far, wait till you see Act 2!

Index

Abie's Irish Rose (play), 14, 31
About Tomorrow (screenplay), 192, 207
Academy of Canadian Cinema and Television, 192, 366, 376–379, 380–381, 382–384, 418, 431
An Actor Prepares (book), 59, 88
acting
  approach to, 88–93, 100–103, 107–108, 109, 110, 135–136, 179, 185, 362–363.
  See also Method acting; movies, theatrical/TV (acts in); plays, stage (acts in); radio shows/dramas (acts in); TV commercials (acts/directs); TV pilots (acts in); TV series (acts in); TV shows/plays/specials (acts in)
Adams, Jack, 415–416
Alexander, Bruce, 33
Alexander, Lincoln, 357
Algonquin Park, 338–339
Alix, Steven, 301
Allan, George, 301
Allan, Ted, 123, 134, 136, 229, 230–231
Allen, Andrew, 60
Allen, Steve, 56, 136

Allen, Woody, 169
All in the Family (TV series), 257, 261, 275
All Quiet on the Western Front (movie), 146
Almond, Paul, 200
Al's Gym (Waxman-led acting class), 111, 390
American Film Theater, 236
American Women in Film, 314
Andrews, Larry, 26
Anspach, Susan, 105
Appleby, George, 203
Arcand, Denys, 379–380
Arowhon, Camp, 338
The Art of Dramatic Writing (book), 160
Ashley, Elizabeth, 88, 220–221
Ashley Famous Talent Agency, 178
Assante, Armand, 417
Astral Films, 299, 374
Atkin, Harvey, 292, 357, 407
Atlantic City (movie), 57, 297
Attenborough, Sir Richard, 380–381, 382
Avedon, Barbara, 306

Backroads and Country Cooking (book by Sara Waxman), 339
British Academy of Film and Television Arts (BAFTA), 379–380, 382

Barney Miller (TV series), 261
Barney's Beanery (restaurant), 176–177, 179, 180
Barrington, Josephine, 57–58, 59, 64, 68, 78, 82
Bates, Alan, 133
Beatty, Warren, 360
The Beginning or The End (movie), 35
Belafonte, Harry, 71
Bell, John Kim, 357
Ben Casey (TV series), 146, 180, 181, 182
Berry, John, 134–135
Berton, Pierre, 241, 268
Bess, Ardon, 261
Beta Sigma Rho (fraternity), 74–75
Between Friends (TV movie), 315, 316
Big Brothers (charity), 274, 286
Billy Liar (play), 145
Black Phoenix (TV movie), 206
Blye, Allan, 113–114
Blye, Gary, 391, 393
B'nai Brith, 285, 356–358
Boa, Bruce, 374
Bochco, Stephen, 313
Bochner, Lloyd, 57
Bogdanovich, Peter, 419–420
Bogus (movie), 419
Boothby, David, 393
Boretski, Peter, 278

432

INDEX

Bottoms, Joseph, 373
Bovaird, Reg, 357
Bowen, Deirdre, 304
The Brady Bunch (TV series), 266
Brinkley, David, 361
Brooks, Richard, 333
Brown, Steve, 313
Bruce, Lenny, 169
Bujold, Geneviève, 200
Burgess, Michael, 357
Burke, Martyn, 206
Burnett, Carol, 316
Burney, Derek, 361, 366
Burnside Drive, 7, 15
Burroughs, Jackie, 244, 245
Burt, Jim, 301
Butch Cassidy and the Sundance Kid (movie), 306

Caan, James, 88, 182, 190, 333
Cadeau, Lally, 292
Cagney and Lacey (TV movie), 304, 307
Cagney and Lacey (TV series), 110–111, 165, 174, 175, 235, 254, 279, 290, 302, 303, 305–315, 328–329, 331, 339, 348–349, 353, 363–364, 379
Calgary Stampede, 337
Callwood, June, 357
Camarie (theatre), 142
Cambridge, Godfrey, 169
Campbell, Douglas, 299
Canada and being Canadian, views on, 10, 11, 93, 101–102, 252, 253–254, 285–287, 299, 376–379
Canada Council, 186–187
Canada Day live performance, 270–272
Canada, Waxman's travels in, 266–272, 285
Canadian Cancer Society, 286, 289
Canadian Film awards, 188
Canadian Film Development Corporation (CFDC), 208, 210, 222
Canadian Native Arts Foundation, 357

Candy, John, 292
Cantor, Eddie, 334
Cap-Ferrat, 335, 338
Carousel (play), 69
Carter, Peter, 191–192, 193
Castellano, Richard S., 190
CBC (Canadian Broadcasting Corporation), 49, 112, 114, 115, 186, 192–193, 253, 266, 277, 293–294, 364
Centre for Maternal and Foetal Medicine, Sara and Al Waxman, 323
Cerro Torre, 369
Chekhov, Michael, 136
Cherry, Alan, 23–24
Chilcott, Barbara, 57
China, travels in, 383–385
Ciccoritti, Jerry, 415, 416
Circus International with Al Waxman (TV series), 280–281
Citytv (TV station), 300
CKEY (radio station), 47–48
Clairman, Arthur, 59–60, 153, 154, 357
Clarkson, Adrienne, 282
Club 22, 196
Cochrane, Elspeth, 124, 142, 143–144
Coe, Liz, 292, 313
Cohen, Nathan, 119–120, 135, 312
Coleman, Dabney, 88, 182
The Colgate Comedy Hour (TV series), 334
Collins, Patricia, 292
Columbia Pictures, 128
commercials, TV. *See* TV commercials
The Connection (play), 118–119
Connors, Carol, 326, 331, 332, 333, 340, 350
Conn Smythe Foundation, 29
Cooke, Jack Kent, 48
Cooke, Lynn, 48
Cooper, Robert, 289, 417
Corday, Barbara, 306
Cosby, Bill, 169
Courtenay, Tom, 133
Couture, Suzette, 292

Cowan, Ed, 242
Crawford, Michael, 128, 129–130
Crawley Films Ltd., 112, 194
Crawley, Francis Radford "Budge," 192, 193
creative consultant, Waxman as, *Tulips* (movie), 299
Crest Theatre, 57
Crime Stoppers, 337
Critical Care (movie), 419
Cronyn, Hume, 79
Cross, Ben, 375
The Crowd Inside (movie), 207–210, 222, 298
Curtis, Tony, 110
Cutler, Bruce, 417

Dagmar, 70
Daly, Tyne, 279, 307, 325, 326, 410
Dancer Fitzgerald Sample (advertising agency), 266
Dane, Lawrence, 113, 216–218, 220, 303
da Silva, Howard, 100, 102–103, 106, 142
Davies, Geraint Wyn, 273–274
Davis, Altavese, 333, 350
Davis, Bette, 80
Davis, Donald, 57
Davis, Murray, 57
Davis, Sammy, Jr., 235, 333–334, 350
Death of a Salesman (play), 12, 95, 313, 418–419, 423–431
Dee, John J., 261
Dee, Sandra, 97
The Defenders (TV series), 172
del Grande, Louis, 251, 262, 265, 347
Deloir, Geneviève, 208
De Niro, Robert, 315
Dennehy, Brian, 375
Dépardieu, Gerard, 419
Destination Unknown (book), 21
DeVito, Danny, 360
Dewhurst, Colleen, 232
Diamond Fleece (TV movie), 373, 374–375, 386

433

INDEX

directing
approach to, 192, 193, 194–195, 360–361, 362–363, 365.
See also movies, theatrical/TV (directs); plays, stage (directs); TV commercials (acts in/directs); TV movies (directs); TV shows/plays/specials (directs)
Directors Guild of Canada, 184, 191
Displaced Persons (DPs), 53–54, 402–403
The Dodo Bird (play), 189–190, 424
Donahue, Troy, 97
Doohan, James, 84, 117
Doorway to Fairyland (radio show), 48–49, 93
Dortort, David, 232, 233, 235
Dougherty, Marion, 99
Douglas, Michael, 20
Drabinsky, Garth, 357
Drainie, John, 60
Dr. Strangelove (movie), 150, 152, 155
Duffy's Tavern (radio show), 31
Durand, Victor, 123
During One Night (movie), 118
Duvall, Robert, 105

Earle Grey Award, 431
Eastwood, Clint, 230, 231, 307
Eastwood, Jayne, 244, 290
Edinborough, Arnold, 203
The Ed Sullivan Show (TV series), 98
Edwards, Vince, 146, 180
Egri, Lajos, 160
Eight Is Enough (TV series), 266
Elgin Theatre, 35
Elizabeth, Queen, 382, 383
Emmy Awards, 337, 373
An Enemy of the People (TV play), 172
The Enforcer (movie), 306
Equity Library Theater, 172
Espionage (TV series), 164
Esposito, Phil, 215

Estrin, Jonathan, 313
Ethnic Squad (TV pilot idea), 300, 301–303

Falk, Peter, 173
Fast, Debbie, 228–229
Feinberg, Abraham, 203
Finestra, Carmen, 293
Ferrier, Garry, 262
Fibber McGee and Molly (radio show), 31
the fifth estate (TV series), 282–283
Finian's Rainbow (play), 69
Finkleman, Ken, 292
Finney, Albert, 133
Fisher, Terry Louise, 313
Flaherty, Joe, 292
Fonda, Peter, 146
Foreman, Carl, 134, 142–143, 144, 147, 148–149, 151, 159, 165, 177, 179
For the People (TV series), 172, 173
For the Record (TV series), 301, 316
Forrester, Bessie, 73–74
Forrester, Maureen, 325
4-H Clubs of West Virginia, 337
Fox, Colin, 244
Fox, Terry, 289–290
France, travels in, 335–337
Franchot, Maude, 66
Freilich, Jeff, 420
Fuchs, Moishe, 138–140
Furie, Sidney J., 48, 117–118, 123, 210

Gardiner, Albert, 178–179
Garnett, Gale, 292
Gascon, Jean, 267
Gemini award, 422
General Motors Presents (TV series), 116
Gerhard, Hans, 340
Gerussi, Bruno, 241, 267, 268
Ghosts (play), 167–168
Gibson, Mel, 360
Glass, Moishe, 357
Glen Cedar Road, 52, 53
Gless, Sharon, 311, 313, 325, 326, 397

Globe (tabloid newspaper), 331–332
Goldberg, Whoopi, 419
Goldman, Bernie, 350
The Gold Shoppe (jewellery shop), 224
Gordone, Charles, 104
Gormé, Eydie, 333
Gotlieb, Allan, 357
"Gotta Hear You Say It Too" (song), 285
Gotti (TV movie), 64, 417
Gowan, Kip, 131–132, 191
Gradidge, Havelock, 203
Graham, Martha, 94–95, 106
Granger, Farley, 71
The Grass is Greener (movie), 131
Greenbaum, Abraham, 140–141
Greenbaum, Hinda (Helen), 68–69
Greenbaum, Luba, 140–141
Greenberg, Harold, 298–299, 357, 374
Greene, Lorne, 233–235
The Green Hornet (radio show), 31
Greenspan, Eddie, 325, 326, 357
Greenspan, Susie, 326
Gregory, Dick, 169
Greshler, Abby, 179, 180, 181–182
Gretsky, Wayne, 274, 305
Group Theatre, 133
Guess Who's Coming to Dinner? (movie), 189
guest, TV talk show, Waxman as, 175, 293
Guttman family, 338

Habimah Theatre, 141, 142
Haddon, Peter, 125, 145
Hall, Monty, 241
Hambourg, Clem, 118
Hamilton, Barbara, 241
Hamilton, George, 146
Hamilton, Pat, 299
Hands, Brian, 346
Hansen's (drugstore), 97
Harnick, Harvey, 189
Harris, Billy, 24

434

INDEX

Harron, Don, 241, 273
Hart, Harvey, 112, 116, 117, 193
Harvey, Denis, 282, 293
Hazzard, Karen, 203
Heartbeat (TV series), 313
Heart and Stroke Foundation, Ontario, 351
Hefner, Hugh, 332–333
Henderson, Paul, 215
Henry, Martha, 367, 426
Henry Street synagogue, 37
He Ran All the Way (movie), 134
Heritage Minute (TV commercial), 404–407
Herriott, Paul, 213, 214
Herrndorf, Peter, 291, 293
Herzog, Werner, 367, 370–371
High Noon (movie), 146
Hillcrest Camerons (hockey team), 24–28
Hillcrest School, 18–19, 24
Hill, Dan, Sr., 357
Hill Street Blues (TV series), 302, 373
Hirsch, John, 193, 248, 251, 253, 255, 270, 293, 325
Hobson, Valerie, 145
Hock, Allison, 313
hockey fan, Waxman as, 13, 215
Hockey Night in Canada (radio show), 13
hockey player, Waxman as, 23–28
Ho, Don, 97
Hollander, Xaviera, 243–247
Hopper, Dennis, 164
Hot and Cold in All Rooms (play), 125
House Un-American Activities Committee, 100
House of Hambourg (theatre), 118–119
Howard, Irene, 130
Howard, Leslie, 130
Howard, Trevor, 130
How Green Was My Valley (book), 38–39
How the West Was Won (movie), 148
Humanitarian Award (B'nai Brith), 356–358
Humphrey, Jack, 251, 262, 265, 288, 292, 301, 346–347
Hunter, John, 206

Icelandia (hockey rink), 23, 25, 26
The Iceman Cometh (movie), 233, 235–236
I Love Lucy (TV series), 266
The Inheritance (play), 171–172
Inmate Training (National Film Board movie), 184–186
Inner Sanctum (radio show), 31
Inniskillin Wines, 318
International Creative Management (ICM), 178
International Ladies Garment Workers Union, 171
Iron Eagle IV (movie), 48
Isabel (movie), 200
Israel Bonds, 285
Israel, state of, 46, 128, 141, 283–284

The Jack Benny Show (radio show), 31
Jacobi, Lou, 291, 350
James, Ken, 292
Jerry K., 54, 55
Jesus Christ Superstar (movie), 396
Jesus of Montreal (movie), 380
Jewish Immigrant Aid Services (JIAS), 53, 54
Jewison, Norman, 123, 396, 419
Gillson, Malca, 81
Joe and the Boy (screenplay), 229–237
Joe Mack, Agent-at-Law (TV pilot idea), 300–301, 303
John and the Missus (screenplay), 223, 231–232, 237
Jolson, Al, 35–37, 50–51, 75–76
The Jolson Story (movie), 35–37
Jones, James Earl, 155
Joshua Then and Now (radio drama), 281
"Journeys in Time" (TV interviews), 299–300
Jutra, Claude, 376

Kane, Janese, 394, 402, 407, 410
Kaplan, Gabe, 297–298, 299
Kaplan, Henry, 193
Karlen, Johnny, 307
Karlin, Miriam "Mims," 133–134
Kastner family, 132
KCOP (TV station), 266
Keeler, Christine, 145
Kelly, Red, 416
Kennedy, Jackie, 149
Kennedy, John (CBC executive), 277
Kennedy, John (U.S. president), 150–151
Kensington Market, 9
Kentucky Derby, 337
Kfar Menachem (kibbutz), 140–141
Kienholz, Edward, 177
King of Kensington (TV series), 63, 111, 242, 248–266, 269, 270, 272, 275, 276–280, 288, 290–293, 306
The King's Wife's Cookbook (book by Sara Waxman), 221, 296
The Kitchen (play), 133
Kleenex commercial, 213
Knapp, Budd, 60
Knox, Alexander, 130
Konvoy, Jerry, 54, 55
Kotcheff, Ted, 123
Kove, Martin, 357, 367, 373
Krugman, Saul, 178
Kubrick, Stanley, 150
Kuper, Jack, 116–117
Kuzik, Mimi, 292, 373

L.A. Law (TV series), 313
Lalonde, Marc, 284
Lancaster, Burt, 297
Landsburg, Alan, 373, 374
Langbord, Eva, 59
Larry, Sheldon, 293
Laskin, Bora, 80–81, 177
The Last Act of Martin Weston (movie), 225

435

INDEX

Lavut, Martin, 111
Lawrence of Arabia (movie), 396
Lawrence, Steve, 333
Law School, University of Toronto, 77–78, 80–81
Lawson, Shannon, 407
Lazarus and the Hurricane (movie), 365
Leach, Robin, 340
League for Human Rights Building, B'nai Brith, 356
Lean, David, 396
LeBlanc, Diana, 424
Lebow, Barbara, 402, 403
Lefcourt, Peter, 313
Leipciger, Bernice (Nathan's wife), 57
Leipciger, Jack (stepfather), 41–46, 56–57, 154, 155–156, 188
Leipciger, Nathan (stepbrother), 42, 43–45, 46, 47, 53, 56–57, 63, 86, 203
Leipciger, Toby. *See* Waxman, Toby
Leone, Sergio, 316
Lévesque, René, 284
Levy, Eugene, 292
Lifestyles of the Rich and Famous (TV series), 340
Lightstone, Marilyn, 292
Linden, Allen, 62–63, 357
Lindsay, Ted, 415
Linehan, Brian, 300
List, Shelley, 313
The Littlest Hobo (TV series), 311
Littlewood, Joan, 133
Lloyd, Christopher, 88
Loews Theatre, 35
Logan, Bob, 405
London School of Film Technique, 162–164
The Lone Ranger (radio show), 31
Lonesome Dove (TV series), 412
The Longest Day (movie), 146
Look Back in Anger (play), 133
Los Angeles
 and consul-general position, 366–367, 372–373, 375–376
 living/working in, 174–183, 330–332
Lost in Yonkers (play), 420, 421–422
Love, Bessie, 124
Love's Labour's Lost (play), 75
Lumet, Sidney, 419
Luminous Award (American Women in Film), 314
Ljungh, Esse, 60
Lux Theater of the Air (radio show), 31

M*A*S*H (TV series), 261, 306
Macdonald, Donald, 380, 381
Maggie's Secret (movie), 373, 386
Maissner, Ben, 325
Makin, Harry, 244
Malle, Louis, 57, 296–297
Mallet, Jane, 292
Mandel, Michele, 372
Man in the Middle (movie), 130–133
Mann, Stanley, 123
Margulies, Donald, 410
Martin, Andrea, 292
Martin, Dean, 97
Marvin, Lee, 233, 235–237
The Mary Tyler Moore Show (TV series), 261
Mayer, Louis B., 399
May, Mathilda, 370
Mayor of Bloor Street, 212
McCartney, Catherine, 276, 277, 297, 304, 357, 394–395
McDougall, Barbara, 397
McKinnon, Catherine, 241
McLuhan, Eric, 405–406
McLuhan, Marshall, 405–407
McManus, Mike, 299–300
McMullen, Bob, 262
McMurtry, Roy, 338
McQueen, Steve, 128, 129, 130
Meisner, Sanford, 89, 94, 106
Melinda Lunch (restaurant), 5, 6, 14, 20
Melinda Street, 5–6
A Memory of Two Mondays (play), 172
Merrill, Gary, 80
Meskin, Aharon, 141
Meskin, Amnon, 141–142
Method acting, 58–59, 89–90, 108, 371
Metropolitan Toronto Police Department, 314, 393
Miami Vice (TV series), 302
Miller, Arthur, 104–105, 172, 423
Miller, Joey, 338, 356
Misery (play), 397
Mishkin, Myer, 235–236
Missing Treasures (TV series), 391–393
Miss New York State (beauty pageant), 275
The Missus (screenplay), 223
Mitchum, James, 146
Mitchum, Robert, 130–131
Moments in Time with Al Waxman (TV series), 316
Monette, Richard, 185, 418–419
Monson, Rabbi David, 158–159, 202, 322
Montalban, Ricardo, 333
The Moral Question (TV movie), 299
Morningside (radio show), 273
Moscow Art Theatre, 141
movies, theatrical/TV (directs)
 The Crowd Inside, 207–210, 222, 298
 Diamond Fleece, 374–375, 386
 Maggie's Secret, 373, 386
 My Pleasure Is My Business, 243–248
 The Moral Question, 299
 Tulips, 297–299
 Tviggy (short film), 186–190, 208
 White Light, 367, 373–374
movies, theatrical/TV (acts in)
 Atlantic City, 57, 297
 Bogus, 419
 Critical Care, 419
 The Crowd Inside, 207–210, 222, 298
 Gotti, 64, 417

Index

Inmate Training, 184–186
Isabel, 200
The Last Act of Martin Weston, 225
Lazarus and the Hurricane, 365
Man in the Middle, 130–133
Net Worth, 28, 415–416, 417, 422
The Rescuers, 419–420
Scream of Stone, 367–371
The Sue Rodriguez Story, 279
Teamster Boss, 57
Tulips, 297–299
The Victors, 142–144, 145–149, 162, 164–166
The War Lover, 128–130, 153–154, 200
When Michael Calls, 220
Wild Horse Hank, 297
movies, theatrical/TV (produces)
  The Crowd Inside, 207–210, 222, 298
  Tviggy (short film), 186–190, 208
movies, theatrical/TV (writes)
  The Crowd Inside, 207–210, 222, 298
  Tviggy (short film), 186–190, 208
  See also screenplays (writes/co-writes); theatrical plays, (writes)
Mulgrew, Kate, 313
Mulroney, Brian, 366
Murder, She Wrote (TV series), 105
Murray, Anne, 280
Music Corporation of America Agency (MCA), 178
Myers, Mike, 292
My Pleasure Is My Business (movie), 243–248

Nancy Susan Reynolds Award, 314
Nash, Knowlton, 293, 357
National Association of Television Program Executives, 275, 337
National Film Board (NFB), 114–115, 184–186, 198–199
Neighborhood Playhouse School of the Theater, 84, 88–92, 93–96, 99, 105–106, 148
Nelligan, Kate, 375, 404
Net Worth (TV movie), 28, 415–416, 417, 422
Newman, Paul, 373
Newman, Sydney, 123
New Yorkers, playing, 110
New York Police Department (NYPD), 110–111, 313–314
New York School of Motion Picture Production, 170
Ngema, Mbongeni, 398
Niagara Falls Summer Theatre, 64–66
Nicholson, Jack, 176
Nielsen, Leslie, 90
No Exit, 134
Nuyen, France, 130

Oakland, Simon, 206–207
Oakwood Collegiate, 60–61
O'Brien, Margaret, 71
Oda, Bev, 241
Odeon Leicester Square (theatre), 164
O'Donnell, Maureen, 258, 259, 260
Ogunquit Playhouse, 79–80
Once Upon a Time in America (movie), 315–316
Only God Knows (movie), 216–219
Ontario Arts Council (OAC), 187
Ontario Film Review Board, 362
Ontario Heart and Stroke Foundation, 351
The Oprah Winfrey Show (TV talk show), 315
Order of Canada, 420–421, 422
Order of Ontario, 418
Orenstein, Leo, 112–113, 193
Orion (production company), 337
Owen, Don, 111

Paperback Hero (movie), 218
Parker 51 incident, 44–45
Parker, Monica, 244, 247, 292
Parks, Larry, 36
parties, 239–240
Paths of Glory (movie), 152
Pearson, Peter, 184–186, 218–219
People's Choice Awards, 337
Peppard, George, 138, 146
Perkins, Elizabeth, 420
Peter and the Dwarf (radio show), 47–48
Peters, Bernadette, 297, 299
Philip, Prince, 382
pilots, TV. *See* TV pilot ideas; TV pilots (acts in)
Pinsent, Gordon, 17, 111, 113, 191, 223, 237
Pitre, Louise, 357
plays, stage (directs)
  first play he wrote, 32–33
  Lost in Yonkers, 420, 421–422
  A Shayna Maidel, 394, 402–404, 407–408, 411
  Sight Unseen, 410–412
plays, stage (acts in)
  Billy Liar, 145
  Carousel, 69
  The Connection, 118–119
  Death of a Salesman, 12, 95, 313, 418–419, 423–431
  The Dodo Bird, 189–190, 424
  Finian's Rainbow, 69
  Hot and Cold in All Rooms, 125
  The Inheritance, 171–172
  Love's Labour's Lost, 75
  A Memory of Two Mondays, 172
  Proposals, 50, 347, 365
  The Rivals, 75
  St. Joan, 59
  Secret of the World, 132–137, 374
  Twelfth Night, 58–59
  A View from the Bridge, 95, 104, 107–110, 172
  While the Sun Shines, 125
plays, stage (writes), 32–33

Index

plays, TV. *See* TV shows/plays/specials
Plaza Hotel, 203–204
The Plouffe Family (TV series), 306
poetry, 82–83, 423
Pogue, Ken, 299
police departments, recognition from, 313–314, 393
Pollack, Sydney, 94
Post, Ted, 232, 233, 304
producing
  approach to, 149
  of first play he writes/directs, 32–33
  See also movies, theatrical/TV (produces)
Profumo, John, 145
Prokop, Skip, 285
Proposals (play), 50, 347, 365
Puff (dog), 270, 320, 385
Purvey, Marjorie, 47, 48

Quant, Mary, 145
Quentin Durgens, MP (TV series), 191

Radcliffe, Rosemary, 279
radio shows/dramas (acts in), 49–50
  Doorway to Fairyland, 48–49, 93
  Joshua Then and Now, 281
  Peter and the Dwarf, 47–48
  Scales of Justice, 49
  Stage, 60
radio shows (hosts), 273
Raincheck (bar), 175–176
Rakoff, Alvin, 123–124
Ramer, Henry, 212, 244, 357
Rathbone, Basil, 235
The Red Badge of Courage (movie), 146
Redford, Robert, 360
The Red Skelton Show (radio show), 31
Regan, Heather, 266
Regis & Kathie Lee (TV talk show), 315
Reid, Fiona, 251, 261, 264, 278–279, 357
Reid, Kate, 57, 297
Reitman, Ivan, 208

The Rescuers (TV movie), 419–420
Revere, Anne, 134, 171–172
Rhodes, Donnelly, 251, 273
Richler, Mordecai, 123
Riel (TV special), 120
Riel, Louis, 120, 223, 230, 232
The Rivals (play), 75
Robbins, Toby, 65, 117
Roberts, John, 266–267
Robinson, Jackie, 334–335
Rogers, Melody, 175
Rosato, Tony, 292
Rosemond, Perry, 111, 113, 248, 249, 251, 262, 301, 393
Rosenberg, Stuart, 164, 172
Rosenzweig, Barney, 304–305, 306, 311, 313, 348–349, 397
The Rose Tattoo (play), 59
Roxy (theatre), 96–97
Rubes, Jan, 292
Rubinek, Saul, 281, 292
Rush (band), 421
Ryan, Claude, 284
Ryan, Robert, 171

Sahl, Mort, 169
St. Joan (play), 59
St. Mark's Playhouse (theatre), 104, 105
St. Vincent de Paul Penitentiary, 185
Salerno, 143–150
Sandor, Anna, 292
Sara and Al Waxman Audio and Visual Library (in B'nai Brith League for Human Rights Building), 356
Sara and Al Waxman Center for Maternal and Fetal Medicine (Shaare Zedek Hospital), 323
Sarafina! (movie), 398
Sassoon, Vidal, 145
Saturday Night (magazine), 203
Savalas, Telly, 110
Scales of Justice (radio drama), 49
Scott, George C., 232
Scott Newman Award, 373

Scream of Stone (movie), 367–371
screenplays (writes/co-writes)
  About Tomorrow, 192, 207
  The Crowd Inside, 207–210, 222, 298
  (with Ted Allan) *Joe and the Boy*, 229–237
  (with Ted Allan) *Them Damn Canadians Hanged Louis Riel*, 223, 229
  Tviggy (short film), 186–190, 208
Secret of the World (play), 132–137, 374
Shaare Zedek Hospital, 322–326
Shack, Eddie, 292
Shapiro, Annie, 202, 409–410
Shapiro, Lorne, 410
Shapiro, Mendel, 200–202, 320–321, 325, 409, 410
Shatner, William, 172
Shaver, Helen, 292
Shawn, Dick, 347
Shaw, Robert, 232
A Shayna Maidel (play), 394, 402–404, 407–408, 411
Shepperton studios, 128
Shuster, Frank, 325, 421. *See also* Wayne and Shuster
Sidestreet (TV series), 251, 273–274
Sight Unseen (play), 410–412
Silver, Liberty, 357
Simcoe Public House (tavern), 42, 155–156
Simon, Neil, 420
Simply Wine and Cheese (TV series), 412–413
Simpson, Denis, 357
Singer, Ron, 255–256, 299
Smith, Eve, 143
Snow, Chief John, 268
Sobel, Harold, 242–243
songwriting, 285
South Africa, travels in, 397–401
Spadina Avenue, childhood on, 7–8, 9
Spector, Maude, 130
Spelling, Aaron, 313
Sperdakos, George, 111–112,

438

INDEX

114, 119, 124, 128, 244, 247, 357
stage plays. *See* plays
Stage (radio show), 60
Stalmaster, Lynn, 182–183
Stander, Lionel, 134, 171
Stanislavsky, Konstantin, 59, 141, 324, 427
Stanley Woolf Players, 107–110
Starsky and Hutch (TV series), 306
Stephenson, Bette, 300
The Story of GI Joe (movie), 131
Strasberg, Lee, 89–90, 103, 106, 170
Strasberg, Paula, 170
Stratford Festival, 418, 423–424, 426
Streisand, Barbra, 283
Stritch, Elaine, 173
The Sue Rodriguez Story (TV movie), 279
Sullivan, Ed, 334
summer stock, 64–66, 79–80, 107–110
The Sundowners (movie), 131
Sun in My Eyes (TV show), 116–117, 118, 123
Susskind, David, 130
Suspense (radio show), 31
Sutherland, Donald, 367, 368, 371
Swit, Loretta, 306, 307, 310

Tadman, Aubrey, 262
Take Thirty (TV talk show), 293
A Tale of Two Cities (book), 38–39, 123
Tandy, Jessica, 79–80
Tarnow, Toby, 65–66, 111
A Taste of Honey (play), 133
Taylor, Elizabeth, 316
Taylor, Mary, 50
teaching, at Al's Gym (acting class), 111, 390
Team Canada (hockey), 215
Teamster Boss (movie), 57
Telegram (newspaper), 5–6
The Terry Fox Story, 289–290
Theatre Royal, 133
Them Damn Canadians

Hanged Louis Riel (book and screenplay), 223, 229
theme parties, 239–240
These Mountains Are Our Sacred Places (book), 268–269
Thomas, Dave, 292
Thomas, Ralph, 301
Three Girls from the Peg (Waxman family singing group), 338
Till, Eric, 210, 297
Titans (TV series), 300
Tivoli Theatre, 35
Tobias, Rose, 130
Top of the Gate (restaurant), 169–170
Toronto
 early memories of, 3, 4, 7, 14
 vs. Los Angeles, 330–332
Toronto Hockey League, 23
Toronto Police Department, 314, 393
Toronto Recycling Action Committee (TRAC), 242
Treacher, Arthur, 70–71
Trent, John, 191, 193
Trials of O'Brien (TV pilot), 172–173
Trudeau, Margaret, 284
Trudeau, Pierre, 284–285
Trueman, Peter, 347
Tsai, Nancy, 357
Tulips (movie), 297–299
Turner, Lana, 97
TV commercials (acts in/directs), 212–216, 241–242, 404–407
TV Guide (magazine), 280
Tviggy (short film), 186–190, 208
TV movies. *See* movies, theatrical/TV.
TV pilots (develops ideas for)
 Ethnic Squad, 300, 301–303
 Joe Mack, Agent-at-Law, 300–301, 303
TV pilots (acts in), *Trials of O'Brien*, 172–173
TV scripts (co-writes with John Trent) *Wojeck*, 191
TV series (directs). *See under*

TV shows/plays/specials (directs)
TV series (hosts)
 Circus International with Al Waxman, 280–281
 Missing Treasures, 391–393
 Moments in Time with Al Waxman, 316
 Simply Wine and Cheese, 412–413
TV series (acts in)
 Cagney and Lacey, 110–111, 165, 174, 175, 235, 254, 279, 290, 302, 303, 305–315, 328–329, 331, 339, 348–349, 353, 363–364, 379
 The Defenders, 172
 Ben Casey, 146, 180, 181, 182
 Espionage, 164
 For the People, 172, 173
 King of Kensington, 63, 111, 242, 248–266, 269, 270, 272, 275, 276–280, 288, 290–293, 306
 The Littlest Hobo, 311
 Murder, She Wrote, 105
 Quentin Durgens, MP, 191
 Sidestreet, 251, 273–274
 Titans, 300
 The Winnings of Frankie Walls, 6, 288, 294, 297, 316
TV shows/plays/specials (directs)
 Black Phoenix, 206
 For the Record episode ("Cop"), 316
 Heartbeat episode, 313
 The Littlest Hobo episodes, 311
 Missing Treasures episodes, 391–393
 Quentin Durgens, MP episode, 191
 Sidestreet episode, 251, 273–274
TV shows/plays/specials (hosts), Variety Club of Ontario telethon, 241
TV shows/plays/specials (acts in)

439

An Enemy of the People, 172
the *fifth estate,* 282–283
Lifestyles of the Rich and Famous (with family), 340
Louis Riel, 120
Sun in My Eyes, 116–117, 118, 123
Twelfth Night (play), 58–59
Twentieth Century-Fox, 130
Two on the Town (TV talk show), 175

United Jewish Appeal, 285
United Way, 285–286
Universal Pictures, 178
University of Toronto Law School, 77–78, 80–81
University of Western Ontario, 73–77
Upsilon Lambda Phi (fraternity), 62
Ussishkin, Menachem, 141

Vaccaro, Brenda, 88
Vaile, Arthur, 62
Valenti, Jack, 361–361
Valentine's Day, 3, 4
Van, Billy, 292
Vanicola, Joanna, 373
Variety Club of Ontario, 241, 274–275, 286, 322, 357
Vaughan Road Collegiate, 62–63
Vernon, John, 252
The Victors (movie), 142–144, 145–149, 162, 164–165
A View from the Bridge (play), 95, 104, 107–110, 172
Village Gate (restaurant), 169, 170–171
Vinci, Bob, 261
Viola, Joe, 313
Voight, Jon, 105

Wagner, Robert, 128, 129
Waldman, Marion, 242
Wales Street, 52–53, 68
Wallach, Eli, 146, 147–148
Walters, Jessica, 88, 172
Wanamaker, Sam, 130, 134
Ward, Stephen, 145
The War Lover (movie),

128–130, 153–154, 200
Watson, Patrick, 300, 404
Waxman, Aaron (father), 4–16, 20, 21–22, 139
Waxman, Adam (son)
 bar mitzvah, 338
 birth, 223–225
 childhood/adolescence, 267, 268, 269–270, 321, 329, 338–339, 346
 relationship with Al, 317, 426–427
Waxman, Al
 as actor. *See* acting. *See also under different genres* (acts in)
 and anti-Semitism, 9, 11, 25–26, 27, 28–29, 163–164, 194
 awards/honours, 294, 314, 356, 373, 393, 418, 420–421, 422, 431
 appointed to Stratford Festival board of directors, 418
 library and medical centre named after, 323, 356
 named honorary NYPD lieutenant, 110–111
 offered position of Canada's consul-general in Los Angeles, 366–367, 372–373, 375–376
 bar mitzvah, 34, 37–38
 birth, 15
 chairs Academy of Canadian Cinema and Television, 366, 376–379, 380–381, 382–384, 418
 charity work, 285–286, 295, 321–326, 351, 356–358
 childhood, memories, 3, 4, 7, 14, 54. *See also* relationships, family
 childhood jobs, 19
 childhood sports involvement, 22–28
 as director. *See* directing. *See also under different genres* (directs)
 early interest/involvement in stage/radio/film, 14, 31–33, 40, 49, 75

early theatre work,
 at University of Western Ontario, 75
 in summer stock, 64–66, 79–80, 107–110
education,
 at Hillcrest School, 18–19, 24
 at Oakwood Collegiate, 60–61
 at University of Toronto Law School, 77–78, 80–81
 at University of Western Ontario, 73–77
 at Vaughan Road Collegiate, 62–63
 at Yeshivah Torath Chaim, 18–19
enjoyments,
 poetry, 82–83, 423
 reading, 38–39
 theme parties, 239–240
financial problems, 354–356, 393–394
as guest on TV talk shows, 175, 293
health problems, 344–345, 346, 347–352
homes,
 Burnside Drive, 7, 15
 Forest Hill Village, 308, 320–321
 Glen Cedar Road, 52, 53
 Rosedale, 238–239, 408–409
 Spadina Avenue, 7–8, 9
 Wales Street, 52–53, 68
as host. *See* radio shows (hosts); TV series (hosts); TV shows/plays/specials (hosts)
influences on,
 Andrea del Sarto (poem), 83, 423
 A Tale of Two Cities, 38–39, 123
 Willy Loman character (*Death of a Salesman*), 12, 395, 423–424, 427–430
 See also Jolson, Al
and Israel, 46, 128, 138–142,

Index

283–384, 396–397
lives/works/studies in England, 121–137, 162–166
lives/works in New York City, 167–173
lives/works in Los Angeles, 174–183
meets/marries Sara, 196–197, 198–204
marriage and fatherhood, 198–204, 221–212, 223–225, 316–317, 329, 335
mother's second marriage, 43–45, 155–156
non-acting jobs,
  bouncer at Top of the Gate (New York), 169–170
  cook at Barney's Beanery (Los Angeles), 176–177, 179, 180
  usher at the Roxy (New York), 96–97
  waiter at Village Gate (New York), 169, 170–171
as producer. *See* producing
relationships, family,
  Aaron Waxman (father), 4–16, 20, 21–22, 139
  Adam Waxman (son), 317, 426–427
  Benny Waxman (brother), 5, 70, 154, 326–327, 343–344, 348, 358–359
  Jack Leipciger (stepfather), 41–46, 56–57, 154, 155–156, 188
  Nathan Leipciger (stepbrother), 42, 43–45, 46, 47, 53, 56–57, 63, 86, 203
  Tobaron Waxman (daughter), 316–318, 329, 357
  Toby Waxman (mother),
    childhood memories, 7, 8, 10, 14, 15, 17–18, 19–20, 29–30
    later memories, 152–153, 162
    reaction to her illness and death, 154–162
    her second husband, 43–45, 155–156

her view of acting, 69–70, 84–86
as songwriter, 285
and storytelling, 425
suffers from self-doubt, 161–162, 387–390, 400–401, 404
teaches at York University, 338, 376, 390–391
theatre/film training, 47, 48, 57, 58
  with Howard da Silva, 100, 101–103, 106
  with Lee Strasberg, 103, 170
  at London School of Film Technique, 162–164
  at Neighborhood Playhouse School of the Theater, 84, 88–92, 93–96, 99, 105–106, 148
  with Martha Graham, 94–96
  at New York School of Motion Picture Production, 170
  in summer stock, 64–66, 79–80, 107–110
temperament, 255–257
tries to enlist in Air Force, 63–64
travels,
  in Canada, 266–272, 285
  to China, 383–385
  to England, 121–137, 162–166
  to France, 335–337
  to South Africa, 397–401
views,
  on Canada and being Canadian, 10, 11, 93, 101–102, 252, 253–254, 285–287, 299, 376–379
  on Canadian TV industry, 115-116
  on the CBC, 193, 293–294, 364
  on hunger vs. desperation, 207, 219
  on Los Angeles vs. Toronto, 330–332
  on "making it," 179
  on marriage, 195, 210

  on talent, 334–335
  on truth and integrity, 364–366
  on work vs. family, 226–227
as writer. *See* writing. *See also under different genres (writes)*
Waxman, Albert A. (cousin), 126–127
Waxman, Benny (brother)
  birth and early years, 9–10, 15, 19
  charity work, 322
  death, 358
  health problems, 342, 351–352
  homosexuality, 343–344
  marriage, 73
  and other family members, 3, 5, 13, 14, 45, 188
  relationship with Al, 5, 70, 326–327, 343–344, 348, 358–359
  Zionism, 46
Waxman, Sara (née Shapiro; wife)
  Al entertains/meets/marries, 51, 196–197, 198–204
  books by, 221, 296, 339
  charity work, 322–326, 356–357
  library and medical centre named after, 323, 356
  marriage and motherhood, 194, 211–212, 220, 221, 223–225, 240–241, 260, 350–351, 409
  relationship with her father, 201, 320–321, 409–410
  travels, 335–337, 358, 397–399
Waxman, Shirley (née Silbert; Benny's wife), 73, 154, 342, 358
Waxman, Tobaron (daughter)
  bat mitzvah, 338
  birth, 211–212
  early life/education, 227–228, 267, 268, 269, 284–285, 335, 338, 358
  on *King of Kensington*, 291–292

relationship with Al, 316–318, 329, 357
Waxman, Toby (mother)
and Aaron Waxman, 16
death, 156–159
early life with, 7, 8, 10, 14, 15, 19–20, 29–30
friendships, 68–69, 73–74
marries Jack Leipciger, 41–45
and reading, 38–39
and surgery, 152–153, 154–156
Wayne and Shuster (comedy team), 31, 32, 280. *See also* Shuster, Frank; Wayne, Johnny
Wayne and Shuster (radio show), 31
Wayne, John, 97, 230
Wayne, Johnny, 325, 350
Wayne, Paul, 217–218
Webster, William, 361
Weinberger, Jack ("Jack W."), 53–54
Weinstein, Seymour, 59–60, 86–87, 153–154, 350, 357

Weintraub, Jerry, 92
Welsh, Jonathan, 273
Wernick, Sandy, 276–278
Wesker, Arnold, 133
Western Ontario, University of, 73–77
West Virginia, 337
When Michael Calls (TV movie), 220
While the Sun Shines (play), 125
White Light (movie), 367, 373–374
Wilde, Cornel, 333
Wild Horse Hank (movie), 297
Wimbledon Repertory Company, 124–127
The Winnings of Frankie Walls (TV series), 6, 288, 294, 297, 316
Winston, Helene, 261, 278
Winter Garden Theatre, 35
Wise, Len, 301
Witkin, Steve, 338, 356
Wojeck (TV series), 191, 252
Woolvett, Jaimz, 373

Worldfest Houston Gold Award, 393
Wright, Mr. (Grade 9 teacher), 61
writing
approach to, 164, 192
See also movies, theatrical/TV (writes); plays, stage (writes); screenplays (writes); songwriting; TV scripts
Wynn, Ed, 130
Wynn, Keenan, 130

Yeshivah Torath Chaim (school), 18–19
Yorkshire Post, 125–126
York University, 338, 376, 390–391
Young, Otis, 176
Young, Stephen, 233

Ziraldo, Donald, 318
Zuckerman, Bernie, 415